Parent Education and Public Policy

CHILD AND FAMILY POLICY

SERIES EDITORS
JAMES J. GALLAGHER AND RON HASKINS

PARENT EDUCATION AND PUBLIC POLICY

RON HASKINS AND DIANE ADAMS
EDITORS

ABLEX Publishing Corporation
Norwood, New Jersey 07648

Copyright © 1983 by Ablex Publishing Corporation.

Printed in the United States of America.

Library of Congress Cataloging in Publication Data

Main entry under title:

Parent education and public policy.

(Child and family policy; v. 3)
Based on papers presented at a conference sponsored
by the National Institute of Education in the spring
of 1980.
Includes indexes.
1. Parenting—Study and teaching—United States—
Congresses. 2. Family policy—United States—Congresses.
I. Haskins, Ron. II. National Institute of
Education (U.S.) III. Series.
HQ755.7.P365   1983   306.8′5   83-12260
ISBN 0-89391-127-5

Ablex Publishing Corporation
355 Chestnut Street
Norwood, New Jersey 07648

CONTENTS

PREFACE TO THE SERIES

JAMES J. GALLAGHER

Emergence of the new field of social policy analysis, starting in the 1960s, but accelerating in the 1970s, is an intriguing phenomenon in the academic world that is worthy of study in its own right. This evolving discipline is clearly multidisciplinary in nature, drawing interest and contributions from such diverse bedfellows as the health sciences, economics, sociology, psychology, and education, among others.

Even more interesting than this multidisciplinary thrust from the academic community is that those in positions of power seem to be aware of this new movement and are generally attentive. The relationship between the keepers of knowledge and holders of power has always been a strained one. Truth, particularly when unpleasant, has rarely been welcomed by those at the seat of power. Those messengers who deliver such unpleasant truths run some very real risks, more psychological than physical these days. On the other hand, the academician rarely has a sense of the multitude of conflicting pressures and compromises that are the daily menu of the practicing politician, and often doesn't appreciate the many changes in directions that often must be taken to reach a political (policy) goal.

To appreciate this continued strain between knowledge and power, one need not invoke the memories of Galileo or Sir Thomas More. The current difficulties are well expressed in the agonies of the atomic scientists, aptly delineated in an extraordinary series of novels by C. P. Snow. Given this obvious and continued strain, why is there a current interest in pursuing what academia can bring to social policy formulation and implementation?

My own view is that the public policies of the 1960s are the stimuli for this review of relationships. Those policies were, by and large, designed to lead to a better life for all our citizens through improving the delivery of health, social, and educational services. The consensus held by both the political community and the lay public appears to be that after 15 years, the programs have largely come to grief, or have attained much less than was originally intended. Whether this outcome is the result of unrealistic expectations, poor policy formulation, or inadequate policy implementation is still a matter of personal interpretation.

Currently, there is a growing realization that attempts to improve American society can no longer be based on a "seat-of-the-pants," largely uncorrelated, and uncontrolled set of innovations. Such a strategy yields uncontrolled budgets and a corrosive cycle of over-expectation, disappointment, and despair. There appears to be a new willingness, tinged with some skepticism, to pursue what academia has to offer in improving policy design and implementation. What does academia have to offer? What it always has—the ability to organize systems of ideas into a pattern that allows us to bring order and new insights to the phenomenon under study.

This series on social policy analysis summarizes some of the latest ideas and methods that are being utilized by those social and health scientists most directly concerned with policy relating to children and families. Each volume in the series will be built around a particular theme so that contributors to a given volume will be focusing on a common topic. In this first volume, the theme is the development of models for analyzing social policy. Such model development is presented from a multidisciplinary perspective as we seek some usable procedures to bring clarity and comprehension to complex policy topics. In subsequent volumes, we will focus upon policy issues such as parent education, the needs of handicapped children and their families, maternal and child health, and children and families in poverty. In each of these volumes, there will be a mixture of general descriptions on the topic area plus the inclusion of specific policy analyses that attempt to bring insight into particular topics within the theme.

It would be inappropriate to conclude these introductory remarks without giving credit to the Bush Foundation of St. Paul, Minnesota, whose forward thinking has provided financial support for much of the analytic work that will be included in these volumes. The Bush Foundation has established training programs at four major universities—Michigan, Yale, UCLA, and North Carolina—and while the papers in this series will be based, to a large degree, on the work at North Carolina, the ideas and concepts in this series will undoubtedly reflect the interests of all four Bush centers.

PREFACE TO VOLUME III

RON HASKINS AND DIANE ADAMS

This volume is based on papers presented at a conference on Parent Education and Public Policy held in the spring of 1980. The conference was sponsored by the National Institute of Education to examine two major questions. First, what is the status of research on the effects of parent education? More specifically, what types of parent education programs have been conducted for parents of preschool and school-age children, and what have been the effects of these various programs on parents themselves and on their children's development? The second question addressed by conference participants was whether these data on parent programs had implications for public policy, and if so, what specific policy recommendations could be made.

The book resulting from the conference is divided into four sections: background on the issue of parent education and public policy; research evidence on parent education; selected policy issues closely associated with parent education; and synthesis and policy recommendations. In the first section, we include three chapters that examine the history of parent education; locate parent programs in the general context of policy for children and families; and portray the policy context, with particular reference to the United States Congress, within which parent programs must be sold if social scientists and advocates have confidence that the programs can be effective in solving social problems.

The second section contains seven chapters that report original research or review previous research on selected aspects of parent education. These chapters range broadly over programs for preschool and school-age children; programs for parents of handicapped, normal, and gifted children; small-scale, quasi-experimental and large-scale, survey research; and several different types of parent education and parent involvement. The section concludes with a review paper by Alison Clarke-Stewart summarizing research on several major assumptions that underlie current interest in parent education and the relation between parent education research and public policy.

Chapters in the third section examine several issues associated with parent programs. These issues include the seemingly inherent tension between professionals and parents, and especially the difficulty professionals often have in relinquishing some control over program and treatment decisions; the types of information about child rearing that parents want and the methods by which such information can be given to them; the need for greater parent involvement in a range of current social programs such as AFDC; and the possibility that ethnic and cultural bias infuses both parent education programs and the social science concepts on which these programs are based.

In the final section, we attempt to synthesize much of the information presented in the chapters, as well as other information on parent education, and apply it to the analysis of parent education policy. The chapter concludes with specific recommendations about parent education and public policy. This chapter was written after the conference and after all the other chapters had been edited. Thus, although it may reflect much of the information discussed at the conference and presented in the book, neither the chapter nor its conclusions were discussed or approved by conference participants. Rather, the chapter reflects solely the views of its authors.

Edited volumes—especially those resulting from a conference—depend on the efforts and ideas of many people. In the case at hand, credit for the original idea of the conference and this volume should go to Hazel Leler, Pat Olmsted, Roberta Rubin, and Earl Schaefer of the University of North Carolina at Chapel Hill. They were primary authors of the grant which funded the conference, and participated heavily in planning the conference and selecting its participants. Thus, much of the credit for the conference and this volume is rightfully theirs.

We also want to thank the staff at the National Institute of Education, and especially Oliver Moles and Lois-ellen Datta, for supporting the conference. Dr. Moles, who was the Project Officer, was especially helpful. His major administrative contribution was to achieve a blend of adherence to the original intentions of the conference with flexibility in the face of changing circumstances. Nor was Dr. Moles' contribution only administrative. His suggestions about conference participants and topics, as well as about the resulting book, demonstrated a solid understanding of parent education as an area of social science research and intervention. We are sincerely indebted to Oliver Moles for his assistance, patience, flexibility, and foresight.

Several people were helpful in planning the conference and in recommending conference participants and themes. We hesitate to single out particular individuals here because of the inevitable need to draw a line in making such citations. Such is our indebtedness, however, that we will do so—with sincere apologies to those who fall on the other side of the line. Mary Robinson, Edith Grotberg, and Lois-ellen Datta were extremely helpful during the early planning stages of the conference. All made excellent suggestions, most of which were subsequently implemented, concerning conference participants and topics for the various papers. Perhaps we would not be overpresumptuous in speaking on behalf of the early childhood education and child development communities in claiming that Robinson, Grotberg, and Datta have set the highest standards for social scientists and educators who make the transition to public program administration. This conference and the field of child and family intervention are indebted to these three remarkable people.

We also acknowledge the efficient and reliable efforts of the people who actually implemented conference plans and helped bring this volume to completion. Flo Purdie and Susann Hutaff did everything from make travel arrangements, keep track of budgets, supervise transportation, prepare conference materials, and in general, do whatever was necessary to keep our wagons in a circle. Flo Purdie has also done a wonderful job of supervising the typing and retyping of manuscripts; Susann Hutaff has helped greatly in editing and proofreading. Both have fulfilled these roles for all three volumes in this series on child development and social policy, and we cannot overstate our gratitude.

Others who assisted with administrative arrangements for the conference and with preparing the manuscripts for this volume included Sherree Payne, Brenda Brady, Sally Scaringelli, Stacy Reynolds, and Katherine Polk.

Finally, we wish to thank the Bush Foundation for continuing support of our policy analysis program, and in particular for their financial assistance with the conference on which this volume is based.

Section I

Policy Background

In this introductory section, we have included three chapters that, taken together, provide an overview of parent education as a movement and of the major policy questions dealt with in other sections of the book. More specifically, Schlossman examines parent education as a social movement during the 1920s; Dokecki and Moroney propose a new and broader role for the state in supporting all families and preventing family breakdown and pathology before it occurs; and Mundel argues that federal policymakers are not convinced that parent programs can have an impact on major social problems. Let us outline each of these chapters in more detail.

As Clarke-Stewart and Apfel (1979) have argued, social science fads are ahistorical. Movements such as parent education tend to offer new solutions to old problems, when, in fact, the solutions have a long history of implementation and even, in some cases, evaluation. Thus, we begin this book with an excellent historical chapter by Steven Schlossman to show that parent education as a strategy to attack social problems has a long and interesting history in the United States. Further, the Schlossman chapter provides a number of insights into the policy context within which parent education policy will be made over the next decade.

Focusing primarily on Lawrence Frank and the Laura Spelman Rockefeller Memorial (LSRM), Schlossman examines the parent education movement of the 1920s. Then, as now, parent education was seen, at least by Frank, as a means of transforming society. Parents could learn to raise their children "scientifically" and in so doing produce children capable of uplifting and reforming American social institutions. In addition to encouraging the belief that research would reveal a technique for meeting the needs of children in the home, Frank played a major role in funding the child development institutes at Columbia, Berkeley, Chicago, and elsewhere that would eventually, he believed, produce such research. Moreover, he pursued a three-part strategy to ensure that scientific knowledge about childrearing would actually be implemented by parents, and more particularly, mothers, in the home.

First, he offered the Child Study Association (CSA) of America as a model organization for promoting systematic child study among mothers. This elite New York organization conducted lectures on child development, prepared bibliographies for its members, and held meetings to discuss scientific approaches to childrearing. Withal, the CSA served as a model for the "mass effort in self-education [Frank] envisioned for mothers throughout the country" (p. 14).

Second, Frank employed several strategies to encourage universities to conduct child development research. He convinced Columbia Teacher's College—probably the leading school of education in the country at the time—to open a research center on preschool children. Once Columbia accepted, Frank was able to use this precedent, plus LSRM money, to convince Iowa, Berkeley, Toronto, and Minnesota to open or expand their own centers. Frank also persuaded the institutes to offer training fellowships to distinguished females with backgrounds in home economics, social work, and teaching. These women, in Frank's plans, would serve as an "elite corps of expert practitioners" who would work in universities, state and local governments, and private educational organizations to spearhead the national movement of child study that he envisioned.

Third, Frank wanted a popular outlet for child study ideas and child development research to help mothers inform themselves about childrearing principles and the scientific application of these principles in their own homes. To this end, LSRM, at Frank's urging, funded a small-circulation parents' magazine owned and edited by George J. Hecht. Operating largely behind the scenes, Frank persuaded LSRM to channel funds through the child development institutes to create a corporation, headed by Hecht, that would publish the magazine. The university backing gave the magazine intellectual legitimacy, and Hecht's experience as a publisher and businessman gave it a sound financial base. After beginning publication in 1926, the magazine very quickly became the largest circulation educational periodical in the world. Interestingly, the magazine, now published under the title *Parents' Magazine*, is still thriving and has a circulation of about 1.7 million.

In weaving this story of Lawrence Frank and LSRM's role in promoting parent education during the 1920's, Schlossman details several similarities and differences between parent education then and now. The similarities include the view that parent education could be used as a strategy in overcoming social problems (including the reform of social institutions), the outpouring of literature directed at parents, the belief that research could provide a scientific basis for childrearing, the emphasis on the importance of the preschool years, and the assumption that parents are the primary socializing force in the lives of children.

These similarities notwithstanding, the differences between parent education in the 1920s and today are even more illuminating, especially for students of public policy. First, there was little consideration by Frank, LSRM, or the universities of a public role in parent education. Indeed, the movement was financed almost entirely by private funds; the money to create the child development institutes, to support child study groups, and to fund popular literature was almost exclusively private. By contrast, as the papers in this volume demonstrate, today there is relatively little consideration of a role for private funds in stimulating parent education. All the research studies reported in this book, not to mention the conference that occasioned its birth, were funded by the federal government. Moreover, nearly all the policy implications—implicit and explicit—drawn by the various authors are directed primarily at the federal government.

Second, there has been a shift, stimulated substantially by President Johnson's Great Society programs, from affective to cognitive objectives for parent education. Again, the studies in this volume focus primarily on the role of parent education in stimulating intellectual development and school achievement. Although many advocates and even researchers talk about adaptive behavior, personality development, and social competence, ye shall know them by what they measure; what they measure is primarily IQ and school achievement.

Third, and closely related to the second difference, researchers, advocates, and policymakers have come to see equality of educational opportunity as a primary objective of parent education. It speaks volumes about contemporary American society, and our view of success and how best to achieve it, that the mystique of intellect and education carries much of the causal burden of America's social ills. If only we could make people smarter and better educated, and if only parents would play their proper role in preparing and encouraging their children to achieve, delinquency and crime would disappear, poverty could be eliminated, and self-fulfillment would be at hand. Not surprisingly, Schlossman's historical insights show the complexity—and persistence—of the social problems for which some think parent education to be the solution.

Dokecki and Moroney, in their chapter on strengthening families, outline a substantial departure from current policies designed to assist families. Traditional American values, which to date have controlled family policy, dictate that government can intervene in family life only in the case of family breakdown, i.e., on occasions when the family fails to adequately perform its childrearing functions. Without evidence of family breakdown, intervention is usually thought to be inappropriate. This "residual" approach to social welfare is the one Dokecki and Moroney see as dominant and the one against which they argue. Thus, social policies that respond to crisis, focus exclusively on pathological or broken individuals and families, and assume that most families can take care of their own problems are no longer adequate. Capitalism and its attendant values of individualism and competition is, in Dokecki and Moroney's view, no longer a tenable ground for American social policy.

What they propose as a more appropriate ground for social policy is a community and human development perspective. Dokecki and Moroney want social policy based on the concept of "shared responsibility between families and the state" to be the major focus on government. Though they deny that this proposed shift is either "new or radical", some might argue that in fact it would constitute a revolution in American social policy.

The most immediate focus of this revolution would be the family. More specifically, Dokecki and Moroney identify four primary goals toward which government social benefits for all families should be directed: (1) helping families execute a broad range of developmental and childrearing tasks; (2) improving the quality of family relations and relations between the family and external systems; (3) minimizing external stress on the family; and (4) improving the quantity and quality of social supports needed by families. The authors elaborate each of these policy goals, with particular attention to creating the conditions that support the development of competence in children.

Finally, the authors identify parent education as a primary means by which these policy goals can be achieved. They call for parent programs that have a theoretical base in the ecology of human and family development, that adopt goals related to parents' needs for information and skills, and that deliver their services through, or in conjunction with, "naturally occurring institutional-family contact points" such as schools, hospitals, and businesses.

The introductory section concludes with a brisk discussion by David Mundel, a former member of the Congressional Budget Office and therefore experienced in working with members of Congress. In many respects, Mundel's chapter represents a challenge to the assumptions and conclusions, not only of the Dokecki and Moroney chapter, but of several other authors who contributed to this volume—and even of the entire field of parent education. Like Dokecki and Moroney, Mundel recognizes that current federal social policy is based on the assumption that low-income and otherwise troubled families are the primary object of social policy. To use Dokecki and Moroney's term, the pervasive view among policymakers is that government policy not only is, but should be, residual.

The straightforward point made by Mundel is that advocates for parent programs have not effectively made themselves heard among policymakers. For the most part, policymakers subscribe to the notion that adult outcomes are correlated with experiences during childhood, but they do not believe that major social problems can be addressed by parent programs.

Mundel goes on to offer several possible reasons for this lack of correlation between social problem-solving and parent programs. Two of these seem especially important. Rights, entitlements, and universalistic perspectives (such as that of Dokecki and Moroney) notwithstanding, parent program advocates must face the fact that budget reductions are necessary. (Indeed, since Mundel wrote his essay, rather severe budget cuts have taken place, particularly in social programs.) Thus, like it or not, advocates are, temporarily at least, in a zero-sum game. If parent programs are to be more heavily funded, other programs must be cut.

Second, as Mundel understates the point, the linkages between policy choices and parent programs have not been well-established. In short, the data are not strong—or at least have not been shown to policymakers to be strong. An important role for social science, then, is to provide data showing the effects that can be expected from increased expenditures on social programs in general and parent programs in particular. We will return to this theme in the second section of this book.

REFERENCE

Clarke-Stewart, K.A., & Apfel, N. Evaluating parental effects on child development. In L. Shulman (Ed.), *Review of research in education*. Ithaca, NY: F. E. Peacock, 1979.

ONE

THE FORMATIVE ERA IN AMERICAN PARENT EDUCATION: OVERVIEW AND INTERPRETATION*

STEVEN L. SCHLOSSMAN

INTRODUCTION

This is a highly selective and, in part, speculative inquiry into the history of American parent education in its formative period: the first three decades of the 20th century. The essay attempts to provide an overview of changing perspectives and programs, while also—relying on a unique and unusually detailed set of historical data—offering insight into the dynamic process by which innovations in parent education first arose and were institutionalized. In particular, the essay examines the creative role played by Lawrence K. Frank and the Laura Spelman Rockefeller Memorial (an autonomous foundation within the Rockefeller philanthropies) in shaping the enormously popular (but largely forgotten) parent education movement of the 1920s. The essay also seeks to explain, more speculatively, why the message of the parent educators was so warmly received when, in retrospect, it appears so doctrinaire, rigid, and unscientific. Finally, the essay suggests that there may be greater continuity between parent education "policy" in the 1920s and today than might at first be apparent.

BACKDROP: THE PRE-WORLD WAR I PERIOD

In historical context much depends, of course, on how we define the rather nebulous notion of "parent education." For example, to define it broadly in terms of its sponsorship—as all formal efforts by public or private agencies to upgrade the attitudes and skills which parents bring to childrearing—the history can fairly be traced to the beginnings of this country in the early 17th century. Church and state then worked in tandem to enforce the child nurture goals sanctioned by the Bible. In Massachusetts, individuals called "tithingmen" were appointed to investigate the family situations of children whose parents were suspected of providing inadequately for their religious and secular education. If the parents were found guilty of neglect and, after being forewarned to educate their children properly, failed to do so, the children could be taken away and placed in other families for proper nurture. Nothing short of a child's soul was at stake.

One can also define parent education in terms of the kinds of publications available to parents as guides to more effective childrearing. A formal literature to aid parents dates back to the ancient Greeks, at least. In the American context, exhortatory books and pamphlets on child nurture were widely read from the late colonial period onward. But for now we need to go back only as far as the mid-19th century, when "advice to parents" books and periodicals first appeared in abundance. These publications were addressed almost exclusively to mothers and portrayed them as the rightful ruling monarchs of the home. At the same time, however—in a classic Victorian paradox—this literature conveyed to mothers one principal message: self-sacrifice. Woman's earthly duty was to sacrifice every personal desire to the needs of her children and the wants of her husband. This domestic message formed a major component of what Barbara Welter (1966) has termed the "cult of true womanhood," which defined the boundaries of acceptable female behavior for most of the 19th century by centering the purpose of her existence in home, husband, and children.

Parent education can also be defined mainly in reference to a variety of organized self-help activities, i.e., activities that went beyond the individual consumption of childrearing literature. Historians have traced the existence of parent self-help organizations to the early 1800s. Not until the 1890s, however, did large numbers of American women—building upon prior organizational experience in social clubs and in temperance campaigns—band together in large numbers in "mothers' study" or "child study" groups to discuss common parental concerns. In 1897, several hundred of these scattered and previously isolated groups joined to form the National Congress of Mothers, which we know today as the National PTA (Parent-Teachers Association).

PTA women did not organize in order to protest their position as society's anointed childrearers. In organizing, these women had different objectives in mind: (1) they hoped to break down their isolation in individual households; (2) to share everyday childrearing frustrations in order to diffuse them; (3) to establish forums for self-instruction in new scientific research on children's physical, psychological, and moral development; (4) to convey basic knowledge on childrearing to impoverished women; and (5) perhaps most distinctively, to serve at local, state, and national levels as political lobbyists to safeguard the special needs of women and children. The PTA urged members to extend their private family values and concerns into the political arena by campaigning for changes in laws and institutions that impinged directly on the quality of children's lives, both at home and in their communities. Political education and political action went hand in hand and were integral to the PTA's definition of parent education. In sum, the PTA—America's archetypal parent self-help organization in the years before World War I—viewed parent education as a vehicle for reinforcing individual and collective female identities, for relieving parental anxieties and burdens, for disseminating scientific advice on childrearing to all social classes, and for changing society by organizing mothers in common political cause (recall that the PTA was organized long before the Suffrage Amendment gave women more conventional political access).

The PTA espoused a view of women and of sex roles that most people today would find unduly constraining: for example, the PTA held mothers directly and fully accountable for their children's destinies. At the same time, however, the PTA's approach to parent education went well beyond traditional definitions of sex roles and significantly extended the sphere of women's legitimate social and political participation. The PTA believed that collective political participation by mothers was essential to the well-being of all children, and urged upon women a role of citizen-activist that seems today boldly unconventional, adventuresome, and certainly not sanctioned by the "cult of true womanhood."

A similar tension was evident in the PTA's approach to the nascent sciences of child development. On the one hand, the PTA considered it essential to convey in popular form to mothers—all mothers, well-to-do and poor alike—the results of recent research in child psychology, pediatric medicine, and nutrition. On the other hand, the PTA's program in parent education was neither dependent on, nor subservient to, the mandates of science. As befits its grassroots origins, the PTA continued to hold traditional, religiously based precepts in equally high regard. In part, this was because the sciences of child development were not very well-grounded empirically in the years prior to World War I, but this, of course, is more easily recognized in retrospect. While the PTA did not question the practical value of new scientific research on child development, it continued to place greater trust in mothers' maternal instincts and moral sensibilities.

We thus see in early 20th-century parent education, as embodied in the work of the PTA, an intriguing balance of perspectives between private domestic responsibility and public political activity, and a reliance on religion and maternal instinct, versus a reliance on science and formal instruction. While there is little reason for nostalgia here, it is important to recognize the existence of this balance and these tensions in the theory and practice of parent education in the pre-World War I era. As we shall see, these features disappeared shortly after the war.

PARENT EDUCATION IN POST-WORLD WAR I AMERICA: THE AGE OF LAWRENCE K. FRANK

During the 1920s, public and professional interest in parent education coalesced into a well-organized social movement which, through myriad programs and publications, reached millions of adults. From scholars, government agencies, foundations, publishers, and a heterogeneous audience, parent education received more systematic and sustained attention than at any time until the 1970s.

In post-World War I America, the knowledge base for parent education progressed to levels of scientific refinement undreamed of in the late 19th century "child study." The field's claim to public attention now came to rest almost entirely on its purported foundation in controlled observations of young children and on its ability to precisely determine "norms" of child development. The nation's leading behavioral scientists contended that their research bore no relation to earlier, largely discredited scientific studies, especially to those by the flamboyant psychologist, G. Stanley Hall. Sponsors of parent education felt similarly: Their programs and philosophy had nothing in common with the educational efforts of the PTA (which relied on Hall as its principal scientific authority). These precedents were embarrassing for their amateurism, their moralism, and their sentimentalism and were better off forgotten.

More shall be said later about the tremendous popular appeal of science in childrearing in the 1920s. For now the key point is simply that the new parent education message reached a much wider audience than ever before. In part its influence was a byproduct of the growing prestige of science generally in postwar America. But even more, I believe, it was the outcome of the concerted, well-financed effort spearheaded by the Laura Spelman Rockefeller Memorial (LSRM), and especially by its chief spokesperson, Lawrence K. Frank.

Frank's role in drawing nationwide attention to the implications of new scientific research on children can hardly be exaggerated. While channeling millions of dollars into a great variety of programs, Frank articulated policy and monitored the organization of the parent education movement as a whole. In an era renowned for "progressive" educational experiments, parent education became one of the most acclaimed innovations of its day.

Frank's background, early ideas, and personality shed important light on his strategy in charting the course of postwar parent education.[1] Born in Cincinnati in 1890, Frank moved (with his mother, after his parents separated) to New York City where he attended public schools before entering Columbia College. Not an outstanding student, Frank nonetheless read widely in the nascent social and behavioral sciences, acquired a vocational skill in statistical economics, and participated in an extracurricular capacity with Frances Perkins (later to be Roosevelt's secretary of labor) in a number of municipal investigations. After graduation, Frank worked for several years as a budget analyst for New York Telephone Company, during which he published several articles dealing with theoretical issues in accounting procedure and monetary analysis from a politically liberal perspective. Soon he also began writing for such publications as *The Dial* and *New Republic* as a social and political commentator at large.

Frank married in 1917, and he and his wife had their first child during the war. While on the staff of the War Industries Board, he became close friends with the brilliant economist, Wesley C. Mitchell. In 1916, Mitchell's wife, Lucy Sprague Mitchell, had founded the Bureau of Educational Experiments (later the Bank Street College of Education), which opened America's first laboratory nursery school in 1919. Throughout Frank's career his intellectual interests shifted in obvious ways to incorporate new personal experiences and friendships. His experience as a father and his close acquaintance with the Mitchells turned him systematically for the first time to educational issues. Probably reflecting Lucy's influence, he championed nursery schools and "progressive" educational ideas in general. Frank's commitment to the field of education grew stronger in 1920 when Wesley Mitchell, a founder of the New School for Social Research, asked him to be the school's business manager. During the same year, Frank and his wife decided to send their child to Lucy's nursery school.

Frank remained at the New School for a little over two years, during which he published two popular articles on educational theory and practice that pointed in the direction of his later work in parent education. His initial piece appeared in the avant-garde periodical *The Freeman* (Frank, 1922a) and dealt critically with efforts by New York public school officials to censor social studies textbooks which reflected the influence of the so-called "new history." The controversy appealed to Frank, because it highlighted a more general tendency of public schools to teach conformity to socially approved ideas and behavior rather than "intelligence." He therefore used it to advance a wholesale attack on American education. Implicit throughout the article was Frank's belief that new educational mechanisms imbued with the spirit of "intelligence" were essential to circumvent the ingrained failures of the public schools.

Frank's (1922b) second popular piece on education appeared in the sober pages of *School and Society* and was a good deal more positive in tone. Following Dewey (with whom he had studied at Columbia), Frank argued the need to divorce schools from "institutional safe-keeping. . . . The world has need of intelligence far beyond the possibilities of its occurrence, and we must insist upon the schools' undertaking the work of emancipating whatever intelligence exists" (p. 657). In a sweeping Jamesian metaphor, he proposed an "educational 'equivalent of war' " to liberate individuals from the "mythical assumptions and conceptions of the past" and instill devotion to "science as the method of intelligence" (pp. 657, 659). "Causality will operate in any case," he concluded, "and intelligence will see to it that, as far as possible, the causalities that operate are the causalities of its choice. Only then can there be a technique for generating a chosen future out of a given present" (p. 659).

In short, Frank held out a vision of a better world and the means to create it. A revitalized school system would play its part, but Frank's (1922b) ideas on the ultimate purpose of education far transcended anything that school reform alone could achieve: "The most formidable obstacle . . . is the almost universal desire to guard the young against a knowledge of their elders' ineptitude" (p. 658). Within a year, Frank would conclude that truly radical change in education required that the elders themselves, as well as the young, acknowledge their own ineptitude and seek to overcome it by acquiring "the habit of intelligent behavior." The parent education movement was already latent in his thought.

Late in 1922 Frank left his post at the New School to become

Beardsley Ruml's second-in-command at LSRM. In its 4 years of existence, LSRM had dispensed several million dollars to advance "child welfare," mainly in the form of block grants to such established organizations as the Boy Scouts and YMCA. This approach no longer satisfied LSRM's trustees, who asked Ruml to develop an alternative philanthropic strategy that would retain, but restructure, the foundation's commitment to improving the quality of children's lives. Ruml then turned to Frank for suggestions. Frank responded with a basic outline of what became the parent education movement: a program of child study for mothers gathered in small groups and based on scientific research in child development, to be implemented by sponsorship of university based research centers, fellowships for training scientists and practitioners, and parent organizations to supervise mothers on the local level. Ruml gave Frank the go-ahead to develop the idea on his own and the assurance that he would support Frank before the trustees.

Frank's comprehensive plan reflected his principal intellectual strength as an integrator, or as he preferred, an "orchestrator" of the unfocused, half-formed ideas of others into fully formed and focused programs of inquiry and action. Having committed himself to science as the key to social progress, to educational innovations as the key to liberating "intelligence," and to the early childhood years as the key to molding healthy personalities, he was able to envision a social movement which, starting at rock bottom with childrearing practices in the home, would radiate outward and eventually transform all social institutions. Frank's vision essentially defined policy in the field of parent education for a decade and a half, and brought to it an unprecedented level of systematization and central coordination.

What were the precedents upon which Frank drew in designing parent education policy? Frank's model for organized child study by mothers was clearly not the PTA, whose educational program he and most social scientists looked down upon as representing a sentimental unscientific approach. Instead, his model was the Federation for Child Study (soon to be renamed the Child Study Association of America, or CSA), a small, exclusive group of women formerly affiliated with the New York Ethical Culture Society, which sponsored lectures, prepared bibliographies, and conducted regular meetings to provide guidance and a forum for parents to discuss childrearing problems. Here, in Frank's view, was a first-class educational organization: It boasted a long tradition (founded in 1888), an established and impressive leadership, proven capacity in adult education, an excellent publications record, and an outspoken commitment to new scientific research as the key to both happier children and social progress.

The CSA, for its part, never doubted its superiority to the PTA.

Indeed, its members held themselves aloof from, and considered themselves superior to, nearly all other women's organizations. There was nothing "clubby" about the CSA's parent education program, its leaders liked to say. There was a seriousness of purpose to the CSA that Frank hoped would inspire the mass effort in self-education which he envisioned for mothers throughout the country.[2]

Precedents for advancing scientific study of the child were both more diffuse and problematic. There were four key institutions: the Yale Psycho-Clinic, directed by Arnold Gesell and founded in 1911; the Bureau of Educational Experiments, directed by Frank's friend, Lucy Sprague Mitchell, and founded in 1916; the Iowa Child Welfare Research Station, directed by Bird Baldwin and founded in 1917; and the Merrill-Palmer Motherhood and Homemaking School, directed by Edna Noble White and founded in 1918 (it actually began operations in 1920).

None of these pioneering ventures, however, provided Frank with quite what he wanted. Gesell's clinic, for example, lacked a nursery school and was dominated by the ego of its founder; the Bureau's fierce commitment to its distinctive research style, plus its close affiliation with the radical wing of the progressive education movement, effectively isolated it from the mainstream scientific community; the Iowa Station's early eugenic orientation, together with its uncertain political/financial base, made its future usefulness uncertain.[3] Merrill-Palmer came closest to providing Frank with a model worthy of emulation, particularly in its strong commitment to community service, its emphasis on interdisciplinary research, and its heavy reliance on a nursery school to focus research and to instruct young women in the most up-to-date techniques of childrearing.[4] But, in Frank's view, Merrill-Palmer's isolation from a university setting presented an insurmountable drawback to its research potential.

Furthermore, however committed it was to the nursery school and to preparental education, Merrill-Palmer sponsored no program in parent education per se (a fact which surprised even Edna White when, in 1940, she reviewed her early annual reports). The nursery school functioned in the manner connoted by the adjective "laboratory": it was a place for observing children by staff and students only. Parents were systematically isolated from the school's activities and hardly recognized as significant actors in their children's education. If parents figured at all in Merrill-Palmer's early annual reports, they were listed as among the "visitors," whose presence was regarded as unnatural and problematic because it disrupted the children's and the researchers' "daily regime." In short, even among the foremost pioneers in early childhood education, the link between the nursery school and parent education had not been clearly drawn.[5]

Frank proceeded slowly at first to make his vision reality. To try to overcome the scorn which universities had traditionally shown toward research on children, LSRM initially funded a Committee on Child Development within the National Research Council, under the leadership of Columbia's prestigious psychologist, Robert S. Woodworth. Among other functions, the Committee sponsored conferences which, by attracting many of the nation's leading scholars, enhanced the academic status of children's studies while raising the confidence of scholars pursuing them. The prestige and scholarly value of these meetings notwithstanding, the Committee mainly provided gloss for the educational movement Frank was engineering behind the scenes. Ultimate success would depend, he felt, on vast expansion of experimental research on children and careful monitoring of the quality of intellectual exchange in child study groups.

To enlist universities in the cause of child development research, Frank decided first to win over Columbia's Teachers College, easily the nation's most distinguished school of education. Early in 1924, he made Dean James Earl Russell a spectacular offer: LSRM would entertain a proposal from Teachers College to fund a research center on young children for 5 years, with a strong possibility of renewal. Interestingly enough, Russell initially was not very enthusiastic, but his faculty (notably Edward L. Thorndike) helped change his mind. Russell (1924) responded to Frank with a full proposal which accentuated the importance of the preschool age: "We realize that education begins far back of the school, and that the school at best is conditioned by influences beyond its control." Through Frank's initiative, then, the first well-funded, university-based, research center on children—the Institute of Child Welfare Research—opened at Teachers College late in 1924. Shortly thereafter, Frank persuaded the nation's foremost woman psychologist, Helen Thompson Woolley of the Merill-Palmer School, to become first permanent director of the Institute.

While the Institute, for a variety of reasons, never quite realized its intellectual promise, it served Frank's immediate purpose quite well. Having "persuaded" the nation's leading school of education to sponsor research on early childhood, and the leading woman psychologist to supervise the research, other universities were more easily persuaded to cooperate. Thus, in short order, LSRM placed Iowa's Child Welfare Research Station on equal financial footing with Teachers College, and during the next few years other institutes followed at Berkeley, Toronto, and Minnesota. As Frank had feared, traditional academicians at these universities sometimes resisted his initiatives as somehow not worthy of, or amenable to, serious intellectual effort. The funding of the research center at Minnesota was delayed, for example, partly due to an attack on the intellectual value of research on children and partly because the reigning academic departments wanted the LSRM money for themselves. At Berkeley, the president and vice president were at first cold to Frank's offer—until he went to Stanford and began negotiations there, whereupon Berkeley warmed to the idea rather quickly.

While research was the main goal of the child development institutes, each initially served also as a training ground for a new profession of woman parent educators. LSRM provided 1-year and 2-year fellowships to advance this goal, selecting for additional study experienced women in such fields as home economics, dietetics, nursing, social work, and teaching with the expectation that they would form an elite corps of expert practitioners for whom there would be great demand by state and local governments and private educational organizations as the parent education movement spread nationwide. At LSRM, Frank took close interest in the fellowship program, for it embodied his commitment to popularization of scientific knowledge as the key to social betterment. While scholars in child development generally remember LSRM's fellowship program mainly for the famous researchers who benefited from it, to Frank the sponsorship of expert practitioners seemed as central to the immediate success of the parent education movement. For they, more than the researchers, were principally responsible for building local support and providing living proof of the value of science in child-rearing. They were Frank's advance guard.

If Frank expected the institutes to help extend knowledge of child development to America's heartland, he was equally concerned with building the movement from the bottom up; that is, instilling in mothers the desire and capacity to apply scientific ideas wisely. Dissemination of information, however valuable, was not enough. To employ new knowledge to their children's best advantage and as a spur to their own continuing education, mothers had to approach the fruits of research "intelligently," in the spirit of scientific investigators themselves.

To realize these goals Frank proposed three major new programs. First, as previously noted, he proposed to make a small, but unusually sophisticated group of New York women (the CSA) the exemplars for organized child study; second, he attempted to encourage women's colleges and women college graduates to incorporate child development into their definition of liberal education and thereby gain the prestige of their example for the movement as a whole; and third, he helped persuade LSRM to fund a mass parent education magazine. Each endeavor met with varying degrees of success, but each attested to the grand scale on which Frank had conceived the movement and to the flexibility of LSRM in approving new methods to achieve his goals.

Concerning LSRM's support of the CSA, only a few additional

comments need be made. The CSA took its mission as seriously as Frank had expected, becoming a model of bold intellectual ecumenicism in the sciences of child development, an energetic and self-conscious elite in upholding standards of child study, and a practical guide to women's organizations interested in acquiring higher educational purpose. The CSA's most important contribution to Frank's grand design, though, may well have come relatively early in the movement when in October, 1925, it organized—with a special grant from LSRM, of course—the first two formal meetings of scholars and practitioners of parent education. The first was a small, select 6-day conference in Bronxville, New York, which, as many participants later recalled, was crucial in building *esprit de corps* and self-conscious identity in a previously nonexistent field. Of even greater impact was the 3-day public conference which followed at the Waldorf-Astoria. Filled to overflowing by several thousand women from the New York area, the conference received considerable publicity, resulted in a major publication (*Concerning Parents*) and, all in all, put parent education on the nation's intellectual map.

Nonetheless, the CSA was never quite comfortable playing its part in the parent education movement. Gradually, a consensus emerged among the CSA's leadership, which placed a ceiling on the height of the organization's fame and influence. Frank offered them the chance to edit a popular childrearing journal (*Parents' Magazine*); the CSA turned him down, choosing instead to publish a journal of higher intellectual quality (*Child Study*) but of little popular appeal. Frank asked them to hire a field agent to increase their influence outside New York and among Protestants (the CSA leadership was mainly Jewish and/or Ethical Culturist); the CSA chose to confine its field agent's activities to New York City alone, focusing attention solely on black parents in Harlem. At Frank's urging the CSA significantly increased the number of affiliated mothers' study groups under its supervision; but after a few years the CSA withdrew its sponsorship from some of them when it became clear that these groups failed to maintain high intellectual standards. The CSA considered itself an elite in parent education and intended to remain one.

In sum, the CSA remained somewhat reluctant to play the more aggressive leadership role that Frank had envisioned for them. Nonetheless, Frank's generous support of the CSA in the 1920s proved to be a shrewd philanthropic gamble. Virtually overnight it created one of the main spark plugs of the parent education movement simply by liberating the latent energies and talents of a small, local, atypical organization to serve broader national goals.

Of all Frank's efforts, his attempt to gain cooperation from the leading women's colleges was least successful. The tightly knit, predominantly liberal arts faculties of the Seven Sisters were understandably suspicious of curriculum changes proposed by outsiders, particularly those which even vaguely threatened to undermine their historic mission of providing women with the same education as men (more on this matter later).

Frank's defeat in the women's colleges was partially compensated for by his success with the American Association of University Women (AAUW). Though dominated by Seven Sisters' graduates, the AAUW gladly assumed a position of leadership in the parent education movement. To be sure, older traditions did not die overnight. When Helen Woolley proclaimed the virtues of scientific study of the child before the annual AAUW convention in 1922, not a few of the classically trained old guard felt betrayed. By the following year, however, her position found wide support, and the AAUW adopted an educational program encouraging individual branches to study scientific literature on preschool and elementary education. Lois Hayden Meek, a recent Teachers College doctoral graduate in child psychology, was chosen to head the program and proved tireless in her efforts to develop new instructional materials, write popular promotional articles, and travel the country several times over spreading the gospel. Until 1929, when Meek returned to Teachers College to assist Woolley in supervising the Institute of Child Development Research, the parent education movement had a staunch ally in the AAUW, and Frank a partial victory in his effort to win college women to his cause.[6]

By the summer of 1925, LSRM had disbursed well over a million dollars to foster the parent education movement. With the creation that fall of the National Council of Parent Education and the beginning of plans for a yearbook on preschool and parent education by the National Society for the Study of Education, the movement had become one of the most widely discussed and visible new forces on the educational scene. As yet, however, LSRM's most far-reaching investment in parent education—the subsidy of *Parents' Magazine*—had not reached fruition.

The initial idea for what eventually became *Parents' Magazine* was George J. Hecht's. After a distinguished performance during World War I as a propagandist for George J. Creel's Committee on Public Information, Hecht had devoted himself to social service pursuits, first as founder of the periodical *Better Times* and later as founder and secretary of the Welfare Council of New York City. Sometime in 1923 (while still a bachelor), he got the idea for a magazine on childrearing to help parents by conveying to them, in popular form, the most recent scientific knowledge on child development. After drumming up minimal financial support among his well-to-do friends and acquaintances, Hecht contacted LSRM director Beardsley Ruml to see whether his venture might be integrated into the fledgling parent education movement and whether he could gain moral and financial support from the Rockefellers.[7]

Frank was kept informed of these preliminary negotiations and advised Ruml to maintain contact with Hecht in order to monitor the growth of his magazine. The potential for distortion and commercialization of new scientific knowledge had long concerned Frank, who feared that parent education might become just another fad. In the spring of 1924, before discussions with Hecht had gone very far, Frank (1924a) tried to anticipate the problem:

> As the number of women engaged in child study and in attending parent classes increases there will arise a host of potential readers for a periodical which will carry information, discussions, reports and the like, written for the lay reader. Inevitably this market will attract commercial capital which has already discovered the profitableness in women's magazines generally. The danger therefore of a meretricious or even vicious publication arising is very real. It can be averted by inaugurating a magazine for parents under the supervision and editorial direction of competent persons and established agencies in the field such as the Federation of Child Study and the Institute of Child Welfare Research at Teachers College. Such a publication would have to be subsidized for several years before it could be put on a self-supporting basis from subscriptions and carefully supervised advertising. The expenditure of funds for the promotion of such a magazine, however, could be carried out so as to give a real impetus to the parent training movement in the states.

After considerable delay and internal doubt, LSRM agreed to finance *Parents' Magazine* (the original title was *Children, the Magazine for Parents*) and, as Frank had suggested, to rely on Teachers College and the CSA to guarantee scientific accuracy in content. This arrangement troubled Hecht somewhat, as he felt he needed a freer hand to make the periodical more commercially viable than academics were likely to approve. As Frank (1924b) reported, Hecht was "rather apprehensive of the success of the publication if the conservative and academic attitude manifested by the Columbia people were to dominate the editorial policy." Nonetheless, LSRM and Hecht reached agreement in late 1924, although the first issue of the magazine did not appear until nearly 2 years later.

The final arrangement was extraordinarily complex and roundabout. It reflected LSRM's reluctance to be publicly identified, or officially connected, with the periodical and to rely on its beneficiaries in the parent education movement to exercise quality control. First, Hecht had to gather $100,000 on his own to subsidize the publication. Then, LSRM offered to channel additional funds discreetly through Teachers College and later through Yale, Minnesota, and Iowa (due in part to Hecht's fears of a Teachers College monopoly) to create a separate business corporation in which the universities held a substantial majority of stock. The corporation agreed in advance to hire Hecht as president and publisher, to allow him considerable latitude in choosing an editor, and to appoint an advisory board of experts to write, solicit, and evaluate articles. In return for their participation, the universities were to receive corporate dividends for the purpose of advancing child development research.

In actuality, the universities' control of the magazine, while substantial on paper and exercised fairly effectively in the 1920s, diminished steadily thereafter. The corporate arrangement basically played into the hands of a brilliant publisher like Hecht, who knew that a good offense—booming circulation—was the best defense against academic conservatism. Periodically, the universities threatened to resign from the enterprise and to forego possible dividends, but the magazine's substantial success with the public (it soon became the largest selling education periodical in the world) made it potentially embarrassing to do so.

Another complication was that while the universities technically owned the majority of stock, it was legally unclear whether they could sell it, or to whom, or how. LSRM had supplied the purchase money in the first place and its successors, the Spelman Fund and then the Rockefeller Foundation itself, refused to take back the stock, assume ownership, or intervene directly in the magazine's affairs. Furthermore, the universities had to proceed most cautiously with their threat to resign, lest they subvert the magazine's intellectual legitimacy and jeopardize future child development grants from the Rockefeller philanthropies. In short, the universities were boxed in, or at best, never adequately resolved basic dilemmas of control and editorial policy. Several decades passed before they were able to extricate themselves from the arrangement and reap a financial reward for their participation—and this came only after Frank, who had long since left the Rockefeller Foundation, came to their aid and threatened to sue Hecht for reneging on the initial agreement.

Whether or not *Parents' Magazine* pleased its sponsors, the fact remained that LSRM's subsidization had made its existence (and the handsome fortune Hecht derived from it) possible. More than any other component of LSRM's parent education policy, this venture revealed the unconventional institutional arrangements it was willing to subsidize in order to disseminate new scientific knowledge and foster a mass education movement.

FRANK'S PARENT EDUCATION POLICY: IMPLICIT ASSUMPTIONS

Such, in broad outline, were the largest basic components of the parent education program which Frank and LSRM engineered in the 1920s. Certain aspects of Frank's governing philosophy are obvious: his faith in "intelligence" as the key to social progress and individual happiness and in scientific method and empirically grounded knowledge as the only true paths to "intelligence"; his hope, tinged with ambivalence, that scientific knowledge could be popularized without being vulgarized; and his confident assumption that the fruits of scientific research would yield immediate practical applications. Yet other elements in Frank's philosophy, as well as in his motivation, are less readily apparent and can be identified best by briefly examining several internal policy memoranda he wrote in order to persuade his superiors at LSRM that parent education was indeed worth "a million or so a year" (for a more critical assessment of Frank, see Shea, 1980).

First, it is essential to recognize that Frank was consciously responding to LSRM's needs as a foundation in selecting parent education as the foundation's alternative child welfare strategy. LSRM's trustees wanted very badly to redefine its basic mission, and to do so as quickly as possible. That is why they had hired both Ruml and Frank. After several disappointing years of supporting scattered projects whose influence could not be easily demonstrated and whose activities often overlapped, the trustees clearly wanted to place their bets on a long-term, focused venture whose potential impact would be greater and more definable.

But there was more to it than that. In the early 1920s, LSRM was only one of several prominent foundations trying to move beyond the 19th century "gospel of wealth" tradition of charity and to integrate the prestigious new social sciences into their philanthropic policy. The Commonwealth Fund, as LSRM and other foundations were very much aware, had been first to act boldly along these lines, by sponsoring in 1921 a long-term, multifaceted experiment in "delinquency prevention," which conspicuously utilized the new science of "mental hygiene" as its knowledge base. No other foundation was likely afterward to encroach on the Fund's "territory" in dealing with children showing "behavior problems" (Cohen, 1980).

Parent education presented LSRM with a similar kind of opportunity to be first in "doing good." It was an area as ripe for development as delinquency prevention, as "modern" in its reliance on social science as the true path to social progress, and equally useful in defining for the foundation a long-term mission through which to establish a distinct public identity. So Frank advised the trustees that they:

> were probably choosing a field of so fundamental an importance to child welfare and of so large an extent that they might look forward for several decades at least to the productive expenditure of a fairly large share of the Memorial's income. . . . Today there are but a few desultory attempts to train parents in the light of the knowledge of physical and mental health which is increasing so rapidly from year to year. The technical literature and popular discussions on the subject are voluminous, but scarcely anything has been done toward the translating of this knowledge into the actual practice of parents in the home. It would seem therefore that in parent training the possibilities of development are practically unlimited. (Frank, 1924c)

There was nothing crass about this kind of competitive foundation gamesmanship, only a genuine desire to spend fortunes wisely, to avoid overlap, to be up-to-date (i.e., promote the social sciences), and to be creative in the choice of benevolent objects.

The parent education program also satisfied the foundation's desire to invest monies in start-up activities only. Thus, even though a private institution (Teachers College) was the first to be funded, the parent education program as a whole centered on state universities, where both a framework and a tradition existed for public support of scientifically based educational programs designed to upgrade the quality of community life (the agricultural experiment stations provided the best example, in Frank's view). Universities capable of pursuing first-class research in child development were few, but in nearly every state, Frank believed, an educational institution already existed which could serve "more or less [as] a leader of public sentiment" for the state as a whole. The philanthropist's key task was one "of integrating the existing facilities and agencies and refocusing their efforts upon the general subject of homemaking and child care so that the additional expenditures for facilities and personnel may be kept to a minimum, at least after the preliminary period of demonstration and experiment" (Frank, 1924d).

These quasipolitical considerations were central to Frank's success in gaining firm support from Ruml and LSRM's trustees for his parent education program. Nevertheless, they were only marginal to other key elements in his philosophy, motivation, and style of leadership.

Perhaps most apparent throughout Frank's general writing and correspondence was his sense of supreme righteousness in pursuing his cause. In Frank's view, there was nothing questionable about offering educational institutions huge sums of money (for the time period) in order to "persuade" them to transform or add to their research agendas and curriculums along lines dictated by the Rockefeller Foundation. The cause of parent education was just, the one true path to enlightenment. Hence, Frank perceived nothing in his "negotiation" that might be considered unwarranted intervention in university affairs, or even a bribe. After all, the educators were "free" to say no.

Frank's attitude and approach toward the elite women's colleges embodied this viewpoint perfectly. Frank refused to admit defeat in his effort to get the Seven Sisters to abide by his wishes and become major instruments of the parent education movement. Even in 1927, after ample experience had demonstrated the improbability, Frank (1927) remained confident he would triumph: "It seems clear that the establishment of a child study major in the women's colleges may be one of the major features in the parent education movement and that it will almost certainly come about either now or later."

The women's colleges' obstinance frustrated Frank for a variety of reasons. Not only did it hamper his effort to win over young women who would soon "occupy a more or less strategic position in the community," it blunted his larger reformist effort to "modernize" higher education for women. Frank considered the traditional college curriculum as hopelessly backward and unrelated to current needs and opportunities. Coursework in applied child development, he anticipated, would provide the wedge for a more thorough transformation. A truly "modern" education would cater much more consciously to women's special needs as future mothers. Women students would no longer study sciences like chemistry, biology, and psychology in the abstract "as isolated academic topics," he suggested, "but rather as means to the handling of the situations set by the care of children, particularly, and the management of homes and institutions." These courses might "at first" be optional, but eventually become mandatory. So he concluded:

> Parent training in the colleges is particularly promising not only because of the character of the students but also because under this name and guise it should be possible to begin that long deferred process of revising the curriculum in women's colleges upon a more intelligent basis. Sooner or later this revision must be undertaken and its accomplishment must wait upon some method or device whereby the present rational, intellectualistic curriculum with its conceptual knowledge can be thrown in sharp contrast with the training in methods and techniques for meeting situations, which is the method of intelligence. (Frank, 1923)

Frank's critique of women's higher education acquires added meaning in light of his corollary belief that American mothers were fundamentally inept at rearing children because they did not know how to utilize the advice of experts:

> In the early years at least, a child's welfare is almost completely controlled by the parents, more especially the mother, who must carry out, in the

daily life of the home, the directions and advice of the doctor, nutrition expert, the psychiatrist and all the other professions and experts concerned with child life. But there has been no large-scale effort to provide the means for the training of parents in the effective discharge of parental responsibilities. (Frank, 1924e)

Frank's mention of psychiatrists among his list of experts deserving deference from mothers was no passing reference. Frank emphasized the need for a psychiatric service oriented especially toward mothers-to-be; his argument was consistent with his critiques of women's colleges and of American mothers, and not a little reminiscent of classic 19th-century stereotypes of the so-called "hysterical woman."

In the development of intelligent and competent parents one of the large contributions to be made is in the resolution of those incipient mental disorders, personality defects and various and sundry hysterias which so largely handicap the mother in providing the proper care and training for her children. We are gradually coming to see that in our educational programs we must provide more and more for what may be called the emancipation of the individual from the coercion both of this individual experience and of the group experience or tradition which so largely impedes and thwarts the realization of a wholesome regime of life. It is therefore quite appropriate to suggest that the provision of what we now call psychiatric service is more or less essential to the training of parents, particularly among women, and it is not unwarranted to remark that a considerable portion of our educational efforts and opportunities are wasted because they are being directed or offered to individuals who are preoccupied, if not more actually constrained, by these hidden conflicts and emotional turmoils. It goes without saying, of course, that a wholesome regimen is essential to a woman who is to bear promising children and the question may be raised whether we are not unsuccessful in obtaining that wholesome regimen of life among young women largely because they are compelled by the unsolved conflicts to pursue modes of living which, however unwholesome, nevertheless bring some escape or alleviation of their difficulties. (Frank, 1924f)

Whether Frank himself thought better of these notions, or whether his superiors demurred from them, is difficult to determine. But Frank eventually dropped his recommendation for a psychiatric service from the memoranda which he circulated among his colleagues. His comments do provide further indication, though, of how deeply rooted in women's ignorance and/or miseducation he considered the problems to be.

Two final points round out the key assumptions in Frank's approach to parent education. If Frank was pessimistic about the current state of American mothering, he was nonetheless remarkably optimistic about the revolution in attitudes and practices which the parent education movement would make possible. One reason was that further research on child development, he felt certain, would dramatically diminish the "diversity of opinions and counsel," which he considered "astonishing" and surely confusing to the average parent. Frank was, at this point in his career, an avid positivist who believed sincerely that the accumulation of facts would dissolve intellectual disagreements. The relative unanimity which characterized research in some of the natural sciences would also come to characterize the social sciences as they matured, he believed. Through the work of the child development research institutes, basic agreement in approach and interpretation would soon emerge and provide parents with "*a* carefully worked out technique for meeting the needs of children in the home" (my italics; Frank, 1924g).

Allied to this view was a faith that parents could, via education, wholly change their basic attitudes and patterns of interaction with their children. When "intelligence" reigned supreme, all was possible, particularly when (in classic Deweyan terms) "intelligence" was activated by "interest." Parents, Frank wrote, were "under the strongest possible incentive to learn that which will benefit the child." "Necessity and desire" combined to make possible what might at first glance seem impossible for adults, namely, "to learn an almost complete set of new habits and methods in taking care of the child" (Frank, 1924c). It was as if scientific truth would cleanse away impurities in parental thought and make feasible, as a goal of public policy, the transformation of parenthood into totally learned behavior.

PARENT EDUCATION AND THE CRISIS OF MIDDLE-CLASS FAMILY LIFE IN THE ROARING TWENTIES: SOME SPECULATIONS

Parent education was extraordinarily popular in the 1920s despite the fact that, compared to the approach of the PTA in the prewar era, it was defined much more narrowly and rigidly. Earlier interest in parent education as a stepping stone to social reform disappeared almost entirely. Parent education became apolitical: It referred, by and large, to the instruction of middle-class women in ways they could rear their own children in accordance with new dictums from the behavioral sciences.

The new dictums were severe indeed. The 1920s witnessed the triumph of a variety of behavioristic psychologies, often but by no means necessarily associated with the work of John Watson. The emphasis in the new parent education—so different from that popularized by Hall and his PTA devotees—was on strict habit formation, particularly in the preschool years. Parents were offered lengthy lists of do's and don't's and enjoined not to let affection divert the application of scientifically derived nurture techniques. What most endangered healthy child development, according to the new conventional wisdom, was the parents' tendency to sentimentalize children. Overall, parent educators in the

1920s stressed the extraordinary amount of control which parents (who were duly deferential to science) could exercise over their children's futures. When children failed to mature properly, it was entirely the parents' fault and, moreover, science would pinpoint the precise cause.

Why—aside from the power and prestige which association with the Rockefellers imparted—were behavioral scientists and parent educators so successful in selling this message to the public? Obviously no single, simple answer will do, and this is not the occasion for an extended discourse on the Zeitgeist of post-World War I America. But I want nonetheless to offer a brief, speculative answer. Educational historians too often simply ignore issues concerning audience appeal, and explain the success or failure of a popular educational movement wholly on the basis of the movement's alleged inherent strengths and weaknesses. Clearly, we need to account for the existence of an audience so anxious to listen to, to reach out for, to put into practice the kind of advice disseminated by the parent education movement.

We often look upon the 1920s as an unusually high-spirited, light-hearted, carefree time for middle America, symbolized by the flapper, the hip-flask, the jazz craze, and the myriad newly omnipresent gadgets to amuse adults in their growing leisure—the radio, the movies, the automobile, the condom. Yet one need not read too far into the era's newspapers, popular magazines, and scholarly literature to recognize how misleading this impression is. Virtually overnight, it seemed, the social and moral codes that had guided middle-class behavior for generations had broken down. Youth everywhere were in revolt, it was said. While the flouting of sexual codes of conduct drew a disproportionate share of the mass media's attention, in the average household it was youth's flippant, cynical, "hard-boiled," smart-aleck attitude toward social convention and adult authority that concerned and confused parents more. In retrospect—as Paula Fass (1977) has argued—it appears that the child's peer group stepped into this breach of parental authority and exerted an effective discipline of its own. Yet, at the same time, the growing influence of young people's peer groups only attested further to the decline of deference and to parents' helplessness before a phenomenon a later era would term the "generation gap."

How devastating this experience must have been for middle-class parents whose children came of age in the 1920s! They had begun child-rearing in the confident prewar years when their family values reigned supreme. In the numerous social uplift movements of the Progressive era, the aim had been to reform lower-class immigrant family life in a Waspish middle-class mold. Serious behavior problems among the young were identified with the poor and unassimilated and explained as the natural, if unfortunate, result of ghetto environments, unworthy parental models, and unfamiliarity with American language and customs. But now, to the pained astonishment of the middle class, their own offspring stood condemned for many of the same behavior vices they had earlier identified exclusively with the underprivileged—and, to make matters worse, their children seemed defiantly proud of their behavior![8]

Social commentary on what ailed modern youth was extensive and focused almost invariably on what ailed the middle-class family. The commentary was nearly as diverse as it was emotional; its major thrusts can be sorted out in a variety of ways. To Paula Fass, for example, opinion fell generally into "traditionalist" or "progressive" camps. The major distinction between the two positions, as Fass is careful to point out, was one of sensibility more than point of view. Both camps depicted the middle-class family in terms of disorder and breakdown. They differed mainly on whether the trend was irreversible or whether coordinated social effort could lay a new foundation for family harmony and social order (Fass, 1977, Chaps. 1–2). As I review social commentary on youth and family breakdown in the 1920s, a somewhat finer set of distinctions seems useful in order to lay a backdrop for the success of the parent education movement. For the sake of convenience and brevity, I shall confine myself to opinions expressed in and by the *New York Times* and isolate four basic positions.

Surely the most common opinion was that mistakes by middle-class parents were directly responsible for the obnoxiousness of modern youth. Clergymen especially enjoyed a field day each Sunday in telling parishioners just how little regard their children had for them as parents. One of the more exuberant critics was the rector of St. James Episcopal Church on New York's upper East Side who, in a series of sermons on the American home, attacked both parents and youth for their failures: "The increase of lawlessness, immodesty and depravity among our youths," was a product of "the breakdown of the home. . . . There is not the slightest doubt that the principal cause of the moral and spiritual failures of boys and girls and growing people is the lack of the powerful influence of Christian homes . . . these ills are directly chargeable to neglectful parents" (*New York Times*, 1925d). In another lecture the good rector grew angrier still. The "old-fashioned sanction of society," he lamented, had been replaced by "the morals of the barnyard." He continued:

> We have been blockheads, we older people, because we forget to look after the young. We forgot that they were immature and needed training and discipline. Parents forgot to sacrifice themselves for the sakes of their boys and girls, as their parents did for them. The chief ambition of too many mothers has been the popularity of their daughters, whatever the

cost, and the cost has often been too great. And too many fathers have been so absorbed in business that they have not given their boys the companionship to which they have a right. (*New York Times*, 1925e)

While the Reverend Edward E. Clarke of Mount Morris Baptist Church in East Harlem described the problem identically, he attributed it to very different causes. It was not that parents were selfish but that they indulged their children too much:

> This is an underdisciplined generation of children. What the child wants he gets, and when he objects to disagreeable tasks he is relieved of them. The result is that he has no backbone of moral force to strengthen him as he grows older. The child has been pampered and spoiled by too much love. (*New York Times*, 1925g)

Now that the damage was done, the only recourse, as Clarke saw it, was to address fallen youth directly: "I appeal to the younger generation, not only for its own sake, but for the sake of generations yet unborn, and ask it to discipline itself so that it may have the strength to meet the world" (*New York Times*, 1925g).

Another line of opinion—not as prominent, but widely held—was that whereas parental failings explained much of the revolt of modern youth, the more fundamental causes were broad social and economic forces which had undermined parental authority and influence. The *New York Times* itself held consistently to this view. Challenging assertions made by Fordham University's dean of the School of Social Service, the editors stated:

> Not much is accomplished by the fierce scolding for the transgressions of their offspring which it is the fashion, just now, to give the parent class. Much said about the breakdown of family discipline is unquestionably true. But if the boys and girls, the young men and maidens of the day are to have the responsibility for what they do transferred to their fathers and mothers, why cannot the fathers and mothers say in turn that they are just what their own fathers and mothers taught them to be, or let them be, and so start a sequence of responsibilities that go back to Adam and Eve? (*New York Times*, 1925f)

To the editors, "the main currents of modern life" and "irresistible social and economic change," not parents' weakness per se, bore prime responsibility for the decline of family order (*New York Times*, 1926a).

Other commentators variously elaborated this line of thought. The dean of Princeton University, for example, argued that "the faults of the younger generation are the natural outgrowth of the 20th century world." More specifically, he contended, "when the present older generation was young there were no radios, movies, telephones, or automobiles, all of which . . . contributed to the disturbed state of the younger generation" (*New York Times*, 1927b). Like so many other commentators, moreover, the dean pinpointed World War I and its aftermath as directly responsible for the emotional imbalances of modern youth.

> The World War had a great influence on youth. Whereas former wars . . . had raised up public idols who were swept into office on waves of hero worship, the World War . . . had a contrary effect of disillusioning youth and engendering a spirit of revolt from the older generation that was responsible for the world conflict. [The hypocrisy surrounding Prohibition] cultivated disrespect for authority and [gave] rise to a belief by young people that anything that was compulsory should be disregarded. [The] morale of youth had broken down. (*New York Times*, 1927b)

Though different in tone from the militant blaming of parents, this line of analysis further reinforced the perception of youth as beyond parental control and an embarrassment to all. Rare indeed were commentators bold enough to claim that modern youth were no worse than generations past in cutting up and flouting their elders' values; bolder still, that modern youth's behavior was admirable and enlightened. Though small in number, such commentators commanded disproportionate influence, and so can be said to constitute a significant line of thought.

One of the best known was Denver's flamboyant Juvenile Court Judge Ben Lindsey, whose espousal of "free love" and "companionate marriage" struck many as merely sanctioning youth's debasing of middle-class values. Most of those who defended the young, however, avoided the issue of sex and emphasized instead youth's courageous efforts to adjust to the "new realities" of postwar society. Observed Albert Shiels of Teachers College:

> Lack of harmony brings about a certain amount of nervous response. Nowadays innumerable things are knocking at the consciousness of children. The radio, the motor, the phonograph all contribute to the tension under which they labor. It was all nonsense to declare that children were going "to the dogs," [for] young people of the present were "getting on their feet" better than they did in the days of their dads and granddads. (*New York Times*, 1926c)

More emphatic in his praise of modern youth was the liberal Rabbi Stephen Wise, who argued in a lecture before the League for Political Action that: "The only trouble with the revolt of youth today is that there isn't enough of it! This lack of revolt is the great danger with youth today. . . . The so-called revolt of youth is precious, because our young people at least deem themselves free to criticize and examine. The rest of us are not always so alert" (*New York Times*, 1927a).

Even among those of obvious "progressive" sensibility, however, such clearcut defenses of youth's behavior and, by implication, of the methods of family nurture and peer surveillance which had shaped it, were rare. Far more common among youth's defenders was a resigned acquiescence in the turbulent state of middle-class family life; a fond hope that with more frequent communication between parents and children, greater empathy on both sides, and the passage of time, the rougher edges of youth's rebellion would be smoothed away; and, above all, a confident belief that new knowledge on human development, especially on the psychological needs of children, would guarantee for the youth of tomorrow a less troubled transition to adulthood. The new science of child development would give parents the tools to reduce and perhaps even eliminate, in the lingo of the day, "maladjustments" (the counterpart on the individual level to "cultural lag" on the societal level). Social scientists would provide a distinctly modern antidote to the unparalleled chaos of middle-class family life, and reassert parental authority on a new foundation of empirically grounded, behaviorist truth.

It is difficult to understand the endless celebrations of the challenge of childrearing in the 1920s without appreciating the profound emotional relief which young middle-class parents felt at knowing that—unlike any group of parents in history—they had easily within grasp the scientific knowledge to assure their children's smooth and painless maturation into adulthood. Through its editorials and choice and slant of feature stories, the *New York Times* served as an important carrier of this pervasive postwar viewpoint.

In the latter half of the 1920s especially, the *New York Times* gave much coverage to the projects and findings of leading researchers, especially those in the New York metropolitan area, and to the activities of public and private agencies which sought to enlighten parents on the practical applications of child development research. Commenting on a large conference sponsored by the CSA at the Waldorf-Astoria, the editors argued that it marked

> a beginning of realization that children are proper objects of scientific research. The scientists, of course, cannot take the place of the mothers, but they can teach them many useful things and enable them to do intelligently not a little that they now do in accord with blind instinct or the advice of women no wiser than themselves. (*New York Times*, 1925a)

A few days later, another editorial, entitled "Modern Parenthood," addressed itself again to the conference and its import for middle-class family happiness: "The modern mother, if we are to believe the popular novel and the scenario writer, is a pleasure-seeking, irresponsible creature who divides her time among bride and dancing and 'parties' [sic], where the conduct is 'advanced'; while the modern father is even less of a father than he used to be." But the recent conference "framed quite a different picture: a renewed sense of parental responsibility and interest which has now reached the proportions of full-fledged national movement. This modern parenthood . . . is quite unlike the old-fash-ioned variety, but it has much to recommend it and merits a thorough understanding" (*New York Times*, 1925b). Into the confusion inspired by unparalleled social and economic change, irresponsible individualism, and feminist extremism has "come a flood of new knowledge of children and adults in their relation to children" which would work to everyone's benefit and peace of mind.

> Modern mothers with time on their hands are seizing upon this material with avidity; they will make the routine training of their own children their profession. Organized child-study groups have grown in numbers prodigiously within the past few years, and books on the care and rearing of children find a much more ready market. Business and professional mothers give their children of pre-school age what they believe to be the more expert care and better material surroundings of the rapidly growing "nursery schools." Whether modern parenthood will produce a finer race of men and women than the old-fashioned father and mother has yet to be demonstrated; but it seems to focus the present set of economic and social change. (*New York Times*, 1925b)

A *New York Times* reporter who covered the same conference was even more hopeful—and thankful:

> By some strange cosmic alchemy the same economic and social forces which have broken up the old-fashioned home and sent women into the world of business and pleasure on much the same terms as men, upsetting the manners and morals of the race, have now distilled a new interest in the business of being a parent. . . . Broadly viewed, [the conference speeches] give an interesting panorama of a new epoch in human devel-opment which may rival the birth of public education in importance for the race (*New York Times*, 1925c).

On another occasion the *New York Times* reached much the same set of sanguine conclusions in commenting on the work of the Com-monwealth Fund on delinquency prevention. The Fund had pioneered in the sponsorship of demonstration child guidance clinics, first only for children referred by juvenile courts, but increasingly for children con-sidered in any way "unhappy or maladjusted . . . regardless of the de-gree of intensity of the problem." The *New York Times* praised the Fund's work as a "countercurrent, as yet small in volume but large in poten-tialities" to the unfortunate tendency of moralists to hold parents directly responsible for the crisis of authority in the middle-class family. From the Fund's work one could be confident that while the decay of the "old fashioned home . . . as a source of character and moral tone presents a problem of vast import to the future of our civilization," fortunately, "modern life, which is destroying so much of value, is [also] tending to give us in its place new sources of health" (*New York Times*, 1926a).

As one would expect, the *New York Times* greeted the appearance in 1926 of *Parents' Magazine* with great enthusiasm, and commented at length on its first two issues:

> The new publication is an indication of the trend of thought which recognizes the importance of knowledge about the very young organism. Parents have always wanted to do the best they could for their boys and girls; now they want to know just what is the best. (*New York Times*, 1926b)

That the editors thought "the best" was easily definable, and that *Parents' Magazine* was ably communicating the results of scientific research, suggests just how much middle-America wanted to believe in the science of child development as a permanent solution to its current family crisis.

From the foregoing synopsis of social commentary in 1920s America, I think we can isolate two main elements that figured centrally in the appeal of the parent education movement. First was the pervasive belief that the family had lost its moral rudder, had failed to provide youth with effective guidelines for a smooth transition to adulthood, and was crying out for help. Second was the burgeoning confidence that a new scientific knowledge base was fast accumulating that would, if absorbed and applied by parents, help reestablish parental authority in the home. The gospel of scientific child development offered beleaguered parents both a safety rope and a beacon: It would mediate between traditional and new values, between the attractions of the traditional family and the enticements of postwar modernity. After a period of severe cultural agitation, science would anchor a new social order. Or so, at least, it seemed as the prosperous 1920s drew to a close, and the 1930s beckoned.

CONCLUSION

How does the history of parent education in its formative period shed light on policy choices today? The most obvious and basic point is that parent education has a longer history than most modern-day practitioners realize. Parent education is not a direct byproduct of new knowledge generated in the 1960s on children's cognitive development, nor is it an original contribution of spokespersons for the Great Society. The roots of parent education reflect our long-term commitments to education as the principal vehicle of economic mobility and social progress, on the one hand, and to mothers as the principal guardians of private morality and public virture, on the other.

At the same time, however, parent education has never been fully legitimated as a social service, whether sponsored by private agencies or by government. There remains today, as in the past, a deeply held suspicion that systematically designed instruction in parenting ignores the instinctive base of family ties, threatens family autonomy, and attempts to impose uniformity on what is quintessentially an individual experience. Parent education is thus at one and the same time an integral, yet suspect, part of American culture. Its history, not surprisingly, is marked by substantial advances followed by major reverses. At two points in our history—the 1920s and the 1970s—it seemed that parent education was about to be accepted as a substantial responsibility of government. That this did not come to pass attests not merely to the fickleness of politics but to a central cultural ambivalence concerning the family as a proper object of educational intervention.

Parent education has meant different things to different people at different times. Obviously, as the essays in this volume attest, the goals, methods, and knowledge base of parent education in the past decade differed sharply from those of the early 20th century, and in particular, from those of the 1920s. The switch in emphasis from the affective to the cognitive realm in child development; the major role which the federal government now plays in sponsoring research and dissemination; and the attempts to use parent training programs as potential equalizers of educational opportunity for poor, minority children, have few counterparts in the past.

Equally apparent, the relation of parent education to "public policy" today is very different. Nowadays when we speak about public policy, we almost invariably refer to policies promulgated by government, especially by the federal government. We tend to assume that *public* policy must be initiated and monitored by *public* agencies. But in earlier periods of our history, the boundaries that separated "public" from "private" activity were not so clearly delineated. This was especially the case in policy areas that dealt with the well-being of children and families. In education, social work, health, and other key areas of public life, vigorous private associations regularly and legitimately performed functions that we today consider clearly the prerogative of government. Thus, the role played by LSRM in the parent education movement was not entirely unprecedented, although the scale and extent of its influence were extraordinary.

While these differences are significant, we dare not jump to the conclusion that past and present experiences in parent education are wholly discontinuous. Just because the auspices under which policy is formulated have shifted more and more to government does not necessarily mean that the policy choices we face today are dramatically different from those in the past. Just because there have been notable changes in the knowledge base, methods, and goals of parent education, does not rule out the possibility of equally impressive continuities in approach, design, expectations, and underlying assumptions. A number of these continuities strike me as particularly important, for example:

1. As in the 1920s, a tremendous outpouring of professional and popular literature urges parents to apply the most "modern" methods of childrearing, at the risk of doing permanent injury to their children.

2. As in the 1920s, parent educators often assume that parental behavior is the single most important determinant of a child's future success and happiness.

3. As in the 1920s, parent educators view "expert" intervention into internal family affairs as desirable in order to improve the quality of children's lives, rather than merely to protect them against blatant harm.

4. As in the 1920s, remarkable deference is paid to science as ultimate arbiter of standards of right and wrong in childrearing.

5. As in the 1920s—although with the emphasis on cognitive development—there is lopsided stress on the preschool years and the irreversibility of patterns established then.

6. As in the 1920s, parent education programs and literature focus almost exclusively on mothers, even while (in both periods) denying the existence of maternal instinct.

7. As in the 1920s, there is inadequate recognition of unique and irreducible differences among children, and a tendency to reify developmental "norms" in assessing parental performance.

8. As in the 1920s, there is a tendency to exaggerate the potential of parent education to transform parent attitudes and behaviors.

9. As in the 1920s, there is a tendency to portray parent education as a panacea for a wide range of nagging social problems.

10. As in the 1920s, parent educators seem less concerned to increase parent self-confidence and allay parental anxieties than to establish new and higher standards of parental performance.

11. Finally, as in the 1920s—but very different from the pre-World War I period—parent education is generally conceived narrowly, privately, and apolitically, as a means to enhance early child care, rather than to encourage adults to see their parental responsibilities as springboards for self-instruction and political activism in all phases of community life that impinge on the well-being of families.

In short, as I compare past and present experience in parent education, it seems apparent that a structure and set of assumptions emerged in the early 20th century which exerted substantial influence on policy and practice a half-century later. By becoming aware of the nature of the formative experience, we may see our way clearer in the future to transcend it in new policies and programs.

FOOTNOTES

*This essay primarily synthesizes my previous research on the history of parent education, as exemplified in Schlossman (1976, 1978a, 1978b, 1978c, 1979, 1980a, 1980b, 1980c).

[1] The following account synthesizes material from diverse published, unpublished, and oral sources, especially from the Milton J. E. Senn Oral History Collection, History of Medicine Division, National Library of Medicine, Bethesda MD.

[2] My impressions of the CSA derive from interviews with several members active in the 1920s, and from a dissertation by Wallons (1983) on CSA President Sidonie Gruenberg.

[3] Gesell's work has never received the attention it deserves from historians. An insightful recent essay on the Bureau is provided by Antler (1982). The Iowa Station will receive thorough analysis in a forthcoming book by Hamilton Cravens, parts of which he has kindly shared with me. Neither Antler nor Cravens should be held responsible for my interpretations of their works.

[4] My interpretation of Merrill-Palmer derives from diverse sources, but especially from the School's annual reports; see White (1940).

[5] Frank viewed the nursery school as both the lynchpin of the entire parent education movement and the quintessence of progressive education principles.

[6] My research on this subject has benefited immeasurably from a personal interview with Dr. Lois Hayden Meek Stolz, Professor Emeritus, Stanford University, and from an invaluable, lengthy series of edited interviews with Dr. Stolz by Ruby Takanishi, on deposit at the Schlesinger Library, Radcliffe College, and selected other libraries.

[7] Though seriously ill, Hecht graciously granted me an interview in 1979 concerning the genesis of his own career and of *Parents' Magazine*. Senn's interview with Hecht is highly revealing of his style, temperament, and intellectual bent. Hecht died early in 1981.

[8] On the Progressive period, see Schlossman (1977).

REFERENCES

Antler, J. *Progressive education and the scientific study of the child: An analysis of the Bureau of Educational Experiments.* Teachers College Record, 1982, *83*, 559–591.

Cohen, S. The mental hygiene movement, the Commonwealth Fund, and public education, 1921–1933. In G. Benjamin (Ed.), *Private philanthropy and public elementary and secondary education.* Pocantico Hills, NY: Rockefeller Archive Center, 1980.

Fass, P. *The damned and the beautiful.* New York: Oxford University Press, 1977.

Frank, L. K. The object of education. *The Freeman,* 1922, *4,* 610–611. (a)

Frank, L. K. Two tasks of education. *School and Society,* 1922, *15,* 655–659. (b)

Frank, L. K. *Memorandum. Child study—parent training program.* Pocantico Hills, NY: LSRM Collection, Box 30 (Folder 315), Series III, Subseries 5, December 21, 1923.

Frank, L. K. *Training personnel and preparing teaching material.* Pocantico Hills, NY: LSRM Collection, Box 30 (Folder 315), Series III, Subseries 5, Spring 1924. (a)

Frank, L. K. *Memorandum of interview with George J. Hecht.* Pocantico Hills, NY: LSRM Collection, Box 37 (Folder 390), Series III, Subseries 5, November 6, 1924. (b)

Frank, L. K. *Parent training.* Pocantico Hills, NY: LSRM Collection, Box 30 (Folder 315), Series III, Subseries 5, March 26, 1924. (c)

Frank, L. K. *Memorandum. Child study and parent training.* Pocantico Hills, NY: LSRM Collection, Box 30 (Folder 315), Series III, Subseries 5, May 23, 1924. (d)

Frank, L. K. *Parent training.* Pocantico Hills, NY: LSRM Collection, Box 30 (Folder 315), Series III, Subseries 5, March 26, 1924. (e)

Frank, L. K. *Memorandum. Projects in parent training.* Pocantico Hills, NY: LSRM Collection, Box 28 (Folder 294), Series III, Subseries 5, January 18, 1924. (f)

Frank, L. K. *Child study and parent training program.* Pocantico Hills, NY: LSRM Collection, Box 30 (Folder 315), Series III, Subseries 5, August 12, 1924. (g)

Frank, L. K. *Child study work in the women's colleges.* Pocantico Hills, NY: LSRM Collection, Box 30 (Folder 315), Series III, Subseries 5, April 1927.

New York Times, p. 24, October 28, 1925. (a)

New York Times, Section 2, p. 8, November 1, 1925. (b)

New York Times, Section 9, p. 10, November 1, 1925. (c)

New York Times, p. 24, November 23, 1925. (d)

New York Times, p. 22, November 30, 1925. (e)

New York Times, p. 22, December 11, 1925. (f)

New York Times, p. 24, December 14, 1925. (g)

New York Times, p. 24, January 14, 1926. (a)

New York Times, p. 24, September 23, 1926. (b)

New York Times, p. 4, September 30, 1926. (c)

New York Times, p. 9, January 7, 1926. (a)

New York Times, p. 5, February 12, 1927. (b)

Russell, J. E. *Letter to the Laura Spelman Rockefeller Memorial.* Institute of Child Welfare Research Files, Teachers College Archives, Columbia University, New York, April 3, 1924.

Schlossman, S. L. Before Home Start: Notes toward a history of parent education in America, 1897–1929. *Harvard Educational Review,* 1976, *46,* 436–467.

Schlossman, S. L. *Love and the American delinquent.* Chicago: University of Chicago Press, 1977.

Schlossman, S. L. The parent education game: The politics of child psychology in the 1970s. *Teachers College Record,* 1978, *79,* 788–808. (a)

Schlossman, S. L. *Family as educator, parent education, and the perennial family crisis.* Paper presented at the conference Parents as Educators, National Institute of Education, Washington, DC, November, 1978. (b)

Schlossman, S. L. *Kids in the saddle: New perspectives on progressive education in the 1920s.* Paper presented at the conference Needs and Opportunities for Research Concerning the History of Education in New York City, Teachers College, Columbia University, New York, December, 1978. (c)

Schlossman, S. L. *Science and the commercialization of parenthood: Notes toward a history of Parents' Magazine.* Paper presented at the biennial meeting of the Society for Research in Child Development, San Francisco, March, 1979.

Schlossman, S. L. Philanthropy and the gospel of child development. In G. Benjamin (Ed.), *Private philanthropy and public elementary and secondary education.* Pocantico Hills, NY: Rockefeller Archive Center, 1980. (a)

Schlossman, S. L. *The multiple possibilities of decency: Family and society in American history.* Keynote address presented at the conference The American Family: Moving Toward the 21st Century, Columbus, GA, May, 1980. (b)

Schlossman, S. L. *The child study association, parent education, and the crisis of the middle-class family.* Paper presented at the conference Beyond the System, Teachers College, Columbia University, New York, December, 1980. (c)

Shea, C. The ideology of mental health and the emergence of the therapeutic liberal state: The American mental hygiene movement, 1900–1930. (Doctoral dissertation, University of Illinois, 1980). *Dissertation Abstracts*, 1980, 41(6), 2476A–2477A.

Welter, B. The cult of true womanhood: 1820–1860. *American Quarterly*, Summer, 1966, pp. 151–174.

White, E. N. *The Merrill-Palmer School*. Detroit, Merrill-Palmer School, 1940.

Wallons, R. *Educating mothers: Sidonie Gruenberg and the Child Study Association of America, 1881–1929*. Doctoral dissertation, University of Chicago, 1983.

Two

To Strengthen All Families: A Human Development and Community Value Framework*

PAUL R. DOKECKI AND ROBERT M. MORONEY

The purpose of this chapter is to provide a framework for developing public policies related to child care and parent education that enable parents to act in their own, their children's, and society's interest. Our position is that public policies that increase the strength of American families will help mitigate an array of vexing societal conditions. Removing obstacles to effective family functioning and fostering competence to master family development tasks may contribute to the national purpose. Involved is facilitation of family capacities and relations—expected to vary in concrete expression by social, economic, and ethnic circumstances—associated with the development of children and other family members.

The family is an important focus for policy because it is a social institution superior to other institutions in performing humanizing and socializing functions. But the family is changing and experiencing stress. Not that the family was better off in the romantically remembered past; rather, it persists in playing a necessary, albeit complex and difficult, function in American society.

The family is an appropriate focus of public policy, but our analysis leads us to prefer strengthening families rather than developing specialized agencies that often seem to weaken families in the discharge of their responsibilities. Of course, social service agencies will and should continue to operate in contemporary American society, but they should support rather than replace family functions. Indeed, agencies have the vital purpose of assisting parents to be competent. Parents, for their part, must have—or be helped to develop through parent education and related programs—knowledge, resources, and authority in order to exercise choice and deal effectively with professionals and service agencies.

Featherstone (1979) relates the burgeoning interest in *family* matters to the fact that the family *matters*. But "the family is such an elusive symbol," he says. "It is perfect for an uncertain age. . . . Ambiguity seems stitched into the family as a topic" (p. 51).

One manifestation of the current interest in the family is the loose coalition of politically diverse individuals and organizations forming around family policy. A very common policy-related assertion heard from this coalition is that families are weak, impaired in their capacity to perform traditional family functions. This view implies that families were stronger at an earlier time and that policies can be developed to restore their former strength. But when were families stronger? And do all or only some families need strengthening? Further, is it possible that strengthening means more than rehabilitating those families not meeting certain expectations or not conforming to socially desirable standards of behavior?

Assertions of family deterioration are based on any number of social indicators—rates of illegitimacy, divorce, family violence, delinquency, adolescent pregnancy, and chronic economic dependency. The resultant list of weak family types, then, includes single-parent and "broken" families, families in which parents abuse themselves or their children, families whose adolescents behave in sexually or violently disruptive ways, and families on public welfare. The family-deterioration argument often is grounded in value-laden concepts of pathology or deviance and leads inevitably to proposals to rehabilitate weak families by making them more like strong families. It is often said that weak families are failures, are deficient, and are the cause of their own problems.

Although an apparent advantage of a dichotomous strong–weak family policy position is that data can be marshaled to help identify needs and indicate policy options, this advantage is often illusory. A fundamental problem inheres in the dichotomy. Mention the term "strong family," and each American has a personal definition. Unlike many areas of policy development that demand technical knowledge, most people consider themselves experts on the family and use personal experiences with their own families as guideposts for thinking and judging. Those who feel that their family experiences were positive tend to define strong families in terms of their personal family histories; even those with negative family experiences often reactively idealize the type of family they would like to have had. Thus, deeply held personal beliefs are likely to shape our definition of "weak" and "strong" as applied to families. These subjective elements inevitably color the views of citizens and policymakers alike in the realm of family policy formulation.

But pursuing clarity through detailed policy analysis may prove disquieting. For example, although most people would agree that spouses should respect and support each other, there is much less agreement on the specific roles, functions, and statuses individuals should assume within the family. Or again, it is agreed that children should grow up in caring environments where their physical, cognitive, social, and emotional needs are met; but there is controversy over the specific characteristics of such environments. When specifics enter the public debate, the current loose, family-oriented coalition is threatened as debate focuses on controversial objectives, and, of greatest importance, values that underlie family policy. But such threats to coalition may be necessary and worthwhile. Conducting explicit value analysis of policy options may result in clearer and more effective policy. At worst, wasteful pursuit of inconsistent or contradictory policies may be avoided; at best, a rationale may be developed that is capable of capturing the imagination of citizens and policymakers so that fresh policy directions may be charted. But how should we think about the role of values in policy?

Values permeate the entire policy process. They influence the selection of specific policy issues that will be addressed and how they will be defined. They are the basis for setting policy goals and objectives, for selecting criteria to compare policy options designed to achieve these goals and objectives, and for evaluating policies once implemented.

Recent analyses of social policies have tended to slight value issues and to stress procedural and technical solutions. Arguments are made about the appropriate focus of responsibility for meeting people's needs. Should it reside in the private or public sector, and, if the latter, at which level of government? Should needs be met directly through services or indirectly through market mechanisms? If through markets, should we develop income maintenance programs such as the Family Assistance Plan or a negative income tax, a family allowance program, a modified public assistance program, or vouchers for categories of resources such as housing, food, child care, or education? The growing emphasis on procedures may reflect discouragement with the perceived failure of previous large-scale programs and distrust of government. It may also reflect reaction to the current fiscal situation and lack of confidence in the nation's ability to deal with complex social conditions. But what it does reflect, for certain, is reluctance to clarify values. Policy people in government and other sectors of society are reluctant to define relationships between means and ends and to explore the nature of present society and its future course. And often overlooked is the fact that procedural and technical issues themselves are value-laden. For example, efficiency, cost-effectiveness, centralized vs. decentralized implementation, and providing benefits to all or only some people are issues related to deeply held values and convictions about the role of public institutions in the lives of people.

The rallying cry that families should be strengthened has been mostly a value-laden slogan and will remain so until the values implicit in the notion are identified and analyzed. It should be stated not only *that* families should be strengthened, but also *why* they should be strengthened. That they should be strengthened expresses a global value preference that neither provides organizing principles for analysis nor clarifies incipient differences between groups in the values that should guide policy-making and implementation.

CURRENT MAINSTREAM POLICY VALUES

Most Americans believe that unnecessary intervention in family life harms both the family and society, invading family privacy and questioning basic family competence. Proliferation of unnecessary intervention renders the family dependent on professionals and bureaucrats, and, in the extreme, undermines the family as the basic unit of society. A very strong version of this widely held belief is presented by Christopher Lasch (1977, 1979), who believes that reducing the family's capability to provide nurturance and protection and preventing the family from performing many important functions leaves the individual at the mercy of the state. The general line of reasoning leads many people (e.g., Bane, 1976; Steiner, 1976) to argue strongly that public involvement in family life should be extensively debated in the public arena before major action is taken.

We accept this widely shared concern over unnecessary intervention into families, but we ask what criteria might be used to discriminate necessary or beneficial intervention from unnecessary or harmful intervention? More broadly, what are the prevailing values in the United

States concerning the relationship between families and public institutions? Dunlop (1978b) offers a set of propositions that attempts to represent mainstream American thinking and valuing, especially regarding child care and parent education. These propositions are not universally shared and are sometimes contradictory, and those who hold them may not agree with all their policy implications once elaborated. But they are instructive and serve as a backdrop for an alternative value position we will advance in later sections of this chapter.

Families, according to Dunlop, are believed to be valuable and important social structures because the socialization, nurturance, and mediation functions they perform cannot be adequately performed by other institutions. Although some forms of professional and state intervention are acceptable, certain family rights and responsibilities should be maintained, including the family's rights to pursue its own concept of socially accepted values for its children, to make certain mistakes if it is acting in the "best interest of the children," to communicate values to its children, and to control childrearing practices. The family is viewed as the best institution for preserving and nurturing cultural differences and for protecting the uniqueness and rights of individuals. Dunlop's basic assumption is that if critical family functions are taken over by government, the family will be seriously compromised and may cease to exist as one of the few remaining institutions that provides a buffer between the individual and large-scale, insensitive bureaucracies.

Many also believe, according to Dunlop, that families should rely on their own resources to the extent possible and should not be dependent on professionals. Implicit in this view is the belief that families know what is best for their members, especially for their children. Parents may consult with professionals, but any relationship that places them in a dependent role is viewed as unnecessary and harmful. Ironically, the actual beliefs and practices of many professionals are inconsistent with this cluster of popular beliefs. Indeed, professionals often act in ways that increase the probability of families becoming dependent on services. And, of course, there are parents who have unbounded faith in professionals.

Another belief described by Dunlop is that preparation for parenthood and childrearing should, in most instances, be achieved within the family setting. In part, this belief seems to be related to distrust of professionals and social agencies, and, in part, to the deeply held conviction that parenthood is a "natural" state. Also central to this belief is the notion that socialization of children is too important to be carried out by nonfamily members, most alternatives being seen by parents as potential infringements on their rights and responsibilities.

If these beliefs are accepted as the value base for policy choices, state intervention to help families fulfill their childrearing function, according to Dunlop, should take the following somewhat circumscribed forms. Government has the responsibility to become involved in childrearing when and if a child's parents are unable to carry out this function. Transfer of responsibility might take many forms—permanent or temporary, complete or partial—depending on why the intervention becomes necessary. Justifiable reasons for complete transfer might include parental illness or death, desertion, serious abuse and neglect, or the parents' desire to divest themselves of responsibility for the child's upbringing. Underlying this position, at least partially, is the idea that intervention is acceptable only when parents are incapable of fulfilling their responsibilities as parents.

Child care, an example of partial transfer, should be made available primarily to those families whose circumstances require parents to be absent from the home. Further, parents should monitor and control the quality of out-of-home care received by their children. Although licensing and other governmental efforts to ensure minimal levels of quality care are acceptable because their purpose is to protect the child, efforts to regulate the quality of care beyond these minimal levels are likely to be questioned. Parents feel they are (or can be) competent enough to identify quality child-care settings for their children. Thus, efforts to increase governmental regulation and supervision are viewed with suspicion, since they imply that parents are neither capable nor trustworthy enough to choose well.

Further, such parents would argue that state involvement in child care and parent education should be accomplished by means of small-scale, neighborhood-based programs. Services provided in familiar settings strengthen the parents' perception that they do, in fact, control the childrearing function, since small local settings and their staffs are accessible.

These values and attendant policies described by Dunlop are compatible with many of the values undergirding past and current American social policies. Two important principles have emerged to shape the state's intervention strategy. Services and supports are usually provided when the family cannot or will not carry out its childrearing functions, leading the state to become the child's surrogate family. But is it legitimate for the state to go beyond this function and develop policies to support all families in childrearing? Intervention is usually deemed inappropriate, except in cases of family breakdown, because it is seen as undermining and weakening the family—and worse still, of producing dependence.

For these reasons, it appears to many that the appropriate role of the state is to intervene only when there is clear evidence of family pathology. It is argued that there is such a fine line between support and substitution, between intervention and interference, that caution is the preferred course. In using this *residual notion* of social welfare, each case is judged on its own merits, and intervention decisions are made by competent professionals. In such a way, the troublesome issue of unnecessary interference in family life is said to be minimized.

The prevailing value framework, then, contains the assumption that limited policies to strengthen families are sufficient to meet existing needs. Involvement by the state should be restrained and indirect, its aim being to increase economic stability and to guard privacy. The primary purpose of social policy, as we have described it thus far, is the amelioration of poverty and other social pathologies. The concern is with families whose financial and personal resources are below some agreed-upon level of subsistence.

Historically, American social policy has been justified by reference to the values of competitive individualism and the related notion of laissez-faire economics. It has usually been claimed that nothing is inherently wrong with the free-enterprise capitalist system, and that the state's primary function is to support the market's continuing operation; however, social policies should humanize the economic system. Social policies, then, have been portrayed as corrective measures in the interest of individual and social welfare. Balancing individual and collective welfare, with an emphasis on utilitarianism and the principle of maximizing overall satisfaction, is consistent with the distinction between dependent people who need assistance and the remainder of people who do not. Social policies should ignore enhancement of the general welfare, because the economic system will allow the vast majority of citizens to earn the resources necessary to achieve self-sufficiency.

Even with the advent of the modern welfare state during the Great Depression, social policy was conceived as part of general economic policy, not as an independent area of policy governed by separate non-economic principles. The Social Security Act in this country and the Beveridge Report in the United Kingdom went far beyond provisions of the Poor Laws, but both remained rooted in the economically derived concept of a social minimum. Although many current social policies seem to contain the recognition that modernization and industrialization have created risks and consequences that potentially affect all people and not just a small percentage of the population, social policies mostly function as attempted correctives to an economic system that has not achieved a just allocation of goods and services. Social policy continues to emphasize provision of a minimum standard of living and reactive, crisis-oriented provision of services. It is controlled by economic concepts, with social services functioning as the ambulance at the bottom of the cliff rather than the fence at the top that prevents people from falling over.

The current approach to social policy may give rise to an anomaly; namely, that social objectives are pursued vigorously only during periods of economic prosperity. During periods of economic retrenchment, however, social objectives may be deferred. For example, in the 1980s we seem to be choosing guns in preference to butter. The logic and effect of this approach are troublesome, since even if the narrow definition of social policy objectives is granted, an increase in social welfare problems will occur during periods of economic downturn, and more rather than fewer social programs will be needed during such periods.

The final value underlying much of current social policy is that the primary justification for increased expenditures on social programs is economic. The primary manifestation of this value is the general application of human investment or human capital theories. For example, it is argued that resources should be allocated to children because they are economic resources for the future. Programs for the handicapped are justified on the grounds that rehabilitated handicapped persons will become independent and contribute to economic productivity, or at least not cost the taxpayers as much to maintain as they would in the absence of such programs. This argument is inevitably cast in benefit–cost terms: for every dollar invested, a given return should be expected. In addition to delegating social concerns to peripheral status, another difficulty with this is that, in practice, some individuals are better risks than others. Such individuals require less investment for better "payoff" in economic terms. Thus, many people with serious needs are overlooked because services would not render them more productive.

If the values shaping current social policies remain unquestioned, then families will continue to be seen as means to—usually economic—ends. Strengthening families will thus be defined as increasing the economic productivity of family members. Policies will continue to be reactive, will focus almost exclusively on the needs of clearly defined target populations, and will assume that most families are able to function adequately without provision of resources and supports. Expanding parent education and child care programs to include a wider spectrum of families will be claimed to weaken some families and to waste scarce resources.

Although current mainstream values exert a powerful influence on the public and on policymakers, we cannot fully accept them. We prefer a more reform-oriented rationale in support of community development (Dunlop, 1978a).

AN ALTERNATIVE POSITION

The historical and current debate on what is the most appropriate approach to social policy ultimately reduces to the issue of how individuals should be related to the collectivity. In the family policy domain, this issue translates to specifying the proper relationship of individuals and their families to the collectivity. The prevailing approach in the United States has emphasized the values of: (1) independent, strong, competitive individuals and families, and (2) a state that operates according to economic principles, intervening primarily to promote the economy and only secondarily to promote humanitarian ends. Although the twentieth century has witnessed a remarkable increase in scope and quantity of social programs—seemingly contrary to the value of minimal state intervention—the individualistic-cum-economic value basis for intervention has remained virtually unchanged.

We propose that traditional social policy values be reevaluated, and that consideration be given to the implications of shifting from valuing the atomistic individual and family to valuing the individual and family within community, and from valuing a society based on economics to valuing a society based on human development. These new value emphases would signal a shift from a reactive and residual approach to social policy to one that is forward-looking, universalistic, and preventive. The purpose of state policy would be expanded, however, to include the enhancement of the general welfare of families and children by going beyond guaranteeing the social minimum.

Social policy based on community and human development requires a new set of first principles. Unnecessary intervention would continue to be avoided, but the concept of "necessary–unnecessary" requires reworking. It would be recognized that industrialization and modernization have given rise to stresses and consequences that affect all people, not just an exceptional portion of the population. Society would be built on the premise that social welfare is a collective responsibility, resting its moral claim on the ethics of mutual aid and cooperation.

This concept is neither new nor radical. Indeed, concepts closely related to it were espoused by Thomas Jefferson (Wills, 1978). It is different from prevailing American social thought, however, in rejecting the concept of an atomistic society with its emphasis on self-interest and competition. It is an image of society built on the ideal of community—a society in which individuals and families avoid alienation and have a sense of social identity and belonging. Self-interest is redefined as being achieved best through concern and action on behalf of the well-being of others.

We argue against the development of future social policies that limit intervention to situations where families are unwilling or unable to perform traditional family functions. We argue instead for *shared responsibility between families and the state* and for social policies that are not limited to crisis intervention (Moroney, 1976). Moreover, we view parents as the key agents for childrearing and family development, with the role of the state being to support rather than substitute for families (Dokecki, Strain, Bernal, Brown, & Robinson, 1975).

Families are accepted as valuable and important social structures because the socialization, nurturance, and mediation functions they perform cannot be performed as well by other institutions. Thus, families do have certain rights and responsibilities that should be respected and protected. The belief that families should rely on their own resources to the extent possible and not become dependent on professionals to carry out primary functions is consistent with these concepts. Finally, we accept the belief that child care and parent education programs should be sensitive to family needs and prerogatives. Our disagreement with mainstream values emerges when these values are translated into pathology-oriented, exceptionalistic policies based on troublesome interpretations of the current situation of family–society relationships.

Despite the increasingly complex demands placed on America's parents, and the continuing pattern of family stress and limited family support, parents are expected to carry out their tasks as if they were automatically capable and autonomous. There is mounting evidence, however, that this expectation is unrealistic (Keniston, 1977). As a result, families need resources and supports to permit adequate parental functioning, and, as has been argued by Dokecki and Strain (1973), this is true of families and parents in general, not just low-income families. This universalistic viewpoint requires elaboration.

Our analysis leads us to believe that all families should be addressed by public policies. Clearly, all families do not experience the same stresses or have the same specific needs, and policies must be designed to be sensitive to such differences. But there are important developmental commonalities among families. We argue for universal entitlement to family supports and services, voluntary participation relative to entitlement, and the need for selective targeting in policy implementation.

Family policy analysts typically limit their concerns to specific and exceptional classes of families; e.g., poor families, minority group families, single-parent families, dual-worker families, families with handicapped children, or otherwise "unlucky" families. Data are marshaled to show that these families experience special stresses, are uniquely "at risk," and have special needs. It is then argued—and often vigorously advocated—that such families be given special consideration in allocating scarce resources. This exceptionalistic approach is not without value, and, in fact, it has a number of advantages. First, by focusing on discrete special groups, analysis can be narrowed and concrete recommendations made. Second, inequities can be pinpointed, including gaps or shortages in needed resources and services. Finally, the exceptionalistic strategy meshes well with our political system wherein—given limited resources—policymakers weigh demands from competing groups, establish priorities, and determine which objectives among many possible ones will be pursued (Steiner, 1976).

Although a persuasive case can be made for the exceptionalistic approach to public policy, its overall and long-range effects are often dysfunctional. First, it encourages the notion that priorities should be determined in an overly competitive fashion, the needs of one group of families being met only at the expense of other groups in an "I win, you lose" zero-sum game. In periods of economic retrenchment, this severely competitive process is volatile and destructive, creating enemy camps among otherwise worthy constituencies. Second, in highlighting the needs of certain types of families, there is an unfortunate tendency to move from the concepts of stress, risk, and need to a view that these families are qualitatively different from normal families, that they are in some way deficient, abnormal, or pathological.

By underestimating the stresses and risks encountered by all families in American society, the exceptionalistic approach encourages stigmatization of families designated by public policies as needing special consideration. Since self-sufficiency and independence are powerfully sanctioned societal values, the stigmatization related to being placed in a dependent position by exceptionalistic policies and programs is often accompanied by substantial loss of perceived status and self-esteem. In addition, families ignored for special consideration within a generally exceptionalistic policy context are not likely to seek external resources and support, even when they experience the inevitable difficulties of American life. Reluctance to seek help is particularly strong among parents (regarding their childrearing responsibilities) who often view it as an admission of weakness or pathology. Lack of these supports can produce negative effects on family and child development.

Kahn and Kamerman (1975) also argue against an exceptionalistic approach and for universalistic provision of services for all families. They point out that rich and relatively fortunate people also receive "benefits and services assigned for important public reasons, in the public interest, and not achieved through marketplace transactions" (p. ix). These social welfare benefits are provided to the more fortunate by policies such as agricultural subsidies, tax deductions for interest on real estate loans and business expenses, and mortgage guarantees. Beyond these two forms of social welfare is a third type—the public social utility—that provides to society-at-large such programs as public schools, public health services, and cultural activities.

Regarding these matters of social welfare for the poor, social welfare for the rich, and public social utilities, Kahn and Kamerman (1975) maintain:

> Government, business, and voluntary social service agencies are active in all three domains; there is intervention, allocation of tax funds, assignment of personnel. Yet history and ideology have caused us to take one attitude toward public or private welfare services for the poor, another toward subsidy for the affluent, and still another toward public social utilities, or social infrastructure for everyone. Society masks realities by distinguishing among what it calls public welfare and social services for the poor and troubled, education and public health protections for everyone, and benefits for the affluent. It fails to recognize that, in a more basic sense, there are really two categories, not three: social services and benefits connected to problems and break-downs (and *these* are not limited to the poor), and *social services and benefits needed by average people under ordinary circumstances.* (p. x, italics in original)

Arguing on the basis of these generally overlooked issues, they conclude that "the assignment of general tax revenues for social programs is morally no different—if the services are in the public interest—from tax revenues for roads, canals, guns, or forest-fire fighting" (pp. 172–173). The Kahn and Kamerman position is more than an appeal to social altruism; national well-being and national productivity are at stake in the development of social policy.

A HUMAN DEVELOPMENT FRAMEWORK

The basic value assertion or first principle implicit in the preceding discussion is that human social development—defined as the continual broadening of human experience and perfection of human social relations over the life cycle—should be the aim of social policy. We should strive in the present to develop ourselves, and especially our children, into socially competent people who will create and support a just, democratic, and caring community and social order. Strengthening families is therefore an important subject of public policy. The conclusion is indisputable that society has a legitimate role to play in the functioning of American families; however, it is equally indisputable that more caution and deliberation must inform public policy than has been the case throughout our nation's history (Bane, 1976; Keniston, 1977; Steiner, 1976).

Given that family life and child development are matters of some public concern, should families or children be the focus of programs and public policy? The preponderance of research evidence suggests that more often than not the family should be a key service delivery vehicle (Dokecki et al., 1975; Moroney, 1976). While there may be instances in which children should be the primary object of social policy (Goldstein, Freud, & Solnit, 1973), evidence from much of the early childhood intervention research of the 1960s and 1970s leads to the conclusion that family level intervention is the more successful strategy, especially for families with young children.

The goal of strengthening families involves, at least in part, the following tasks: (1) improving the capacity of families to master a broad range of developmental tasks; (2) improving the quality of intrafamily systems and family relations with external systems; (3) minimizing potentially harmful stresses affecting the family; and (4) improving the operation of liaison or linkage functions related to social resources and supports needed by families (Newbrough et al., 1978). Let us briefly explore these four tasks of social policy.

First, within a human development framework, families are viewed as moving through developmental phases from childless married couples, through several phases defined by the presence of children of varying ages, and finally to aging. Each phase requires family tasks to be mastered, such as physical maintenance, protection, socialization, social control, reproduction, and development of independent behavior (Hill & Mattessich, 1977). Social policies to strengthen families would involve supporting family members in their ability to master these developmental tasks.

Second, families are also viewed as small systems operating in relationship to societal institutions. Intrafamily systems include units such as the individual, marital dyad, parent–child dyad, sibling subsystem, and the nuclear family. The family system also transacts with extrafamily systems, such as the extended family, the neighborhood, schools and other service bureaucracies, the community, the world of work, and the marketplace (Mattessich, 1976). Strengthening families here would involve facilitating the operation of this network of social systems.

A third aspect of strengthening families would involve developing their capacity to handle stress constructively. Family stress has two components: tension and overload. Chronic interference with daily family functioning produces tension or strain, and acute stress that requires extraordinary family coping and the use of reserve resources to preserve family stability results in a potentially dangerous overload. It is not that stress can or should be completely eliminated, because it can be a source of challenge and growth.

Fourth, liaison theory and practice (Dokecki, 1977; Hobbs, 1975; Newbrough, 1977; Williams, 1977) have underscored the importance of linkages (shared plans of action) between families in need of help and available social supports. Strengthening families, therefore, requires the development of liaison functions to identify and mobilize family resources and supports.

Beyond these four aspects of strengthening families, Bronfenbrenner's (1978) developmental propositions derived from the behavioral research literature help elaborate our human development framework. He places particular emphasis on the development of competence during the early childhood years:

> *Proposition I.* In order to develop, a child needs the enduring, irrational involvement of one or more adults in care and joint activity with the child. (pp. 773–774)
>
> *Proposition II.* The psychological development of the child is brought about through his continuing involvement in progressively more complex patterns of reciprocal activity with persons with whom the child develops a strong and enduring mutual emotional attachment. (p. 774)
>
> *Proposition III.* The involvement of caretaker and child in patterns of progressively more complex reciprocal activity generates an emotional bond, enhanced motivation, and cognitive and manipulative skills that are mutually reinforcing to both participants, are then reflected in the child's competence and cooperation in other situations, and thereby facilitate the child's future development. (p. 775)
>
> *Proposition IV.* To develop the enduring involvement of one or more adults in care, activity, and so forth, requires social policies and practices that provide opportunity, status, encouragement, example, and approval for parenthood. (p. 776)

Although children's needs relative to the specifics of their development vary across cultural, racial, economic, and ethnic groups, Bronfenbrenner's four propositions describe generalizations supported by the preponderance of research findings, and suggest that developmental needs are best met for children in meaningful relationships with primary caregivers in the context of a family or familylike setting. The environment provided in such settings is probably the single most important influence on the development of children's cognitive, affective, and social competence, particularly during the first 6 years of life (Bloom, 1964; Bronfenbrenner, 1974; Clarke & Clarke, 1976; Hunt, 1961).

Besides providing for a developing child's primary needs, parents also serve a crucial "executive function" for the family in mediating between the child and the larger society (Berger & Neuhaus, 1977; Keniston, 1977). Thus, socialization and transaction with society are key functions of families, functions that can have largely negative or positive developmental outcomes, depending on the stresses and supports experienced by each family unit (Goodson & Hess, 1977).

In concluding the presentation of our human development framework, it should be noted that it is in the spirit of John Dewey's social thought, especially on the topic of democracy as a social and individual way of life. Says Dewey (1968):

> The keynote of democracy as a way of life may be expressed, it seems to me, as the necessity for the participation of every mature human being in formation of the values that regulate the living of men together; which is necessary from the standpoint of both the general social welfare and the full development of human beings as individuals. (p. 236)

AN HISTORICAL OVERVIEW OF CHILDREARING INTERVENTIONS[1]

One area in which we are attempting to apply the value framework outlined above is parent education. The history of parent education has been, and continues to be, marked by major shifts in purposes, approaches, and contents. Moreover, its history is also intertwined with other childrearing interventions such as child care and early childhood education. In order to help trace the changes that have occurred in the development of parent education, an historical framework identifying the variables involved may prove helpful. There are two levels to such an historical framework—one involving the Broad Societal Context within which interventions develop, the other involving a more focused perspective that deals with Intervention Components themselves.

The Broad Societal Context perspective identifies four major variables that have influenced the development of interventions in childrearing: (1) the goal of the intervention, which is based upon; (2) a societal problem defined by a discrepancy between what is (the present social reality) and (3) a societal value or ideal about what should be and (4) the intervention strategy which is the translation of goals into specific activities and programs. This outline greatly simplifies the forces that interact to influence the specific form of interventions. But as we outline the history and recent developments associated with childrearing interventions, we shall see how changes in these four basic variables have changed the nature of interventions.

The Intervention Components consist of: (1) the knowledge base that supports a particular intervention, which leads to (2) selection of program goals to be achieved through (3) the use of a core approach to intervention, with (4) the focus placed upon particular persons. The fact that goals are mentioned in both levels of the framework suggests that although these variables and components appear to be linear and sequential, they actually represent a field of forces that interact in complex, dynamic ways. Changes in any one of the variables or components can lead to different intervention approaches that generate a new knowledge base. Conversely, the knowledge base developed from existing interventions can lead to switches in program focus and goals which can in turn alter values.

A summary of the historical framework, much of which is adapted from Fein (1980), is presented in Table 1. This table lays out in broad strokes the evolution in childrearing interventions that has culminated in a situation very closely related to the value framework outlined in this chapter. The suggestion that parent education may be one approach to strengthening and supporting the functioning of all families—and not just families thought to be pathological, deviant, or at risk—emerges from several sources:

1. Rationales based on a belief that knowledge ordinarily accumulated by parents has been made obsolete by rapid economic, cultural, and social change, and that new knowledge from scientific developments can help families adapt to America's technological and continuously changing environment (Luscher, 1977);
2. The idea that becoming a parent is a crucial role transition, which in the modern American family has been made more stressful by the decline of traditional (e.g., the extended family) social support networks;
3. Rationales based upon social indicators believed to reflect increased pressures on all families (Minnesota Council on Quality Education, 1979);
4. Parent education needs expressed by large percentages of parents from all social and economic levels in society (Le Masters, 1957; Yankelovich, Skelly, & White, 1977);
5. Primary prevention arguments, in which parent training is seen as a way of helping parents promote the development of competence in children and thus prevent subsequent mental health problems (Cowen, 1977; Gordon, 1977; Hobbs, 1978); and
6. Results of empirical research which indicate that effective childrearing styles are not simply related to socioeconomic status (Epstein & Evans, 1979; Shipman, McKee, & Bridgeman, 1977).

The combination of these six sources is creating a shift to a concern for all families. This shift suggests a new framework—only dimly apparent now—for parent and family education programs. The major characteristics of this framework are as follows: (1) the major goal at the societal level is the strengthening of all families; (2) the major societal problem needing attention is the stress presently experienced by all families as revealed by social indicators of family disruption and turbulence; (3) the value sought is strong families as a means of building a caring and competent society; (4) the primary target of intervention programs is family functioning; and (5) one of the useful intervention strategies is parent and family education. Further, the most promising intervention programs are those that have (1) a theoretical base in the

Table 1:   An Historical Overview of Childrearing Interventions

Intervention variables	1600–1800	1800–1850	1850–1880	1880–1900	1900–1920
			Broad societal context		
Goals	Socialize; to instill moral values	Socialize	Acculturation (mainstreaming)	Socialize	Massive reform of societal institutions and individuals
Societal problems	Crime and corruption	Immorality and corruption	Waves of immigrants and rapidly growing cities produce disorder and an underclass not socialized in dominant values	Corruption (especially political) and immorality in society	Waves of immigrants largely uneducated and unsocialized; uninformed and politically irresponsible citizens; rising divorce rates
Values	Moral (religious) citizenry	Morally responsible citizens	Stable society	Moral and decent society	Decent, stable society; socially and politically responsible citizens
Intervention area/strategy	Childrearing/parent education	Childrearing/child centers for lower class; parent education for middle class	Childrearing/infant schools for immigrants	Childrearing/parent education (middle class)	Maternal role (childrearing and awareness); maternal education (middle and lower class)

Intervention components

Knowledge base and philosophical/theoretical underpinnings	Two emergent philosophies: Calvinistic doctrine of infant depravity; Comenius-emphasis on first six years of life; child held to be innocent and in need of guidance	Two movements based on Comenius: Reform philosophies with regard to poor popular early in the 1800s; a belief in the ultimate authority of the individual and legitimacy of self-interest; the assumption that social benefits will be gained when self-interest is exercised	Calvinistic approach dominant Stress on obedience, compliance, and order in children	Philosophical shift with G. Stanley Hall's *Laws of Mental Development* and first empirical studies of child behavior; his laissez-faire policy stressed child's need for freedom to explore and develop; emphasis on early ages; first time cognitive and emotional development of children recognized	Hall still important but his emphasis shifts to adolescence; Dewey's social philosophy and pedagogical theory; first mention of executive function of parents; parents have broader responsibilities than child rearing
Program goals	Teach parent to be effective shaper of child's moral development		Change child's behavior	Use behavioral science to create a science of pedagogy; effective parents and self-improvement of mothers	Translate professional information to mothers; increase self and political awareness of mothers
Core approach to intervention	Religious sermons (occasional religious tracts)	Sunday schools expanded to weekdays; pamphlets, tracts, magazines, and sermons; first maternal association (1820)	Day nurseries run by nurses	Books, pamphlets, and discussion groups	Group discussions; socio-political action groups; home instruction for poor
Focus of intervention	Mother	Child—lower class Mother—middle class	Child	Mother	Mother

Table 1 (continued)

1920–1940	1940–Late 1950s	Late 1950s–mid 1960s	Mid-1960s–early 1970s	Mid 1970s–present
		Broad societal context		
Socialize	Help parents fill their role in child care	Redress of inequalities in society through governmental affirmative action	Redress of inequalities in society through governmental affirmative action	Strengthening all families
An adolescent population unprepared to assume moral responsibility or recognize social norms; parents inept in role	Depression and World War lead to industrial mobilization forcing women into labor force making them unable to care for children full-time	Disenfranchised urban poor; institutional racism	Disenfranchised urban poor; institutional racism	Social indicators of familial disruptions and turbulence in response to modern society
Morally responsible citizens and stable society	Adequate environment for child development	Equal rights; just society	Equal rights; just society	Strong families as means to a caring and competent society
Childrearing/parent education (middle class)	Child care/day care	Antipoverty interventions; compensatory education	Antipoverty interventions; compensatory education	Influences on family functioning and parent/family education

Intervention components

Watson, Dewey, Gesell, and Freud; focus on early childhood; personality traits fixed by age 5; children should be deferential to authority, socially conformist, and in control of their emotions; emphasis on social and emotional (not cognitive) development	Watson, Dewey, Gessel, and Freud; focus on early childhood; personality traits fixed by age 5; children should be deferential to authority, socially conformist, and in control of their emotions; emphasis on social and emotional (not cognitive) development	Development research focused on enriching environment and promoting early cognitive development	Research indicating importance of parental influence	Ecology of human and family development
Bring childrearing information to mothers; target on child's behavior, habit formation, personality, integration, and social adjustment; Nursery schools to give parents lessons in child rearing	Day care to allow mothers to be employed outside the home	Equalize educational opportunity; promote school success	Equalize educational opportunity; promote school success	Nurture family development through supporting parent roles (direct and executive) and parents' needs as adults
	Nursery schools (parent participation not encouraged)	Center-based programs run by professionals stressing stimulation of children	Impart knowledge/skills to parents; mostly didactic	Variety of program needs defined by family, with professional as resource
Mother	Child	Child	Child through parents	Family as an organized system

ecology of human and family development (still in its infancy as an empirical knowledge base); (2) goals related to the needs of parents for information or skills in either their parenting or executive functions; (3) a core approach of community compatible programs integrated within naturally occurring institutional–family contact points (such as schools, hospitals, and businesses); and (4) a focus on the family as a whole.

CONCLUSION

We do not argue that our human development and community approach represents a complete agenda for family policy. Much of the stress experienced by families is caused by external factors, factors that must be addressed if families are to become effective caregivers. Such external factors include insufficient income, inadequate housing, poor health, and meaningless or dehumanizing employment. Although this discussion has not addressed these critical areas of social policy, we recognize their influence. The decision to focus on human development was made for two reasons. First, other studies have made recommendations related to income, housing, health, and employment policies (e.g., Keniston, 1977; National Academy of Sciences, 1976). The second reason for this decision is more fundamental.

Economic recommendations, if implemented without attention to such issues as child care and parent education, affirm the historical view that social welfare policies have as their primary purpose the provision of an economic minimum. We grant that current economic recommendations are more sensitive to actual need than many previous policies have been, and that they are often properly concerned with guaranteeing economic benefits as rights. But from our viewpoint they are troublesome for three reasons: (1) they continue to define as the purpose of intervention the elimination of poverty and social pathology and not the enhancement of general social welfare; (2) they continue to emphasize and stigmatize subgroups within the general population; and (3) they emphasize the idea that families with adequate income, housing, health provision, and meaningful work are unlikely to need support in carrying out family functions. It is our contention that even if better equalization of economic resources is achieved through a redistribution strategy, even if economic stresses are minimized, and even if the material well-being of families is improved, families will still need support in carrying out their childrearing functions. In a sense, these economic policies should be seen as prerequisite and necessary—not final and sufficient—solutions. Thus, it will be necessary in the remaining decades of this century to address the situation of all American families from the value perspectives of human and community development.

FOOTNOTE

*This paper was prepared in conjunction with a project funded by the Carnegie Corporation and carried out at the Center for the Study of Families and Children of the Vanderbilt Institute for Public Policy Studies.
[1] This section contains material that also appears in Florin & Dokecki (in press).

REFERENCES

Bane, M. J. *Here to stay: American families in the twentieth century*. New York: Basic Books, 1976.

Berger, P. L., & Neuhaus, R. J. *To empower people: The role of mediating structures in public policy*. Washington, DC: American Enterprise Institute for Public Policy Research, 1977.

Bloom, B. S. *Stability and change in human characteristics*. New York: Wiley, 1964.

Bronfenbrenner, U. Is early intervention effective? *Day Care and Early Education*, 1974, 2, 14–18, 44.

Bronfenbrenner, U. Who needs parent education? *Teachers College Record*, 1978, 79, 767–787.

Clarke, A. M., & Clarke, A. D. B. *Early experience: Myth and evidence*. New York: Free Press, 1976.

Cowen, E. L. Baby-steps toward primary prevention. *American Journal of Community Psychology*, 1977, 5, 1.

Dewey, J. John Dewey. In E. Fromm & R. Xirau (Eds.), *The nature of man*. New York: Macmillan, 1968.

Dokecki, P. R. The liaison perspective on the enhancement of human development. *Journal of Community Psychology*, 1977, 5, 13–17.

Dokecki, P. R., & Strain, B. A. Intervention 2001: Transactional and developmental perspectives. *Peabody Journal of Education*, 1973, 50, 175–183.

Dokecki, P. R., Strain, B. A., Bernal, J., Brown, C., & Robinson, M.E. Low-income and minority groups. In N. Hobbs (Ed.), *Issues in the classification of children* (Vol. 1). San Francisco: Jossey-Bass, 1975.

Dunlop, K. H. *Rationales for governmental intervention into child care and parent education*. Nashville: Vanderbilt Institute for Public Policy Studies, 1978. (a)

Dunlop, K. H. *Social values in the United States: Implications for the development of policy options*. Nashville: Vanderbilt Institute for Public Policy Studies, 1978. (b)

Epstein, A. S., & Evans, J. Parent–child interaction and children's learning. *The High/Scope Report*, 1979, No. 4, 39–43.

Featherstone, J. Family matters. *Harvard Educational Review*, 1979, 49, 20–52.

Fein, G. G. The informed parent. In S. Kilmer (Ed.), *Advances in early education and day care* (Vol. 1). Greenwich, CT: JAI Press, 1980.

Florin, P. R., & Dokecki, P. R. Changing families through parent and family education: Review and analysis. In I. Sigel & L. Laosa (Eds.), *Changing families*. New York: Plenum, in press.

Goldstein, J., Freud, A., & Solnit, A. J. *Beyond the best interests of the child*. New York: Free Press, 1973.

Goodson, B. D., & Hess, R. D. *The effects of parent training programs on child performance and parent behavior*. Unpublished manuscript, Stanford Univ., 1977.

Gordon, T. Parent effectiveness training: A prospective program and its delivery system. In G. Albee & J. J. Cedil (Eds.), *Primary prevention of psychopathology* (Vol. 1). Hanover, NH: University Press of New England, 1977.

Hill, R., & Mattessich, P. *Reconstruction of family development theories: A progress report*. Paper presented at the meeting of the National Council on Family Relations, San Diego, 1977.

Hobbs, N. *The futures of children*. San Francisco: Jossey-Bass, 1975.

Hobbs, N. Families, schools, and communities: An ecosystem for children. *Teachers College Record*, 1978, 79, 756–766.

Hunt, J. McV. *Intelligence and experience*. New York: Ronald Press, 1961.

Kahn, A. J., & Kamerman, S. B. *Not for the poor alone*. Philadelphia: Temple University Press, 1975.

Keniston, K. *All our children: The American family under pressure*. New York: Harcourt Brace Jovanovich, 1977.

Lasch, C. *Haven in a heartless world: The family besieged*. New York: Basic Books, 1977.

Lasch, C. *The culture of narcissism*. New York: Norton, 1979.

Le Masters, E. E. Parenthood as crisis. *Marriage and Family Living*, 1957, 19, 352–355.

Luscher, K. *Knowledge on socialization*. Paper presented at the Cornell University conference, "Research perspectives in the ecology of human development," Ithaca, New York, 1977.

Mattessich, P. *Taxonomies for family impact analysis*. Minneapolis: Minnesota Family Study Center, 1976.

Minnesota Council on Quality Education. *A policy study of issues related to early childhood and family education in Minnesota*. St. Paul, MN: State Department of Education, 1979.

Moroney, R. *The family and the state: Considerations for social policy*. New York: Longmans, 1976.

National Academy of Sciences. *Toward a national policy for children and families*. Washington, DC: Author, 1976.

Newbrough, J. R. Liaison services in the community context. *Journal of Community Psychology*, 1977, 5, 24–27.

Newbrough, J. R., Dokecki, P. R., Dunlop, K. H., Hogge, J. H., Simpkins, C. G., Barnes, L., Boggs, B., Innes, S., Percey, J., & Robinson, S. *Families and family–institution transactions in child development.* Nashville: George Peabody College Center for Community Studies, 1978.

Shipman, V. C., McKee, D., & Bridgeman, B. *Stability and change in family status, situational and process variables, and their relationship to children.* Princeton, NJ: Educational Testing Service, 1977.

Steiner, G. Y. *The children's cause.* Washington, DC: Brookings, 1976.

Williams, J. S. Liaison functions as reflected in a case study. *Journal of Community Psychology*, 1977, *5*, 18–23.

Wills, G. *Inventing America: Jefferson's Declaration of Independence.* New York: Doubleday, 1978.

Yankelovich, Skelly, and White, Inc. *Raising children in a changing society.* Minneapolis: General Mills, 1977.

Three

The Apparent Lack of Connection Between Congressional Concerns and Those of Parent Program Proponents

DAVID S. MUNDEL

Are policymakers in Washington leaving parents out of the picture when they draw up legislation for children?

The correlations between children's backgrounds and their current and future characteristics are all too apparent for policymakers to ignore parents in the design of public interventions. Numerous studies have shown the correlation between parent and family characteristics and children's health status, nutritional intake, school performance, employment success, and antisocial behavior. Most children's programs are directed at children whose parents are socially or economically disadvantaged; many other programs provide cash and in-kind income to reduce the poverty among families with children in order to improve the environments within which children develop.

If the correlations between family backgrounds and childhood outcomes are evident to policymakers and a principal aspect or focus of the policies they design, why do the major problems confronting Congressional decision-makers seem to have little, if any, connection to parent programs? In the 1980s, the Congress is addressing the problems of high inflation, continuing unemployment, declining productivity, and rising international tensions. Most of the domestic policy alternatives under discussion are proposals to constrain the growth and improve the productivity or effectiveness of federal involvement. But people involved in operating, designing, and advocating parent programs concentrate on expansion, rather than reduction, of the federal role.

There are several reasons for this apparent lack of connection: (1) the lack of connection may be more apparent than real; (2) program proponents may be unable or unwilling to participate in budget reduction or reallocation politics; (3) many of the needed linkages between policy choices and parent involvement may not have been established; and (4) many potential family problems may not have reached the level of severity that elicits public attention. Each of these reasons suggests the need for different responses by those who wish the Congress to consider more carefully the role and development of parent programs.

One reason for the apparent lack of connection between Congressional concerns and those of parent program advocates may simply be inadequate understanding or reporting of Congressional concerns. Although the Congress appears to be primarily addressing the problems of inflation and unemployment, it is also considering new programs for youth education and training, as well as proposals to expand the funding for Head Start and social service programs. These latter discussions have not had the attention that their significance deserves. Efforts to reduce the federal budget receive extensive journalistic review, but expansions in welfare benefits (such as those passed in 1979 by the House of Representatives) and the growth in federal support for education have been relatively unnoticed or unreported. Outside observers all too often take the public image of Congressional interest at face value. Although Congress may appear to be primarily interested in cutting back, it is also interested in continuing to develop and support major programs that ameliorate domestic problems. Program advocates and designers would be well-advised not to discount the value of dealing with a fiscally conservative Congress.

A second reason for the apparent lack of connection between policymakers and the parent program community is that program proponents may be failing to help policymakers with their current problems.

Congress is now concerned with constraining and redirecting the patterns of federal involvement. Program developers, advocates, and operators do not effectively contribute to the resolution of these issues when they continue to recommend program expansions. Their recommendations are particularly ineffective when they appear to be based on a desire to maintain or expand status, income, or staffing levels, rather than on evidence of usefulness or need. Often, program advocates are unwilling to help like-minded Congressmen when the heat is on. If advocates do not help their friends when times are tough, good times may come less often.

A third reason for the apparent lack of connection between parent education programs and Congressional concerns is that many of the needed connections have not been established. In considering ways to improve the efficacy of a wide range of public programs, little Congressional attention is devoted to improving parent behavior or expanding the direct involvement of parents in programs. Parent program proponents narrowly focus much of their attention on parent involvement in education. But there seems to be a large and relatively unexplored potential for improving children's health by stimulating parents to make wiser use of existing systems for health care and disease prevention. Similarly, because most children eat most of their meals at home, the impact of federal child nutrition activities could be greater if more resources were devoted to improving the nutritional decisions of parents, rather than focusing on the few meals that children consume in child care institutions and schools. Other children and youth policies might also be improved through greater parent involvement.

Two sets of biases are found among most program advocates and policymakers—biases in favor of professional and institutional service delivery and biases against involving disadvantaged parents in the control of programs. The service-providing community and the groups that lobby on its behalf are dominated by professionals. These professionals—doctors, nurses, nurse practitioners, nutritionists, social workers, and teachers—are taught that their services are not only highly valuable but also beyond the understanding of lay people, particularly everyday, ordinary parents. It seems not to occur to them that parents could be encouraged or taught to provide many of the same services or at least be helpful to their provision.

Most program proponents also favor institutionally provided services; i.e., those that are provided by hospitals, neighborhood health centers, school lunchrooms, and child care centers. These institutionalized settings appear to be more predictable providers; their behavior can be more easily monitored and analyzed by government officials. All too often we assume that when the federal government provides funds to these institutions, such funds represent a net gain to, rather than a substitute for, funding that would have been provided by others. It is also easy to believe—mistakenly—that the quantity and quality of institutional inputs is a good indicator of the quantity and quality of institutional outputs. The food left in school lunchroom garbage cans should militate against this belief.

In short, professionals and many policymakers are likely to feel that efforts to educate and involve parents in improving a program are less apt to succeed than expanding the use of professional and institutional resources. Consequently, more informal efforts involving parents are likely to receive less political attention.

Not only are there biases in favor of professionally and institutionally provided services, but there is also a bias against parents. Program advocates argue that parents are inadequate. Greater public attention to education, health care, and nutrition is needed, because families are inadequately providing or arranging these services for their children. Low incomes account for part of this inadequacy. Even if family incomes were increased, however, most human service program proponents would not expect parents to make appropriate choices. In some cases they might be right, but in most it would seem productive to try to help parents do a better job.

Another bias or fear exists among policymakers that also needs to be understood by parent program advocates—a fear of involving the government explicitly in family life. Proponents of increased parent education and greater parent involvement should not underestimate the desire of policymakers to avoid involvement in this issue.

Expanding the role of parents in human services programs calls for making more apparent the connections between the success of programs and parent involvement, and combating the biases against parent involvement and against government involvement with families. Serious program development and evaluation efforts are likely to be more effective in this effort than are political or religious claims of need or effectiveness.

The fourth reason for the apparent lack of connection between Congressional concerns and parent programs is that many family or parent problems may not have reached the level of severity that elicits public attention. Policymakers generally like to avoid problems. Problems require attention, time, and political capital, and "solving" them always upsets some people and frequently makes no one very happy. Consequently, if problems are not severe and visible, they will not be dealt with. This happens with many severe problems as well.

Parents and their children face problems, but these problems have not become so publicly threatening or visible as to elicit public response.

For example, while real family incomes have grown over the last decade—because of increases in wages, in the number of wage earners per family, and the level of public assistance—the quality of family life has probably declined. More children have divorced parents. More children are growing up in families where both parents work, and parental time available for child development is consequently less than it once was. More children are being born to unwed teenage mothers. A large proportion of all children are being born in minority and otherwise disadvantaged families who face greater social and economic problems and thus experience more difficult childrearing problems.

These trends in family conditions are likely to continue throughout the 1980s. The negative effects are likely to be made worse by slower growth in family incomes. Moreover, public assistance benefits are unlikely to increase as rapidly during the 1980s as they did during the 1970s. Wages are now growing more slowly than prices, and higher payroll taxes in the near future will reduce net incomes still further. Families with two wage earners continue to face a "marriage penalty" in the income tax law that reduces the net income resulting from a second earner. The baby boom that once crowded the nation's high schools, and more recently its colleges and universities, is now crowding the younger segment of the labor force. This crowding will further reduce the growth in earnings among younger workers and will make their support of children more difficult.

These demographic and labor force trends, together with the harsh new economic realities of the 1980s, are likely to worsen the problems facing parents and children. But the problems may not become bad or visible enough to arouse public concern. If the parent program community wishes to increase that concern, it will have to find ways to make these problems more visible to those in the political arena, or else await the problems' eruption.

The implications of my arguments are very simply that the parent program community needs to take stock and increase its role within the public policymaking process. The lack of apparent Congressional interest should not be construed as a lack of concern on the part of legislators. The fact that Congress is searching for budget reduction strategies does not mean that it is unwilling to tackle new problems or undertake new and more productive solutions. If problems are to be dealt with, they must first be known to exist.

Section II

Research Studies

In this second and longest section, we include seven chapters dealing with various aspects of research on parent education.

Paul Dokecki and his colleagues Erwin Hargrove and Howard Sandler open this section with a summary of research on the Parent Child Development Centers (PCDC). Although some critics have had less than favorable views of the PCDC's (Steiner, 1976), perhaps the most interesting aspect of PCDC history is that the underlying concepts represent a very advanced model for social experimentation. One might quibble about interpretations of the data, but the planning and execution of this experiment bear close examination, which is precisely what Dokecki and his associates provide.

Four aspects of the PCDC are of special note. First, the theory and logic of the overall design were well-thought-out in advance by Mary Robinson, whose planning papers provided not only a blueprint for the experiment, but commentary on many problems of implementation as well. Second, the plan called for experimental sites to initiate and conduct the parent programs, and then to replicate their results by working directly with replication sites in other cities. Elaborate statistical techniques not excepted, there is no better way to demonstrate the validity of a finding than to replicate it, and the PCDCs represent one of the very few systematic attempts to examine replicability in social policy experimentation.

A third noteworthy aspect of the PCDC experiment was the invention and use of something called a Replication Management Organization (RMO), which (1) helped monitor the communication of the intervention program and its theoretical basis from original sites to replication sites; (2) helped original sites provide training and other assistance to replication sites; and (3) documented and analyzed problems and successes of the replication process.

Finally, the PCDC experiment was important because it provided an excellent example of cooperative funding between the public and private sectors, in this case between the Administration for Children, Youth, and Families and the Lilly Endowment. Given the current and likely future emphasis on private sector involvement in social programs, this aspect of the PCDC experiment was especially timely. Successful experiments that are as carefully planned as the PCDC study could begin to supply the kinds of data on social interventions that policymakers would find persuasive.

Whereas the PCDC experiment focused on education and support for parents of preschool children, another major intervention program of the late 1960s focused on parents of school-age children. This intervention program, known as Follow Through (FT), included a rather elaborate evaluation study that eventually produced a set of controversial results (in a word, that Follow Through had no significant effects on achievement; see Anderson, St. Pierre, Proper, & Stebbins, 1978; House, Glass, McLean, & Walker, 1978) concerning the effects of Follow Through on educational achievement. The chapter by Olmsted and Rubin, however, focuses only on the parent involvement aspects of the FT program.

Interestingly, FT legislation and regulations, originally conceived in 1967 primarily to help poor children achieve well in the lower elementary grades, contain quite substantial requirements for parent involvement. In particular, the regulations require every program to have: a Policy Advisory Committee (PAC) with heavy parent representation; parents participating in the classroom as observers, volunteers, or paid employees; and home visits and other parent contacts by project staff. Taken together, these regulations constitute one of the strongest requirements for parent involvement of any federal education program. Thus, the chapter by Olmsted and Rubin examining parent involvement in FT seems especially appropriate for this volume.

After a brief overview of FT and a summary of its parent involvement requirements, Olmsted and Rubin examine evidence concerning the effects of parent involvement on FT programs and children. To do so, they examine two types of information: (1) information generated by national surveys and other national FT activities; and (2) information from local FT sponsors. Based on this information about effects of FT parent programs, Olmsted and Rubin draw several policy recommendations. These recommendations focus primarily on the particular characteristics of parent program that should be required; e.g., parents should be involved in program development and management as well as advocacy roles.

The chapter by Hazel Leler is a valuable addition to this volume because she reviews studies of programs for parents of school-age children. A consequence of the long-standing emphasis among researchers and professionals on the importance of the preschool years is that most reviews of parent programs focus on the preschool years. However, the school-age years are also important because during the first 3 or 4 years of public schooling, children are exposed to, and expected to learn, fundamental academic skills that will shape the remainder of their school careers.

Leler first proposes an organizational framework for the studies of parent involvement. Citing Ira Gordon, she notes that there are three general types of parent involvement: (1) family impact programs in which outside agencies, such as the schools, attempt to influence parents; (2) school impact programs that attempt to facilitate the influence of parents in the schools and other agencies; and (3) community impact programs that conceive of the home, school, and community as interrelated sources of influence on children.

Not surprisingly, most studies concern the more traditional type of family impact programs. On the whole, most studies reviewed by Leler found some positive results on children's school achievement, usually in reading performance. These effects, however, were not very large, and as Leler notes, almost none were measured at long-term followup.

The review of school impact studies is more diffuse, largely because the variables by which one can measure impacts on the school are not well understood. Nevertheless, several studies show that parents, teachers, and administrators say they want more parent impact on the schools. Although Leler interprets these findings to mean that most people favor parent influence in schools, it seems possible that there are actually some serious differences among administrators, teachers, and parents in this regard and that these differences may constitute barriers to parent involvement. Whitaker (1977), for example, in a study reviewed by Leler, found that although parents and school administrators agreed that more school involvement by parents would be good, the groups differed widely in their views on the causes of low parent involvement. Thus, whereas administrators saw parent apathy as the major barrier to parent involvement, parents thought the major problem was that they didn't get information on school policies. These and similar differences may suggest that professionals in the schools and elsewhere jealously protect "their" turf against parent infringement, and that this force could stand as a major barrier to an expansion of parent programs (see Chap. 11).

The very few published studies of the Community Impact approach are difficult to evaluate because they are so broad and consider information on so many measures. Leler's review suggests that these programs are effective, but perhaps a decision should await publication of more studies.

The next two chapters concern programs for parents of handicapped children. Recent claims that modern American families are under exceptional stress, signified most clearly by the Keniston (1977) Report (subtitled "The American Family Under Pressure"), should not distract us from the realization that families with a handicapped child, regardless of the family's financial condition, have always experienced stress (Bristol & Gallagher, 1982; Moroney, 1980). These families often have extra financial burdens, suffer mightily from stigma, and face a host of complications ranging from such banal considerations as sleeping arrangements to more potent problems such as child care. Thus, programs for handicapped children have a long history of emphasizing parent participation—if for no other reason than these parents need support in coping with the mundane problem of day-to-day existence.

The chapter by Karnes, Linnemeyer, and Myles reports the results of a survey of projects participating in the Handicapped Children's Early Education Program (HCEEP). This federal program, enacted by Congress in 1968, has now funded over 300 preschool programs for all types of handicapped children in each of the 50 states. Like the federal programs studied by Keesling and Melaragno (Chap. 9), the HCEEP legislation and regulations require rather substantial levels of parent participation. The purpose of the survey conducted by Karnes et al. was to examine these parent participation programs in some detail. Of the 139 HCEEP projects asked to participate in the survey, 71 returned usable questionnaires by mail, and these constitute the data base summarized in the first section of the Karnes et al. chapter.

Several interesting descriptive findings were revealed by the survey. In particular, over 85% of the 71 projects had specific goals for their parent programs, and a similar percentage based their goals on a needs assessment process engaged in with parents. In general, the needs assessments revealed that parents of handicapped children wanted: to participate in educational planning for their child, to learn techniques of fostering their child's development, to learn child management skills, and to learn as much as possible about their child's handicapping condition.

The survey also revealed six types of parent participation used by 85% or more of the projects: conducting group meetings, training parents in skills needed to work with their child, involving parents in planning their child's educational program, holding parent–teacher conferences, teaching parents to participate in child assessment, and training parents to engage in direct teaching of their child. Though strong data to support the following generalization does not seem to be available, one has the impression that HCEEP programs, unlike parent involvement programs in the public schools, train parents to acquire and use skills normally reserved for professionals, including child assessment and direct teaching. An optimist might conclude that this finding demonstrates that, at least under some circumstances, professionals are capable of sharing their expertise with parents and of treating parents as partners in the educational process (see Chap. 11).

In the second and largest section of their chapter, Karnes and her colleagues provide concrete descriptions of several exemplary parent participation programs. A compelling feature of this section is the broad range of parent program types represented, including center-based and home-based models, models that focus on fathers, and models for the gifted and talented handicapped as well as the severely and profoundly handicapped. Several of these projects collected outcome data on children's development to demonstrate the effectiveness of their parent programs.

In the final section of the chapter, Karnes and her colleagues discuss a number of public policy questions raised by their survey. Although they offer few specific recommendations, they offer enlightening discussions of key program issues. These include: (1) funding of programs for handicapped children under 3 years of age; (2) characteristics of parent programs that should be mandated by legislation or program regulations; and (3) obstacles professionals often put in the way of expanded parent participation.

Like Karnes et al., Hocutt and Wiegerink examine parent participation in the HCEEP network. More specifically, these authors present three empirical studies of HCEEP parent programs. In the first study, they assembled five groups of experts who, using a type of Delphi procedure, were asked to identify specific types of parent participation that would define more specifically the four categories of participation mentioned in HCEEP legislation. Of these four categories—which included: (1) parents receiving information; (2) parents engaging in passive educational activities, such as receiving reports and participating in counseling; (3) parents engaging in active educational activities such as administering curriculum items or therapy routines with their child; and (4) parents engaging in decision-making and program planning or operation—there was remarkable agreement among the Delphi panelists that parents participating in educational activities was the most important type of participation and that participating in program decision-making was the least important. Further, panelists agreed that most parents would actually participate in educational activities and fewest parents would actually participate in decision-making activities.

The second study was a survey of 23 HCEEP third-year projects to determine the actual types of parent activities offered by projects, the percentage of parents participating in these activities, and the correlates of parent participation. Interestingly, the highest levels of actual parent participation were in educational activities—the very type of participation rated most important by Delphi panelists. Similarly, the lowest level of actual parent involvement was in program decision-making—the participation category rated least important by panelists. This study also produced the somewhat troubling finding that HCEEP projects with lowest levels of parent participation were associated with public school systems.

Logically enough, the third study was a survey of HCEEP parents. This survey demonstrated that, overall, parents were highly satisfied with the parent participation activities offered by the projects. There were, however, interesting correlates of parent participation levels across projects. Most notably, parents of children with the severest handicaps and parents in projects associated with the public schools were least satisfied, while parents who believed they had substantial influence on project operation were the most satisfied.

The chapter by Keesling and Melaragno of the System Development Corporation represents a very different kind of research than the other chapters in this section. Whereas all the other papers are concerned with the characteristics and effects of parent programs, this chapter provides descriptive information on the actual extent of parent participation in four federal programs that mandate parent participation; namely, Title I of the Elementary and Secondary Education Act, Title VI of the same Act (also known as the Emergency School Assistance Act), Title VII of the same Act (also known as Bilingual Education), and Follow Through (see Chap. 5). In addition, the chapter carefully examines the relationship between legislation and regulations for each program and the type and extent of parent participation revealed by the survey.

Among the most interesting data reported by Keesling and Melaragno is that on the percentage of schools having particular types of parent participation in each of the four programs. On the average, 32%

of the schools used parents as volunteers, 50% had them involved in training their children at home, and 29% hired parents as paraprofessionals. These figures actually seem somewhat inflated, because FT data is much higher than that for the other three programs for all three types of parent participation. Removing Follow Through data reduces the above figures to 20%, 41%, and 14%, respectively. Critics might conclude that these are surprisingly low percentages and that parent participation is not widely practiced—even in programs where it is mandated by legislation and regulation.

On the other hand, the comparable figures for the FT program are 67%, 76%, and 74%. A reasonable response to critics, then, might be that the FT program demonstrates the high levels of parent participation that can be achieved under some circumstances. After all, in each of these three parent participation categories, including the two that represent very sophisticated levels of parent participation (delivering the curriculum and serving as paid paraprofessionals), nearly three quarters of the schools surveyed had parent programs.

What we want to know, of course, is what circumstances promote such high levels of parent participation. The answer given by Keesling and Melaragno is that the legislation and regulation of a given program can play a major role in creating high levels of parent participation. Indeed, the primary policy conclusion they draw from their survey is that high levels of parent participation can be produced by: (1) using strong and clear language in the legislation and regulations; (2) specifying the precise activities in which parent participation is required; and (3) providing incentives for maintaining certain types or levels of parent participation. The Keesling and Melaragno data seem quite persuasive in supporting the notion that federal mandates can, under some circumstances, produce high levels of parent involvement at the local level.

Taken together, the first six chapters in this section provide a strong justification for parent education. This very positive evaluation of parent programs, however, is challenged by Clarke-Stewart in the final chapter in this section.

Clarke-Stewart, in an extremely concise and compact analysis, examines what she regards as the five major assumptions underlying parent programs. These assumptions are that: (1) researchers have provided an empirical ground supporting the edifice of positive developmental effects produced by parent education; (2) parent programs have been evaluated and their effects documented; (3) we know what types of parent programs work best; (4) we understand how parent education works; and (5) parent education is more effective than other forms of social reform.

Detailed examination of the empirical evidence for these five assumptions causes Clarke-Stewart to conclude that none of them are well supported by data. The assumption that parent education programs have been evaluated and shown to be effective (assumption "2" above) is perhaps the most strongly supported by research data, but even here Clarke-Stewart raises a number of caveats. Among these: (1) relatively few parent programs have been carefully evaluated, and those that have represent a biased sample of very good, highly expensive, often university based programs; thus, whether the documented results would generalize to "run-of-the-mill" programs is unknown; (2) most evaluations have been extremely simple and have used questionable control or comparison groups and rather gross outcome measures such as IQ or school achievement; (3) experimental-control group differences, though significant, are usually not very large; and (4) very few studies have shown long-term effects. One can understand Clarke-Stewart's position on the other four assumptions underlying parent education by recognizing that this is the assumption for which she finds the strongest empirical support. Indeed, she outright rejects the last three assumptions: "The assumption that we know what kind of parent education works best is simply unfounded" (p. 410); "Clearly, we are a long way from understanding the process by which parent education works" (p. 415); "The suggestion that parent-focused programs are more effective than those involving the child or focused exclusively on the child . . . is simply not supported" (p. 416).

Advocates of parent education may examine the same data as that studied by Clarke-Stewart and come to different conclusions; some may even charge her with bias. Nonetheless, Clarke-Stewart's chapter, in conjunction with her previous work (especially Clarke-Stewart & Apfel, 1978), show her to be among the most knowledgeable people in the country on this topic. Thus, advocates of parent programs are forced to deal with her reasoning and conclusions if for no other reason than, as Clarke-Stewart wisely remarks:

> It looks as if the facts are in: we have seen parent education and it is good; we have tried parent education and it works.
>
> But before we expand our parent education efforts in this era of scarce resources, I suggest we make sure we've got our facts straight. Support for parent education will inevitably come at the expense of other social programs; we need to make the most of our limited opportunities for social change. We will not get away for long with promising outcomes we can't deliver, and there is danger in basing parent education on the claim that it is "scientifically proven," if it is not. If the rationale for parent education were merely good will or good intentions, there would be no problem. But it is not—witness the many pages of program evaluations in this volume. Therefore, we need to examine very carefully this presumed empirical basis for parent education before we proceed. (pp. 257–258)

REFERENCES

Anderson, R. B., St. Pierre, R. G., Proper, E. C., & Stebbins, L. B. Pardon us, but what was that question again?: A response to the critique of the Follow Through evaluation. *Harvard Educational Review*, 1978, *48*, 161–170.

Bristol, M. M., & Gallagher, J. J. A family focus for intervention. In C. T. Ramey & P. L. Trohanis (Eds.), *Finding and educating high-risk and handicapped infants*. Baltimore: University Park Press, 1982.

Clarke-Stewart, K., & Apfel, N. Evaluating parental effects on child development. In L. Shulman (Ed.), *Review of research in education*. Ithaca, NY: F. E. Peacock, 1978.

House, E. R., Glass, G. V., McLean, L. D., & Walker, D. F. No single answer: Critique of the Follow Through evaluation. *Harvard Educational Review*, 1978, *48*, 128–160.

Keniston, K. *All our children: The American family under pressure*. New York: Harcourt Brace Jovanovich, 1977.

Moroney, R. M. *Families, social services, and social policy: The issue of shared responsibilities* [DHHS Publication No. (ADM) 80-846]. Washington, DC: U.S. Government Printing Office, 1980.

Steiner, G. *The children's cause*. Washington, DC: Brookings, 1976.

Whitaker, B. I. Citizen participation in educational decision making in an urban school district as perceived by parents and administrators (Doctoral dissertation, Georgia State University School of Education, 1977). *Dissertation Abstracts International*, 1978, *38*, 3893A-3894A. (University Microfilms No. 77-29,322)

FOUR

AN OVERVIEW OF THE PARENT CHILD DEVELOPMENT CENTER SOCIAL EXPERIMENT*

PAUL R. DOKECKI, ERWIN C. HARGROVE, & HOWARD M. SANDLER

INTRODUCTION

From the vantage point of the mid 1960s when the Parent Child Development Centers (PCDC) social experiment was conceived, its achievements have largely confirmed the expectations of its planners. After careful planning, attention to the state-of-the-art in theory and research, and allocation of reasonable time and money to research and development, several model parent education programs for low-income families with young (birth to age 3) children were developed, evaluated, and replicated (Andrews, Blumenthal, Johnson, Kahn, Ferguson, Lasater, Malone, & Wallace, 1982). From the vantage point of the early 1980s—scarcely 15 years since the surge of optimism about social innovation of the Kennedy–Johnson years—the fulfillment of expectations by PCDC's is a rare event.

The experiment is noteworthy for two major reasons. First, it is one of the few carefully evaluated intervention programs for young children and their families. Second, it demonstrates that research and development in the behavioral and social sciences can be used to create valid programs with potential for influencing social policy.

RATIONALE FOR THE PCDC PROGRAM

The PCDC social experiment was conceived in the Great Society, but it was born in the early Nixon years. Originally proposed within the Office of Economic Opportunity (OEO), PCDC-like interventions were seen as one of the promising service strategies thought necessary to complement economic strategies (e.g., jobs and income maintenance) in framing a comprehensive poverty policy for the nation. The decline of OEO, the emerging skepticism about the effectiveness of social programs, and the rise of the New Federalism led to both a reduction in scope of the PCDC experiment and the failure to test the efficacy of a combined service and economic approach to the problems of low-income families and children. As a result, the PCDC program has operated as a controlled research and development program, albeit one with significantly fewer dollars and on a smaller scale than originally intended.

Key Ideas in PCDC Planning

Several strands of thinking were woven together to form the PCDC planning rationale. These included: (1) the emerging understanding of infant development; (2) the recognition of parental influences on child development; (3) the determination that parents, especially but not exclusively low-income parents, need and can profit from the latest information on childrearing; (4) the belief that developmental programs are particularly needed for poverty families during the child's earliest years; and (5) the suggestion that adult education with a parent focus can have favorable consequences for child development and the economic condition of the family.

Regarding the last point, Mary Robinson, former PCDC project officer, maintained that there was a great need for programs that share knowledge of child development with parents, especially the parents of infants. In the early 1970s, census data indicated that some 1.2 million families with poverty-level incomes were rearing about 1.8 million children under 3 years of age, plus another 2.4 million children ages 3 to 16 years. In only about 12% of these families were mothers employed full time. Given the average number of children in these families (3.26 children under 16 years of age in two-parent families; 2.97 in one-parent families), demographic data strongly suggested that the employment of mothers in 80% of families at or below the poverty level promised few, if any, income or social benefits to the families themselves or to the public in the form of decreased dependency. On the other hand, the presence of these mothers in the home meant they were available to participate in parent education programs in order to increase their effectiveness as parents, and at very low opportunity costs. That is, mother's foregone earnings would generally be less than the cost of surrogate care were mothers to begin work. When the near poor (families with incomes up to 150% of poverty level) were included, according to Robinson, the universe of need almost doubled to 1.0 million families with 1.2 million children under age 3 and a total of 3.1 million children under age 16. In this group, 78% of mothers in two-parent families and 60% of mothers in one-parent families were not employed and, hence, could concentrate on the development of their children. Although there has been an increase in female labor force participation since the early 1970s, it seems probable that the basic outline of Robinson's argument still holds.

Another dimension of the need for and utility of parent-oriented intervention involved findings that, due to a variety of income-related factors, stress in low-income families was such that developmentally stimulating experiences often seemed to be lacking. Consequently, it was believed that encouragement of positive parent–child interactions at the earliest phases of development might lead to enhanced development of both parents and children. The infusion of new and tested developmental knowledge and help in reducing poverty-related stress was required.

Unlike many early intervention programs, PCDCs put primary emphasis on the education of mothers alongside their children. It was believed that through the mothers, the child receives many immediate and sustained aids to development. Parent involvement has repeatedly been deemed crucial in intervention efforts, and PCDCs answer that need by relying heavily on techniques of adult pedagogy (see Dokecki, Roberts, & Moroney, 1979; Knox, 1977). Adult development and growth is central in the PCDC conception, with the emphasis that parents may change their styles and beliefs over time to suit their own needs. At the same time, the bodies of knowledge that PCDCs deliver are constantly changing. Thus, a dynamic interaction between parents as information-seekers and a valid knowledge base is fostered. Learning is made relevant to daily life experiences. Participants are in control of their own education and can see results from their actions in their everyday lives.

Another important focus for PCDCs that has often been lacking in early intervention and parent education efforts is the provision of a comprehensive program, focusing on the entire family environment, instead of solely on the young child. It is assumed that participating families have many serious needs, and that their local communities and sociocultural circumstances should be taken into account in understanding these needs. Besides learning activities relevant for young children, PCDCs offer a broad array of services for mothers and families, such as classes in nutrition, arts and crafts, financial budgeting, and local politics, as well as social services, recreation, medical care, home visits, and peer support groups. Since financial need is inherent in the low-income family system, modest stipends are given to help alleviate the stresses and costs of attending the program.

Research and Development Strategy for the PCDC Social Experiment

Regarding future relationships between social policy and research, Henry Aaron (1978), former assistant secretary for planning and evaluation in the Department of Health, Education, and Welfare, maintains that:

> The critical questions are likely to remain how government policies can effectively achieve objectives most Americans feel should be handled collectively and how the results of social science research should be used best to help in that quest. (p. 169)

Such questions are indeed critical in the wake of several recent failures of research to contribute to the public purpose—especially in the area of compensatory education, the most noteworthy example being Follow Through (see Chap. 5).

It makes sense to use pilot experiments to fashion social programs. Persistent and strong forces in American politics and government, however, make it very difficult to do so. For example, the Model Cities program was, in its conception, to be a pilot program in urban social development for one to two cities. But the ambitions of President Johnson and the requirements of Congressional passage eventually brought the number of Model Cities to over 100. A thinly diluted program of services replaced the ideal of an experiment. Most Great Society programs were originally envisioned as experiments, but were quickly transformed into service programs lacking in clear theoretical formulation about the relations between cause and effect in treatment and outcomes. Such was the case with the Parent–Child Centers (PCC), the service-oriented forerunners of the PCDCs.

The dominant theme of the politics of American social policy is that of distribution—or more specifically, of three types of distribution. First, the geographic structure of representation in Congress mandates the wide distribution of programs across constituencies and provides little incentive for pilot programs. Second, the emphasis on distribution of services obstructs the use of control groups and other experimental devices. Finally, because funding is seldom adequate for programs of national distribution to be effective, the division of funds among as many constituencies as possible often becomes an end in itself. The political incentives for presidents and members of Congress usually lead to the launching of new programs that emphasize grand hopes and provide tangible goods. The question of effectiveness in meeting problems is for the long run; political accountability governs the short run.

Of course, research and development divisions of agencies give their support to pilot experiments that are conceived and developed by universities and other private institutions. The problem is that too little attention is given to the task of systematically testing the early, fragile experiment in a variety of settings. The incentives to rush into full-scale delivery have been too strong.

Recognition of this missing stage has prompted efforts to fashion parts of existing operational programs into experiments. Head Start was built on a national scale without the benefit of pilot programs in different settings, and an experiment in planned variations of Head Start projects was begun as a corrective. The Follow Through program, intended as a reinforcement to Head Start, was also adapted to include planned variations. And such was the case when PCDCs were developed after PCCs were rushed into action in the mid-1960s.

These efforts at quasiexperimentation had great difficulty overcoming the problems of implementation which were endemic in the larger programs (see, for example, Anderson, St. Pierre, Proper, & Stebbins, 1978; House, Glass, McLean, & Walker, 1978). As laid out by Rivlin and Timpane (1975) in discussing the Head Start Planned Variations and Follow Through, and as foreseen in the Robinson (1966–1971) planning papers,[1] the problems of implementing planned variations are surprisingly diverse.

First, each of the programs of planned variation was based on a number of alternative theories and strategies of delivery with the common goal of helping disadvantaged children overcome educational deficiencies. In the case of the Head Start Planned Variation, planners faced the quandry of whether the models were to be compared and ranked according to effectiveness or tested and assessed in terms of the specific goals each set for itself. The answer to this question had consequences for the development of outcome measures for evaluation. Different specific objectives require different measures. But the desire to achieve standardization in evaluation led to the creation of tests that were not keyed to model differences. The problem here was not with the evaluation, but with the failure to resolve the question of comparison.

A second implementation problem illustrated by the Head Start Planned Variation was the lack of clarity about whether models were to be replicated as precisely as possible or whether adaptation to local setting and situation was to be permissible. The virtue of replication is that, if properly done, it permits measurement of what actually happens. Thus, one can know if the theoretical model and its actual implementation are the same. However, the political and service pressures in such experiments favor adapting the program to local settings.

Third, few of the Head Start Planned Variation models had been well tested initially. The theories underlying them were similarly untested, and it was not possible to say precisely how treatment variables were related to theory. This made it difficult to know what was essential to the model.

Fourth, there are usually tensions between the goals of service and the goals of research. For example, Follow Through was originally conceived as a service program that would reinforce the educational gains achieved by Head Start. When parts of Follow Through were redirected to become experiments, this shift in objectives was not always clear to lower-level federal, state, and local officials. They continued to see the programs as a service, and often did not conform to experimental requirements.

Fifth, as again illustrated by Follow Through, planned variations may be subject to federal regulations. In the case of Follow Through, the necessity of complying with regulations ensured a pro forma standardization, but precluded a range of experimentation. For example, a requirement for "community participation" prevented variation from that norm.

Finally, the various models being tested were often located in communities with very different characteristics so that populations receiving treatment were quite different. This, of course, represents a possible confounding of models with populations served, thereby minimizing the possibility of comparing effects of the various models.

OEO planners anticipated these problems and therefore designed the PCDC social experiment to minimize their impact. Planners of the PCDCs began with the belief that the use of program evaluation procedures as a sole means for improving compensatory education was based on the following tenuous and unproven assumptions: (1) a sufficient number of exemplary programs or models existed; (2) existing models were fully developed and could be effectively replicated; (3) evaluation procedures were robust enough to identify exemplary programs; and (4) critical program characteristics could be revealed and described in terms that would permit replication.

The corrective prescription for the tenuous nature of these assumptions offered by PCDC planners involved two propositions. First, applied research and development tasks (i.e., the formulation and initial testing of treatments and treatment mixes) and replication tasks (i.e., experimental field testing of exemplary programs and previously developed models) would be recognized as successive stages of a single innovation process. Second, valid experimental field testing (i.e., controlled replication and comparison of previously developed models or exemplary programs) required the existence of a stock of models as a critical precondition of the controlled experimental effort (Robinson, 1966–1971). These propositions have provided a continuing framework for the PCDC research design. Applied research and development tasks have preceded a controlled replication phase of the overall project. In contrasting the PCDC research strategy with earlier large-scale efforts (e.g., PCC, Head Start, Follow Through), it should be recognized that the controlled replication stage was defined explicitly from the beginning of program development (Robinson, 1966–1971), thereby making the PCDC treatment approach more rigorous and specific than the initial stages of other demonstration efforts.

Use of the two-phase research and development strategy defined above and implemented by PCDC planners has certain advantages in establishing large-scale programs. First, the greatest experimental risks occur during the first phase when numbers of participants and expenses are lower. Second, identifying stages of problem development with respect to treatment, testing, documentation, and production of curriculum materials helps the program remain on schedule. Additionally, this strategy is designed to yield successive sets of answers to increasingly more difficult and expensive questions under conditions of reduced risk.

The mission of PCDCs was to develop theoretically-based program models that would link child development and adult (parent) education principles. To this end, the following objectives were defined for developing theoretically sound models of infant and parent education to identify, develop, and test a variety of replicable program elements that:

1. stimulate the intellectual, emotional, and physical development of infants from low-income families in order to prevent cumulative developmental lags;

2. provide parents with a broad range of substantive knowledge and skills related to the stimulation of infant development (e.g., child development and learning, use of community resources);

3. meet parents' basic adult education needs; and

4. lead to effective child rearing by reducing potential liabilities of low-income home environments; e.g., by providing education and job-training for fathers, income maintenance, family planning (Robinson, 1966–1971).

OVERVIEW OF THE HISTORY OF THE PCDC SOCIAL EXPERIMENT

The three initial PCDCs in Houston, New Orleans, and Birmingham were established in 1969–70 by means of program competition among the large number of existing Parent–Child Centers. As mentioned earlier, the PCCs were begun under OEO sponsorship as service rather than research programs.

The three PCDCs were to develop theory-based practices that could be evaluated and eventually replicated. In fact, the three centers did develop somewhat different intervention strategies during their first 5 years of operation. The findings from evaluation as of 1976 (to be presented subsequently) were positive. These positive findings encouraged moving to the next planned stage in which three more centers were to be created, each as a replication of an original program.

The most important question for the second stage of development was how the replication was to be implemented. From the beginning (Robinson, 1966–1971), program sponsors in OEO and subsequently in the Office of Child Development (now renamed the Administration for Children, Youth, and Families [ACYF]) believed very strongly that it was essential to reproduce the initial models in new settings. They wanted to learn what was required for replication in order to know how to design a subsequent national program which, while being implemented in a variety of settings, would be true to the original theories and models. The replication experiment was therefore a crucial link in program development. If replication could be achieved, several of the past problems of implementation might be surmounted.

Recall Rivlin and Timpane's (1975) six problems in the implementation of social experiments:

1. The tension between comparing models and testing them individually;
2. The tension between replication and adaptation to local settings;
3. The tension between research and service orientations;
4. The failure to test models carefully in the initial stages of development;
5. The failure to match communities as well as models in replication; and
6. The insensitivity of uniform federal regulations to the need for experimentation.

With regard to the last three problems, the PCDC programs had met the task of initial development; there was the intention of matching communities as well as models; and the status of being a research and development program reduced problems of formal rules and regulations.

The first three difficulties, however, remained to be faced.

Thus, the idea of a Replication Management Organization (RMO) was conceived by government staff people. The RMO would be the agent of the federal government in implementing the three replications. Invention of the RMO was necessitated by two facts about government. First, public agencies are seldom staffed to conduct experiments directly. Second, private organizations have often been effective intermediaries between the federal government and other bodies in the utilization of research and development findings from experiments supported by government. The latter point is important not only for the initial replication but for subsequent enlarging of the program. One or more RMOs, acting as agents of the federal—or eventually state—government, could be more sensitive instruments for replication than government bureaucracy itself. In short, the RMOs would be specialized to the task of the replication stage.

The Bank Street College of Education in New York City, operating as a separate and external entity from the PCDC local project sites, was selected to function as the RMO. Pooling of federal (ACYF) and foundation (the Lilly Endowment) funds permitted Bank Street to undertake a number of crucial and expensive tasks which are necessary in the replication of program elements. These tasks included: (1) supporting and monitoring the transmission of original theoretical models to replication sites; (2) supporting staff members from the original centers in providing training and technical assistance to the replication sponsors and program staffs; (3) documenting and analyzing problems of the replication process; and (4) assessing the establishment and maintenance of essential elements of the original models across successive waves of program replications, as well as identifying procedures by which the original models are adapted to their replication sites.

A second part of the replication stage of the PCDC project was the planning of three successive waves of PCDC replication models. The first of the three replication waves, funded by the Lilly Endowment in 1976, established programs in three different geographic sites. The Birmingham model was replicated in Indianapolis, the Houston model in San Antonio, and the New Orleans model in Detroit. In selecting replication sites for the three original models, three criteria were considered: (1) characteristics of the community and the potential clientele of the replication model were to be similar to those of the original model; (2) the replication sites were to be established in a geographic area different from the original model; and (3) the replication model was to be established under local, private sector sponsorship. At least two criteria were planned for selecting sites for the second and third replication waves. First, characteristics of the community and clientele would vary substantially from those of the original models. Second, sponsors of the replication models would include public, state, and local organizations which attempt to prevent developmental delays in very young low-income children through parent education.

A third aspect of the replication stage of the PCDC project was the continuation of the original sites as operational programs and as training resources for replication models. Continued support of the three original models was maintained through ACYF funding. These three sites largely completed their research and development tasks in 1975 and continued to serve a low-income population of parents and infants as operational centers. In addition, the three original centers were used by the RMO as training resources for the replication models.

The final aspect of the replication stage of the PCDC project was an external evaluation of overall effectiveness across all program models. This evaluation was conducted by the Educational Testing Service.

PCDC PROGRAM ESSENTIALS[2]

A key aspect of the PCDC operational philosophy is the concept of model development. Each of the original sites (Houston, New Orleans, Birmingham) was to have staff members responsible for creating a model program consistent with the needs and characteristics of the local community. Each model was to be based on the best available research on parent education and early child development and to be theoretically coherent. Further, the model was to guide the selection and use of specific intervention practices, first in the original site, and then in a series of controlled replications. In order to give the overall project coherence, PCDC planners required each local site to incorporate certain shared features into its model (Robinson, 1966–1971).

The PCDC project was originally designed to serve low-income families, the conviction being that families in poverty have multiple needs and stresses that are best met through multicomponent, comprehensive programs. Benefits expected to accrue to participating parents, children, and families included: (1) a wide range of social skills and intellectual competencies; (2) more positive attitudes and motivations; (3) increased potential for employment of mothers when infants reach school age; (4) involvement of fathers and their increased understanding and psychological support of mothers in the child-rearing task; (5) greater family solidarity; and (6) positive effects on older children and on subsequent children born to participant families.

The three original sites in Birmingham, Houston, New Orleans each were to serve 60 to 70 families with children from birth to 3 years of age. The actual number of families served at any given time has varied from site to site. Families were invited to participate, and those who accepted were randomly placed in either the program or a control group.

Program effects are hypothesized to occur through a chain-of-effects from program to parents (usually mothers) to children. Mothers are considered the most powerful agents in child development and, thus, are the primary targets of program efforts. "Mother" here actually denotes primary caregiver, since grandmothers, aunts, and other relatives are frequently the principal participants in the programs. It is believed that positive changes in the primary caregiver's attitudes, beliefs, and knowledge will bring later positive changes in the child and other family members. Fathers and other appropriate male figures are included in program activities whenever possible.

Simultaneous programs are offered to mothers and children that provide both the opportunity for practice in new interaction patterns and child care when the mother is involved in adult education activities. But the central intervention strategy in the PCDC approach is adult pedagogy, wherein parents are exposed to bodies of knowledge and skill, and are encouraged to react critically to the material while applying it to their own lives. The process takes place in three stages: *description*, where educational material is provided to the mother; *validation*, where she thinks about, discusses with peers, and experiments with the material at the center; and *translation*, where she adapts and applies the material to match her particular family and personal needs. Thus, the PCDCs trust the capacity of parents to learn and put their knowledge to appropriate use, and such efforts are encouraged in an atmosphere of autonomy and peer support. Central to adult pedagogy is a belief that the information presented is constantly changing, as are the needs of families. Thus, the program is flexible, and opportunities to participate in a variety of ways are provided.

Modes of learning include modeling demonstrations, peer discussion groups, films, didactic classes, workshops, individual tutoring, and home visiting. Several topical areas are covered in an attempt to encompass the broad range of needs experienced by low-income families. Aspects of the curriculum include: child development classes, preparation for high school equivalency exams, participation on parent advisory boards, health and nutrition classes, instruction in relating to community and government agencies, and development of other competencies that help mothers and fathers become more effective adults.

In addition to these learning experiences, supportive services are offered to aid in alleviating the many stresses that impoverished environments may inflict upon families. The supportive services include: health, social, and medical services; transportation; day care for siblings; and clothing where needed. A stipend is also given to participating mothers to help alleviate stress, to provide an incentive for attendance, and to compensate for possible foregone work.

The continual awareness that research and development is an integral part of the program has been present in all PCDCs. Staff and parents have been asked to adapt to constraints imposed on programs by the design of the evaluation structure. These constraints include making decisions based on data derived from the research literature in infant development, adult learning, and education; randomly assigning participants to program or control groups; codifying and evaluating the program; and planning for replication.

Finer program specifications are tailored to the local community and population served. For example, from site to site mothers participate from 2 to 5 days a week in various activities depending on the age of the child, status of the mother in the program, and needs of the family. Program locales vary between providing home- and center-based experiences. In addition, PCDC staff members—including paraprofessionals—are from varied educational and professional backgrounds and are mostly of the same ethnic background as the population served. Staff development is an integral part of the programs; staff members, like the participating mothers, continually learn and adapt new materials and information for use in the program.

Since this chapter emphasizes the overall PCDC experiment, we will give only brief attention to the particulars of individual models. The Birmingham PCDC serves black and white families in a 32-month program beginning when infants are 3-5 months of age. Using a systems theory approach, the program is center-based and progresses over levels of increasing intensity for the mothers, with the more experienced mothers becoming the teachers of newer mothers. The Houston PCDC serves Mexican-American families over a 2-year period beginning when infants are 1 year old. It is home-based during the first year, center-based during the second year, and uses a variety of adult and family group activities throughout. The New Orleans PCDC serves black families in a 34-month program beginning when infants are 2 months old. The program is center-based and uses a two-way learning model that emphasizes equality, mutuality, and supportive relationships between parents and staff members.

The shared features characterize the operation at each model program site, and they are expected to be present in every program replication. In effect, these shared features express in practice the overarching theory developed by PCDC program planners and tested by ACYF. The particulars of these three program models are consistent with these shared features and are the specific operationalizations of the overarching theory adapted to the unique aspects of the original development sites in Birmingham, Houston, and New Orleans. Program replications are adaptations of a given model's particulars (in effect, its theory) to fit the unique aspects of the replication communities. Thus, the entire PCDC experiment involves theory-into-practice, ever recognizing that general theory is only useful when adapted to the realities of specific community environments (Robinson, 1966–1971).

THE 5-YEAR PCDC EVALUATION

Overall Design

Rather than yield to the inevitable difficulties of evaluating the implementation of federal social programs (Aaron, 1978) by compromising the rigor of evaluation, the PCDCs used true experimental designs, which are infrequently used in program evaluation. The important decision to use randomization led to fewer methodological and interpretive problems than has often been the case in program evaluations.

In their evaluation program, all three PCDCs used variations of the two-group (program group and control group) repeated measures (pretest and posttest) design with multiple measures of program impact. There were, however, variations across programs in such things as the number of data collection points, what data were collected at which points, and whether the design was replicated across cohorts (successive waves of program participants). In addition, the population sampled the method of sampling (i.e., recruitment), and the maintenance of the sample (i.e., attrition) differed across sites and influenced conclusions drawn from the data. Strict random assignment was used at all three centers, a particular strength of the evaluation. There was also sensitivity to language, cultural, and background factors in measurement of participants. For example, differing literacy levels and problems with English often led to oral administration of particular measures.

Basic demographic characteristics of participants in the three PCDCs are presented in Table 1. As can be seen, there were differences among the three samples. In addition to ethnic composition, there were differences in maternal age, maternal education, per capita income, and family composition. The sample of mothers in Houston was older and less well educated, and almost all Houston families had the father present (and employed), and consequently had higher incomes. Additionally, although the Birmingham staff was able to recruit whites into their program, they were not able to recruit a white control group. Thus, all program/control comparisons were based on the black sample only.

Of those families originally recruited into the three PCDCs, approximately 45% "graduated" from each program. Differences in length

TABLE 1:   DEMOGRAPHIC CHARACTERISTICS OF THE PCDCS

Variable	New Orleans	Birmingham	Houston
Mother's education	11.0	10.9	7.8
Mother's age (years)	23.5	22.0	28.0
Per capita income (yearly)	$1150	$850	$1400
Head of household			
Father (%)	25	25	94
Mother (%)	55	33	6
Other (%)	20	42	0
Ethnic composition	Black	Black	Mexican American

of time required by each program did not influence rates of attrition. In both Birmingham and New Orleans, a higher percentage dropped out of the program group than the control group, while in Houston the attrition percentages were about equal in both groups. Staff members in Birmingham and New Orleans attribute the higher dropout rate among families in the program to the greater demands made on their time than on control families' time. Across all three programs, it was also reported by staff that program mothers who dropped out after a year or more expressed regret that job-market pressures forced them to leave.

None of the three PCDCs reported statistically significant differences in characteristics between those who dropped out of the program and those who dropped out of the control groups. Consequently, it appears that differential attrition is not an issue in the PCDC evaluation. In addition, the demographic characteristics of those who dropped out of either the program or control groups were not found to differ significantly from those who remained, suggesting that those who completed the experiment were representative of those who began.

Evaluation Designs of the Individual Programs

New Orleans. In addition to the program/control classification, a distinction was made between those who entered the study in 1971 and those who entered in 1972. The New Orleans evaluation included: measures of mother–child interaction in a structured situation (at 2, 12, 24, and 36 months of age); measures of infant cognitive development from the Uzgiris-Hunt test (visual pursuit and object permanence, means for achieving ends, schemes exhibited, construction of objects in space, and initiation—taken every 2 months starting at age 2 months and continuing until completion of all scale items, usually in the 16-20-month period);

the Bayley mental and psychomotor scales (at 7, 13, 19, and 25 mos.); measures of perceptual and abstract abilities from the Meyers Pacific Test (at 24, 30, 36 mos.); measures of receptive language ability from the Ammons Picture Vocabulary Test (at 24, 30, 36, and 48 mos.); the Concept Familiarity Index (at 36 mos.); the Sanford-Binet (at 36 and 48 mos.); measures of effectance motivation (curiosity for novel stimulation, preference for response variation, at 48 mos.); the Purdue Self-Concept Scale (at 48 mos.); and measures of attitudes toward peers, school, home, and community from the Purdue Social Attitudes Scale (at 48 mos.). The data analysis plan was based on multivariate and univariate analyses of variance.

Birmingham. In Birmingham, participants entered the study in either 1972, 1973, or 1974. However, these demarcations were not carried over into the analysis as a consequence of the continuous recruitment used. The Bayley (at intake, 10, 16, and 22 mos.) and the Stanford-Binet (at 30 and 36 mos.) were among the measures used in Birmingham. Observations of mother–child interactions in structured situations were made at 13½, 24, and 36 months. Finally, a structured interview was administered to all program participants upon graduation at about 36 months in an attempt to assess changes in the mother's interactions with her child and others, as well as her problem-solving style. Multivariate and univariate analyses of variance were used in data analysis.

Houston. In Houston, participants entered the study when infants were 12 months old and were assigned to either the program group or to one of two control groups. Since the program group was to have educational, medical, and social services, it was initially thought necessary to have two control groups—one of which would receive medical and social services only, and one of which would have no services at all. The former control group would allow evaluators to isolate effects attributable specifically to the educational component of the Houston program; the no-services control group would allow detection of effects attributable to all three components of the intervention. However, as it turned out, families in the medical and social services control group received only minimal services, and only a few families agreed to participate in the no-service control group. Thus, the two control groups were combined for analytic purposes. In addition to the Stanford-Binet (at 15 and 36 mos.), the Bayley Scales (at 12 and 24 mos.), and the Concept Familiarity Index (at 36 mos.), the Houston evaluation used measures of mother–child interaction (at 24 and 36 mos.) and measures of cognitive and social stimulation in the child's home (using the Home Observation for Measurement of the Environment Scale at 12, 24, and

36 mos.). Again, both multivariate and univariate analyses of variance were employed in the data analysis plan.

Results and Discussion of the 5-Year Evaluation

Social competence is an important developmental and evaluation concept. Zigler and Trickett (1978) have strongly argued that policies and programs with human development objectives should be evaluated by this concept, operationalized through measures of physical well-being (e.g., incidence of childhood diseases, innoculation history, height and weight relative to age), cognitive ability (e.g., an intelligence test or measure of cognitive development), motivation and emotion (e.g., self-image), and achievement (e.g., preschool or school-aged standardized academic achievement tests). In addition, Zigler and Trickett emphasize the importance of longer-range and policy-related indicators such as rate of school dropout, grade retention in school, placement in special education, juvenile delinquency rates, teenage pregnancy rates, and participation in the welfare system. And one might add to these indicators eventual effectiveness of children as parents.

The PCDC 5-year evaluation was carried out in the spirit of the social competence concept. The observation that children from low-income circumstances frequently reveal both early developmental problems in physical, cognitive, or motivational areas as well as later achievement and social adaptation problems formed an important part of the justification for PCDCs. Moreover, the belief that socially competent parents are necessary agents for adequate early child development, and that the ongoing quality of life of parents and their families is itself related to the social competence of parents, formed the core of the PCDC evaluation (Robinson, 1966–1971). As we have seen, the measures were mostly of two sorts: parent social competence as indexed by observations of the quality of parent–child interactions, and child social competence as indexed mostly by measures of cognitive development. The child's physical well-being was of concern, but since both program and control groups were served in this regard, it was not evaluated. Some measurement of motivation was attempted, but because of the primitive state of measurement in this area, little assessment was possible. The longer-term impact of PCDCs on children, especially in school, was planned for future evaluation.

The data summarized here were taken from 5-year reports by Blumenthal, Andrews, and Weiner (1976), Johnson, Kahn, and Leler (1976), and Lasater, Malone, Ferguson, and Weisberg (1976), and from drafts of a monograph prepared by the RMO in collaboration with researchers in the original centers. The completed monograph has just been published (Andrews et al., 1982). No new analyses of these data have been performed for this chapter. Since the above-mentioned reports presented only some of the statistical analyses conducted by the researchers, and since we present here only a subset of these analyses, a caveat to keep in mind is the technical problem of inflation of the experiment-wise error rate. In other words, some number of results we present may be significant by chance beyond the reported probability levels. A factor that helps mitigate this problem is that all program/control differences reported by the original researchers favored the program groups.[3] Even so, the pattern of program/control differences was complicated. In general, only scattered differences were found before 36 months; however, at graduation the pattern appeared more clearly.

Program effects on mothers. Analyses of mother–child interactions at all three PCDCs indicated that program mothers engaged in more positive maternal behaviors at graduation than did control mothers. At 2 and 12 months of age, there were few measures taken and no significant differences. At 24 months of age, however, significant differences favoring program dyads were found for measures of comforting ($p < .01$) and positive interaction ($p < .01$) in the Birmingham sample; there were no significant differences between the Houston groups; and positive interaction favoring program dyads ($p < .01$) was significant for the New Orleans sample. At age 36 months (graduation), positive interaction ($p < .001$) was significant at Houston; and positive interaction ($p < .01$) was significant at New Orleans, with a trend on negative interaction ($p = .06$) suggesting that program mothers were less negative.

Regarding these findings, it is interesting to note that both 3-year programs (Birmingham and New Orleans), starting at or near birth, began to show significant effects by age 24 months, while the 2-year program (Houston), starting at age 12 months, showed effects at age 36 months. There were no followup data collected on the mothers.

As the original researchers concluded: "Thus, although the PCDCs differed in Program intensity, some of the program elements, and Program structure, the critical mass of PCDC model elements was generally effective in providing mothers with increased skill for childrearing" (Andrews, 1979).

Program effects on children. The pattern of significant children's effects (namely, few if any early in the program, the emergence of effects at 24 months, and the clearest pattern of effects at 36 months) was the same as that for the mothers, but not as strong and clear. Before 12 months of age, there were few measures taken and no significant program/control differences. At age 12 months, there also were no significant differences. At age 24 months, however, the child's positive behavior in a nonsocial stress situation ($p < .001$) and in a waiting room ($p < .05$), and scores on the Bayley ($p < .001$) were significant for the Birmingham sample; the child's verbalization ($p < .001$) and scores on the Bayley ($p < .01$) were significant for the Houston sample; and there were no significant differences for the New Orleans sample. At age 36 months (graduation), the child's positive behavior in a waiting room ($p < .01$) and scores on the Stanford-Binet ($p < .001$) were significant for the Birmingham sample; there were no differences for the Houston program, though scores on the Concept Familiarity Index and Stanford-Binet approached significance ($p < .10$); and scores on the Pacific ($p < .05$) and Stanford-Binet ($p < .05$) were significant for the New Orleans sample. All these differences favored experimental children.

There were some followup data collected at age 48 months. At Birmingham, Stanford-Binet scores for program children increased from 97.96 at 36 months to 99.55 at 48 months; the respective scores for control children were 90.50 and 95.02. The program/control difference was highly significant ($p < .001$) at 36 months, as noted above, and approached significance ($p < .06$) at 48 months. Followup data were not collected at Houston for the 48 month period. At New Orleans, with both cohorts combined, there was a significant program control difference at age 48 months on effectance motivation ($p < .05$) and the Purdue Self-Concept Scale ($p < .05$), while the difference on the Stanford-Binet was no longer significant. When the second cohort was examined separately, however, both the Purdue ($p < .01$) and the Stanford-Binet ($p < .05$) followup scores significantly favored the program group.

An interpretive comment concerning effects of the PCDC programs on children made by the original researchers is appropriate here:

> There are many possible reasons for the evidence of program impact on the children not being as impressive [although it is not unimpressive] as that on the mothers. PCDCs are parent education programs. The effects on the child are intended to derive primarily from the mother's participation in the program and not so much on the child's experience in the program. The cause and effect relationships between mother's increased knowledge about child development and childrearing techniques and the child's later or concurrent developmental progress are difficult to untangle and are confounded by many variables. It does seem likely, however, that children wouldn't derive direct benefits from the experience. The PCDC results do seem to indicate that mothers profit from the experience before their children. (Andrews, 1979)[4]

There are three important points to make with regard to the results of the evaluation. First, one way of conceptualizing the results is in terms of the "signal-to-noise ratio" present in the data. Despite the difficulties (i.e., the noise) of evaluating a large, federally funded, field-based project, with its inevitable implementation and management problems (Aaron, 1978), significant[5] positive effects (i.e., the signal) kept cropping up. Most importantly, the signals virtually all carried the same message: the program is working. This in itself was enough encouragement to pursue the strategy inherent in the PCDC model. Second, in setting up large experimental programs like the PCDC, the focus should be on finding things that work and finding places to concentrate our efforts; thus, it is far more important to make sure nothing has been overlooked than it is to adhere rigidly to statistically nonsignificant findings (cf. Carver, 1978). Third, we find it encouraging that a positive pattern emerged from the operationalization of the PCDC program theory at different locations by different people serving diverse populations.

In light of these points, let us summarize the general results of the 5-year PCDC evaluation. By program's end, PCDC mothers exhibited enhanced positive interactions with their children, and PCDC children had enhanced cognitive, language, conceptual, and abstraction skills compared to control group mothers and children. Further, there was some evidence that child effects were still present one year after the program.

THE REPLICATION PROCESS[6]

Results and implications such as those just presented signalled the desirability of beginning the second phase of the PCDC social experiment—the replication experiment. Having demonstrated the effectiveness of PCDC philosophy as operationalized in the three model programs, multiple tests of the three models were begun under controlled conditions in order to learn: (1) what effects of the several models would generalize to what subgroups of the poverty population; and (2) what supportive assistance would be required in the transmission of the program to new sites and new user groups. The replication experiment was intended to enable local, state, and federal planners to assess the probable benefits and costs of widespread use of the model programs before committing resources to large-scale program expansion. The experiment was also designed to show what types of existing service organizations could carry out programs most effectively with differing communities and clientele.

A Model of Authority

Each of the PCDC models presents a package of program elements which, if adapted, must be used in totality. This requirement is a problem for replication, because it is not easy to reach agreement on the essential aspects of each model. Since the individual program elements have not been assessed, there is room for disagreement about the importance of any one of them to a given model. Thus, the very first problem faced by the RMO was to define what was essential for replication. There are three parties to such a definition; namely, the original centers (Birmingham, Houston, New Orleans), the RMO (Bank Street), and the new centers (Indianapolis, San Antonio, Detroit). Uncertainty about the models causes a reluctance to delegate authority on the part of either the RMO or the original centers.

Out of a myriad of field experiences, however, a general set of loose and open authority relationships and decision rules gradually developed among the six centers and the RMO; these became the framework of authority under which the replication is being conducted. The principal technique in the exercise of authority by the RMO, including its New York staff and its field staff, is leadership by suggestion and moral suasion, rather than by command. This leadership by indirection takes two forms. First, the field coordinator and training specialists from the RMO observe the operations of new centers and make suggestions about improvement to center directors. These suggestions are accepted or not according to the credibility of the individual RMO staff members who make them. Second, the RMO director, associate director, and senior research associate meet regularly in New York with the field coordinators and training specialists to assess the state of the replication and develop ideas for improvement. Their conclusions are communicated to directors of the new centers and implementation is achieved through a process of negotiation. At the other end, the centers do not make important changes in their operations without consulting the RMO.

This system of authority is both flexible and fragile. It is flexible in that staff members at the various centers can protect their own interests through a process of negotiation with the RMO; neither the RMO nor any of its staff can impose decisions on the individual centers. On the other hand, an authority system with this flexibility and absence of centralized decision-making is fragile because a lack of sensitivity to personal or institutional relationships or an arbitrary action can bring the decision system to a halt. The key to effective functioning of such a system is for the RMO to help insure that strong, effective leadership exists in each of the new centers, to leave operational decisions to the centers, and yet to exercise ultimate authority over the replication. Without such a system of authority, the replication cannot succeed.

There are some differences in perception as to whether the original sites require the assistance of the RMO in operating their own model.

Center staff admit that without the poking and prodding of an RMO there might be a tendency for each of the centers to falter and move away from model specifications. The original model might eventually be eroded. The original centers, however, see themselves as generally operating at high levels of effectiveness. They tend not to regard the RMO as essential for their daily functioning. The RMO, on the other hand, sometimes sees deficiencies which need correcting and feels responsible for doing so.

Key staff in the new centers eventually believe that they have gone beyond the early period of dependence on the parent site. Some believe that they have improved the model in ways that might even benefit the original centers. It is assumed by all participants in the PCDC social experiment that the models are not fixed for all time. Learning from experience is to be incorporated into curricula. In minor matters the centers may proceed on their own. For example, the director of the New Orleans Center has added material on child abuse to her curriculum and has informed the social worker in Detroit of the addition. Detroit added the serving of meals to their program, with RMO assent, but New Orleans has not followed suit. More important changes, such as dropping a health education component or altering the time spent by mothers in the center, require RMO approval.

These more important areas of program change are primarily the concern of the RMO. The RMO has latitude to improve as well as replicate, but not to change the essential features of each model. If the RMO were to see itself as an agent for improving the models by altering their essential features, and were to begin exerting authority in this direction, then we would have the problem of who is to guard the guardian. The essential features of the models might be altered beyond recognition, though this is not likely because the six centers act as checks on the RMO. There must be agreement on innovations, and such agreement must be worked out through the loosely jointed system of authority described earlier. Nevertheless, it is important for the experiment that there be an RMO to worry about improvement because static models will not thrive long. There must be learning from experience and that learning must be shared.

Assessing the Degree of Replication

In order to know whether the replication is succeeding, it is necessary to do more than merely insure that essential features of the models have been set in place. One must also assess the degree of actual implementation of services delivered to families.

Such an assessment would have two other uses. It might be a

vehicle to cause center staff to be more self-conscious about their effectiveness and for measuring actual service delivery which would provide useful information for evaluating outcomes. Thus, for example, evidence concerning changes in the interactive behavior of mothers with their infants may be associated with changes in infant test scores.

The RMO has been developing techniques that both assess replication site performance and encourage improvement without being threatening, thereby permitting mutual use of the surveys between the RMO and the centers. This is an illustration of the kinds of conceptual and methodological problems involved in a social experiment. It is not likely that a federal agency or regional office would be able to carry out such tasks.

Tentative Conclusions Regarding RMO Operation

The structure of the PCDC project overcame, at the outset, some of the problems of social experiments discussed earlier. The models had been carefully tested. Communities were reasonably well matched. Federal bureaucracy was bypassed. But, as pointed out earlier, three problems remain. We must now ask if the RMO has coped with these problems satisfactorily.

Tension between comparing the three models and assessing them separately. Some believe that the different strategies of service delivery among the centers are not crucial to the theoretical soundness of the general PCDC approach. In this view, it might even be possible to reach agreement on a common model for future replication. Others, however, see the treatment strategies as very different. For example, all activity during the first year of the Houston model takes place in the home. Fathers as well as mothers are active participants. There is also an emphasis upon Spanish-speaking people achieving competence in English. These features are not present in the other models. The Birmingham model takes longer to start up than the New Orleans model because many of the teachers are mothers who have been in the program for some time. In New Orleans, the teachers are women drawn from the same society as the mothers. If the number of replications expands to a wider variety of settings and to different populations, the task of adapting essential characteristics of each model to new localities increases in difficulty.

Tension between replication and adaptation to local settings. The RMO has proved to be a sensitive device for balancing general and particular practices. However, many subtle problems have yet to be faced. For example, despite surface similarities, the teachers and mothers in New Orleans and Detroit may be very different. The New Orleans participants come from a stable, traditional black society with roots in the past. The Detroit participants are not so rooted in their geographical area. Moreover, they have been influenced by the labor union subculture of Michigan to be sensitive to their rights. Such social differences may affect the two programs in unanticipated ways. The RMO must develop means to detect such subtleties and, more importantly, decide how they should be handled. If the program spreads, it will be necessary to investigate the permissible degree of adaptation of service strategies to local situations. Such flexibility is important, but the RMO should ensure that such adaptation is purposive and not a simple cooptation of centers into existing social norms and structures.

Tension between research and service orientations. The assignment to replicate the delivery of services has been guided by a research purpose. The concept of replication breaks down the barrier between research and service and requires each goal to serve the other. Ties between research and operations can be fostered, if future program directors see the importance of linking process research about replication to impact research about outcomes. This is a great methodological challenge to evaluation research which will surely be very difficult to meet. Nonetheless, it is important to try.

Rivlin and Timpane (1975) cited an additional problem in the politics of experiments. A sound experimental strategy should build up from rigorously controlled experiments to ever widening replications, they suggest, until the program becomes a national one (see also Robinson, 1966–1971). The PCDC program is well on its way in this regard. Nevertheless, the hard test of political acceptability in Congress and the federal agencies has not yet been met.

This raises a fundamental question about the political economy of social science research. Do we have the patience and the resources to act according to our intelligence in a democratic society, or are the demands of economy and representativeness too strong? If the latter is the case, then we are fated to have popular but ineffective social programs. One hesitates to pose the dichotomy in this way. The challenge faced in the PCDC experiment has been to find a politically and economically acceptable way to do what is intelligent. It is to this and other public policy questions that we now turn.

POLICY IMPLICATIONS OF THE PCDC SOCIAL EXPERIMENT

Having reviewed the more than 10 years of PCDC operation—from planning, through program development, implementation, evaluation, and finally to the replication process—policy questions must now be raised.

The PCDC results are highly suggestive. It has been empirically demonstrated that parent behaviors related to the development of young children can be meaningfully enhanced. Moreover, such effects can be achieved while the autonomy and cultural traditions of families are respected. The PCDC social experiment offers a validated piece for the mosaic of policies that might be developed for families, especially low-income families. In concert with economic policies (e.g., jobs, income, taxation), the PCDC approach to service delivery has great potential for social policy development.

The PCDC social experiment also has many policy implications for research and development; these are emphasized in this final section. Over the last 10 years, there has been growing skepticism about the utility of a model-building and testing strategy to improve the quality of human service delivery. As discussed earlier, there have been several failures of this strategy, perhaps the most noteworthy being Follow Through.

To be fair, Follow Through was not a total failure; rather, it was highly controversial. Earlier in this chapter, we drew several contrasts between the PCDC and strategies using as an analytic device the Rivlin and Timpane (1975) report of issues raised by a 1973 Brookings conference on Follow Through. Recent data on Follow Through and discussion of their interpretation (Anderson et al., 1978; Hodges, 1978; House et al., 1978; Wisler, Burns, & Iwamoto, 1978) also help place in perspective some of the strategies of the PCDC social experiment. In particular, one of the few points of agreement in an otherwise vituperative exchange between Anderson et al. (the FT evaluators) and House et al. (the evaluators of these evaluators) is instructive. Anderson and his colleagues (1978) found that:

> Each Follow Through model had very different effects on test scores in the various communities in which it was implemented. Differences in effectiveness between sites within each model were greater than overall differences in effectiveness between models. (p. 163)

This finding led them to urge researchers to consider "the characteristics that distinguish localities; they [researchers] must learn not to treat programs as black boxes, with money and theories as inputs and achievement changes as outputs" (Anderson et al., p. 162). House (1978) and his colleagues totally accepted this view and maintained that it was:

> An important confirmation of contentions that the success of any educational innovation is dependent on contextual factors. . . . This does not mean that model programs are worthless but only that their effects will

vary substantially, depending on interaction with local circumstances. (p. 154)

We have seen that the PCDC program planners anticipated this contextual effect. Indeed, the overarching program theory developed in Washington was expected to be operationalized in community-specific ways during phase one work in the original model development sites. Further, the original models were expected to be operationalized in community-specific ways during phase two work in replication sites (Robinson, 1966–1971).

But the model-program-by-community interaction issue has at least two separable subissues. One involves the recognition that exact duplication of model program functions in different communities is not possible—nor would it be desirable even if it were possible. Research and development specialists have finally come to understand this fact which was driven home strongly by Follow Through. The second subissue involves not model program functions, but program outcomes. House et al. (1978) argue:

> If the concentrated effort of highly competent and well-funded sponsors working with a few sites cannot produce uniform results from locality to locality, it seems doubtful that any model program could do so. (p. 154)

We believe this conclusion regarding uniform results is premature. The "highly competent sponsors" in Follow Through were competent in education research, practice, and program design. But very few were competent in the transmission of complex programs to distant replication sites. Indeed, the demand for such transmission is new, and the sponsors could not have been expected to be expert in managing the multifaceted and demanding replication process. It is on this score that the second phase of the PCDC experiment—a replication experiment testing a new organizational form, the RMO, to manage the replication—is so important. The RMO holds promise of better standardizing both model program functions and outcomes across communities.

The PCDC program could have been expanded by stages into a national program. Additional replication sites might have been developed in order to experiment with a greater variety of sponsor organizations. But at some point in such an expansion, the capacities of the RMO would have been severely taxed. Bank Street could not have handled more than six centers with its staff. Increased resources would have permitted the addition of more centers, but there is surely an outer limit to the number of centers an RMO can oversee without encountering problems of bureaucratic layering, faulty communication, and erosion of authority at the top.

Yet, a large program—certainly a national one supported by federal funds—would require organizations like the RMO to assure replication. Otherwise, the program would proceed in many different directions and the benefits of the initial experiment would be eroded.

It is therefore important to conceptualize new RMO forms and tasks. One could conceive of a central RMO which would train the staff of regional RMOs. The central RMO might operate a model center that would experiment with different delivery components. Experimental findings could be transmitted to the field through the network of RMOs. The regional RMOs would then be responsible for the implementation of replications. This would be a less intensive activity than at present if the number of centers were greater. Periodic visits and reports might suffice as centers built up capabilities over time.

Such an approach for the future is superior to a plan for the federal bureaucracy and its regional offices to assume the replication task. Such agencies lack professional capabilities, are too easily swayed by Congressional and local political demands, and are so constituted that they confuse conformity to standardized regulations with actual implementation. The use of private organizations as intermediaries for the implementation of federal programs is an accepted device. The RMO is an invention for the implementation task, which can improve the capabilities of government by performing assignments which government itself does not do well.

There is the question of the accountability of such a private organization to public authority in a democratic society. The central RMO would be charged with reporting to the federal agency about its work, and the agency should direct independent evaluation of the program. This is the kind of supervision for which federal bureaucracy is well suited.

One suggestion might have been to replicate the three models with different ethnic and cultural populations and service adaptations, using public authorities as sponsor organizations for the new centers. Each of the original centers was sponsored by a private organization such as a university, which has had experience in the area of child or parent education. The experiment could have been extended to new populations and new host organizations. New problems of authority, of course, would have arisen. How is a private RMO to exercise sanctions over a public body such as a state department of education, if the latter is a sponsor organization? The history of the PCDC social experiment indicates that constructive cooperation of government and private organizations is possible. Thus, for example, the replication stage of the experiment was financed at one point by a joint partnership between the Administration for Children, Youth, and Families and the Lilly Endowment. ACYF supported the three original sites and Lilly funded the three replication sites and the RMO. This complex funding relationship worked—mostly because of the good relationship that developed between ACYF and Lilly. Such relationships could have been fostered in an expanded program, but might have been difficult to duplicate on a wide scale.

If replications are to proceed effectively, they must proceed slowly and in stages so that the authority questions which occur at each stage can be worked out. The two key issues here are timing and scale. The programs must also be of reasonable and manageable size for as long as possible. There should be an effort to duplicate at the regional level what was replicated on a small, pilot basis with the three PCDC program replications. This regional expansion might involve a regional RMO and a few local sponsors in the region. In any case, the point here is that program expansion should be accomplished in a deliberate and incremental fashion.

Is not the RMO experience a fragile precedent which depends for its success on good personal relationships? How can such relationships be institutionalized on a national scale? What are the preconditions for such institutionalization, as seen on a small scale?

1. A program which works, that is, gets practical results (bureaucratic politics might destroy a mediocre program; the sense of pride fosters unity).
2. A sophisticated RMO organization with considerable backup resources.
3. A sponsoring government agency that will keep tabs, but not intervene arbitrarily.
4. Sponsor organizations for centers that have institutional capabilities for administration and research orientation but which, like the government agency, will foster center responsibility.

These conditions can be achieved by careful selection of the organizations which are to be RMOs or sponsors. Wrong choices cannot be repaired and programs will probably fail in such instances. This is the responsibility of the federal agency. Very careful estimates must be made of the capacities of organizations to carry out the programs as intended before such selections are made. It might be necessary to do further analysis on the essential characteristics of an RMO and to make sure that federal staff possess clear criteria to guide them in their choices.

SUMMARY AND CONCLUSIONS

Having reviewed and analyzed the PCDC experience, we close by drawing five conclusions for public policy.

First, as one aspect of a cautiously developed public policy for children and families, PCDC-like parent education programs can have positive and lasting effects on parents and their young children. Such programs should be viewed as complementing economic policies in such areas as jobs, income support, and taxation.

Second, a carefully conceived research and development plan that is consistently executed over a long period of time, and that receives funds adequate to the relatively expensive processes of model development, validation, and replication, can produce workable and generalizable human service programs.

Third, continuity of program goals and management/monitoring strategies are required for a research and development program to progress through the many stages necessary for its successful completion. Particularly important here is continuity of federal level staffing. It is readily acknowledged that such requirements are difficult to achieve in the face of the continually shifting federal scene; however, the PCDC social experiment is one instance where these requirements have been met.

Fourth, theory into practice can be a useful guiding principle of program research and development. However, the essential program theory must be adapted to local conditions faced by developers of the initial model programs and by those involved in each phase of program replication. But despite such adaptation to local conditions, the theoretical bases—or program essentials as we have called them—must remain intact.

Fifth, the process of transmitting complex social systems, such as model programs, from development site to replication site, and eventually to service sites, requires sensitivity to local conditions and management capabilities not generally possessed by government or the research and development community. New organizational forms, exemplified by the RMO, must be developed, if a model development and testing strategy is to be successful in improving the nation's human service delivery capacity.

Much has been learned and demonstrated by the PCDC social experiment. Its results have important implications for child and family policy as well as federal research and development policy—topics of great concern in the 1980s.

Footnotes

* The authors would like to thank Sharon Innes and Jennifer McDowell for their assistance with this manuscript. Work on the paper was supported in part by a contract from the Administration for Children, Youth, and Families. We have drawn heavily on the remarkable series of planning documents written by Mary Robinson (1966, 1967, 1968, 1969, 1970a, 1970b, 1970c, 1970d, 1970e, 1971). Hereafter we will refer to this set of documents as "Robinson, 1966–1971."

[1] The Robinson Planning Papers (1966–1971) are a series of unpublished staff memos and planning documents written by Mary Robinson during her tenure at the Office of Economic Opportunity. She kindly let the senior author examine these documents in preparation for writing this chapter.

[2] The three original PCDCs now operate at Parent Child Centers (PCCs) within the Head Start program.

[3] Given the large number of dependent measures used in the evaluation, it was appropriate to depend on multivariate analyses of variance rather than univariate analyses. But where multivariate analyses were used, full advantage was not taken of the information available from the analyses. The multivariate Fs appear to have served primarily a protective function; that is, to have kept the Type I error rate (i.e., the probability of rejecting the null hypothesis when it is true) within reasonable bounds.

[4] Although reliable improvements have been found in program mothers and their children through the analysis of group data, it is still possible that only some of the mothers and only some of the children actually changed while the rest remained unchanged. Further, it is conceivable that children who

changed were those whose mothers were unaffected by the program, and vice versa. Such linking of mothers and children is possible through the use of path analyses, or, as a special case, cross-lagged panel analysis. Although other correlational techniques might be appropriate, our goal is simply to point out the importance of linking the choice of technique with the nature of the hoped-for answer. In setting up the PCDC program, it was hoped that changing the mothers would change the children, but the analyses chosen did not fully answer this question. Nonetheless, the data in New Orleans were consistent with the chain-of-effects model in that group differences for mothers did precede group differences for children.

[5] It is not only statistical significance that should be judged in this evaluation, but also the size of the effect. In order to judge whether the benefits attributable to the program are large enough to warrant continued spending, we must have some a priori decisions about what size effect is meaningful. We are all able to understand a 13 point difference on the Stanford-Binet (as reported for Cohort II in New Orleans at 48 months), but it is much more difficult to judge the importance of a given difference in, for example, positive maternal behavior. What is the least number of additional behaviors necessary to make a positive contribution to the child's behavior?

[6] One of the authors (Hargrove) conducted a brief field investigation of the replication process, which forms the basis for this section. This summary of the replication process was written while the PCDC experiment was still in operation.

REFERENCES

Aaron, H. J. *Politics and the professors: The great society in perspective.* Washington, DC: Brookings, 1978.

Anderson, R. B., St. Pierre, R. G., Proper, E. C., & Stebbins, L. B. Pardon us, but what was that question again? A response to the critique of the Follow Through evaluation. *Harvard Educational Review,* 1978, *48,* 161–170.

Andrews, S. R. Personal communication, August, 1979.

Andrews, S. R., Blumenthal, J. B., Johnson, D. L., Kahn, A. J., Ferguson, C. J., Lasater, T. M., Malone, P. E., & Wallace, D. B. The skills of mothering: A study of Parent Child Development Centers. *Monographs of the Society for Research in Child Development,* 1982, *47* (6, Serial No. 198).

Blumenthal, J. B., Andrews, S. R., & Weiner, G. *Five year summary of the New Orleans Parent-Child Development Center* (Report for Grant DHEW-90-C-381). Washington, DC: Office of Child Development, 1976.

Carver, R. P. The case against statistical significance testing. *Harvard Educational Review,* 1978, *48,* 378–399.

Dokecki, P. R., Roberts, F. B., & Moroney, R. M. *Families and professional psychology: Policy implications for training and service.* Paper presented at the annual meetings of the American Psychological Association, New York City, August, 1979.

Hodges, W. L. The worth of the Follow Through experience. *Harvard Educational Review,* 1978, *48,* 186–192.

House, E. R., Glass, G. V., McLean, T. D., & Walker, D. F. No simple answer: Critique of the Follow Through evaluation. *Harvard Educational Review,* 1978, *48,* 128–160.

Johnson, D. L., Kahn, A., & Leler, H. *Houston Parent-Child Development Center* (Report for Grant DHEW-90-C-379). Washington, DC: Office of Child Development, 1976.

Knox, A. B. *Adult development and learning*. San Francisco: Jossey-Bass, 1977.

Lasater, T. M., Malone, P., Ferguson, C., & Weisberg, P. *Birmingham Parent–Child Development Center: Five year progress report* (Report for Grant DHEW-90-C-380). Washington, DC: Office of Child Development, 1976.

Rivlin, A., & Timpane, M. P. (Eds.). *Planned variation in education: Should we give up or try harder?* Washington, DC: Brookings, 1975.

Wisler, C. E., Burns, G. P., & Iwamoto, D. Follow Through redux: A response to the critique by House, Glass, McLean, and Walker. *Harvard Educational Review*, 1978, *48*, 171–185.

Zigler, E., & Trickett, P. K. IQ, social competence, and evaluation of early childhood intervention programs. *American Psychologist*, 1978, *33*, 789–798.

FIVE

PARENT INVOLVEMENT: PERSPECTIVES FROM THE FOLLOW THROUGH EXPERIENCE*

PATRICIA P. OLMSTED AND
ROBERTA I. RUBIN[1]

INTRODUCTION AND RATIONALE

This chapter focuses on parent education and involvement within one of the longest running federal education programs for school-age children and their families. Each year, the national Follow Through program has served approximately 75,000 low-income children in over 150 communities across the United States. Although this program has been in existence since 1968, it enjoys the reputation of being "the best kept secret in federal compensatory education." The major reason for this reputation is that the program was considered an educational experiment during the first several years of its operation and consequently, publicity was kept to a minimum.

One of the primary components of the national Follow Through

(FT) program is the involvement of parents and community in its implementation (Office of Education, 1977). This component constitutes a major emphasis on parent involvement in Follow Through that is greater than the parental involvement emphases in other federal compensatory education programs for school-age children. One might ask why a major federal education program, aimed at improving the life chances of children, would require parent involvement as one of its major implementation components. The answers to this question serve as the basic assumptions about parent involvement that are made by the authors. These assumptions present the rationale and lay the foundation for reviewing the parent involvement data from Follow Through.

One of the most well-accepted and fundamental suppositions underlying the acceptance of parent involvement in education is that parent involvement affects children and enables them to excel in the cognitive and affective domains (Bradley & Caldwell, 1978; Bronfenbrenner, 1979; Gordon, 1979; Hanson, 1975; Keeves, 1972; Marjoribanks, 1974, 1979; Walberg, 1979; Walberg, Schiller, & Haertel, 1979; Williams, 1976). Improving the family environment and getting parents involved in the education of their children, by changing the various systems (i.e., educational, economic, and political) which are reciprocally related to the family, positively influence the child. As Gordon (1978b) has stated:

> Children learn from modeling . . . and as they see their parents in influential roles vis-à-vis the school, this enhances their motivation to achieve, and thus is reflected in their achievement. There are two additional elements in this. One recent book by Ogbu (1978) indicated that there is the sociological–anthropological position that only as fundamental changes are made in the class and caste arrangements will minority children see the necessity to achieve and thus achieve. From this position, broad scale intervention programs such as Follow Through need to help low-income parents develop new attitudes and skills so that their children can see possibilities for their own participation in this society. Further, the recent work by Brookover et al. (1978) indicates that the pupils' own feeling of hopelessness was the major variable affecting their achievement. Our rationale is that as parents become involved in a variety of ways, their own sense of potency is enlarged, which then should impact upon the child's sense of purpose and thus upon the child's sense of achievement. (p. 1)

Other evidence for the supposition that parent involvement in education impacts upon children's performance includes studies and surveys both in the United States and other countries. In 1966, Coleman, Campbell, Hobson, McPartland, Mood, Weinfeld, and York found that the influence of the home environment seems more critical to school achievement measures than the quality of education the child receives at school. The reanalyses of Coleman's data (Jencks et al., 1972; Mayeske et al., 1973; Mosteller & Moynihan, 1972) confirmed the same findings;

namely, that family background was more important than school characteristics in explaining differences in child achievement. Several studies investigating the relationships between measures of family environments and the cognitive and affective characteristics of children have reported these relationships to be positive (Marjoribanks, 1974, 1979; Walberg, 1979; Walberg et al., 1979; Williams, 1976). Further support for this contention was stated by Gordon (1978b) in his observation that, "From our extensive reviews of the educational achievement literature . . . , it is clear that a considerable portion of the variance in child achievement has been demonstrated to be a function of family process variables" (p. 1). Therefore, it appears that certain characteristics of the family environment are integrally related to child achievement and child affect.

With the foregoing framework in place, it becomes clear why efforts aimed at helping children should include an emphasis on parent education and involvement with a special focus on communication between parents and systems, such as those in the educational, economic, and political arenas. Research and experience, particularly within the federal program highlighted in this chapter, tell us that targeting children is not enough. We must also target the parents and the home environment in order to maximally influence the child's development. Project Follow Through represents a remarkable and unique program within the pool of federally funded educational projects, because it systematically includes a parent involvement component across all participating sites. Although threats of financial cutbacks have plagued the program and thus thwarted efforts aimed at examining, researching, and evaluating this important component, data have been collected across the participating stakeholders of the program. The remainder of this chapter will be devoted to a brief description of the FT program with emphasis on the parent involvement component, a review of findings related to this component, and a discussion of implications for public policy decisions.

THE FOLLOW THROUGH PROGRAM

Program Definition and Brief History

> Follow Through is a community services program established in 1967 under an amendment to the Economic Opportunity Act of 1964 for children in kindergarten and the primary grades who are from low-income families. The program was designed to sustain and expand upon the gains made by children in Head Start or similar preschool programs. (Office of Education, 1977, p. 33146)

Follow Through was originally planned as a social action program similar to Head Start, but because of massive cuts made in the Office of Economic Opportunity budget in 1967, the focus of the program was changed in the second year of operation to an educational experiment. This experiment consisted of implementing and evaluating a variety of compensatory education programs to ascertain which approaches might be more effective with which children and families in which communities. This program format, called planned variation, originally included 13 approaches or sponsors (including self-sponsored). A sponsor was generally a group of persons at a university or institute who had developed a particular approach to early childhood education. Sponsors worked closely with communities to insure maximum implementation of their particular educational approach. During the next 2 years, 10 more sponsors were invited to join the program bringing the total number to 23. The number of sponsors currently participating in the FT program is 19. A list of sponsors with their institutional affiliations and number of sites is presented in Table 1.

Planned variation was not in operation during 1967–68, the first year of implementation of the FT program. During that year, each of 39 communities, serving a total of 3,000 low-income children, designed and implemented its own local program. In 1968–69, planned variation began and sites and sponsors were paired at two national meetings. At these meetings, sponsors made brief presentations about their programs and community representatives selected the one which seemed to best meet the needs of their community. During 1968–69, the Follow Through program was implemented in 82 communities with approximately 15,500 low-income children. Currently the program serves about 75,000 low-income children in over 150 communities.

Guidelines for Parent Involvement in the Follow Through Program

The FT Program Rules and Regulations (Office of Education, 1977) specify the following general components for every Follow Through project: (1) instructional program; (2) parent and community involvement; (3) comprehensive services; and (4) staff development. Every FT community, regardless of its sponsor's affiliation, is required to implement a program consisting of *all* of these components. In many cases, the sponsor's approach only involves the instructional and staff development components; in these situations it is the responsibility of the community to ensure that the other two components are effectively implemented.

The important role of parent involvement in the FT program can be seen in two sections of the Follow Through Program Rules and Regulations (Office of Education, 1977). In one section, 15 criteria for refunding of local projects are listed and six of these are directly related

TABLE 1:   FOLLOW THROUGH SPONSORS[a]

Title of sponsor's model	Most recent institutional affiliation	Number of sites[b]
Responsive Education Model	Far West Laboratory for Educational Research and Development	15
Tucson Early Education Model	University of Arizona	20
Rank Street Model	Bank Street College of Education	14
Mathemagenic Activities Program	University of Georgia	7
Direct Instruction Model	University of Oregon	20
Behavior Analysis Approach	University of Kansas	13
Cognitively Oriented Curriculum Model	High/Scope Foundation	10
Parent Education Follow Through Program	University of North Carolina	11
EDC Open Education Model	Education Development Center	10
Individualized Early Learning Program	University of Pittsburgh	7
Interdependent Learning Model	Fordham University	3
Language Development (Bilingual Education) Approach	Southwest Educational Development Laboratory	5
Hampton Institute Non-graded Model	Hampton Institute	6
Culturally Linguistic Approach	Northeastern Illinois University	5
Parent Supported Diagnostic Approach	Georgia State University	2
Personalized Instruction Model	Prentice-Hall Developmental Learning Centers	1
Home-School Partnership Model	Clark College	2
New School Approach	University of North Dakota	4
Culturally Democratic Learning Environments	University of California-Santa Cruz	1
California Process Model[c]	California State Department of Education	6
Parent Implementation Educational Model[c]	AFRAM Associates	9
Role Trade Model[d]	Western Behavioral Sciences Institute	1
Self-Sponsored		13

[a]Adapted from Haney (1977).
[b]Number indicates maximum number of sites implementing a sponsor's program; some of these sites have dropped out of the program.
[c] Discontinued as sponsors in 1975.
[d] Discontinued as a sponsor in 1977.

to the parent involvement component of the program, while in another section seven criteria for evaluation are given and two of these seven pertain to parent involvement.

The major vehicle for parent involvement in a FT project is the Policy Advisory Committee, or PAC. Program regulations specify the purpose, membership, advisors, funding, and duties of PAC, with the latter including such activities as proposal preparation and personnel selection. In addition to the PAC, the regulations list three other forms of parent involvement including: "(2) participation in the classroom as observers or volunteers, or as paid employees; (3) regular home visits and other contacts initiated by project staff; and (4) participation in educational and community activities, developed through other program components" (Office of Education, 1977, p. 33151).

INFORMATION CONCERNING PARENT INVOLVEMENT IN FOLLOW THROUGH: NATIONAL LEVEL

Unfortunately, parent involvement as a program component has not received the attention in the national evaluation of Follow Through which one would expect after reading the program regulations. The many reasons for this are discussed in detail by Walt Haney in two reports (Haney, 1977; Haney & Pennington, 1978). Briefly, the reasons are that the national evaluation in the early years of Follow Through was fairly comprehensive and included interviewing parents as one technique of data collection. However, with changes in personnel in the national FT office, with criticisms regarding both the instrumentation and the purposes for this data collection with parents, and with increasing emphasis on the instructional component, less and less effort was devoted over the years to assessing the parent involvement component.

Between 1969 and 1975, over 60,000 parent interviews were conducted with both Follow Through and non-Follow Through (NFT) parents, but other than returning descriptive data to each community involved, little use was made of this massive set of information (Haney, 1977). Modifications were made to the interviewing instrument each year which made it difficult, if not impossible, to examine the data longitudinally. Also, data of this type are extremely expensive to analyze and during the early 1970s there were mounting criticisms regarding the cost of the national evaluation. In 1978, Walt Haney and Nancy Pennington of the Huron Institute received funds to reexamine a subset of the original 60,000 parent interviews. A summary of their findings will be presented later in this chapter.

Another type of involvement by FT parents was their participation in two national conferences and their reaction to the planned phase-out of Follow Through. Although this information is not part of any evaluation, it provides clear examples of the deep commitment parents felt for the program and the strong feelings they had about their involvement in it.

In October, 1968, a national FT meeting was held in Atlanta with the Washington staff, sponsors, local community staff, and parents present. By this time the planned variation format was underway and there was a decreased emphasis on the social action elements (e.g., parental and community involvement) of the program. The parents, as well as a group of general consultants who worked with the communities, were generally unhappy about this basic change in direction and expressed their dissatisfaction. According to people who were present at the meeting, the parents' comments had a definite effect on both the FT program and the evaluation. As reported by Haney (1977), changes in the program included the addition of several sponsors, many from minority institutions, and a strengthening of the guidelines regarding parent involvement. In the area of evaluation, changes included the addition of parent interviews and community case studies as data collection methods.

Four years later, FT parents were even more vocal at the national meeting held in Denver. Shortly before the Denver meeting, the Office of Education had announced that the FT program would be phased out. Many of the parents' comments concerned this issue, as well as the issue that the national evaluation was not sufficiently inclusive. The parents generally felt that the program was successful, but that the evaluators had done a poor job of showing this success, thereby contributing to the phase-out of the program.

There were two significant aftereffects of the Denver meeting. First, national Follow Through meetings were discontinued. Second, parents went home from the meeting and mobilized other parents in their own as well as in other FT communities to fight the planned phase-out of the program.

Parents played a major role in reversing the phase-out planned for the early 1970s. As Hodges, Branden, Feldman, Follins, Love, Sheehan, Lumbley, Osborn, Rentfrow, Houston, & Lee (1980) stated:

> Parents have brought unique skills to the implementation process and, through involvement in their children's education, have become strong advocates of Follow Through. A single illustration is indicative of this advocacy. During the years 1973–75, when the federal administration rescinded or attempted to reduce the appropriation for Follow Through, the parents mobilized and, through letters to their respective legislators, were perhaps most responsible for the restoration of federal funding. (pp. 21–22)

During spring, 1980, a similar funding crisis occurred and once again the parents played a major role in saving the program. In addition to writing letters and making phone calls to members of Congress, a 3-week series of meetings was held in Washington, D.C., during which FT parents traveled to the city for personal visits with their representatives. On June 3, 1980, a national Follow Through rally was held. More than 1,000 program supporters (mainly parents) attended this rally at the Capitol and marched to the White House (Ramp & Altman, 1980). Many members of Congress (e.g., Natcher of Kentucky; Obey of Wisconsin; Conte of Massachusetts; McDade of Pennsylvania; DeConcini of Arizona; Laehy of Vermont; Hatfield of Oregon; Weicker of Connecticut) became more supportive of the program after discussing it with parents from their districts or states. During these meetings, parents presented information about the program in areas other than child achievement, such as how the program had changed the lives of parents through career development and employment, and how the parents felt they had an effective voice in decision-making in the programs and in the schools.

In a way, these threats to program survival were the ultimate tests of the parents' decision-making ability and their ability to function as advocates for themselves and their children—skills which were a part of the parent involvement component of the FT program. The parents passed these tests with flying colors. Through their collective efforts, the parents were able to reverse both the phase-out decision, which had already been made by the Office of Education during the early 1970s, and the 1980 funding threat from Congress.

Reexamination of Parent Interview Data

As stated earlier, although 60,000 parent interviews were completed over 7 years as part of the national evaluation, there was very little analysis of these data. To remedy this situation, the Huron Institute received a contract to reexamine and perform additional analyses on a subset of both parent and teacher interview data which had been collected.

This reexamination was done using the spring, 1975 parent and teacher interview questionnaires. Data from 68 sites affiliated with 15 different sponsors were included in the reanalysis (Haney & Pennington, 1978). A total of 3,911 parent interviews was examined, with approximately half (1,996) from Follow Through parents and half (1,915) from non-Follow Through (NFT) parents. As the authors point out, these data are not entirely representative of the total Follow Through population since sites affiliated with some sponsors were not included. Also, the demographic data available suggest that although there were some differences between the FT and NFT samples of parents, the two samples:

> . . . resemble each other far more closely than either sample resembles the national population. In other words, these samples are alike in that relative to the national population they represent populations disadvantaged in terms of income, having high proportions of single-parent families, and also having high proportions of non-white families. (Haney & Pennington, 1978, pp. 15, 17)

The technical quality of these data are moderate, but Haney and Pennington (1978) state:

> The main justification for carrying out this reanalysis is that the . . . data, whatever their technical quality, provide the sole opportunity for us to examine the success of Follow Through from two perspectives which heretofore have been almost completely ignored in the national Follow Through evaluation; namely, the views of Follow Through as a comprehensive service program and Follow Through as a social action-parent involvement program. (p. 20)

Because there was limited information available concerning the quality of the interview data and because of problems such as response bias, Haney and Pennington felt the most suitable format for data presentation was to compare the two groups of parents in terms of the percentages responding a certain way to each item. Of the 252 separate items on the original interview, 157 were included in the Huron reanalysis; only a few of these reanalyzed items will be presented here.

Most of the interview questions had a response format of three to five categories from which the parent was asked to select one. However, a few questions were open-ended. One of these was "What are the things you *like* most about Follow Through?" The words "child's school" were substituted for the words "Follow Through" when NFT parents were interviewed. A maximum of three responses was recorded for each parent. Parent participation was the second most frequent response among FT parents with 22% mentioning it as one of their three answers. Among NFT parents, parent participation was the seventh most frequent response with 14% giving it as a response. These data suggest more positive feelings toward parent involvement among FT parents than among NFT parents.

Knowledge of and involvement in PAC (Policy Advisory Committee) were assessed through several interview questions. In many communities, NFT families participated in federal education programs other than FT (e.g., Title I) which also have PACs, so the comparison is to some degree between programs. When parents were asked if they had ever heard of PAC, 72% of FT parents and 31% of NFT parents responded "yes." Data for questions concerning PAC participation and the percentage of the two groups responding "yes" were as follows: (1) Have you ever gone to a PAC meeting? FT = 43%; NFT = 8%; (2) Have you ever voted in a PAC election? FT = 30%; NFT = 5%; and (3) Have you ever been an officer of PAC? FT = 9%; NFT = 2% (Haney & Pennington, 1978, p. 37). Although the percentages for FT parents may not seem high at first glance, it is useful to consider them relative to those for NFT parents. When this is done, it is clear that FT as a program has been reasonably successful in involving parents in the decision-making aspects of parent involvement.

Traditionally, low-income parents have felt uncomfortable in their relationships with schools. Often, one consequence of this is little or no involvement in parent groups (e.g., see NFT percentages for participation). The findings that 72% of the FT parents report they are aware of PAC and that 43% report they have attended a meeting are indicative of the comparatively high level of parent involvement in the FT program.

In addition to PAC, the federal FT regulations mandate that parents be involved in the school and classroom as observers, volunteers, or paid employees. When parents were asked if they worked in school either as a volunteer or for pay, 28% of the FT parents and 13% of the NFT parents answered "yes." Haney & Pennington (1978) noted that:

> Those parents who reported working in school were then asked whether or not they work in a *classroom* at school. Of those parents working in a school, FT parents were much more likely (72%) than NFT parents (50%) to respond yes. (p. 34)

This finding may be related to the fact that FT parents are given first consideration for nonprofessional and paraprofessional positions as mandated by federal FT regulations. These data provide some evidence to suggest successful implementation of that portion of the program regulations.

Several questions on the parent interview pertained to the amount of direct contact among parents, teachers, and other school personnel at school and in the home. Responses to these questions indicated that there was more direct contact among these groups in both home and school for FT parents than for NFT parents. A higher percentage of FT parents (52%) than NFT parents (38%) visited the classroom. Of those parents who did visit the classroom, FT parents visited nearly twice as frequently as NFT parents. Finally, FT parents visited more often as a result of their own decision rather than in response to a request from the teacher to discuss a problem.

Also, although FT and NFT parents are "equally likely to go to school to talk with the teacher (82%), FT parents average about one more visit per year (4.5) than NFT parents (3.4)" (Haney & Pennington, 1978,

p. 35). For parents who had visited the school to talk with someone other than the teacher, FT parents averaged 10.6 visits per year as compared to 4.5 visits per year for NFT parents.

Direct contact in the home consisted of visits by teachers and by other school personnel. Home visits by teachers were reported by 12% of FT parents and only 4% of NFT parents. More home visits by school personnel other than the teacher were also reported by FT parents than NFT parents, with the average number of visits per year by other personnel averaging 7.9 for FT parents and 1.9 for NFT parents. Haney & Pennington (1978) concluded:

> In sum, both parent and teacher data indicate that direct contact, both at school and at home, between parents, teachers and other school personnel not only consistently involves *more* FT parents than NFT parents, but is more frequent for the FT parents than for the NFT parents. (p. 36)

FT Parent Involvement Needs Assessment

FT sponsors, as a group, have formed several task forces to assist in the planning of the national FT program. Areas of concentration for these task forces include evaluation, criteria for refunding of sites, and parent involvement. As one activity, the Parent Involvement Task Force, which consists of three sponsors, three parents, and one local FT coordinator, developed a needs assessment questionnaire and distributed it to FT participants throughout the country. One copy was sent to each Washington FT project officer ($N = 13$), each sponsor ($N = 19$), and to a randomly selected sample of 21 of the 39 state FT coordinators. In addition, 100 FT sites were selected for inclusion, with an attempt made to ensure equal representation of all sponsors. Each site received six copies of the questionnaire to be completed by the following: two parents, one teacher, one paraprofessional, one school administrator, and the local FT coordinator.

The questionnaires were completed during fall, 1979, and returns were received from 41 states and the District of Columbia. Because respondents were only required to note their role in the program (e.g., parent, teacher), but not their site or sponsor affiliation, little information is available regarding the representativeness of the respondents. The percentage of returns for the various respondent groups varied between 54% and 86%; of 653 questionnaires distributed, 423 (65%) were completed and returned (Parent Involvement Task Force, 1979). The questionnaire consisted of 31 items; for each item there was a four-point scale on which the respondent was asked to indicate how important he or she felt this aspect of parent involvement to be. The items covered various types of parent involvement such as decision-making, volunteering, and serving as political advocates. The data were analyzed within respondent groups with the items ranked in importance from #1 to #31 for each group according to the points given on the four-point scale by respondents. For example, the item "Parents as teachers of their own child" was #4 in importance (out of 31 items) for the Washington staff as a group, while it was #13 in importance for school administrators. Because of little information about the representativeness of the respondents, large differences in group sizes, and problems of response bias, the data will be presented in terms of comparisons of rankings of importance among the various groups of respondents.

Since PAC is the major vehicle of parent involvement in FT, it is interesting to see how different groups ranked this type of involvement. Five groups (parents, sponsors, Washington staff, paraprofessionals, and local FT coordinators) ranked this item as #2 in importance while school administrators, teachers and state FT coordinators ranked the item #11, #13, and #13, respectively. There appears to be general agreement between the key role given to PAC in the program regulations and the ranking of importance given by the groups most closely involved in actual program functioning.

Another major role for parents is in the classroom, either as volunteers or employees. The rankings of importance for these two items are shown in Table 2. Generally, respondents felt that it is more important for parents to serve as volunteers than as employees. Only the sponsor group gave similar rankings to the two roles. It is surprising to see how "low" the role of employee was ranked by nearly every group,

TABLE 2:   RANKINGS OF IMPORTANCE FOR PARENT ROLES IN THE CLASSROOM[a]

	Parent role in classroom	
Respondent Group	Volunteer	Employee
Parents	5	21
Sponsors	15	14
Washington staff	12	23
Local FT coordinators	9	19
State FT coordinators	10	24
School administrators	8	24
Teachers	4	23
Paraprofessionals	6	22

[a]Each respondent group ranked 31 items by importance. Thus, for the parents, classroom volunteer was ranked as the 5th most important type of parent involvement, while employee was ranked as 21st in importance.

particularly since the FT regulations clearly specify that FT parents are to be given first consideration for nonprofessional jobs.

In an earlier section there was a discussion of the successful effort by FT parents in fighting two planned phase-outs of the program. One item on the needs assessment questionnaire asked respondents how important it is to "acquaint parents with political advocacy skills." The ranking of this item for seven of the eight respondent groups ranged between #24 and #28 (out of 31). Only the sponsor group deviated from this range by giving the item a #19, still a fairly low ranking.

This brief summary illustrates some of the interesting information resulting from the FT parent involvement needs assessment. Although the questionnaire was restricted to FT, a variety of program stakeholders was included which allowed for the comparison of rankings of importance among the various groups. This set of data from 41 states and 8 different groups of respondents is probably the most comprehensive collection of parent involvement needs assessment data in existence.

SPONSOR SPECIFIC ACCOUNTS OF PARENT INVOLVEMENT IN FOLLOW THROUGH[1]

As previously mentioned, Project Follow Through is a planned variation program, with different approaches and implementation strategies. Realizing the diverse nature of the program, individual descriptions of several sponsor approaches to parent involvement will be presented. Although there are 19 sponsor models, in the interest of space only three sponsor approaches are presented (in alphabetical order) in this chapter.

Each program synopsis includes a brief description of the: (1) philosophy of the sponsor approach and the parent involvement component; (2) activities of the parent involvement component congruent with the particular philosophy of the model; (3) evidence of success as described by the sponsor; and (4) evidence of success as reported by Haney and Pennington (1978) in their reanalysis of parent and teacher interview data.

The data vary in scope, and the reader will note the paucity of "hard" data on parental involvement within sponsor evaluations. "Hard" data refers to the statistical examination of the relationship between parent involvement and child outcomes. As stated in previous sections, collection of parent involvement data was not encouraged during the history of Follow Through. In addition, it was thought that future funding of federal programs would be contingent on positive evidence of success pertaining to child outcome measures. It is of no surprise, then, that sponsors have focused their data monitoring and program evaluation efforts in the area of child outcome, and more specifically, of child achievement. Although attempts were made by a few sponsors to tie parent involvement data to child achievement measures, the information was not readily available, easily collectible, or easily isolated. For these reasons, available data are primarily descriptive, although a few studies focus on certain parent involvement predictors of child achievement.

Whenever possible, all pertinent data which reflect individual sponsor approaches are presented in this chapter. In addition, portions of individual sponsor descriptions of relevant data included in the Haney and Pennington report (1978) are given. These data were collected in the spring of 1975 and focus on four areas of concern derived from items on parent and teacher interviews: (1) perceived importance of parent involvement; (2) helpfulness of school to parents and parents to schools; (3) degree of parent involvement; and (4) PAC (Haney & Pennington, 1978).

For the sponsor level analysis in the Haney and Pennington report, one-tailed tests of significance were applied separately for large and small sponsors. Haney and Pennington (1978) stated that "the question addressed in such tests was of the sort, 'Is the proportion of respondents answering in a particular way for Sponsor A significantly greater [or less] than the corresponding proportion of respondents for FT [or NFT] overall?' " (pp. 51–52). Taking this one step further, questionnaire items bearing on the four areas of concern which revealed significant results for three out of four of Haney and Pennington's comparisons were reported as positive effects for the sponsor. Haney and Pennington's four comparisons included the sponsor average as compared with: (1) the NFT comparison group average for that sponsor; (2) the overall NFT average across all comparison sites; (3) the overall FT average; and (4) the response levels of all sites affiliated with a particular sponsor. In the fourth comparison, the response levels were compared to the NFT response levels. Haney and Pennington (1978) admonished that "these tests of statistical significance are merely heuristic devices—they are *not* formal tests of statistical significance in the sense of confirmatory data analysis" (p. 51).

No attempt is made in this chapter to present data as it specifically relates to child achievement. Parent involvement data, in its own regard, are presented and discussed, and it is from these data that policy considerations will be advanced.

Bank Street Follow Through Model

Philosophy with emphasis on parent involvement. The Bank Street model emphasizes the personal growth of children, parents, and teachers. It has as its major goals the stimulation of children's cognitive and affective development and community change (Bock, Stebbins, & Proper, 1977, p. 53). Children participate actively within the classroom and are supported by adults who help them acquire academic skills through their direct experiences in the environment.

Bank Street's process of carrying out its educational philosophy relies heavily on parent participation. In carrying out and expanding on the federal regulations for parent involvement, both the Bank Street sponsor and its communities and schools have worked together to create resources for parents to support their children's learning (Weisberg, 1978). A partnership between home and school is formed by having parents volunteer in school-related activities, actively participate in PAC and community activities relating to the school, and confer closely and frequently with teachers. Other interesting parent involvement activities include: newsletters which are sent home to parents to provide information about the program; a career development program; a Parent-Assisted Learning program aimed at having parent volunteers work with the social service and educational components of the model; and a Parent Internship Program in which parents have direct access to early childhood classrooms for 2 full days per week for 4 weeks (Smith, 1978).

Evidence of success of the parent involvement component: Sponsor reports. Evidence of success has been reported in the following areas (Weisberg, 1976):

1. PAC—Parent activities reported across sites include political, cultural and educational groups;
2. Intake—the vital place where parents and FT staff initiate relationships. Parents were reported to have helped with registration;
3. Parents learning about children's program—workshops, meetings, newsletters and videotape films have been reported as evidence in this area;
4. Child study—discussion groups, coffee hours, meetings, workshops, and individual conferences were the settings for discussions on child development;
5. Parents working in classrooms—involvement varied across communities with different training across sites;
6. Parents in political activity—a great amount of activity was reported across all sites particularly when federal funding was threatened. Letters were written by parents to Congress to save Follow Through. Local involvement was also successful with reports of parents appearing before the school boards on various issues;
7. Career development programs for parents—developed with community colleges where degrees were obtained. In addition, organized non-credit classes were formed; and

8. Parent interview—79% of parents interviewed during the spring of 1973 had visited the classroom at least once during the year; 77% of all parents had been visited in their home by a FT staff member; 82% indicated that Follow Through had influenced their child's development in specific ways; 91% expressed a desire for the continuation of the FT program into the fourth grade instead of terminating after grade three; and parents indicated that their children had positive feelings about school and that involvement in Follow Through broadened their lives through decision making, opportunities for social and educational training, and increased child-parent interaction at home (Bank Street Follow Through Model, 1973).

Evidence of success of the parent involvement component: Haney and Pennington report. The Bank Street model shows up well in terms of parent involvement as reported by parents and teachers. Parents indicated that they agreed that parents had a say in how the school was run. Further, they indicated that the school was helpful to parents in the following ways: learning about teaching; getting to know the teacher; helping the parent help the child with school work; understanding how children learn; and meeting other parents. Sixty-one percent of Bank Street's parents reported having gone to watch their child's class. Both parents and teachers indicated a high level of implementation of PACs in their schools (Haney & Pennington, 1978, p. 71).

University of Kansas Behavior Analysis Model

Philosophy with special emphasis on parent involvement. The primary objectives of this model are the mastery of reading, arithmetic, handwriting, and spelling skills by children. The objectives are accomplished partially through team teaching and individualized teaching, programmed instruction, an instructional system, and a token reinforcement system (Bock et al., 1977).

Parent participation in the model takes various forms. Parents, employed as aides, engage in specific teaching roles in the classroom. Parents also receive monthly progress reports of their children's academic behavior. Fueyo, Ramp, and Bushell (1979) stated, "The sole purpose is to provide a standard set of information on a regular basis, that allows educators and parents to assess the impact of their decisions on the academic performance of each pupil" (p. 3). In addition to these activities, parents respond to an annual questionnaire which is composed of items relating to the local acceptance of the program and the areas of perceived refinement of the program. Lastly, parents participate in the locally established PAC.

Evidence of success of the parent involvement component: Sponsor reports. Between 1974 and 1978, results of the annual parent questionnaire indicated that 80% or more parents indicated satisfaction with the program. Among the areas of satisfaction were: the education provided by the Behavior Analysis Program; the cost of the program; children's happiness at school; and the parents' influence over school policy (Fueyo et al., 1979).

Data pertaining to PAC focus on the decision-making behavior of parents. In one Behavior Analysis site, decisions made by parents increased from 15% in 1969 to 80% in 1978. This particular site's PAC was responsible for the removal of unsatisfactory staff personnel as well as the support of achievement testing during financial crises (Fueyo et al., 1979).

During the 1979–80 academic year, a system was implemented by the model sponsor to record the training and employment opportunities for parents. Data generated from this effort summarized the number of parents employed; the number of parents completing training; the number of parents employed for the first time; and the total funding expended by the project to employ parents (Fueyo et al., 1979).

Evidence of success of the parent involvement component: Haney and Pennington report. The University of Kansas Behavior Analysis Model appeared strong on items concerning PAC in Haney and Pennington's (1978) analysis. Parents had heard of PAC, attended PAC meetings, and indicated that PAC helps parents. The analysis also revealed that parents learned to help their children with school work and to find jobs.

University of North Carolina Parent Education FT Program (PEFTP)[2]

Philosophy with special emphasis on parent involvement. "Basic to the [philosophy of the Parent Education Follow Through] Program is the assumption that parents exert a major influence upon the intellectual development of their children, and that these parents serve as a vehicle by which new learning behaviors are passed on" (Rubin, True, & Pezzano, 1979, p. 4). To this end, the PEFTP targets the home environment as well as its ambient environments (agencies and systems). Linkages are formed among the home, school, school system, and community through the implementation of several key features of the program. These key features, as outlined by Rubin et al. (1979, p. 4), include:

1. Parent educators who visit parents in their homes and work in the classrooms with these parents' children;
2. Home learning activities, which are developed by parents and

staff at various PEFTP sites are brought into the home by the parent educator, with the emphasis placed on parental teaching behavior when demonstrating these activities;

3. Parent committees and meetings which are organized to facilitate increased parent involvement, allowing parents to become partners, along with teachers, in the educational development of their children;

4. Teachers working cooperatively with parents who volunteer in the classroom; and

5. Comprehensive services for participating families (social, psychological, and medical).

These features of parental involvement underscore six major roles of parents in the education of their children: teachers of their children, paid paraprofessionals, decision-makers and policy advisors through PAC, adult learners of new skills, audience or recipients of information, and volunteers in the classroom (Rubin et al., 1979). Further, as Rubin (1981) notes, implementing these six roles produces desirable changes in teachers and children, as well as parents.

Evidence of success of the parent involvement component: Sponsor reports. Due to the comprehensiveness of this parent education program, numerous types of evaluative studies have been performed by the sponsor. Evidence of success has been reported for children, parents, and the school and community.[3]

The effects of this parent involvement program which relate to child achievement have been documented by Stebbins, St. Pierre, Proper, Anderson, & Cerva (1977) at Abt Associates; House, Glass, McLean, and Walker (1978); and the sponsor (Olmsted, Rubin, True, & Revicki, 1980; Olmsted, Rubin, & Revicki, 1981). According to Stebbins et al. (1977), the PEFTP ranks in the top four (of the 13 sponsors studied in their report) on the three outcome domains of basic skills, cognitive conceptual skills, and affective outcomes. Data included in the Stebbins report were collected by Stanford Research Institute during the period from 1971–72 to 1974–75. Results reported by House et al. (1978), in a reanalysis of the evaluation conducted by Stebbins et al. (1977), indicated favorable results with a ranking of the PEFTP in first position in Total Reading on the Metropolitan Achievement Test. With respect to the Total Math, Spelling, and Language scores, the PEFTP ranked 5, 3, and 6, respectively, of the 13 sponsors (Olmsted, Rubin, Revicki, Stuck, & Wetherby, 1979). Sponsor accounts of child achievement during the period from 1973–74 through 1978–79, revealed that 38.6% of all the statistical analyses favored the PEFTP group, 20.5% of the analyses favored the comparison groups, and 40.9% of the analyses indicated no significant differences (Olmsted et al., 1980; Olmsted et al., 1981).

Other related studies investigated the use of desirable teaching behaviors by parents in the home, and the diffusion of program effects to members of the family other than the targeted child. Results indicated that PEFTP parents used significantly more desirable teaching behaviors (M = 24.0) as compared to non-PEFTP parents (M = 14.5), F (1, 63) = 6.35, $p < .05$. In addition, the number of desirable teaching behaviors used by parents correlated with child Reading and Math scores on the Stanford Achievement Test, Reading: r = .50, $p < .001$; Math: r = .35, $p < .05$ (Olmsted, 1981). Results from two studies which addressed vertical diffusion indicated that younger siblings of PEFTP children scored higher on the Preschool Inventory as compared to comparable children from non-PEFTP homes (Moreno, 1974; Ware, Organ, Olmsted, & Moreno, 1974).

Data pertaining to parents have been summarized by the sponsor in the areas of PAC attendance, decisions made by parents at PAC meetings, parent volunteering, engagement of parents in instructional activities during classroom volunteering, and home visitation. Information derived from one of these areas indicated that during a typical school year, over 8,000 children are in the program and approximately 150,000 home visits are made.

Effects of the program in relation to the school and community have been documented in the areas of child attendance rates, time spent planning for home visits with the teacher by the paraprofessional, teacher and paraprofessional time spent in instructional activities in the classroom, and the diversity of home learning activities brought into the home by the paraprofessional. Positive findings have been reported in these areas as well as in the area of impact reported in seven ethnographic case studies conducted in PEFTP sites. Information from these qualitative evaluation studies showed the model's social, political, and economic effects in the areas of career development of parents, program development, cross-cultural communication, and comprehensive services (Olmsted et al., 1979).

Evidence of success of the parent involvement component: Haney and Pennington report. Haney and Pennington (1978) report that PEFTP produced high levels of parent involvement: "This is, of course, precisely what we would expect since the Florida [now University of North Carolina] approach is called the Parent Education Model and gives primary emphasis to parent involvement" (p. 70).

According to PEFTP teachers, parent involvement in the areas of decisions about school and social activities is very important. The summary of comparisons for items concerning helpfulness of school to parents and parent to school indicated 47% of the PEFTP parents mentioned that one of the things they liked most about Follow Through was parent participation (as compared to 22% for FT parents overall). In addition, parents indicated that they had worked as a volunteer or paid worker and thought the school was generally helpful to the parent in terms of learning about teaching, helping parents to help their children with school work, and meeting other parents. PEFTP teachers indicated that a mean number of 5.90 children in their class had their parent serve as a classroom volunteer at least once as compared to a mean number of 3.85 for FT teachers overall. Sixty-five percent of the PEFTP parents reported that they had gone to watch their child's class versus 37% for PEFTP NFT comparison parents and 52% for FT parents overall (Haney & Pennington, 1978, p. 70). Haney and Pennington (1978), also found that "in one of the most striking contrasts in these data, 71 percent of Florida [now the University of North Carolina FT project] parents reported that a teacher's aide had gone to talk with the parent in her home (the proportion reporting the same for FT overall was 14 percent and for NFT just 1 percent)" (pp. 70–71). In the area of PAC, 91% of the PEFTP parents said that they had heard of PAC (compared to 72% FT overall), 62% indicated that they had attended a PAC meeting (compared to 43% FT overall), and 68% indicated that they thought PAC would help a parent solve a problem about the schools (as compared to 52% FT parents overall).

Summary of Sponsor Specific Accounts

Perusal of information contained in the sponsor specific accounts on parent involvement in Follow Through reveals widespread positive findings. Although the data are not considered to be "hard" data, evidence of success is observed. These parent involvement data found by several sponsors are important in their own regard based on the primary assumption, stated earlier in this chapter, that helping parents ultimately helps children.

In spite of the different emphases of FT models, the parent involvement component is a vital and operative one within each program described in this chapter. Sponsor accounts show that parents were actively involved in several FT programs; Haney and Pennington (1978) report this finding supports the perspective of Follow Through as a social action endeavor which has impacted on parents, children, and communities. Notable effects indicate that it is possible for low-income parents to become actively involved in the education of their children. Further, this involvement leads to a spiraling effect on other institutions affecting children and their families. School boards, school districts, and entire school systems have been influenced due to the involvement and decision-making role of parents.

These effects for individual sponsors, coupled with findings on the national level, suggest several strategies for public policy.

POLICY CONSIDERATIONS

Both specific and general policy considerations for parent education can be drawn from the Follow Through program. As was stated in the introduction of this chapter, parent education programs are based on the assumption that making changes in parents results in changes in children. These changes in children may occur in a variety of areas such as self-concept, motivation, and academic achievement. There are little "hard" data in this field at the present time, but the data which are available support the assumption of the relationship between changes in parent attitudes and behavior and changes in child behavior.

With regard to the Follow Through program, the situation is very similar. The same assumption is applicable and little "hard" data are available. Parent participation is heavily emphasized in the FT program regulations and one would expect significantly more data to be in existence after reading these regulations. The problems seem to lie in two areas: monitoring implementation of the regulations and evaluation of this program component. Over the years only moderate effort has been given to ensure that the various elements of parent participation have been implemented by FT programs. There have been changes in the actual emphasis given to this program component during the history of Follow Through, as well as some degree of uncertainty regarding who was actually responsible for monitoring the implementation (i.e., project officers, sponsors, or general consultants).

The more serious problem has been in the evaluation of parent involvement in the FT programs. In the early years, there was some effort to include parents in the national FT evaluation, but this effort was small and consisted mainly of data collection without accompanying data analysis and dissemination of results. Existing data come mainly from sponsor evaluations.

During 1979–80, the Parent Education Follow Through Program received funds to conduct a special study on the relationships among various forms of parent involvement and several measures of child behavior. Funding of this special study may be an indication of increased emphasis on the part of the national office to investigate and evaluate parent involvement in Follow Through.

There are three specific policy considerations which can be drawn from the parent involvement component of the FT program. First, local FT communities should be encouraged to implement the program regulations regarding parent involvement, since this generally results in a high level of parent involvement. A mechanism has been found then, that, when put into operation, can result in a high degree of parent participation. This is a very important finding regarding the Follow Through program and one which has received virtually no publicity.

Second, as Gordon (1978a) has argued:

> The concept of sponsorship in the design, execution and evolution of programs as demonstrated by the Follow Through approach is a viable and powerful vehicle for change. . . . Since parent education is different from adopting a new textbook, or curriculum, and includes outreach activities, it seems even more essential that there be research, demonstration and diffusion efforts which use a model sponsor approach. (p. 5)

Third, parents should be involved in an advocacy role in the program. Probably the most significant events thus far in Follow Through are the two successful reversals of program phase-out accomplished by parents. These events illustrated that low-income parents could work cooperatively and could function as effective political advocates for themselves and their children. These actions on the part of parents were directly related to the key roles they played in programs at the local level. In most FT programs, parents have functioned as decision-makers and thus felt directly threatened when the phase-outs were announced. As a response to these threats, parents banded together to save "their" program. The intense commitment, the large amount of work done, and the skills involved in these activities all have implications for public policy in parent education.

The remaining policy considerations are more general than the ones just presented, but are related, directly or indirectly, to the FT program. First, parents should be considered as equals in a parent education program. They should be seen as people who have skills and experience. Parents have just as much, if not more, to offer parent education programs as do the professionals involved.

Second, parents should be involved in the development of parent programs. This does not mean that hundreds of parents should be involved, but parent representatives should participate in meetings to plan program content, criteria for program participation, and criteria for selection of program personnel. Parent input is especially valuable in designing ways to inform other parents about the program and determining what kind of programs might be most appropriate.

Third, parents should be actively involved in the management of parent programs. Small groups, of which parents are active members, should supervise every aspect of parent programs, from budgeting and personnel selection to evaluation and report writing. In this way there is continuous communication between parents and other program personnel, and problems are resolved quickly while they are still minor.

Parents and program personnel alike feel a sense of ownership in the program and are more committed to having a successful, effective program.

Fourth, parent programs should involve many forms of participation to enable parents to select those which best meet their needs and circumstances. Some parents may prefer to be actively involved in program decision-making, while others may prefer to function as a volunteer or tutor.

Fifth, if a parent program operates in conjunction with a school system, it is important to have administrative support for the program. A parent program of this type generally involves teachers, parents, principals, and other school administrative staff and requires openness and a willingness to change on the part of each participant. As Ira Gordon (1978a) once stated: "If administrators are not willing for schools to change, and teachers are not willing for their roles to change, then it would be best if they never get involved in parent involvement" (pp. 6–7).

Sixth, parent programs should be given adequate time to become institutionalized and to have an impact. Since parent programs generally require changes in attitudes as well as changes in behavior on the part of both program personnel and participants, sufficient time must be given before summative evaluation is conducted.

Seventh, the evaluation of parent programs should be comprehensive and should include monitoring of program implementation in addition to assessment of outcomes. Monitoring provides information regarding the actual level of implementation for various program components. This formative evaluation should include continuous record-keeping as well as periodic comparisons between what should be happening and what actually is happening in the program. The summative program evaluation has to encompass all stakeholders as well as all program components. For example, if a parent program operates within a school system, teachers and school administrators as well as parents and children need to be included in the evaluation. If the program is designed to have an impact on the school system and community as well as the home, then each of these institutions must be part of the overall evaluation.

In order to have effective program evaluation, both formative and summative, two things are necessary. First, the evaluation design and methodology must be developed in conjunction with the program development. As each program component is designed, the evaluation for this component should also be designed. Second, there should be adequate funding for program evaluation. When funds are expended on a program, it is as important to use a portion of those funds to assess the implementation and effects of the program, as it is to use funds to actually implement the program. Only through information and data collected about a program can decisions regarding its effectiveness be made.

The underlying threads running through these policy considerations are that parent involvement is important and feasible, that parents should be involved in all aspects of parent programs, and that evaluation of parent programs needs to be given more attention and more funding.

CONCLUSIONS

Positive results from the parent involvement data have been reported across the spectrum of sponsors as well as on the national level of the FT program. Evidence of success has been accumulated from a variety of data collection procedures including descriptive, ethnographic, and inferential.

These positive findings, along with the mandate of parent involvement in the FT program, suggest a farsighted stance to be taken among decision-makers in setting funding priorities for future federal programs. Decision-makers should look at the positive results and use the information derived from these results in planning new and expanded strategies in the development of parent programs. We have learned a great deal from the Follow Through experience and it is now time to more closely examine two elements of this experience.

One element concerns the evaluation paradigm of the program and focuses on the monitoring of the parent involvement component. Assessment of the degree of implementation of this component within Follow Through has not been accomplished on a systematic basis. If a parent component is legislatively mandated in a program, then a necessary part of program evaluation is assessment of the implementation of that program component. The next step in the evaluation would be to expand the evaluation to include the study of relationships among parent involvement, child performance, and program impacts in the school, school system, and community. Different types of evaluative efforts would have to be used to accomplish this objective. Alternative methods of data collection and analysis would have to be employed in order to investigate the many diverse impacts of the parent program (e.g., family stability and juvenile delinquency).

Another element concerns funding patterns and allocations within the program. Funding should be commensurate with the emphasis put on each component of the program. For too long, parent involvement has been stressed in federal programs without any concomitant structure for a support system for implementation, research, and evaluation. In other words, we must ensure that a potentially very positive and productive abstract social policy, namely parent involvement, is supported by the necessary administrative, political, and financial backing.

A great potential exists for positively impacting upon the development of children in relation to educational outcomes and other significant variables. At least for the Follow Through models included in this chapter, we know that the framework may be developed for exploring these relationships, but it is crucial that all relevant programs be implemented using updated feedback. As stated earlier, we need to pay more attention to issues of methodology, data generation, monitoring, record keeping, and evaluation. Most importantly, we must recognize the needs of the stakeholders in this entire process by involving them in the policy development, implementation, evaluation, and research of the program. Involvement of stakeholders in all phases of the program will probably allow the program ideals to be more adequately, validly, and reliably put into practice.

FOOTNOTES

* The data presented in this chapter come from the national Follow Through Program which is now administered through the Department of Education. The opinions expressed are those of the authors.

[1] The authors wish to thank the Follow Through sponsors who provided information and data for this chapter.

[2] The description of this sponsor's approach is lengthier than the other sponsors' descriptions because the main thrust of this program was primarily implemented in the home with a concomitant larger pool of reported information on parents. This model was referred to as the "Florida Model" prior to 1977.

[3] Although there are three parent models within this FT program (Clark College Home-School Partnership Model (HSPM), Georgia State University Parent Supported Diagnostic Approach, and the University of North Carolina Parent Education Follow Through Program (PEFTP), data relating to child achievement are only reported for the PEFTP. The PEFTP functions primarily in the home and tangentially in the classroom, whereas the HSPM and the Georgia State University Supported Diagnostic Approach funntion mainly as parent programs but have stronger classroom components. Therefore, the authors feel that it is legitimate to present the child achievement data for the PEFTP only, under the assumption that these child achievement effects are directly related to the home and parent focus of the PEFTP.

References

Bank Street Follow Through Model. *Report of Follow Through parent interview project*, New York: Bank Street College of Education, 1973.

Bock, G., Stebbins, L. B., & Proper, E. C. Effects of Follow Through Models, Vol. IV-B (Report No. 76-196B). *Education as experimentation: A planned variation model* (U.S. Office of Education, Contract No. 300-75-0134). Cambridge, MA: Abt Associates, 1977.

Bradley R., & Caldwell, B. Screening the environment. *Journal of Orthopsychiatry*, 1978, *48* (1), 114–130.

Bronfenbrenner, U. *The ecology of human development: Experiments by nature and design*. Cambridge, MA: Harvard University Press, 1979.

Brookover, W. B., Schweitzer, J. H., Schneider, J. M., Beady, C. H., Flood, P. K., & Wisenbaker, J. M. Elementary school social climate and school achievement. *American Educational Research Journal*, 1978, *15*, 301–318.

Coleman, J. S., Campbell, E. Q., Hobson, C. J., McPartland, J., Mood, A., Weinfeld, F. D., & York, R. L. *Equality of educational opportunity*. Washington: U.S. Government Printing Office, 1966.

Fueyo, V., Ramp, E. A., & Bushell, D., Jr. *Evaluating parent involvement in behavior analysis model*. In P. Olmsted (Chair), Parent involvement in education: The Follow Through experience. Symposium presented at the meeting of the American Educational Research Association, San Francisco, April, 1979.

Gordon, I. J. *Parent education* (A position paper for the Education Commission of the States, Office of Education). Aspen, CO, April 1978. (a)

Gordon, I. J. *Request for proposal, 78-101* (Technical Proposal: Planning Information for Follow Through Experiments, HEW/OE, Contract No. 300-78-0458). Washington, D.C.: U.S. Office of Health, Education, and Welfare, Office of Education, Follow Through Branch, 1978. (b)

Gordon, I. J. The effects of parent involvement on schooling. In R. S. Brandt (Ed.), *Partners: Parents and schools.* Alexandria, VA: Association for Supervision and Curriculum Development, 1979.

Haney, W. *The Follow Through planned variation experiment. Vol. 5, A technical history of the national Follow Through evaluation* (Report to the U.S. Office of Education, Office of Planning, Budgeting, and Evaluation). Cambridge, MA: The Huron Institute, August 1977.

Haney, W., & Pennington, N. *Reanalysis of Follow Through parent and teacher data from spring 1975* (Report to the U.S. Office of Education). Cambridge, MA: The Huron Institute, October 1978.

Hanson, R. Consistency and stability of home environmental measures related to IQ. *Child Development*, 1975, 46, 470–480.

Hodges, W., Branden, A., Feldman, R., Follins, J., Love, J., Sheehan, R., Lumbley, J., Osborn, J., Rentfrow, R. K., Houston, J., & Lee, C. *Follow Through: Forces for change in the primary schools.* Ypsilanti, MI: High/Scope Press, 1980.

House, E. R., Glass, G. V., McLean, L. D., & Walker, D. F. No simple answer: Critique of the Follow Through evaluation. *Harvard Educational Review*, 1978, *48*, 128–160.

Jencks, C., Smith, M., Acland, A., Bane, M. J., Cohen, D., Gintes, H., Heyns, B., & Michelson, S. *Inequality: A reassessment of the effect of family and schooling in America.* New York: Basic Books, 1972.

Keeves, J. *Education environment and student achievement.* Stockholm: Almquist & Wiksell, 1972.

Marjoribanks, K. (Ed.). *Environments for learning.* Slough, NFER, 1974.

Marjoribanks, K. *Families and their learning environments.* London: Routledge & Kegan Paul, 1979.

Mayeske, G. W., Okada, T., Cohen, W., Beaton Jr., A. E., & Wisler, C. E. *A study of the achievement of our nation's students.* Washington, DC: U.S. Department of Health, Education, and Welfare, 1973.

Moreno, P. R. *Vertical diffusion effects within Black and Mexican-American families participating in Florida parent education model.* Unpublished doctoral dissertation, University of Florida, 1974.

Mosteller, F., & Moynihan, D. (Eds.). *On equality of educational opportunity.* New York: Random House, 1972.

Office of Education, Department of Health, Education, and Welfare Follow Through Program Rules and Regulations. *Federal Register, 42* (125). (June 29, 1977), 33146-33155.

Ogbu, J. *Minority education and caste: The American system in cross-cultural perspective.* New York: Academic Press, 1978.

Olmsted, P. P. An observational study of parental teaching behaviors and their relationships to child achievement. JSAS *Catalog of Selected Documents in Psychology*, August 1981.

Olmsted, P. P., Rubin, R. I. & Revicki, D. A. Assistance to local Follow Through programs, annual report (HEW/OE Grant No. G00-770-1691). JSAS *Catalog of Selected Documents in Psychology*, 1981, 11, 88 (Ms. No. 2382).

Olmsted, P. P., Rubin, R. I., Revicki, D., Stuck, G., & Wetherby, M. *Model issues for planning information for Follow Through experiments* (HEW/OE Contract No. 300-78-0458). Washington, DC: U.S. Department of Health Education, and Welfare, Office of Education, Follow Through Branch, November 1979.

Olmsted, P. P., Rubin, R. I., True, J. H., & Revicki, D. A. Parent education: The contributions of Ira J. Gordon. *Monographs of the Association for Childhood Education International*, 1980. (IBSN 0-87173-0944)

Parent Involvement Task Force. *A report on Follow Through parent involvement needs assessment*. Lawrence, KS: University of Kansas, Follow Through, Department of Human Development, December 1979.

Ramp, E., & Altman, N. *SCAN: Sponsors/sites/states, communication advisory network* (newsletter). Ypsilanti, MI, August 22, 1980.

Rubin, R. I. Parent involvement results of the six parent roles in the Parent Education Follow Through Program. JSAS *Catalog of Selected Documents in Psychology*, August 1981.

Rubin, R. I., True, J. H., & Pezzano, J. D. *Comprehensive model for child services: Parent Education Follow Through Program*. Paper presented at the annual meeting of the American Psychological Association, New York, September, 1979.

Smith, B. J. *An account of the Parent Internship Program (1976–77), Cambridge, Massachusetts Follow Through*. New York: Bank Street College of Education, 1978.

Stebbins, L. B., St. Pierre, R. G., Proper, E. C., Anderson, R. B., & Cerva, T. R. An evaluation of Follow Through, Vol. IV-A (Report No. 76-196A). *Education as experimentation: A planned variation model* (U.S. Office of Education, Contract No. 300-75-0134). Cambridge, MA: Abt Associates, 1977.

Walberg, H. J. *Educational environments and effects: Evaluation, policy and productivity*. Berkeley, CA: McCutchan, 1979.

Walberg, H. J., Schiller, D. E., & Haertel, G. D. The quiet revolution in educational research. *Phi Delta Kappan*, 1979, *61*(3), 179–182.

Ware, W. B., Organ, D., Olmsted, P. P., & Moreno, P. Vertical diffusion in a family-centered intervention program. *Childhood Education*, 1974, *51*, 111–115.

Weisberg, A. *Report on review of the parent component in Bank Street Follow Through projects*. New York: Bank Street College of Education, 1976.

Weisberg, A. *The active partnership of family and school: Bank Street Follow Through approach to parent programs*. New York: Bank Street College of Education, 1978.

Williams, T. Abilities and environments. In W. Sewell, R. E. Hauser, D. Featherman, (Eds.) *Schooling and achievement in American society*. New York: Academic Press, 1976.

Six

Parent Education and Involvement in Relation to the Schools and to Parents of School-Aged Children

HAZEL LELER

This chapter will attempt to answer the following questions: What is the research in parent education and involvement in relation to the efforts of the schools and the parents of school-aged children? What are the kinds of programs which have been studied? What are the results? Which parent education approaches appear most promising?

THREE MODELS OF PARENT INVOLVEMENT

Gordon (1977, 1978) has identified three models of parent involvement. These are: the Parent Impact Model, the School Impact Model, and the Community Impact Model. The following descriptions of these three models have been drawn largely from Gordon's work.

Parent or Family Impact Model

In this model most of the influence goes from the school to the home. The effort is "to improve the family's capabilities to provide the type of learning environment in the home that accentuates the positive elements of the cognitive and emotional factors" (Gordon, 1978, p. 4). The impetus for this model was provided by research reports such as those by Coleman et al. (1966) and Mayeske et al. (1973) that the home environment accounts for almost 50% of the variance in children's school achievement. Gordon points out that many parent involvement efforts aim toward this goal and have been accused of operating from a deficit view of the family. Gordon (1978) believes that "one who holds this view actually believes strongly in the family and in the parents' ability to learn, to grow, to accept information and use it for the family's own good" (p. 4).

The Parent Impact Model assumes that parent educators or agencies can influence roles and relationships within the family. This model is the basic one for all formal education. According to Gordon (1977), underlying this model are assumptions that there is a body of information essential for life, that teachers know and teach it, and that individuals, including parents, learn and apply it. This model assumes that the right way to rear children can be learned from books or experts, and parents who apply these learnings can be successful childrearers.

The Family Impact Model is used both among middle-class parents where a parent education group is often voluntary, self-selective, and group self-directed, with the content often based upon the parents' perceptions of need, and among lower-income parents where the parent education may be funded or connected with government agency and based upon "expert" perception of parents' needs. This model may include comprehensive services to families, such as health, dental, and mental health services, and counseling and guidance services. Thus the school may attempt to provide nonacademic services and information to families which will enable the child to come to school more able to learn.

There are a number of questions one needs to ask and answer about the Parent or Family Impact Model: How do agencies or schools know what parents want or need? How do we reconcile differing views as to what families need? Does this model promote condescension to parents, thus lowering self-esteem? Do parent educators impose their values on parents in using this model? Gordon (1977) states: "With some justification, some people feel that this strategy treats symptoms (parent–child behaviors, family transactional patterns) without attacking root causes, without clearly understanding subcultural strengths, and/or without recognizing the varieties of positive ways of childrearing" (p. 74). An additional concern of this author is that programs operating under this model are one-way, with knowledge going from teacher to parent, for the most part. The rich knowledge and experience of the parent is often ignored.

Many parent education efforts use this model. This includes some, but not all, of the following: home visit programs, group classes, Head Start parent involvement, Home Start, and Title III programs. It is essential to specify that not all of these programs use this model, because in some individual programs the influence goes both ways, from school to home and from home to school.

Although we have questions and concerns about this model, research findings as summarized in Palmer (1977) and Goodson and Hess (1975) show that such an approach can have lasting effects on the intellectual and academic performance of children.

School or Agency Impact Model

In this model, most of the influence goes from the home to the school. This model attempts to make schools and other agencies more responsive to parents. Parents may try to change the schools. The hope is that if educators and other agency workers become more attuned to, and understanding of, the family and the culture of the home, they can teach and serve the child more effectively. In this model, according to Gordon (1978), parent involvement means involvement in the classroom and school aimed at modifying the teacher and the school system. Parents serve on policy or advisory councils, committees, and boards. Comprehensive services are still important. There is parent involvement in, and even parent control of, the delivery of such services.

In the Parent Impact Model, the family learns to deal with agencies and schools as they are; in the School or Agency Impact Model, the goal of parent involvement is to change the school or agency and make it more responsive to the family as it is.

Some programs combine the Family Impact and the School Impact Models in the same project; e.g., Head Start, and to some degree Follow Through and Title I. Thus, parents learn knowledge and skills in childrearing, and also serve on the policy council to influence the program. Parents develop skill in group decision-making processes and in dealing with the power structure.

Gordon (1977) believes that the School Impact Model can lead to conflict unless both parents and educators recognize their mutual needs to learn from each other. This model also requires modifications in the education or training of agency or school personnel who need to learn new attitudes toward parents and new skills in communication, group processes, and sharing. According to Gordon, the School or Agency Impact Model may intrude heavily on the Parent Impact Model. Parents may not see the need for the parent education which professionals design, or they may see needs to change the behavior of agency or school staff, rather than their own.

This model also raises a number of questions: How do we reconcile the views of parents and the views of schools as to what families need? What happens if the school system wants parent involvement in decision-making if it enhances the school system as is, but parents want to make major modifications in the school system? What happens in a program where the parents are the learners and also the decision-makers? Some say that neither of the above models is a permanent answer but that what is needed to help the family is to change the larger systems in which the family operates.

Community Impact Model

In this model, the influence goes to and from home, school, and the larger community. This model works on the assumption that factors in the home, school, and community are all interrelated. In the process, Gordon (1978) states, all agencies change internally as well as in their relationships to each other.

In this model, there are six roles parents should play, not only to influence their own behavior, but also to influence the agencies with which they come in contact. Gordon (1978, 1979) pictures these six parent roles as spokes on a wheel with all spokes necessary. These roles include the roles of parents as: volunteer, paid employee, teacher at home, audience, decision-maker, and adult learner. In the Community Impact Model, parents must play all of these roles in order for the wheel to turn effectively.

Some of the principal examples of the Community Impact Model are comprehensive Head Start centers with parents active on policy councils, the Parent-Child Development Centers (see Chap. 4), and many of the Parent-Child Centers, as well as Gordon's Parent Education Follow Through model (see Chap. 5).

Gordon (1977) comments that the Community Impact Model may make us feel overwhelmed, like Sisyphus rolling the rock up the hill. There is so much to do. It may imply that other models should be abandoned. However, Gordon points out that much that is good and useful can be found in the variety of parent education and parent involvement efforts which have been made, and results show that the Family Impact Model works. The School Impact Model has also led to legislative and school district changes. The Community Impact Model, as used in Head Start, improved the health of many children and brought many formerly powerless people into the political mainstream. The Kirschner Report (Lazar et al., 1970) claimed that there seemed to be a relationship between the degree of parent participation in Head Start centers and the extent of centers' involvement in the institutional change process.

Gordon (1977) concludes that efforts in all three models need to continue and to be enlarged. Prospects are improved for the development and use of the Community Impact Model as well as for the continuation and strengthening of the other two models. His overriding concern was that efforts not be piecemeal, unsynthesized, small-scale, and sporadic, but that they be placed in the broader social systems context. Where possible, parent education efforts need to be tied to employment, family income, housing programs, health and medical programs, and professional education (see Chap. 13). We need to be concerned not only with "how-to" questions, but with strategic issues: Why are we doing this? How does it fit into the larger social scheme? What are our basic assumptions about people—what do they need and want, how do they learn and grow, what do we desire for them?

Levels of Involvement

Before moving into the research, it will be useful to consider three levels of parent involvement in the schools which have been described by Schickedanz (1977). She defines these levels of involvement in terms of the degree to which the involvement alters the role of the teacher as "expert" and the role of school personnel as decision-makers.

Level One, or low parent involvement, is characterized by "parental activities that do not challenge the expertise of the teacher or the decision-making power of the school" (Schickedanz, 1977, p. 332). Activities on this level include newsletters which are produced by teachers or schools to inform parents about school life and activities, parent meetings called to inform parents, individual parent conferences, and items provided by parents such as snacks or waste items (cloth scraps, for example). Level One activities keep parents out of the special territory of the teacher and the school. Parents obtain information secondhand from school personnel.

Level Two, according to Schickedanz (1977), is characterized by "parental presence and participation in the educational setting" (p. 332). Activities on this level include parent visitation and observation in the classroom and using parents as aides under the supervision of the teacher. In such roles, parents may relieve the teachers by performing clerical or housekeeping tasks, by supervising playground, art, or other classroom activities, or helping with field trips. On this level, parents are represented physically in the school and gain firsthand information about their children's school experiences. However, what goes on in the classroom is determined largely by the teacher and the school. Assistance from parents can free teachers to perform more of the educational tasks they were specifically trained to perform.

At Level Three, both teachers and parents are seen as having expertise and as decision-makers. This level, according to Schickedanz (1977), is characterized by "activities that involve parents in teaching their own children and in making decisions concerning educational policy" (p. 332). Although teachers may at first have more expertise in teaching than many of the parents, they consider it their responsibility to help parents develop expertise, too. Work is organized to decrease the differences in skill between parents and teachers, not to maintain these differences. Parents at this level may serve as volunteers in the classroom, but the duties assigned to them are not trivial. They may also be involved in workshops and meetings designed to help them learn about teaching their children. At this level, parents are members of school policy councils or governing boards. Such membership involves them in a decision-making role with school personnel, making decisions about curriculum, budget, staff, and other administrative areas. It is evident that in Level Three, the role of teacher as "expert" and the role of school as "decision-maker" are altered. The teacher is still an expert, but the expertise is no longer guarded; rather it is actively shared with parents learning to educate their children.

Referring back to the three models of parent involvement developed by Gordon (1977, 1978), we see that the first two levels of parent involvement described by Schickedanz are variations of the Family Impact Model. Level Three, the highest involvement of parents, relates to some elements of the Family and School Impact Models, but actually is more like the Community Impact Model.

In the research which follows, we will see studies in which parents play a variety of roles in elementary and secondary education. Some studies focus on a specific role, for example, the role of parents as tutors of their own children; others focus on several roles, and some focus on multiple roles.

RESEARCH IN PARENT EDUCATION AND INVOLVEMENT RELATED TO SCHOOLS

Research studies of parent involvement in public schools have increased dramatically within the last decade. What has precipitated this increase? According to McKinney (1975), one factor is the failure of urban school children to achieve in reading and mathematics at anticipated national norm levels. Extensive time, energy and resources have been spent on new programs and approaches, but there is still a lag. The blame at times has been placed on everyone involved: parents, teachers, and school officials.

Another factor which precipitated research efforts has been the work of Coleman and his colleagues (1966), mentioned previously, who reported that the home environment accounts for almost 50% of the variance in school achievement.

A third factor that has helped increase public school research has been the success with parents at preschool levels. Bronfenbrenner (1974) and others have concluded on the basis of research studies that programs involving parents have the best long-term results. School staff have tried new approaches and research studies are beginning to demonstrate effective programs.

Not all studies in the literature are included in the research reviewed below. An attempt has been made to include primarily the studies which are the most unbiased in design and methodology. The most rigorous designs are those which include random assignment to experimental and control groups. In the educational arena this is not always feasible. Studies which do not include random assignment to experimental and control groups have been included if they have other redeeming features, such as comparisons of methods or innovative treatments. The design description is included in the research summary so the reader can note the lack of a randomized assignment or other sources of bias and judge the results accordingly.

Parent or Family Impact Model

The first set of studies reviewed are based on the Parent or Family Impact Model, in which the effort is to improve the family's capabilities to provide learning environments in the home. Most of these studies concern reading because it is assumed that reading is a crucial skill for success in school as well as in occupations and everyday adult living. Others reviewed below have studied achievement and changes in school behavior, as well as several different parent education models.

Family impact studies and school achievement. Della-Piana, Stahmann, & Allen (1966) conducted a study which focused upon a parent training program in which behavior modification principles were applied to improving children's reading achievement and behavior. Parents of 40 students in the third and sixth grades with reading achievements 1 year or more below grade level agreed to participate in a reading improvement program. Students were randomly assigned to experimental and control groups; the control group received the program after the experiment was completed. Parents in the experimental group attended group training sessions and received at least two home visits in which parent–child tutoring sessions and interaction were observed. These tutoring sessions worked on reading as well as the child's home- and school-related behaviors. The program was individualized to each child's needs and school program. A pretest–posttest control group design was used. The principal finding was that experimental children gained significantly more than controls on both oral reading and comprehension.

In a widely quoted study by Smith (1968), a parental support program focusing upon the reading achievement of elementary school children from low-income, inner-city families was conducted. Children in the second and fifth grades in two elementary schools made up the experimental group and children in another "matched" school served as a comparison group. Parents of children in the experimental group attended group meetings at school in which they were instructed to establish routines at home which would model regard for learning and facilitate homework completion. Among other activities parents were asked to (1) read to their children; (2) read in the presence of their children; (3) ask questions about their children's work and praise their efforts; and (4) arrange a quiet place for homework at the same time each day. Among the findings: Experimental children made significantly greater gains in reading vocabulary over the 5-month period than their matched comparison group. Comprehension tests showed inconsistent results. Parents who were surveyed revealed overwhelmingly favorable attitudes toward the program.

According to Niedermeyer (1969), several studies have established that pupil performance may be enhanced through the use of parent-administered practice following classroom instruction. However, one of the difficulties has been to maintain a high level of parent participation beyond very short time periods. Therefore, Niedermeyer designed a study which include two treatment variables relevant to this problem: (1) school-to-home feedback where parents receive weekly teacher comments and/or pupil test scores, and (2) parent accountability, where records of competed home instruction are returned to school daily. The parent participation program developed for this study operated in Los Angeles in conjunction with the Southwest Regional Laboratory's First-Year Communication Skills Program. From a population of schools using this kindergarten reading program, one was designated as the parent participation school and two others were used to form comparison groups. Parents of 74 out of 89 kindergarten children at the parent participation school volunteered to participate by attending a 90-minute training session on conducting home practice. After training, these parents were blocked high or low on the basis of their children's score on a reading achievement test given prior to parent participation. They were then randomly assigned to one of four parent treatment conditions: (1) school-to-home feedback; (2) parent accountability; (3) both feedback and accountability; (4) neither feedback nor accountability. Thus, the study compared four treatment conditions and these groups in turn were compared to the two comparison schools. Results showed that the parent participation program promoted a high level of reading achievement, with students in the parent program school averaging 83% on the measure, compared to an average of 60% in the two comparison groups. The high levels on the evaluation measures were obtained in all parent treatment groups. No significant differences were found among the four experimental parent groups which varied in treatment on school-to-home feedback and parent accountability. One interesting finding was that pupils of the parents conducting home practice chose these home instructional activities over television viewing and school instructional activities.

A Parent Participation in Reading Program for low socioeconomic black parents and their first-grade children in Cincinnati has been described and analyzed by Crosset (1972). Experimental subjects were 63 children in three first-grade classrooms and their parents. Reading achievement scores of first-grade children from the previous year were used for comparison. Parents observed their child at school in a reading group under the guidance of a teacher for parents. They also received instruction and materials for home tutoring. Seventy percent of the parents participated actively in this program. At the end of the school year, results showed no significant differences between reading achievement scores of the 29 untreated first-grade children from the previous year and the scores of the 44 children whose parents participated actively.

Hirst (1972) conducted research to determine whether repeated sessions of reading practice within the home conducted by parent tutors would result in a significant increase in reading achievement. Eight boys and eight girls were selected at random from each of six second-grade classrooms in two elementary schools in Kentucky and were randomly divided into experimental and control groups. Four boys and four girls from each of the six classrooms were in the experimental group with four boys and four girls from each classroom in the control group, making a total of 24 boys and 24 girls (48 pupils) in each group. All were Caucasians with parents of varied socieconomic backgrounds. Mean intelligence of the pupils was 100 IQ. Parents serving as tutors gave the experimental students five, 30-minute periods of reading practice at home each week for 16 weeks. The parents were instructed at an orientation meeting to help the child read over the story he had learned at school that day one or more times. The same basal reading text was used at home as at school. The parent–tutor kept a record of oral word errors and gave specific verbal reinforcement to the student for performance. Results showed no significant differences between experimental and control students on reading and achievement tests, either on the posttest or on the delayed posttest, given after 3 months of summer vacation. However, responses to a questionnaire showed that over 95% of the parents liked the practice of helping with their child's reading, wanted to continue, and would recommend the home practice to other parents.

Another study investigating whether participation of parents as their children's tutors would affect reading achievement was conducted by Murray (1972). The parents of 26 second-graders who were having reading problems in the public schools and in a school for Army dependents in Tennessee volunteered to participate. The families included both lower- and middle-income families. Of the 26 children, 14 were randomly assigned to an experimental group and 12 to a control group. The training consisted of a 2-week comprehensive program in which parents were taught reading methods and the diagnosis of strengths and weaknesses, and were exposed to learning theories. They also observed demonstrations of children being taught. Parents then taught their children during 12, 1-hour sessions which were supervised by a professional who modeled, guided the parents, and served as a resource. Children in the experimental group made significantly greater gains on an oral reading measure than control children, but did not make significant gains on an achievement measure.

In 1972, Wise reported a study designed to explore the possibility of developing a home-based instructional model for assisting in the teaching of reading to low-income elementary school children. Working within a community-based child health agency in an inner city area of Washington, D.C., the Parent Participation Reading Clinic offered a model for providing remedial educational assistance to low-income black children through involvement of the child's parent or older sibling as a "home instructor" in the teaching process. The sample consisted of 19 experimental children in grades 2–5 and 19 "matched" controls, who participated in the study over an 8-month period. Experimental subjects were secured through voluntary enrollment of parents who chose to participate. Control subjects were obtained by selecting another child from the same class as an experimental subject, matched by sex, age, and similar scores on a test of basic skills. The classroom teacher was not informed which children were in experimental or control groups.

The parent or home instructor observed his/her child through a one-way mirror during assessment sessions, and was then given a initial task to perform with the child. An educational prescription specifying the instructional program, objectives, duration of program and followup evaluation was then signed by parent, child, and reading specialist, thus serving as a contract. The prescription called for up to 30 minutes of instruction with the child daily. Regular weekly contacts were made with the home instructor at the clinic or through home visits. Periodic home-instructor meetings were held to discuss individual problems and strategies. Instructional materials included those which emphasized phonetic rules, a programmed reading primer, readers, phonetic drill cards, word-picture games, and a booklet developed by staff entitled "Let's Make Reading a Family Affair," containing suggested materials and activities. Results showed a significant increase on a measure of words learned and on an achievement test after 6 months, but no increase on a vocabulary measure. Experimental children showed significant gains over the matched control group on an 8-month reevaluation of vocabulary and comprehension. Experimental group parents reported improvement in parent–child relationships since involvement in the project. One problem in this study was attrition, with approximately 45% of the families discontinuing the program. Multiple reasons for this existed, including moving and difficulties some parents had with the materials. The evaluation of this author is that some words and concepts in the materials were too difficult for parents of low-educational levels. A possible source of bias in this study stems from the fact that parents in the experimental group chose to participate in the program, whereas parents of control subjects did not.

According to Henry (1974), professional reading practitioners generally agree that boys comprise from 75–90% of cases referred for remedial reading, and reading is viewed by the male sex as mostly feminine. He cites child development literature indicating that children between 3 and 4 change from favoring mother to favoring father. Therefore, he designed a study in which the overall thrust is the reading role of the father and its relationship to the son's subsequent likelihood of trouble in reading. All boys in the kindergarten sections of a school in Syracuse, New York, were assigned to a father-read-to, a mother-read-to, a father-not-participating, and a control of unplanned reading group for a 6-month treatment period. The treatment was being read to by the assigned parent reader about two or three times a week. Results indicated that father-read-to boys had significantly higher mean scores on a words in context measure than the mother-read-to, the father nonparticipant, or the control boys. There were no significant differences among the group means on isolated word and letter-naming measures.

A study to assess the influence of parent participation in school on the assistance parents could give their children outside the classroom was conducted by Woods, Barnard, and TeSelle (1974). They developed a Parent Involvement Program in the Mesa, Arizona, Title I schools to help raise the consistently low reading scores of kindergarten children. A random proportional stratified sample was selected from 14 kindergarten classrooms in five of these schools. The research sample which completed criteria consisted of 39 experimental students whose parents participated in the program and 38 control students whose parents did not participate. Twice a week for the entire school year, parents attended instruction in working effectively with their children, making reading games, and teaching in the kindergarten classroom with groups of 2–4 children one day a week for about 40 minutes. Teachers worked equally with children whose parents participated and with children whose parents did not participate. Results showed that all children taught by parents in the classroom mastered letter recognition skills, whether or not their own parents participated, and both groups made significant gains in letter recognition skills with parental assistance. Results on a reading readiness test on phonemes, used only as a posttest, showed that children whose own parents attended the program learned more letter sounds than children whose own parents did not attend. This assumes, however, that both groups were equal in their pretest scores. This assumption can be questioned, in the opinion of this writer, because children whose parents attended were significantly higher on the letter recognition pretest than children whose parents did not attend, and they might well have been higher also on letter sounds.

O'Neil (1975) conducted a comparison of performance by reading disabled students when (1) parents tutored with little or no supervision, and (2) when parents tutored with continued close supervision by a reading specialist. A second comparison was made to determine if parent tutoring in either form, supervised or unsupervised, was significantly more effective when compared with a nontutored control group. The subject pool was 159 first-, second-, and third-grade children in seven elementary schools in Eugene, Oregon. Each was at least 1 year below grade level in reading. The pool was randomly assigned to one of three groups, two experimental and one control. Twenty-three parent–child tutorial teams elected to participate and completed the study. All participants in the two experimental groups tutored their own child in reading using the instructional guide, Helping a Child to Learn, for a 10-week period during the summer. Participants in Group A attended weekly instructional meetings to hear presentations regarding the program. Individualized supervision was provided both at the meetings and during the week as needed and requested by parents. Participants in Group B tutored their own child without supervision or guidance in any form other than the instruction guide. Participants in Group C served as the control group. The design used for evaluation of this study was the posttest-only control group design. The results suggested that while extensive supervision was not significantly more effective in most instances than no supervision, the supervised group demonstrated greater confidence, tutored more regularly, and worked at a faster pace, covering more materials than the unsupervised group. The supervised group showed significant differences over the control group on four decoding subskills, and the unsupervised group showed significant differences over the control group on two decoding subskills. This study demonstrated that having parents tutor their own children in reading appears to be a viable solution to the remedial needs of the reading disabled child.

Hobson (1976) reported a study to determine the effect of a summer parent-guided at-home project on the reading skills of second-graders in the Title I Program in the District of Columbia. It was hypothesized that the experimental group would demonstrate significantly higher achievement in reading skills after exposure to the project than before this exposure, and would demonstrate significantly higher achievement than a comparable group of second-grade students participating in the regular Title I Summer School. A pretest–posttest control group design was used. Both hypotheses were supported.

Three degrees of parental involvement were the focus of a study by Burnett (1977) to determine which was the most effective in enhancing the reading performance of second- and third-graders. The sample was 120 children in a Virginia public school representing a wide socioeconomic range, the majority of them Caucasian. Subjects were randomly assigned to three groups. Parents received their children's pretest scores on diagnostic, achievement, word knowledge, and comprehension measures. Two groups of parents received materials for use in the home to help their children with reading. Parents in Group I were invited to the school for meetings and received followup notes and telephone calls from the researcher. Group II parents received the same materials but no followup materials. Group III parents received no materials. After three months, posttests were administered. No significant group differences were found on any of the four measures. There were some grade by sex and treatment by grade interactions on the diagnostic measure which were significant. Females in second grade seemed to have benefited most from the treatment. Second graders in Groups I and II showed greatest growth. Males in Group II showed marked improvement over other males in word knowledge, while females in Group II showed less improvement than females in other groups. Parental attitudes toward the project were positive in general, but no differences occurred among groups. Parents found the materials appropriate and easy to use, and thought their child's reading had improved.

Gillum, Schooley, and Novak (1977) report a study of student achievement in three Michigan performance-contracting programs. The reading achievement of 600 students in grades 2–6 in three school districts was determined, using two achievement tests at the beginning and end of the school year. The performance contract for each district included a parent involvement component. Analysis of results indicated that students in the programs achieved at a significantly higher rate than was expected on the basis of national norms. There were also differences in the reading achievement scores of the three districts. District C children scored significantly higher than District A and District B children. Analysis of the contracting programs revealed the major difference existing between District C and the other districts which may have caused the difference in reading achievement was in relation to parent involvement/participation.

In District A, the parent involvement component consisted of a community information program to assure that parents understood the performance-contracting program and its implication for their children. Each school's principal was responsible for informing the community through community meetings, with at least four such meetings held during the school year. In District B, the parent component consisted mainly of an open house at the beginning of the school year. In addition, demonstrations regarding the contracting program's educational delivery system were presented at a PTA meeting. District C's performance contract stipulated that parents of participating students would receive in-service education on how they could assist their children in achieving project objectives. In-service sessions were designed so that parents and teachers could work together as a team. District C provided intensive in-service training for 40 parents who served as parent leaders. These parent leaders conducted in-service sessions for other parents who had children involved in the program. Parent in-service sessions were geared to the following areas: (1) understanding the child's educational program; (2) parents and schools working together to assist children in achieving reading objectives; and (3) parents being able to assist and reinforce the child's learning in the home. Intensive in-service education was also provided for teachers designed to improve their management of an individualized reading program. Further analysis of contracts in District C revealed that parents and teachers shared profits earned as a result of student achievement. The profits earned in Districts A and B went solely to the contractor.

Wade (1977) conducted a study to determine whether a planned program of parent education would result in improvement of the reading achievement of first-grade children. The study was conducted in a rural school district in Georgia in which the school population was 74% black and 26% white. A large portion of the participating parents were from a low socioeconomic level. The parents of 45 first-graders volunteered to take part in the program. The parents of 35 children were randomly selected from the remainder of the population. Parents took part in a series of 10, 2-hour meetings. The meetings taught parents ways they could reinforce the reading skills their children had learned in school. Parents were then asked to work 15 minutes daily with their children for approximately 24 weeks. A tutorial kit was one type of instructional material used. Parents could check out books, games, and other materials from a parent outreach center. Parent meetings were conducted by the researcher and by two college consultants. A teacher's aide set up meetings, provided transportation for parents, distributed materials to parents, and maintained contact between the school and home. School principals and first-grade teachers also cooperated and participated. The period between the pre- and posttests was a full academic year, but the treatment period was only about half the school year. Results showed no significant differences between experimental and control groups on basic skills and language measures.

Two studies have been concerned with the achievement in both reading and mathematics. McKinney (1975) reported a research project in Miami, Florida, designed to teach parents tutoring skills so they could help raise their children's achievement in reading and mathematics. The pupils and parents represented an inner-city triethnic population of blacks, whites, and Spanish-surnamed in three elementary schools. The sample was a random selection of 100 parents from a group of about 600 parents who indicated a desire to participate. The first 50 of these 600 were randomly assigned to the experimental group, and the second 50 randomly assigned to the control group. Experimental group parents attended a practicum 2 hours a week for 15 weeks, in which they were trained to tutor their children in reading and mathematics at home. Home visitations were made to observe the parents working with their children. Telephone conferences helped determine the degree of success experienced by the parents. Experimental students showed a significant increase in achievement over the students in the control group and their parents evidenced a more positive attitude toward the school.

The staff of the Exceptional Child Center at Utah State University (1976) developed a parent training model with rural Utah parents whose children had been identified as having learning problems. The parent training consisted of self-contained paper and pencil instructional packages. Administrative manuals, placement tests, and procedures had also been developed and field-tested. In the summative evaluation, 40 teachers selected a total of 150 students from 50 classes, whom the teachers identified as the lowest three in reading and/or mathematics performance in their classes. The students were in grades 2–6 in nine rural schools. Of the nine schools, five were randomly assigned to the treatment group and four to the control group. The students were pretested with an achievement test and a parent-teaching package test. Teachers then readministered the second test to determine the instructional package most appropriate for the students' skills. This test assessed 11 areas, including sound symbols, word recognition, number skills, and computations. Posttest results showed no significant findings. Procedures designed to monitor implementation indicated that the treatment was not fully implemented; for example, the telephone followup, an important treatment aspect, was conducted in less than 30% of the required cases. This study did generate a related study in which a different set of instructional packages was used with parents of severely handicapped children in rural areas. In this study, significant changes in pupil behavior and parent attitudes were observed in favor of the experimental group.

The following studies of behavior and attitude change also follow the Family Impact Model. An investigation by Duff (1972) consisted of three stages in an attempt to develop a treatment method for counseling parents of underachieving elementary school students in an economically deprived area in Los Angeles. The initial task was the development of a catalog of behaviors and strategies parents could use to enhance the school achievement of their children. The second test consisted of developing a method for approaching parents in the home. Since the field survey revealed that parents in economically deprived areas tend to avoid coming to the school, it was resolved to carry the instructional sessions into the home. Assertion training was developed to help interviewers gain entrance to the home, and a technique was devised to motivate parent involvement, using trading stamp books as rewards. The third stage consisted of an experiment in which nine behaviors believed to be most effective were taught to parents, testing whether such home intervention could result in academic achievement for the underachieving child. Eight pupils were selected from each of two fifth-grade classrooms by teachers using three criteria for underachievement, and assigned randomly to treatment and control groups, with eight in each group. All students were black. The parents of the eight treatment group pupils received home visits, consisting of two base-period interviews followed by four treatment visits. Classroom scores and teacher satisfaction were recorded before the first visit, and these two measures plus parent charting were recorded after the interviews and after the final charting. A followup interview was held 3 months after treatment completion to measure parent reaction and obtain an estimation of behaviors still in use. Results show significant gains for classroom scores in English but not in mathematics, for teacher satisfaction (homework completion only), and for six of nine behaviors charted by parents. Duff concluded that so limited a series of interventions cannot effect permanent or major changes. A full-scale program was recommended to extend throughout the school year with weekly visits, preferably at the first-grade level. This study demonstrated that parents can be taught to facilitate the school achievement of underachieving students in an economically deprived area.

The purposes of a study by Bar-Lev (1976) were to determine whether parent participation in a parent training program could increase motivation, desirable classroom behavior, and achievement in elementary age children, and whether parent training was effective for non-helping parents or only for helping parents. A list of parents of students from third to eighth grade who lived with both parents was divided into two groups: helping parents and nonhelping parents, based on teachers' evaluations. From each group 24 parents were randomly selected. Sixteen parents from each group were assigned to the experimental group (32 in all). The other 16 parents (8 helping and 8 nonhelping) were assigned to the control group. Research design was pretest–posttest control group design. A model for parental training was developed, derived from several motivational theories and from other models. Measures used were a motivation measure, school behavior scale, and an achievement test. Findings indicated that it is possible for parents to increase motivation and desirable classroom behavior in their children. It was also concluded that the parent training program was effective for both helping and nonhelping parents.

Of the 18 studies reviewed above focusing upon academic achievement of children as a result of parent involvement, 13 showed positive results on one or more variables as a result of the parent involvement; and five showed no differences between experimental and controls on any measure. None showed negative results.

Parenting gains and school achievement.   During the last decade, numerous approaches have been developed for parent groups, primarily centering on childrearing issues. It is important to cover these in this review because of their effects upon parent attitudes and practices, and child outcomes, such as classroom behavior, self-concept, and achievement.

At present there are three primary models. Each model relies on methods drawn from a conceptual framework. One model includes discussion programs built on the personality theory of Adler (1957). At first, groups following this approach based their discussions on *Children: The Challenge* by Dreikurs and Soltz (1964). Recently, a packaged program called Systematic Training for Effective Parenting (STEP), based on the ideas of Adler and Dreikurs, has been developed by Dinkmeyer and McKay (1976). This approach stresses that parents practice democratic methods in childrearing and such techniques as encouragement, rather than rewards and use of natural and logical consequences. It helps parents understand the reasons why children behave or misbehave.

A second model is based upon the nondirective interpersonal relationships concepts developed by Rogers (1951). These groups formerly used the works of Ginott (1965), but now seem more inclined to use the widely read *P.E.T.: Parent Effectiveness Training* by Thomas Gordon (1970). This approach stresses parental understanding and acceptance of children's behavior and feelings and teaches such techniques as "active listening."

A third model, based on behavioral concepts, helps parents learn how to apply the principles of behavior modification to childrearing and child-learning situations. Works by Becker (1971) and Patterson and Guillion (1971) are frequently used. Some of the research studies reviewed earlier in this chapter used behavior management techniques (see Della-Piana et al., 1966; Niedermeyer, 1969).

Seven studies are reviewed of programs based on the Adlerian model. De Laurier (1975) directed a study to investigate the effect of Adlerian parent study group participation on children's reading achievement and classroom behavior and on parents' attitudes toward childrearing. All parents of fourth graders in six schools were invited to participate in a group led by the school counselor. Parents who expressed willingness were randomly assigned to an Experimental Group or to Control Group I. Control Group II consisted of a randomized sample of parents who did not volunteer. Following attrition, there were 25 child–parent dyads in each of the three groups. Experimental group parents attended sessions using Dreikurs's (1964) book for 10 weekly sessions of 1½ hours each. Pre- and posttests were administered. No significant differences resulted in reading achievement or classroom behavior of the children, or in parental attitudes toward childrearing, although parents reacted positively to the study group.

A study by Turrall (1975) investigated the differential effects of sensitivity training with children and Adlerian Parent Study groups for their parents upon grade point averages and self-esteem of underachieving males and upon parental attitudes toward childrearing. In four Canadian secondary schools, 135 students in grades 9–11 and their parents were randomly assigned to one of four groups: (1) students exposed to 6, 2½-hour sessions of sensitivity training; (2) parents with the same amount of exposure in Adlerian Parent Group sessions; (3) students exposed to sensitivity training and parents exposed to Adlerian Parent Group sessions separately but simultaneously; and (4) control group. Each group was led by a professional group leader. Pre- and posttests with followup on students three months later were administered. Results were: (1) little or no differential effects upon grade point averages, self-esteem and parental attitudes toward childrearing as a result of sensitivity training and Adlerian Parent Group sessions; and (2) self-esteem increases significantly when fathers participate in parent training and sons participate in sensitivity training, but only on followup.

Goula's (1976) study evaluated the effect of an Adlerian Parent Study Group approach with and without a communication training component. The sample consisted of 42 volunteer mothers in a middle- to upper-middle socioeconomic area of Tucson who had children in the age range 4 to 11. Random assignment was made to two experimental groups and a control group. Mothers who attended at least five meetings and completed all measures were included in data analysis. This resulted in 10 mothers in the experimental group with communication training, 11 in the experimental group without communication training, and 10 in the control group. Measures used were a child behavior scale measuring the mothers' perception of their child's behavior and a mother–child interaction exercise, designed to measure the number of facilitating and nonfacilitating statements made by the mothers to the child. A pre-test–posttest control group design was utilized. Results indicated no significant differences among the groups in mothers' perception of their child's behavior and number of facilitating and nonfacilitating statements.

The remainder of the studies reviewed based on Adlerian concepts have used the STEP program, Systematic Training for Effective Parenting, mentioned previously. This nine-session, multimedia program blends communication skills with basic Adlerian principles; it consists of posters, tapes, reading assignments, and discussion. McKay (1976) conducted a study to assess the effectiveness of this new program. The sample involved 26 volunteer mothers from a middle- to upper-middle socioeconomic area of Tucson who had a child between 4 and 13. They were randomly assigned to the STEP Group and to a control group. Mothers who attended at least seven of the nine sessions were included in the data analysis; this resulted in 10 mothers in each group. A pre-test–posttest control group design was used. Findings: STEP was effective in changing the mothers' perceptions of their child's behavior. There were no significant differences in number of facilitating and nonfacilitating statements made by the mothers of the two groups.

Bauer (1977) focused her study on delivery systems and a comparison of STEP with the Dreikurs program. Subjects included 44 parents from one school system and 46 parents from a second school system. Intact groups with random assignment to treatment/control was used. The four groups were: (1) 31 parents in a STEP program using a didactic approach; (2) 33 parents in a STEP program using a process-oriented approach; (3) 11 parents in a Dreikurs group, and 15 parents in a control group. All three experimental groups received a 9-week treatment course which included lecture, discussion, reading assignments, and homework. Pre- and posttests were carried out, using a self-concept scale and a parental assessment of child behavior. STEP was effective, in changing parent's interactions with their children but not generally effective in changing self-concepts. The two STEP approaches and the Dreikurs program were equally effective.

Mize (1977) studied a program which combined the STEP approach with a motivation approach. Subjects were parents of 34 children from third and fourth grades of four elementary schools in a small mid-western industrial city and their parents. A pretest–posttest, randomized, two-group (control and experimental) design was employed. Parents attended a 7-week program of activities guided through three in-service training sessions for parents and teachers. Parents received instruction and guidance on how to conduct adult–child learning activities and how to apply the relevant motivational communication principles specified in the Individually Guided Motivation system and the STEP program. Parents, teachers, and children completed behavioral contracts to guide their participation in the various learning activities throughout the treatment program. Posttest analysis comparing experimental and control groups indicated that parent–teacher rapport and parental involvement in their child's learning activities significantly increased for those participating in the treatment program. The parents showed improved educational attitudes. Significant differences between experimental and control children were observed on virtually all child variables. The impact of the treatment program was evidenced by children's significantly increased levels of self-esteem, motivation to learn, improved academic attitudes, and higher levels of reading achievement.

An investigation conducted by Fain (1976) compared the effectiveness of three methods and combinations of methods in teaching two Adlerian parent skills and improving parent attitudes. The two skills focused upon were "encouraging" and "applying natural and logical consequences." The parent education methods compared were microtraining, verbal reinforcement via immediate feedback, and the more traditional Adlerian training of lecture–discussion. The subjects were 36 parents who volunteered to attend parent skill group sessions. The three treatment groups were divided into six groups of 4–8 subjects who met in eight weekly sessions of two hours each. Pretest measures were administered at the beginning of the first session for all groups and consisted of a parent attitude survey and a 5-minute taped, structured situation in which each parent role-played with a child actor. One pretest consisted of frequency data of desired behavior from this tape. The microtraining method stressed explanation, modeling, and discussion of the desired behaviors. The positive verbal reinforcement via immediate feedback method included an explanation of the desired behavior, and parents were verbally reinforced through small receivers worn in their ears. Following the instruction on each skill, another 5-minute session with a child actor was taped as a posttest of the taught skill. The second two 5-minute tapes and scores on a second parent attitude survey made up the first posttest. The parents in the traditional parent group began a group discussion after completing the pretest. The second posttest was conducted at the end of the eighth session, consisting of data from two more 5-minute taped sessions and a repeat of the parent attitude survey. Findings were: all three methods were effective in teaching the two parenting skills. No one of the three procedures was clearly superior to the others in teaching the parenting skills or improving parent attitudes.

These studies can be summarized as follows: Three studies showed no significant differences between experimental and control, one showed significant positive results, and three showed mixed results, that is, the experimental group showed positive change on some measures and not on others.

We turn now to studies of the Parent Effectiveness Training program (P.E.T.) developed by Thomas Gordon (1970). An experimental study by Uhl (1975) was devoted to the development of an economical parent education program and evaluation of its effects on parent attitudes and self-esteem and child self-esteem and achievement. Tape cassettes, class notes, and homework activities were developed to incorporate P.E.T. principles in an inexpensive program of Tape Assisted Parent Education Discussions. Subjects consisted of 14 experimental couples and 12 control couples in Chicago, randomly assigned, all parents of fifth-grade children. Experimental couples listened to tapes and discussed them in nine, 2-hour sessions. Parental attitudes of democracy, acceptance, and autonomy, along with parental self-esteem, were examined on pre- and posttests, and on a 3-month followup. Child self-esteem, reading, and mathematics were tested. Results showed that experimental parents became appreciably more democratic and encouraging of autonomy. There was only a slight increase in parental acceptance attitudes, and no change was found in parent self-esteem over the 5-month period of the experiment and followup. Experimental parents improved in their perceptions of their children's behavior. The experimental group parents were enthusiastic and positive in their evaluation of the course; 73% found it very helpful for them, and all rated it very good or excellent as a communication and problem-solving skills building course. Experimental children showed growth in self-esteem and achievement. Their self-esteem growth was not evident in post-testing but was at followup. In the 5-month period, experimental children showed 9.3 months of growth in reading achievement and 8.0 in mathematics, compared to 2.2 months' growth in reading and 5.8 in mathematics on the part of control children.

Pelkey (1976) examined attitudinal changes in both parents and teachers who participated in Parent and Teacher Effectiveness Training. The subjects, 66 elementary children, were divided into two equal groups: Group 1, students whose parents participated in Parent Effectiveness Training, and Group 2, students whose parents did not (there was no indication of whether assignment was random). Ten teachers who participated in Teacher Effectiveness Training made up a third group. Pre- and posttests were carried out. Among the findings were the following: Teachers and parents participating in effectiveness training programs showed significant changes in attitude toward children. Parents' and teachers' attitudes were correlated significantly with student self-image. Boys and girls whose parents and teachers participated in effectiveness training programs showed significant changes in self-image.

To summarize these two studies, it appears that the P.E.T. Program changes children's self-esteem and achievement, as well as parental attitudes.

Other studies of P.E.T. have compared this strategy with behavior modification. Schofield (1976) found P.E.T. a superior approach to parent training in behavior modification for raising children's self-esteem and changing parental attitudes toward childrearing. Pinsker (1977) conducted a similar study and found no significant differences in parental self-concept between experimental groups using behavior modification and P.E.T. However, deviant behaviors of children whose parents were in the behavior modification group decreased significantly but not those of children whose parents were in the P.E.T. group.

One other study combined behavior modification with other approaches. James (1974) designed a study which combined behavior management and communication skills in a parent group education program. Subjects were 102 seventh- and eighth-grade Illinois students who had been designated as socially maladjusted and underachieving on the basis of psychological reports and achievement test scores. Students formed three groups: Group A, 32 students whose parents made a commitment and participated; Group B, 26 students whose parents made a commitment but did not participate (motivated control group); and Group C, 45 students whose parents made no commitment and did not participate (nonmotivated control group). Group A attended eight, 2-hour training sessions of 2 hours each in behavior management and communication skills. Pre- and posttest measures administered to the students consisted of achievement tests, adjustment tests, sociograms, and behavioral measures. Significant differences in favor of students whose parents participated were found in relation to adjustment, family relations, acting out, and off-task behaviors, and responses in academic discussion. No significant differences were found in achievement and interpersonal relationships.

In summary, the studies of parenting groups show generally favorable results. In fact, 8 of 12 studies showed at least some positive effects on achievement on parenting skills or attitudes. Combined with the 18 studies of the Family Impact Model and school achievement reviewed in the previous section, we find that 21 of 30 studies revealed positive effects on one or more outcomes, and 9 showed no differences between experimental and control groups. None had significant negative results. The approaches which seem most promising are those in which parents are trained in home instruction with their children and approaches focusing on communications, such as Parent Effectiveness Training.

School Impact Model

There have been no experimental studies which followed the School Impact Model. There are, however, three studies which surveyed the situation as it actually exists in relation to the inclusion of parents in decision-making roles, and several additional studies on the attitudes of parents, teachers, and others toward parent participation in the schools.

Heck (1977) studied parent participation in policy formation in California elementary schools. About half of California elementary schools have parent participation groups called School Advisory Committees, set up in response to federal and state requirements. Questionnaires were sent to a random sample of 285 California elementary schools. The study found that most School Advisory Committee time is spent on planning and evaluation activities required by the state and on activities affecting learning. Least time is spent on clerical tasks. Committee members perceive that they have influence on activities required or supported by state and federal agencies, but less influence on matters for which already established procedures exist within the schools. Factors most related to perceived influence include the openness of the principal to the committee and the role defined for a committee with a school. Conclusions made include the following: (1) what a committee does bears directly upon its perceived influence; (2) the posture of the principal toward the committee is critical in determining a committee's influence; (3) the ability of a committee to circumscribe and specify its role enhances its perceived influence; and (4) support from outside the school encourages influence. In brief, a committee perceives influence when it has support from outside the school (government), when it has support from within the school (principal), and when it devotes itself to specific and limited tasks.

A study seeking to determine the nature and extent of Title I parent council member participation in the planning, developing, operating, and evaluation of Title I programs was conducted by Dawson (1977). A questionnaire was administered to 99 Title I parent council members in a New Jersey county. Among the findings: Title I parent council members vary both in the types of decisions they make and in participation rates. Parents play a limited role in decision-making activities of all kinds but have the most input on program evaluation and preparation of the Title I application. Urban and suburban council members have more input than rural members; members of higher socioeconomic status occupy the key positions on advisory councils. Many members do not participate in council meetings because there are not enough Title I funds allocated for babysitting and transportation, though both are required by Title I regulations. Most members do not want full official responsibility for planning, developing, operating, and evaluating the Title I program. However, they desire greater responsibility than they presently have.

Novak (1975) conducted an exploratory study to investigate parent representativeness and factors affecting the participation of lower socioeconomic group members on school advisory councils in a Florida city. Information was obtained from most of the 195 active parent members on the city's 20 school advisory councils. Among the findings: Lower socioeconomic group parents were not on the majority of councils and were proportionally underrepresented on those councils in which they were present. The school's location and percent of lower socioeconomic group student were significant factors in parent recruitment. Moreover, information from interviews with school staff and council chairpersons revealed that councils were dependent on the principal for their functioning.

Seven studies focused on attitudes toward parent and citizen participation in schools held by parents, teachers, administrators, and school board members. A study by Dromisky (1974) attempted to determine whether there is a significant difference in attitudes toward school revealed by teachers, parents, and students in schools with and without parental involvement in curriculum development. In four Florida counties, seven elementary and middle schools with parental decision-making involvement in curriculum development were studied. Some of the findings from an analysis of teacher, parent, and student responses were: (1) responses from parents indicated significantly more favorable attitudes toward school among parents from involved schools; (2) the teacher group from noninvolved schools revealed significantly more favorable attitudes toward the principal; (3) the teacher group from involved schools revealed significantly more favorable attitudes toward the community; (4) the student group from involved schools revealed significantly more favorable attitudes towards teachers; and (5) the parent groups revealed no significant difference in attitudes toward participation. The authors reached several conclusions and recommendations: In schools where parents are frequently and meaningfully involved, parents, educators, and students become more knowledgeable and understanding of each other, the school, and the home. Parents can become a part of the curriculum planning team and can supplement the instructional program. Public confidence in schools is more readily gained through meaningful home–school relationships. School boards should establish policies and practices that will nurture home, school and community interrelationships, and legislatures should provide financial support and consultative services.

Dickson (1976) compared the attitudes of teachers and parents of children involved in the early childhood programs in a California county about parent participation programs in public schools, and further compared the attitudes of parents participating in the program with nonparticipating parents. Ten schools that were 1-year participants in a state-funded early childhood education program were surveyed. From a survey of teachers, participating parents, and nonparticipating parents, some of the conclusions were as follows: (1) teachers and parents differed in their selection of appropriate duties for classroom aides with teachers more inclined to select tutorial duties in addition to clerical duties, whereas parents selected clerical duties more often; (2) teachers and parents differed in opinions on the amount of decision-making power appropriate for advisory committees with parents approving of greater power for parents in decision-making; (3) participating and nonparticipating parents differed in their selection of appropriate duties for classroom aides with participating parents selecting tutorial tasks more often than nonparticipating parents; (4) participating and nonparticipating parents did not differ in the amount of decision-making power appropriate for advisory committees; and (5) teachers, participating parents, and nonparticipating parents did not differ in their judgment of the success of the parent participation program in their schools.

Hightower (1977) analyzed the perceptions of Title I coordinators and parent advisory council members regarding ideal and actual levels of parent involvement in educational decision-making. Information was received from 63 of 75 school district Title I coordinators and 49 of 320 parent advisory council members included in the survey. No overall differences were found between ideal and actual levels of parent involvement. However, there was a significant difference between ideal and actual mean scores of coordinators in the area of community involvement and in scores of parents in the area of management and budget. In each case the ideal mean was significantly higher than the actual mean. Additionally, a significant difference existed between the perceptions of coordinators and parents in relation to the ideal level of parent involvement in the area of management and budget. The major conclusion drawn from the study was that, although there were several instances of significant differences between perceptions of parents and coordinators, neither group saw ideal involvement exceeding the level of "making suggestions."

A study of the literature by Whitaker (1977) revealed general agreement on the importance of citizen involvement in educational decision-making, but disagreement among administrators, teachers, school boards, and citizens on specific involvement. A citizen participation inventory was administered to 1,200 parents and 348 administrators in Atlanta. The inventory solicited demographic data, responses to roles of citizens in making decisions in 79 selected tasks, and requested information about the extent and amount of participation, barriers to effective participation, and means to encourage effective participation. The 697 parents who responded were predominantly black mothers with high school education or less and yearly incomes of less than $10,000. The 284 administrators who responded were predominantly black males with 14 years or less of administrative experience, most with education beyond the master's degree. Parents generally perceived no active role for citizens in educational decision-making. Only middle school parents perceived active roles for citizens in school–community relations. Administrators perceived a more active role for citizens. This was true in areas traditionally perceived as exclusively or predominantly duties of administrators (e.g., evaluating the principal, deciding on textbooks) as well as those in which citizens might get involved (e.g., planning school events, developing parent involvement programs). Parents felt that citizens had little influence or policies and decisions, but administrators felt that citizens had some influence. Administrators perceived community apathy to be the major barrier to effective participation, whereas parents saw difficulty in getting information about school policies and issues as the major barrier. The researcher recommended that administrators need additional training to assist them in developing school–community programs.

Berreen (1976) sought to compare the perceptions of parents and principals in Catholic elementary schools in two New York Counties in relation to parental involvement. Data from 37 principals and 402 parents were secured. Some of the conclusions of the study: (1) There was little or no opportunity for parents to be involved in decision-making. This was seen as an area of latent conflict between parents and principals; (2) Opportunities for parental involvement in implementation did exist, especially in program development, school finance, and public relations; (3) There was no real parental involvement in decision making and implementation, and therefore no true home–school partnership existed; (4) Both parents and principals believed that parents ought to become more involved in these areas; (5) The more administrative experience a principal had, the more likely he was to perceive decision-making as an area to be kept primarily in the hand of professional educators; (6) The more active a parent was in the local home–school association the more involved she was in decision-making; and (7) In-service training is needed by principals in parental involvement.

A study comparing the attitudes of school administrators, secondary school principals, and school board members toward the involvement of teachers, parents, and students in decision-making was carried out by Capie (1977). Completed response forms to a questionnaire were received from at least one member of each of the subject groups from 112 school districts in New York State, or 75% of the sample—150 randomly selected school districts, excluding New York City. Perhaps the most important finding of this study was that whereas mean attitude scores of all subject groups revealed positive attitudes toward the involvement of teachers, parents, and students, school board members believed in significantly less involvement than did administrators and secondary school principals.

Lucas and Lusthaus (1978) point out that interest in school–community relations has intensified. There are differences between the extent and quality of school involvement at the elementary and secondary school levels. Typical reports indicate that mothers of children in grades 1–6 are most active, but PTAs have difficulties in maintaining junior and senior high school units. Parents seem discouraged by the greater organizational specialization and complexity of the secondary school, and by the fact that secondary school youth are often more independent. Lucas and Lusthaus designed a study to investigate the perceptions of elementary- and secondary-school parents in relation to their present and desired levels of decision-making, their satisfaction in this area, and their feelings of being able to effect change in their community and schools. The study setting was an urban school district in Canada. A random selection of parents was surveyed. Responses were received from 47% of 549 parents surveyed. Of this number, 89 were parents of elementary school pupils, 76 were parents of secondary school pupils, and 92 had children in both. Only the first two groups were compared. Parents were asked their decision-making role in relation to 14 situations including selection of tests, disciplinary procedures, instructional methods, subject areas, and budget. Among the results: Elementary parents indicated significantly more overall participation in the 14 decisionary situations than did secondary parents. There was no significant difference between the two groups of parents in their overall scores in relation to their desired level of decisional participation. However, both groups of parents were dissatisfied with their present levels of decisional participation. Contrary to expectations, the two groups did not differ significantly in their perceptions of the welcome extended by their schools, nor did they differ in feelings about being able to change their schools and community. These results have questioned previous assumptions of declining parental interest in the schools as children grow older.

From the above studies of parent involvement in decision-making, there is substantial evidence that parents, teachers, principals, higher administrators, and school board members desire greater participation of parents in decision making or more impact of parents in the schools. Although this is a difficult area for experimental research, more studies should be attempted.

Community Impact Model

The most intensive efforts in parent involvement in public schools following the Community Impact Model have been in Follow Through (FT) programs, especially in the parent education Follow Through program (see Chap. 5). This program, developed by Ira Gordon and associates (1974) is an especially intensive effort, with parents playing all six of the roles outlined by Gordon (see Gordon et al., 1974, p. 5). This program has had positive results in relation to children's achievement and other outcomes. No attempt will be made to describe this community impact program further or to describe any of the other FT parent education efforts since they are reviewed in Chapter Five by Olmsted and Rubin.

Two other research programs have followed the Community Impact Model. McConnell (1976, 1979) describes a program established to provide bilingual multicultural education to children, preschool through third grade, of migrant and seasonal farm workers. This program was started in 1971. It has been called "Training Migrant Paraprofessionals in Bilingual Mini Head Start," but in 1978, the title was changed to "Individualized Bilingual Instruction" (IBI) because of efforts to make the program more applicable for adoption at other sites. A year-round program is operated at two sites in Washington State and one site in Texas. The Texas site is also the origin of the families who move in the migrant stream north from Texas. This site operates a mobile component in which staff provide continuing services to migrant families and children. The children who move with their families in the migrant streams are called "continuity children." The mobile component normally follows from 60 to 80 children. Over 90% of the families served in the program have been Mexican or Mexican-American. In 1978, 46% of the children served were monolingual Spanish speakers, 26% were Spanish-dominant bilingual speakers, and 27% were "primary language English" speakers. The teaching staff is composed entirely of adults from the target population. The project employs paraprofessionals (previously untrained and inexperienced bilingual adults) backed up by certified staff who work as supervisors and trainers. By working cooperatively with the public schools which the children attend, the mobile project staff arranges to work with the children on released time from their regular classes or after school, providing supplementary education in mathematics, reading, bilingual skills, and cultural concepts and activities, as nearly as possible year-round to a moving population.

Families and community members participate in program management and decision-making. There is an organized parent/community advisory group at each of the three sites. In the Washington sites, all parents of children enrolled in the program are members. In the Texas site, the parents' group incorporated so it could apply for grant funds for related programs and elected a five-member board. General parent meetings are held frequently. The parents are active in decision-making at each site in the following policy making areas specified in project goals: (1) organizational matters (voting for officers, etc.); (2) input into and review of proposals; (3) personnel actions (the board of the administrative school district has final hiring authority, but personnel recommendations by a committee of parents and staff have always been honored); (4) use of funds (parent groups have the sole authority over the use of funds earned through voucher payments for volunteer services); (5) discussion of educational program; and (6) evaluation of progress. During the year covered in the 1976 report, in two of the three sites parents participated in all six of the policy-making areas above, and in the third, all but evaluation. Family members participated in the children's educational program by acting as teachers or teaching assistants, assisting with cultural heritage activities, participating in parent–child educational games, or providing support services such as making or repairing equipment. Altogether, in the year of the 1976 report, 195 family members helped the program in one of the four ways specified. The staff reported to parent/community groups. Staff members attended each parent meeting, and made presentations about various aspects of the program. In the 1976 report, every goal in relation to parent and community involvement was met. Parents served in all six of the roles specified by Gordon (1978, 1979).

Research findings on the children's achievement revealed increases in mathematics and in reading. Achievement of kindergarten continuity children is more than twice as high in mathematics and reading when compared with another group from a Texas community which is also Spanish dominant, has the same socioeconomic level, and also migrates. Of the project children, 83% improved their bilingual capability. Project children were significantly superior to comparison children on a test of cultural concepts.

In the 1977–78 program year, the achievement of the IBI children in the two Washington sites was compared to a national norm group and to a project norm group, the expected level of achievement project children would have had without the bilingual program. At age 7, the achievement of IBI children in mathematics was markedly higher than the project norm group. It was also above the national norms at age 7, but slightly below at age 8. At all age levels, IBI children, whose primary language was Spanish and who attended at least 200 days, had a superiority in reading achievement to the project norm group statistically significant beyond the .001 level. The scores of IBI children were somewhat below national norms, but came closer to the norms as the children got older. On a test measuring knowledge of U.S. and Mexican cultures, IBI children showed a superiority over the project norm group which was statistically significant. The IBI continuity children, in the 1977–78 program year, showed a small superiority in Spanish and a great superiority in English to the comparison group, with the gap widening at every grade level. At every grade level, IBI continuity children were superior to the comparison group in both reading and mathematics beyond the .001 level of significance. They were also within the average range of national norms. Almost all of the goals set for this community program have been met or exceeded.

Gross, Ridgley, and Gross (1974) planned and implemented a comprehensive development program for the staff, parents, and community at an inner-city Washington, D.C., elementary school serving a disadvantaged, segregated student population. The program included a variety of activities, workshops, group efforts, and meetings, which encouraged participation in the educational process. Parental involvement, student activities, community development, and in-service programs for the staff were developed and implemented.

Parental involvement in the school was increased, and a parent corps was organized. Parents provided the following services: holding classes while teachers attended workshops; helping prepare scenery for plays; tutoring individual students and small groups; correcting papers; chaperoning field trips; and assisting in the lunchroom. An attempt was made to secure one room parent for each classroom. These room parents helped with a PTA membership drive. Two parent discussions were held during the school year to discuss a decentralization plan for district schools. A two-day open house was held during American Education Week during which parents observed and participated in mini-workshops. An after-school parental program and workshop was held for 12 weeks to equip parents with simple teaching techniques for helping their children in grades 4–6. Each group of parents attended a two-week session twice a week by grade levels; during the last two weeks, a culminating activity was held during which each parent demonstrated a technique learned, using his/her child in the session. A total of 34 parents participated in this workshop. An alternative strategy was a mini-workshop to give help to parents and teachers in the construction of materials and instructional aids. Adults were also recruited for continuing education classes leading to better jobs, self-improvement, and helping children at home. A total of 173 adults responded to these classes. The usual high school continuing education classes were held and new courses (such as Health and Family Learning, and Consumer Education) were offered. Extended evening counseling services for parents were offered two days per week for hard-to-reach parents.

Activities for teachers included monthly discussions on such professional topics as report cards, individualizing instruction, media, tests, and parent–teacher sharing. Teachers were given time to observe classrooms and travel for professional growth. Teachers also had workshops and in-service training in such areas as behavior management, cooperative action, and communication skills. New or improved activities for students included a peer tutoring program; an improved student council; interest grous in such areas as newspaper, drama, and creative arts; safety patrols; and skill development in leadership, interests, and service. Award assemblies recognized academic excellence, citizenship, and attendance.

Evaluation of these efforts showed the following results: The number of parents receiving credit toward a high school diploma or General Education Development certificate, the number of persons referred for community services, and the number of parents involved in the total school program all increased. The average daily participation of parents increased from 17.3 to 57.6. Adults improved buying habits and family budgeting and took instruction in income tax preparation. Teachers enrolled in more classes for professional development and implemented ideas from staff development workshops. The achievement of students in mathematics and reading was elevated. More parents joined the PTA and attended open houses. Conclusions were that the combining of human efforts made significant differences in the lives of students, school staff, parents, and community persons; created more positive attitudes on the part of students, teachers, and parents toward school goals; and improved interpersonal skills of the staff and community.

The two studies described above and the Parent Education FT Program show positive results for those programs following a Community Impact Model. All of these studies obtained data on parents involvement and outcomes at the elementary school level, but the Washington, D.C., program also involved adult education and high school activities. These two studies point the way to the possibilities and potential values of intensive parent involvement in public schools.

RELATED CONCERNS

A number of the studies reviewed above point to the key role of the principal in relation to parent involvement. For example, Novak (1975) pointed out that parent advisory council were dependent upon the principal for their functioning. In the studies reporting the attitudes of teachers and principals toward parent participation, there is a shift from attitudes in previous years. There is an obvious need for principals and teachers to receive more training in this area, both pre-service and in-service (Berreen, 1976; Whitaker, 1977). both point out the need for more training for principals.

A study by Windle (1977) points up the role of the principal and the teachers related to the level of parent participation in a school. The purpose of his study was to identify the relationship between various components of parent participation programs and early childhood education program effectiveness as perceived by principals, teachers, paraprofessionals, and parents, to analyze these relationships through case studies, and to present recommendations for the improvement of parent participation programs in early childhood education schools throughout California. Windle conducted 100 structured interviews with principals and early childhood education staff of ten selected schools in eight districts in Los Angeles County. Selected findings and conclusions were: (1) the principal's communication skills and enthusiasm are the most important competencies and characteristics for effective work with parents; (2) the involvement of parents in the evaluation of a program contributed heavily to its effectiveness; (3) parent assistance in subject areas of reading, mathematics, and language contributed to program effectiveness; and (4) parents who volunteered their time and talent without pay contributed more to program effectiveness than parents who were compensated.

Based on these findings and conclusions Windle (1977) recommended: (1) improving management competencies and skills of administrators in working with parents through more effective professional development projects; (2) improving human resource management skills of teachers for more effective utilization of volunteer parents in the program; (3) increasing parents' assistance in more curriculum subject areas through in-service training; (4) increasing the number of parent paraprofessionals and volunteers in the early childhood programs in all schools statewide; and (5) encouraging colleges, universities, and teaching training institutions all over California to provide training for prospective teachers on the utilization of parents as instructional aides and volunteers. The findings of this study indicate that one of the crucial needs is for more training of school personnel in the area of parent education and involvement.

CONCLUSIONS

The research studies summarized in this chapter seem to indicate that the fuller the participation of parents, the more effective were the results obtained. Of the 30 Parent Impact Model studies, 70% had positive results on one or more variables or outcomes. All of the Community Impact Model studies, including the Parent Education Follow Through program, had positive outcomes.

One can often see why some of the studies reviewed above failed to find significant program effects. For example, in the Hirst study the pupils were already achieving at grade level. In the Utah study, the treatment was not fully implemented. Furthermore, it has been the experience of this author that materials frequently contain terms or educational jargon which parents with low educational levels cannot understand.

The approaches which seem to have the most potential are those in which the parents have a definite role in the decision-making. Other approaches with potential are those which expose the parents to a somewhat structured program of training. These include programs in which parents receive training in tutoring their children or in programs which follow a planned sequence, such as Parent Effectiveness Training.

Many of the studies reviewed in this chapter are doctoral dissertations. This means that they were usually short-term studies with no longitudinal followup. The Parent Education FT program and the Individualized Bilingual Instruction program are two major exceptions. More long-term longitudinal studies are needed so that we can evaluate various approaches in terms of long-term goals. This is essential, especially with low-income populations, in an effort to bridge the gap between the achievement of these children and more advantaged children.

In conclusion, the review indicates that the preponderance of research shows the effectiveness of parent education and involvement. Now we need to work out effective long-term strategies.

REFERENCES

Adler, A. *Understanding human nature*. New York: Premier Books, 1957.

Bar-Lev, Y. The effectiveness of parent training programs on their children's motivation, classroom behavior, and achievement (Doctoral dissertation, Arizona State University, 1976). *Dissertation Abstracts International*, 1976, *37*, 2521A-2522A.

Bauer, M. T. A study of the effects of a group education program, systematic training for effective parenting, upon parental self-concept and assessment of behavior (Doctoral dissertation, College of William and Mary in Virginia, 1977). *Dissertation Abstracts International*, 1978, *38*, 4511A. (University Microfilms No. 7731783)

Becker, W. C. *Parents are teachers: A child management program*. Champaign, IL: Research Press, 1971.

Berreen, V. C. F. Administrators' and parents' perceptions of real and ideal parental involvement in selected Catholic Westchester and Putnam elementary schools of the Archdiocese of New York (Doctoral dissertation, Fordham University, 1976). *Dissertation Abstracts International*, 1976, *37*, 2522A-2523A. (University Microfilms No. 76-25, 758)

Bronfenbrenner, U. Is early intervention effective? Volume II of *A report on longitudinal evaluatios of preschool programs*. Washington, DC: DHEW Publication No. (OHD) 74–25, 1974.

Burnett, N. C. The design, implementation and evaluation of a program for involving parents of second and third grade students in the teaching of reading (Doctoral dissertation, Catholic University of America, 1977). *Dissertation Abstracts International*, 1977, *38*, 87A-88A.

Capie, R. M. A study of the attitudes and opinions of administrators and board members with respect to the involvement of teachers, parents, and students in decision-making (Doctoral dissertation, St. John's University, 1977). *Dissertation Abstracts International*, 1977, *38*, 560-561A. (University Microfilms No. 77–17, 746)

Coleman, J. S., Campbell, E. Q., Hobson, C. J., McPartland, J., Mood, A. M., Weinfeld, F. D., & York, R. L. *Equality of educational opportunity*. Washington, DC: U.S. Government Printing Office, 1966.

Crosset, R. J. The extent and effect of parents' participation in their children's beginning reading program: An inner-city project (Doctoral dissertation, University of Cincinnati, 1972). *Dissertation Abstracts International*, 1973, *33*, 3148A. (University Microfilms No. 72–31, 922)

Dawson, R. J., Jr. A study of Title I Parent Council member participation in selected Title I programs (Doctoral dissertation, Rutgers University, 1977). *Dissertation Abstracts International*, 1978, *38*, 6965A-6966A. (University Microfilms No. 7804590)

DeLaurier, A. M. N. An investigation of the effect of Adlerian parent study groups upon children's reading achievement (Doctoral dissertation, University of Oregon, 1975). *Dissertation Abstracts International*, 1976, *36*, 4254A. (University Microfilms No. 76-920)

Della-Piana, G., Stahmann, R. F., & Allen, J. E. *The influence of parental attitudes and child–parent interaction upon remedial reading progress.* (Report No. CRPs-266-1). Salt Lake City, UT: Cooperative Research Program of the Office of Education, 1966. (ERIC Document Reproduction Service No. ED 012 689)

Dickson, S. S. A study of the views of teachers and the views of parents toward parent participation in public schools (Doctoral dissertation, University of Illinois at Urbana-Champaign, 1976). *Dissertation Abstracts International*, 1976, *37*, 121A. (University Microfilms No. 76-16, 120)

Dinkmeyer, D., & McKay, G. D. *Systematic training for effective parenting*. Circle Pines, MN: American Guidance Service, 1976.

Dreikurs, R., & Soltz, V. *Children: The challenge*. New York: Hawthorn, 1964.

Dromisky, S. P. Parent, student, teacher attitudes toward school in schools with and without parental involvement in curriculum development (Doctoral dissertation, University of Florida, 1974). *Dissertation Abstracts International*, 1976, *36*, 680A–68aA. (University Microfilms No. 75–16, 376)

Duff, W. A. Counseling disadvantaged parents in the home: Measuring change in parent behavior and its effect upon the child's scholastic achievement (Doctoral dissertation, University of California, Los Angeles, 1972). *Dissertation Abstracts International*, 1972, *33*, 1432A. (University Microfilms No. 72-25, 767)

Fain, C. A. A comparison of the effectiveness of micro-training, positive verbal reinforcement via immediate feedback, and traditional parent skill groups in teaching specific parent skills and improving parent attitudes (Doctoral dissertation, North Texas State University, 1976). *Dissertation Abstracts International*, 1976, *37*, 3416A-3417A. (University Microfilms No. 76-29, 135)

Gillum, R. M., Schooley, D. E., & Novak, P. D. *The effects of parental involvement on student achievement in three Michigan Performance Contracting Programs.* Paper presented at the annual meeting of the American Educational Research Association, New York City, April 1977. (ERIC Document Reproduction Service No. ED 144 007)

Ginott, H. *Between parent and child*. New York: MacMillan, 1965.

Goodson, B. D., & Hess, R. D. *Parents as teachers of very young children: An evaluative review of some contemporary concepts and programs.* Washington, DC: Bureau of Educational Personnel Development, Office of Education, 1975. (ERIC Document Reproduction Service No. ED 136 967)

Gordon, I. J. Parent education and parent involvement: Retrospect and prospect. *Childhood Education,* 1977, *54,* 71–79.

Gordon, I. J. *What does research say about the effects of parent involvement on schooling?* Occasional papers, School of Education, University of North Carolina, Chapel Hill, 1978.

Gordon, I. J., Greenwood, G. E., Ware, W. B., & Olmsted, P. P. *The Florida Parent Education Follow Through Program.* Gainesville, FL: Institute for Development of Human Resources, University of Florida and the Florida Educational Research and Development Council, 1974.

Gordon, I. J., Olmsted, P. P., Rubin, R. I., & True, J. H. How has Follow Through promoted parent involvement? *Young Children,* 1979, *34*(5), 49–53.

Gordon, T. *P.E.T.: Parent effectiveness training.* New York: Wyden, 1970.

Goula, J. R. The effect of Adlerian parent study groups with and without communication training on the behavior of parents and children (Doctoral dissertation, University of Arizona, 1976). *Dissertation Abstracts International,* 1976, *37,* 1985A-1986A. (University Microfilms No. 76-22,473)

Gross, M. J., Ridgley, E. M., & Gross, A. E. *Combined human efforts in elevating achievement at the Wheatley School,* Washington, DC, (Ed.D. Practicum, Nova University) 1974. (ERIC Document Reproduction Service No. ED 102 666)

Heck, S. Perceived outcomes and concurrent conditions of parent participation in school policy-making (Doctoral dissertation, Stanford University, 1977). *Dissertation Abstracts International,* 1978, *38,* 5384A-5385A. (University Microfilms No. 7802169)

Henry, B. Father to son reading: Its effect on boys' reading achievement (Doctoral dissertation, Syracuse University, 1974). *Dissertation Abstracts International,* 1975, *36,* 41A-42A. (University Microfilms, No. 75-13, 990)

Hightower, H. H. Perceptions of ideal and actual parent involvement in educational decision-making (Doctoral dissertation, Arizona State University, 1977). *Dissertation Abstracts International,* 1978, *38,* 4480A. (University Microfilms No. 77-32,414)

Hirst, L. T. An investigation of the effects of daily, thirty-minute home practice sessions upon reading achievement with second year elementary pupils (Doctoral dissertation, University of Kentucky, 1972). *Dissertation Abstracts International,* 1973, *34,* 1001A. (University Microfilms No. 73-20, 591)

Hobson, P. J. W. Structured parental involvement: An analysis of a Title I summer parent guided AT-HOME Project (Doctoral dissertation, George Washington University, 1976). *Dissertation Abstracts International, 1977, 37,* 5489A. (University Microfilms No. 77-6,000)

James, R. K. A study of the effects of parent participation in a parent group education program on seventh and eighth grade underachieving, socially maladjusted students (Doctoral dissertation, Indiana State University, 1974). *Dissertation Abstracts International,* 1976, *36,* 4263A. (University Microfilms No. 75-29,895)

Lazar, I., Anchel, G., Gethard, E., Lazar, J., & Sale, J. *A national survey of the Parent-Child Center Program* (The Kirschner Report). Prepared for Project Head Start, Office of Child Development, U.S. Department of Health, Education and Welfare, by Kirschner Associates, New York, 1970.

Lucas, B. G., & Lusthaus, C. S. The decisional participation of parents in elementary and secondary schools. *The High School Journal*, February, 1978, *61*(5), 211–220.

Mayeske, G. W., Okada, T., Cohen, W. M., Beaton, A., Jr., & Wisler, C. E. *A study of the achievement of our nation's students*. Washington, DC: U.S. Government Printing Office, 1973.

McConnell, B. *Bilingual mini-school tutoring project. A State of Washington URRD (Urban, Rural, Racial, Disadvantaged) Program. Final evaluation, 1975–76 Program Year*. Olympia: Washington Office of the State Superintendent of Public Instruction, 1976. (ERIC Reproduction Service No. ED 135 508)

McConnell, B. *Individualized Bilingual Instruction*. Final evaluation, 1977–78 Program Year. Report to the U.S. Office of Education, Division of Bilingual Education. Pullman, WA: Evaluation Office, 1979.

McKay, G. D. Systematic Training for Effective Parenting: Effects of behavior change of parents and children (Doctoral dissertation, University of Arizona, 1976). *Dissertation Abstracts International*, 1976, *37*, 3423A-3424A. (University Microfilms No. 76-28, 215)

McKinney, J. A. *The development and implementation of a tutorial program for parents to improve the reading and mathematics achievement of their children* (Ed.D. Practicum, Nova University, 1975). (ERIC Document Reproduction Service No. ED 113 703)

Mize, G. K. The influence of increased parental involvement in the educational process of their children (Doctoral dissertation, University of Wisconsin–Madison, 1977). *Dissertation Abstracts International*, 1978, *38*, 6018A. (University Microfilms No. 7717747)

Murray, B. B. *Individualized amelioration of learning disability through parent helper-pupil involvement. Final report*. Clarksville, TN: Austin Peay State University, 1972. (ERIC Document Reproduction Service No. ED 068 497)

Niedermeyer, F. C. Effects of school-to-home feedback and parent accountability on kindergarten reading performance, parent participation, and pupil attitude (Doctoral dissertation, University of California, Los Angeles, 1969). *Dissertation Abstracts International*, 1970, *30*, 3198A. (University Microfilms No. 70-2240)

Novak, J. M. An investigation of parent representativeness and factors affecting the participation of lower socioeconomic group members on school advisory councils in a North Florida city (Doctoral dissertation, The University of Florida, 1975). *Dissertation Abstracts International*, 1976, *36*, 7825A. (University Microfilms No. 76-12,102)

Olmsted, P. P., & Rubin, R. I. *Parent involvement: Perspectives from the Follow Through experience*. Paper presented for Conference on Parent Education and Public Policy. Chapel Hill, NC: Parent Education Follow Through Project, School of Education, University of North Carolina at Chapel Hill, March 1980.

O'Neil, A. L. An investigation of parent tutorial intervention as a means of improving reading skills in the primary age child (Doctoral dissertation, University of Oregon, 1975). *Dissertation Abstracts International*, 1976, *37*, 124A-125A. (University Microfilms No. 76–15, 050)

Palmer, F. H. *The effects of early childhood intervention*. Paper presented at the annual meeting of the American Association for the Advancement of Science, Denver, 1977.

Patterson, G. R., & Gullion, E. M. *Living with children: New methods for parents and teachers*. Champaign, IL: Research Press, 1971.

Pelkey, G. F. The effect of Parent Effectiveness Training and Teacher Effectiveness Training on student self-image (Doctoral dissertation, University of California, 1976). *Dissertation Abstracts International*, 1977, *37*, 5590A.

Pinsker, M. A. A comparison of Parent Effectiveness Training and Behavior Modification Parent Training groups on behavior change in target children: self-concept, family interaction and patterns of behavior change (Doctoral dissertation, College of William and Mary in Virginia, 1977). *Dissertation Abstracts International*, 1978, *38*, 4694A-4695A. (University Microfilms No. 7731781)

Rogers, C. *Client-centered therapy*. Boston: Houghton Mifflin, 1951.

Schickedanz, J. A. Parents, teachers, and early education. In B. Persky & L. Colubcheck (Eds.), *Early Childhood*. Wayne, NJ: Avery Publishing Group, 1977.

Schofield, R. G. A comparison of two parent education programs: Parent effectiveness training and behavior modification and their effects on the child's self-esteem (Doctoral dissertation, University of Northern Colorado, 1976). *Dissertation Abstracts International*, 1976, *37*, 2087A. (University Microfilms No. 76-23,193)

Smith, M. B. School and Home: Focus on achievement. In A. H. Passow (Ed.), *Developing programs for the educationally disadvantaged*. New York: Teachers College Press, Columbia University, 1968.

Turrall, G. M. Differential effects of Sensitivity Training and Adlerian Parent Training upon the self-esteem of academic underachievers (Doctoral dissertation, Boston University School of Education, 1975). *Dissertation Abstracts International*, 1975, *36*, 2113A-2114A. (University Microfilms No. 75-20, 933)

Uhl, S. F. The effects of tape assisted parent education discussions on fifth grade children's self-esteem and achievement levels (Doctoral dissertation, Loyola University of Chicago, 1975). *Dissertation Abstracts International*, 1975, *36*, 2113A-2114A. (University Microfilms No. 75-22,369)

Utah State University, Exceptional Child Center. *Effectiveness of parents as a treatment resource in rural areas. Final report, November 1976*. Logan, Utah: 1976. (ERIC Document Reproduction Service No. ED 139 569)

Wade, B. B. An inquiry into the effects of a parent education program on the reading achievement of first grade children in a rural school system (Doctoral dissertation, University of Georgia, 1977). *Dissertation Abstracts International*, 1978, *38*, 4460A. (University microfilms No. 7730519)

Wade, B. B. *Parent education: Does it make a difference?* Paper presented at the Southeastern Regional Conference of the International Reading Association, Nashville, TN, February 1980. (ERIC Document Reproduction Service No. ED 190 990)

Whitaker, B. I. Citizen participation in educational decision making in an urban school district as perceived by parents and administrators (Doctoral dissertation, Georgia State University School of Education, 1977). *Dissertation Abstracts International*, 1978, *38*, 3893A–3894A. (University Microfilms No. 77-29,322)

Windle, J. L. Parent participation in selected early childhood education programs in Los Angeles County in 1975–76 as perceived by principals and staff (Doctoral dissertation, University of Southern California, 1977). *Dissertation Abstracts International*, 1978, *38*, 4507A-4508A. (Micrographics Department, Doheny Library, USC, Los Angeles, CA 90007)

Wise, J. H. *Parent participation reading clinic—a research demonstration project*. Final Report. Washington, DC: Children's Hospital of the District of Columbia, 1972. (ERIC Document Reproduction Service No. ED 072 174)

Woods, C., Barnard, D. P., & TeSelle, E. *The effect of the Parent Involvement Program on reading readiness scores*. Mesa, AR, Public Schools, 1974. (ERIC Document Reproduction Service No. ED 104 527)

Seven

Programs for Parents of Handicapped Children

Merle B. Karnes, Susan A. Linnemeyer, and Gloria Myles

INTRODUCTION

Special educators have long believed that parent involvement is important to the education of handicapped children; yet, over the years parents have generally been minimally involved. The Bureau of Education for the Handicapped (now Special Education Programs; SEP), in implementing the Early Childhood Assistance Act (1968), made it clear that no project would be funded unless a parent or family component was written into the proposal. Thus, since 1969 SEP has funded over 200 demonstration programs—collectively referred to as the Handicapped Children's Early Education Program (HCEEP)—all of which have parent involvement components. Every state has at least one such project, and some states have had as many as 10 or more. Since the purpose of these projects is to demonstrate viable models for educating handicapped children, impact on the entire country has been great.

In this chapter, we survey the HCEEP projects. All of these projects require parent involvement, and all have reported at least some outcome data in their progress reports. These projects are especially important because BEH-funded projects have had a marked effect on legislation. Prior to 1969, relatively few preschool programs for the handicapped existed, and those few that did exist had little emphasis on parent involvement. After 1969, however, involvement of parents was considered important and beneficial, largely because research began to demonstrate the effectiveness of parent participation in programs for disadvantaged children (Gordon, 1969; Gray, 1970; Karnes, Studley, Wright, and Hodgins, 1968; Levenstein, 1971; Weikart & Lambie, 1969).

Data on parent involvement reported here were obtained from a questionnaire sent to all second-year ($N = 38$) and third-year ($N = 55$) HCEEP projects and to all projects in the outreach[1] phase ($N = 46$). Those who returned questionnaires represented 42% of the second-year projects ($N = 16$), 47% of the third-year projects ($N = 26$), and 67% of the outreach projects ($N = 31$). Questionnaires from two projects had to be discarded, because the nature of these projects precluded answers to most items on the questionnaire.

The questionnaire obtained information on the following issues:

1. Do programs for young handicapped children set goals for their parent programs?
2. What techniques are used to determine the needs of parents as they involve themselves in the education of their handicapped child?
3. What are the primary needs of the parents?
4. What strategies are most frequently used in involving parents?
5. Are projects deliberately training parents to be advocates for their child?
6. Do projects provide parents with printed materials to enhance their understanding of their handicapped child and their effectiveness in working with the child?
7. What percentage of projects employ a full-time parent coordinator?
8. To what extent are parent involvement programs being evaluated? And what types of evaluation data are being obtained?
9. Do the evaluation data demonstrate the effectiveness of parent involvement?

This chapter first considers answers to these nine questions. Second, brief descriptions of selected parent involvement programs are presented. These programs are categorized under the following headings:

1. Center-based models: projects which provide services to children in a center; parents work either in the center or in the center and at home.

2. Home-based models: projects in which the major service is delivered to parents and children in the home.
3. Home-based and center-based models: projects including both a home-based and a center-based program. For example, from age 0–3 a child may be in a home-based program, but at the age of 3 may attend a center-based program. Another example is the parent who has an option to enroll the child in a center-based or a home-based program. Both groups of parents may go to the center for meetings.
4. Models that focus on fathers.
5. Models for severely and profoundly handicapped.
6. Gifted/talented/handicapped models.
7. Parent involvement models in medical centers.

Projects reported in this section were selected from among those which returned the questionnaire because they offered innovative parent involvement programs and because they reported data for evaluating the effectiveness of this component of their program. Following the review of exemplary parent involvement programs, a final section considers the implications of parent involvement for public policy.

CHARACTERSTICS OF PARENT INVOLVEMENT IN HCEEP PROJECTS

Do Programs for Young Handicapped Set Goals for Their Parent Programs?

Of the 71 programs that returned usable questionnaires, 61 (86%) indicated they had specific goals for their parent programs. These goals were general goals that applied to all parents; a few programs indicated that they set specific goals for each parent; a few set goals for each family member. Programs that did not delineate goals usually did not have well-defined evaluation procedures.

How Were Parents Needs Determined?

Sixty-one of the responding projects (86%) conducted a needs assessment with parents to determine their needs; the assessment is an ongoing procedure rather than a yearly assessment. Some assessments were more informal than others; however, a majority of the projects have developed an instrument for assessing parent needs. Some had developed a plan for determining individual goals of parents, strategies for achieving goals, and procedures for evaluating parental progress toward achieving goals.

What are the Primary Needs of HCEEP Parents?

Parents of handicapped children in most projects indicated that they wanted to be part of the educational planning for their child, to learn techniques for fostering child development, to acquire skills for effective child management, and to learn more about their child's handicapping condition.

What Strategies are Most Frequently Used in Involving Parents?

Of the options open to parents, group meetings were used most frequent (100%); parent training was the next most-used strategy (67 projects, 94%). Sixty-three projects (89%) involved parents in child assessment. Next in frequency were involvement of parents in program evaluation (81%) and development of the child's Individualized Education Plan (IEP; 78%). Infant programs were less likely to use this strategy than projects serving 3- to 5-year-old children. Next in frequency was the parent-teacher conference (41 projects, 58%). Sixty projects (85%) involved parents in the assessment of the child, and an equal number involved parents in the direct teaching of their child. Forty-seven projects (66%) provided counseling for parents, while parents served on advisory boards in 47 projects (66%).

Are Projects Deliberately Training Parents to be Advocates for Their Child?

Deliberate advocacy training was reported by 33 of the 71 projects (46%).

Do Projects Provide Parents with Printed Materials?

Forty-two (59%) of the projects have a parent library, although many more projects provide some written materials for parents. An organized library for parents, however, is not one of the major strategies for involving the parents.

What Percentage of Projects Employ a Full-time Coordinator?

Only 28 (39%) of the projects had full-time parent coordinators. Often a social worker or the director of the program served in a coordinating capacity, but this was not their full-time responsibility.

To What Extent Are Parent Involvement Programs Being Evaluated?

A total of 57 (78%) projects used soft data in evaluating the effectiveness of parent involvement. These data consisted largely of spontaneous statements by parents; such statements reported in the questionnaire were generally positive. Forty-one (56%) of the projects gathered hard data to evaluate their parent involvement programs. Thirty-seven (51%) of the projects collecting soft data also collected hard data. Ten projects (14%) reported no evaluation of the parent program. Older projects, especially those in the outreach phase, tended to have more refined procedures for evaluating the parent involvement component than did newer programs.

It is difficult, obviously, to evaluate parent effectiveness as reflected in child growth when a number of other variables also contribute to development. This is especially true in center-based programs where professionals work directly with the child.

What Does Evaluation Tell Us About Parent Involvement?

The evaluation of parent involvement on the basis of both hard and soft data indicates that parents do want to become involved in activities that promise to be of benefit to their child. The more remote the involvement is from the individual child, such as serving on an advisory board, the less value parents place on the activity.

It seems apparent that a needs assessment involving the parents helps to ensure an effective program. One reason parent involvement may not have been successful in the past is that professionals have tried to outguess parents; oftentimes professionals' assessment of parent need was not valid. Finally, parents are more apt to engage in activities if they have a part in the decision-making process.

EXEMPLARY PARENT INVOLVEMENT PROGRAMS

Center-based models

Three center-based models with family involvement components are reviewed in this section. These include the Model Preschool Center at the University of Washington, the Model Preschool Project in Spokane, Washington, and the Precise Early Education of Children with Handicaps (PEECH) Project at the University of Illinois.

Model Preschool Center for Handicapped Children.   This program, located at the University of Washington in Seattle, annually serves approximately 200 developmentally delayed and other handicapped children from birth to 6. Within the Model Preschool Center for Handicapped Children, there are two programs—the Communication Program and the Program for Children with Down's syndrome—that have been approved for adoption or adaptation by the Joint Dissemination Review Panel. The major goal of parent involvement is to provide parents with current information about their child's progress and about classroom intervention strategies, as well as the adaptation of these procedures to the home setting. Parents are also involved in community projects and activities on behalf of handicapped children.

Parents are an integral part of the interdisciplinary team in both programs. For instance, in the Communication Program, the team is composed of the child's family, the classroom teaching staff, and the communication disorders specialist. During initial contact with the Communication Program staff, parents are asked to identify their child's developmental strengths and needs as well as their own concerns and priorities for the child. This information is enlightening for parents as well as for classroom staff, because it sets the stage for later parent participation in the development, implementation, and evaluation of their child's IEP.

Parent training varies according to the needs of the family. However, information on the following subjects is consistently requested by parents: (1) patterns of normal child development in the major skill areas of gross and fine motor development, communication, cognition, and social/self-help; (2) identification of skills within the developmental sequence that their child should master; and (3) intervention strategies that can be implemented at home. Regular conferences with the classroom staff, directed observation, information exchange, acquisition of teaching strategies and behavior management techniques, and updated information on child progress have proven to be successful parent involvement activities.

Model Preschool Project. A program similar to the Seattle program is the Model Preschool Project in Spokane, Washington. This program serves 40 developmentally delayed children from birth to 5. The program objectives are to increase the knowledge of parents about the development of their child's communication skills, fine and gross motor skills, self-help skills, and language development; to increase the awareness of parents about community resources; and to facilitate parents' adjustment to having a child who is handicapped.

Needs are assessed by an interdisciplinary team, and workshops are designed to meet the shared needs of parents and children. Parents engage in directed observation, in skill development training, and in staff conferences to learn strategies for working with their children. Different parents participate at different levels, depending on their needs.

The infant component provides for a therapist or teacher to work with each parent and their infant 1 day weekly for approximately 1 hour. The focus here is on training parents to work with their infant in all areas of skill development in preparation for an increased level of functioning.

A parent/staff newsletter is sent out bimonthly, and handouts and notes are sent home by individual teachers or therapists to exchange information among parents and staff.

Precise Early Education of Children with Handicaps (PEECH). The PEECH Project, located at the University of Illinois and initially funded in 1970, has been nationally validated. Currently, PEECH is in the outreach phase and is being replicated in some 35 states. PEECH stresses the importance of flexibility and individualization in working with parents. Karnes and Zehrbach (1972) have listed various alternatives available to parents and have provided guidelines to ensure that each activity is successful.

A family involvement planning guide is used to help parents assess their needs, to set goals, and to plan activities that will help parents achieve those goals. Through a questionnaire, parents assess the educational program in which their child is enrolled and the parent involvement program in which they themselves participate. The questionnaire is also completed by parents whose children are enrolled in PEECH replication sites.

The following information was obtained from 32 parents in six replication site. Items which measure parent beliefs about their child's educational progress on 5-item scales (Very Outstanding Progress = 5 to No Progress = 1) revealed the following results for five areas of development: (1) speech and language, $M = 4.00$; (2) social, $M = 4.00$; (3) self-help, $M = 3.74$; (4) fine motor, $M = 3.60$; and (5) gross motor, $M = 4.20$. These data indicate that parents perceived their child's progress to have been more than adequate in all five areas.

Three additional Likert-type items (Strongly Agree = 5 to Strongly Disagree = 1) assess satisfaction with the program in general. They are (1) "This program has provided services to meet most of my child's educational needs," $M = 4.40$; (2) "I am very pleased with this educational program," $M = 4.59$; and (3) "I would recommend to my legislator that continued support be provided to preschool programs like this one," $M = 4.78$. These data indicate a high degree of satisfaction with the PEECH program in general.

Two open-ended questions ask parents to identify their favorite program activity and program changes they think would be beneficial. Of the 32 parents interviewed, the most common responses to the question, "What do you like best about this program?": (1) appreciation of staff commitment ($N = 8$); (2) small group size ($N = 7$); and (3) much contact with the staff ($N = 3$). Common responses to the question, "What would you change about the program?" included: (1) nothing ($N = 5$); (2) need for more staff to provide individualized attention, test, and consult ($N = 5$); and (3) need for better communication about parent meetings ($N = 2$).

Satisfaction with the parent involvement program was assessed in three areas. The first area was attitudes about specific program activities in which parents had participated. Parents were asked to rate 12 such events on a 5-point scale from Extremely Successful $= 5$ to Extremely Unsuccessful $= 1$. The events to which the fewest parents responded were: (1) writing a newsletter ($N = 6$; $M = 3.66$), and (2) making materials for classroom use ($N = 7$; $M = 4.28$). The events to which parents most frequently responded were: (1) meeting with staff members at the time of enrollment ($N = 31$; $M = 4.45$); and (2) conferences with school personnel ($N = 29$; $M = 4.55$).

In terms of frequency, then, the least successful aspect of the parent involvement program was newsletter writing. This activity received the second lowest overall mean rating (the lowest mean rating was "serving as an Advisory Board member," $N = 9$; $M = 3.33$). The aspect of the parent involvement program in which parents participated most frequently was meeting with staff members, while the highest overall mean rating went to "meeting to discuss goals for the child," $N = 28$; $M = 4.71$. These data clearly indicate that activities directly related to the child's education are not only the most frequently attended, but also the ones considered most successful by parents.

Attitudes toward interactions with staff members were further assessed by statements rated on a 5-point scale (Strongly Agree $= 5$ to Strongly Disagree $= 1$). The statements referred to availability and cooperation of staff members. The mean ratings ranged from 4.50 to 4.61, indicating strong positive attitudes on the part of parents toward staff with whom they were involved.

The second area of parent satisfaction—skills parents acquired which enabled them to help their child at home—were measured by three items. The first requested parents to indicate the presence or absence of ability to help their children in five areas of skill development.

These areas were: (1) speech and language (26 yes; 1 no); (2) social behavior (26 yes; 3 no); (3) self-help (22 yes; 5 no); (4) fine motor control (22 yes; 5 no); and (5) gross motor control (23 yes; 5 no). By far, most parents perceived themselves to be capable of providing help for their children.

Two Likert-type items also addressed gains in acquired parental skills. These were: (1) "I now know a lot more about my child's development," $M = 4.17$; and (2) "I now know a lot more about how to help my child at home," $M = 4.16$. These results show overall agreement with two positive statements concerning parental development.

The third item which addressed the acquisition of skills by parents was an open-ended question asking, "What things have you learned that have helped you the most?" In response to this item, parents most frequently cited newly acquired skills in various areas of remediation (speech, social behavior, self-help, and so on). The second most frequent response indicated that parents gained a more realistic assessment of their child's capabilities.

On the whole, then, questionnaire responses indicated a high degree of satisfaction with the parent involvement program at PEECH replication sites.

Home-based Models

Three home-based programs will be examined in this section. These include: the Portage Project of Portage, Wisconsin; the Macomb 0-3 Regional Project in Macomb, Illinois; and the Home-Based Preschool Project in Ferndale, Washington.

The Portage Project. The Portage Project in rural southern Wisconsin is nationally validated and has served as a model for projects across the nation and outside the United States. Originally funded by the BEH in 1969, it now also receives funding from the Wisconsin State Department of Education and local school districts. The project serves multihandicapped children from 0 to 6 years, all of whom demonstrate at least a year's delay in developmental age before being accepted into the program.

The instructional program centers around the Portage Guide to Early Education, an ongoing assessment and curriculum planning instrument divided into the developmental areas of cognition, self-help, motor, language, and socialization. Three to four emerging behaviors are selected from one or more of these areas each week, and curriculum objectives are written cooperatively by a professional or paraprofessional home teacher and the parent. Each teaching activity is modeled by the home teacher, after which the parent performs the activity with the child.

The weekly home visit lasts 90 minutes, and the parent works with the child approximately 15 minutes daily. An activity chart is used to record behavioral objectives, instructional procedures, daily responses of the child, and activities for the coming week. Parent and teacher comments and additional activities are also added.

Each full-time teacher, who serves approximately 14 families, receives pre-service and in-service training. Preservice training includes an orientation to the Portage Project and its goals; an introduction to behavioral assessment, curriculum planning, instruction (including the writing of behavioral objectives), behavior modification, and learning theory; an explanation of the home visit process; a summary of community resources; and an overview of agency policies and the use of reporting forms. In-service training, which reviews and expands on the topics just listed, occurs one half day per week.

Child progress is measured by pre- and posttest performance on the Alpern-Boll Development Profile. Gains of 1.2 to 1.8 months in all five developmental areas have been demonstrated by program children. Other testing instruments have included the Cattell Infant Test and the Stanford-Binet Intelligence Test.

A unique component of the project is the Portage Parent Program. Its goal is to make each parent as functionally independent of the home teacher as possible by showing the parents how to instruct their child and to manage the child's behavior. The Parental Behavior Inventory lists the specific behaviors used by parents in teaching, and each parent is assessed by the home teacher as to whether these behaviors are present. Each week the home teacher models the desired behaviors and provides reinforcement or corrective feedback for parental behaviors.

Macomb 0–3 Regional Project. Another home-based program that uses weekly home visits is the Macomb 0-3 Regional Project, a rural child-parent service in Macomb, Illinois. The program serves approximately 50 children who are high risk or developmentally delayed.

The two major objectives of this project are: (1) to provide an effective educational and remediation program for the optimal development of handicapped infants and young children in rural areas, and (2) to help parents who live in rural areas acquire skills and knowledge to become more effective in rearing their handicapped child.

The Macomb Project operates on the premise that the involvement, cooperation, and enthusiasm of parents is essential. Weekly 1-hour visits are made to parents by Child Development Specialists (CDS's). Biyearly goals and weekly activity plans are selected from the core curriculum which was developed by the project. From the activity plans, the CDS and the parent choose an activity for each week. Since parents are the primary change agents for their children, the parent works with the child daily, and the child's responses are charted.

Another component of the program in which parents are actively involved is the Sharing Center. Every two weeks, parents are given the opportunity to meet with other parents. Once formed, Sharing Center groups remain stable. Program children, their siblings, and nonhandicapped children are included in the various activities, so that the Sharing Center environment becomes a kind of "least restrictive" alternative. Training in implementing sharing activities is provided for the parents. Sharing Center groups in two counties have a water activities program weekly or biweekly at the local YMCA. The CDS's employ various techniques of stimulation, relaxation, and body control in working with parents and children in the water.

Another feature of the Macomb Project is its mobile unit. In addition to being part of the home visit component, the unit is used to transport children and parents to medical appointments and to house mini-sharing centers; it is also used to disseminate information about the Project in rural areas.

Evaluation of the parent component is based on a Parent Satisfaction Questionnaire administered by an independent evaluator after parents have been in the program for 3 months and thereafter at 6-month intervals. The 1978 evaluation found that 72% of the parents reported gains in knowledge of their child's problems; 80% reported a greater knowledge of techniques for working with their child; and 94% reported overall satisfaction with project services. Additional means of evaluating the parent component are the videotaping of parent behaviors, and analysis of parent–child interaction according to specific behaviors (e.g., parent modeling of desired behavior, parent praise).

Home-based Preschool Project. The Home-based Preschool sponsored by the Ferndale (Washington) School District enrolls approximately 40 children from 3 to 8 years of age who display significant delays in the developmental areas of self-help, social, communication, physical, academic skills, or behavior.

The goals of the program are twofold: (1) to develop and deliver appropriate intervention services for the preschool child and his parents based on a team effort between parents and teaching personnel; and (2) to increase parent teaching and management skills.

The program's parent component is based on a three-level plan. Level one aims to facilitate parent teaching skills by providing one-to-one instruction. The objective of the second level is to formulate an

Individualized Parent Program, based on a needs assessment, and aimed at increasing parent knowledge of community resources. The third level attempts to develop an informal support group system.

The parent component is evaluated by use of a parent questionnaire. Results for one recent year found a majority of the parents (1) believed the Home-Based Preschool program was working well for their children; (2) were satisfied with the service their children were receiving from the program; and (3) participated in weekly sessions with their children and the home teacher.

Home-based and Center-based Models

The programs to be reviewed in this section are early childhood programs for handicapped children that have both home-based and center-based components. Three programs that represent this category are Project KIDS (Kindling Individual Development Systems) of Dallas, Texas, the Infant "Care" Program of Merced, California, and Project First Chance Parent–Family Participation of Tucson, Arizona. Both of these programs serve children with multiple handicaps.

Project KIDS (Kindling Individual Development Systems). Projects KIDS is a component of the special education program of the Dallas Independent School System and serves handicapped students from birth to 6 years of age. Project KIDS was initiated in 1975 as a demonstration project in the Handicapped Children's Early Education Program. Following the 3-year demonstration period, funding was continued by the school district and federal funds were provided to initiate an outreach program.

The Program serves approximately 300 students each year in three instructional settings: home-based training program (0–2 years); center-based infant education class (2–3 years); and school-based preschool classes (3–6 years). The program utilizes a developmental prescription approach and has developed five dissemination packages: staff development, appraisal, curriculum, parent involvement, and program evaluation.

A major component of Project KIDS has been parent involvement. Because of the diversity of the parent population, an individualized, competency-based instructional approach was designed. A list of 69 competencies pertinent to parenting with handicapped children was devised by project staff and parents. Parents gave higher priority to competencies relating to their role as facilitators of their child's learning and development, while professionals saw these as less important for parents. Fourteen of the highest ranking competencies were used as the basis of the Parent Self-Assessment Inventory (PSAI), an instrument by which parents rate their level of competencies.

After responding to the PSAI, parents were asked to select training activities from an array of diverse learning programs designed to improve their performance of each competency. The number of activities selected corresponds directly to their self-assessed ratings. Almost 80% of the activities chosen by parents were of an individual nature. The areas of most preferred activities included language acquisition, behavior management, parent as teacher, self-care, and assessment.

Parental reactions to the program were obtained from 83 parents through the use of a 23-item questionnaire. Overall, a majority of the respondents expressed positive reactions to every item on the questionnaire. The highest percentage of respondents (89.7% in the school-based program and 96.0% in the home- and center-based program) agreed they were "happy with Project KIDS." Respondents agreed (86.3% in the school-based program and 92.0% in the home- and center-based programs) that the children "had made progress in KIDS."

Infant "Care" Program. The Infant "Care" Program of Merced, California, enrolls 23 children from birth to 3 years. Handicapping conditions include deafness, language delay, ammonemia, cerebral palsy, muscular dystrophy, blindness, spina bifida, Down's syndrome, Erbs-Cuchenne palsy, herpes simplex II, anencephalous, and moderate and profound delays sometimes coupled with seizure.

Active participation of the parent is an essential component of "Care." Based on the premise that parents make the best teachers, parents in the center-based program attend twice a week to help implement their child's program and to share concerns with the psychiatric social worker who works directly with the parents. Parents in the home-based program and those unable to travel to the center are visited by the staff once a week.

Evaluation of child progress indicated that the children demonstrated continuous growth and development in all skill areas measured by the Denver Developmental Screening Test and/or the Learning Accomplishment Profile. In addition, there was significant growth in parent interaction skills as measured by a parent behavior scale that concerned progressional parenting. No attempt was made to compare the progress of parents and children in the home-based and center-based programs.

Project First Chance Parent–Family Participation. This project is located in Tucson, Arizona, and serves moderately handicapped children, cross-categorical with the exception of deafness. Some children are in a home-only program and others are in a center-based program with a home component.

   This family participation program places primary emphasis on individual contacts with parents. A Home Teacher works with parents to extend the content of class instruction into the home and concentrates on generalizing the behaviors learned at school and developing parents' teaching skills. All phases of the school curriculum, which combines cognitive, developmental, and behavioral philosophies, are developed in this home/school program. A major emphasis on language and communication skills is a first priority of home programming.

   Parents are asked to rate their child's skills prior to the initial in-school evaluation and IEP conference. This parent rating serves as a training device for parents in the observation of their child's current performance and is used by the Home Teacher in order to develop a dialogue concerning the parents' goals for the child. The goals are further delineated at an in-school IEP conference.

   During the first few weeks of school, the Home Teacher meets with each parent at school and provides them with a "guided" observation of daily school activities. Parents are encouraged to volunteer to work as teaching aides in the classroom. Whether or not parents volunteer in the classroom, they are provided with a "Home Teaching Manual" and taught the basic principles of instructional programming. Parents are also taught to collect data on opportunities to learn so that the school program can be replicated at home with ongoing data collection. Initially, the Home Teacher provides parents with structured teaching programs and "Just for Fun" activities. In addition, teachers are responsible for assisting parents in making contacts with various community support agencies.

   While these parent involvement activities seek to individualize an approach to parent–child needs, group meetings are also held throughout the year. These meetings focus on special topics taken from the family needs assessment. An advocacy training component is also made available to each parent individually or in a small group setting. Throughout the year, parents are also invited by their children to be guests at special holiday parties, field trips, and open house activities.

   In summary, this program follows the principle of showing parents what to do, since modeling is an important step in learning new skills. The project staff also provides ideas and suggestions to carry out at home. Every aspect of the teaching paradigm is modeled for parents to ensure success in home teaching; e.g., cues, placement of material, criteria for success, and delivery of consequences, with the end goal of the parents working both in partnership with the classroom teacher and teaching their child independently at home.

   The number of home programs run during the year and the number of teaching behaviors gained and maintained over selected time periods provide this program with a primary data base. Data reflecting child change in learning behaviors is collected for both home/school and home-only programs. In addition to home teaching data, the Home Teacher's Daily Log indicates the percent of time spent in direct parent contact, either in the home, at the project site, in the classroom, in parents' group meetings, on the phone, or in agency contact with or for parents. The Parent Assessment of Child Skills given at the beginning of each semester and at the end of the year yields data regarding change in the parents' perception of their child's level of functioning. Consumer satisfaction data are also gathered from parents, along with the entry assessment of parent training needs. Each group meeting is also evaluated by parents. Where possible, observational time sampling of parent–child interactions in the home provides a means for analyzing parenting style. A parent attitude survey is also conducted on a pre–post basis.

Models that Focus on Fathers

In most programs, the mother of the preschool handicapped child is the central figure in parent involvement activities. But three programs sponsored by SEP do offer a notable focus on the fathers of young handicapped children: Project REACH (Rural Early Assistance to Children) in Northampton, Massachusetts; Fathers and Infants Class: A Model for Facilitating Attachment between Fathers and Their Handicapped Infants in Seattle, Washington; and Parent and Infant Program in Columbus, Ohio.

Project REACH. REACH serves approximately 60–70 children yearly, ages birth to 3 years, who are handicapped, developmentally delayed, or at-risk for developmental problems. The chief objectives of this home- and center-based program are to help parents encourage their child's development, to offer support in achieving parental adjustment to the child's handicap, and to help coordinate other community services and resources. Following initial screening of the child, an interview with the family by a staff member, and a multidisciplinary developmental assessment, the REACH team meets with parents to determine appropriate home- or center-based activities for the child and family.

Parent program activities involve the development of parent goals through individual needs assessment and the training of parents as teachers via home visitation. Parents' cooperative play groups, evening education events for parents, and social and support activities are other ongoing components of the parent program.

REACH has also developed an approach to fathers which is intended to encourage better parenting competencies as well as more involvement in program activities. These project efforts include home visits arranged at times convenient to work schedules, a father's support and discussion group, male professional staff for individual counseling and support, and informational materials addressing fathers' issues.

Program evaluation data, collected through interviews and questionnaires at the end of the year, indicated that parents were extremely satisfied with the program services received. Parents indicated they had made some achievement on 86 of 97 goals (89%).

Project Fathers and Infants Class: A model for facilitating attachment between fathers and their handicapped infants. This center-based project serves 10 fathers and 10 infants (0–18 months) with Down's syndrome and associated handicapping conditions. The program is designed to increase the father's awareness of child development and in so doing cause an increase in a prescribed set of behaviors indicative of attachment by the father to the infant.

The project maintains two classes for fathers and their infants in the Seattle area. Classes are held on Saturdays from 10:00 a.m. to noon, the time and day selected by the fathers. Both fathers and infants attend the class. Scheduled activities involve sharing time, linger (thought for the day), music and exercise, snack, guest speaker (Child/Family Development), and previewing the coming week's activities. Effort is made to accommodate parent requests and to provide followups to ensure that what is offered is appropriate and of assistance. The class is not locked into a rigid regime, and the key to its effectiveness is staff awareness of individual needs and the willingness to adapt the model to meet these needs.

An indication of class impact is that absenteeism is low; when a child is ill and cannot attend, the father comes without the child. If the father is out of town, the mother attends.

Parent Infant Program (PIP). This program serves families with children (birth to 3 years) having Down's syndrome or multiple handicaps, as well as infants "at risk" for later disabilities. The project operates through the Nisonger Center for Mental Retardation and Developmental Disabilities, Ohio State University, Columbus, Ohio.

PIP is primarily parent focused. It emphasizes parent and child needs during the child's infancy and facilitates effective parenting by building skills, by providing information to increase awareness, and by offering support in dealing with past, present, and future concerns. PIP is designed as a first program for families who have children with developmental problems and as a precursor to more child-oriented programs offered in the communities.

The evening program provides activities specially designed for fathers, as well as for mothers and siblings. Program participation involves a 2-hour evening session each week at the Nisonger Center and the ongoing implementation of program activities by the family at home. Each session is divided into a developmental class and a parent group. The developmental classes provide a team of professionals and students from various disciplines who work with parents in planning, carrying out, and monitoring learning strategies tailored to the needs of their children and family. Activities are designed to be carried out in the home during the week, and home visits and supplemental services are provided for families as needed. Parent group sessions help parents deal with problems associated with raising a special-needs child, provide information concerning developmental problems and community resources, and give parents an opportunity to share their experiences with each other.

In the yearly evaluations of the program, both fathers and mothers of PIP infants indicate that they are "satisfied" or "very satisfied" with program managers and activities. Most ratings regarding parent expectations, goals, therapeutic and skill development, and infant performance fall between 3.0 and 4.0 out of a possible 4.0 on Likert-type scales.

Models for Severely and Profoundly Handicapped

The programs reviewed in this section serve the severely and profoundly, multiply handicapped and have a home-based component. The projects examined are Project RUN (Reaching Us Now) in Oxford, Mississippi; the Education for Severely Handicapped Outreach Pogram, in Foster, Rhode Island; and the Early Childhood Education for the Severely/Multiply Handicapped Program, in Tempe, Arizona.

Project RUN (Reaching Us Now). Project RUN serves 20 children from 0–8 years old in Oxford, Mississippi. The parent program is based on the belief that parents are a vital force in maximizing development in children. Project RUN views parents and schools as partners in the education process. Through involvement in its programs, Project RUN suggests that parents receive the following benefits: (1) they are active participants in their child's progress; (2) they receive information on their child's handicapping condition; (3) they receive support from the staff and other parents; and (4) they learn techniques to use in teaching their child at home.

Components of the parent program are classroom observation, classroom participation, home training, monthly parent meetings, and representation on the RUN advisory board. Home training consists of home visits every 2 weeks by a parent educator who models teaching activities for the parent. The parent subsequently works with the child daily and records data.

Parents provide input on the overall effectiveness of the program though written evaluations and during parent meetings. Needs assessments are completed by the parents every 8 weeks.

Education for Severely Handicapped Outreach. This project, located in Foster, Rhode Island, is a center-based program serving children from birth to 8 years who are multihandicapped (e.g., severely or profoundly mentally retarded and physically handicapped). The program uses the Trudeau-Zambarano Active Stimulation Program (TZASP) Parent Needs Assessment as a needs assessment device. This 15-item checklist can be broken down into four areas: technical knowledge, attitudes, ease in relating to others, and parental time constraints. Needs of parents as determined by the checklist are subsequently used as topics for inservice meetings. A decrease in expressed needs by parents in all four areas of the TZASP Parent Needs Assessment, especially in technical knowledge, has occurred during the program's implementation. These data are interpreted to mean that needs of parents are being met.

Home visits are an important element of the program. A home visitation record is used to record the parent's and child's progress and to specify the home visit activities. The form is completed after each home visit and includes the date, the time spent on the contact, the planned intervention of the home activity, and informal comments by the teacher.

Home visits are evaluated through the Opinion Scale. Results of the 1979 survey indicate that 71% of the parents felt they had learned a great deal. One hundred percent of the parents responded that home visits had helped in their understanding of their child's program.

The Early Childhood Education for the Severely/Multiply Handicapped Program. This program, located at Arizona State University in Tempe, Arizona, is composed of an infant center- and home-based component for infants 0 to 3 years of age, and a center-based program for children 3 to 6 years of age. The 18 children enrolled in the program have severe multiple handicaps.

The program's goal is to create a partnership between parents and staff that will enhance the development of severely multiply handicapped children. In the infant component, parents meet at the center twice weekly to learn instructional skills. They also receive a weekly home visit. In the program for older children, parents participate once a week in the classroom, working directly with their own child or with other children. Parents also meet weekly with the Parent Program Co-ordinator for 1 hour and are involved with the Advisory Council.

Comments from parents concerning program effectiveness show their enthusiasm: "I feel the . . . program is an excellent one, and extremely effective," and "In the past 4 months my son has been in this program, he has progressed more than we had hoped. This program teaches us what and how to teach our children and how to cope and handle problems we have in our homes."

Gifted/Talented/Handicapped Models

SEP funded two projects to develop models for gifted handicapped preschoolers. The Chapel Hill Model, funded as a demonstration classroom from 1975 to 1978, was located at the Division for Disorders of Development and Learning at the University of North Carolina at Chapel Hill. Materials from the project are still being disseminated. The other project, Retrieval and Acceleration of Promising Young Handicapped and Talented (RAPYHT), began in 1975 and is located at the University of Illinois.

The Chapel Hill Model. This classroom-based program includes a family component that serves a supportive and ancillary role. Bloom's (1956) taxonomy is used to specify program objectives for each child. Parents are involved in the assessment procedure and in program evaluation, in addition to receiving project services. The basic functions of the family program have included: supportive counseling, liaison between parents and the classroom, parent skill development, referral services, and advocacy training (Leonard, 1978, pp. 730–734).

The project has a family coordinator who is a trained social worker. Activities in which families are engaged include home visits, group meetings, parent–teacher conferences, home activities, use of a parent library, and classroom observation and participation. There are a total of 20 options. Of the 20 options for parents, no parent participated in fewer than 7, with 13 being the highest. The mean was 12.8.

The evaluation of the parent component focused on parent participation, parent change, parent perception of child change, and parent satisfaction. Parents were asked to rate on a scale of 1 to 5 the usefulness of the various options open to them. The following items were considered the most used in rank order: printed materials regarding children's special needs or parenting skills; parent–staff conferences; weekly mothers' meetings; special classroom days (e.g., Christmas, Thanksgiving, birthdays); classroom observation; and participation in IEP conferences.

The parents' assessment of personal change was in acquisition of information, in attitudes, and in expectations. The two areas in which parents noted greatest change were "Knowledge of services available to my child" and "Knowledge of ways to be an effective advocate for my child."

All parents stated that their children had made positive changes during the year. Ten of the 14 parents attributed this change to participation in the program. The greatest changes noted by parents were in their child's relationships with other children, in attentiveness, in language and communication, and in motor (large and small muscle) development.

In response to a program satisfaction questionnaire, all parents indicated positive reactions for both themselves and their children. Among the experiences that parents appreciated most were daily, informal feedback from staff, group experiences for the child, emotional support from contacts with other parents, and individual counseling by staff members.

University of Illinois Retrieval and Acceleration of Promising Young Handicapped and Talented (RAPYHT). This project serves gifted and talented, handicapped children ages 3 to 5 who are mainstreamed with nongifted, handicapped children and with nonhandicapped, gifted children. Two approaches are used: an informal, open classroom approach and a teacher-directed approach which relies on the Guilford Structure of the Intellect (Guilford, 1967) as a framework for curriculum development. The project serves a total of 35 gifted/talented handicapped children in the demonstration site at the University of Illinois and in nine replication sites. Essentially 10% of mild and moderately handicapped children are identified as potentially or actually gifted/talented using instruments developed by the project. These children are provided with special programming at school and at home.

Parent and family participation is an important component of RAPYHT, and an effort is made to provide families with a number of alternative activities designed to achieve program and family goals. Family and staff work together to plan the individualized involvement of each family member. Most often, the family members involved are the child's mother and father, but grandparents, brothers and sisters, and aunts have also participated in certain activities.

Documentation of the effectiveness of the family involvement program is obtained from records kept by the teachers and from a questionnaire ("Confidential Parent Report") completed by the parent. A variety of teacher–parent interactions occur over the year; the effectiveness of these activities is indicated in part by how successful parents feel such activities have been. Twelve activities were listed on the parent questionnaire (activities which ranged from "meeting to discuss goals for the child" to "serving as an advisory board member"). Five responses were possible: Extremely Successful = 5, Successful = 4, Neutral = 3, Unsuccessful = 2, Extremely Unsuccessful = 1. Overall, items averaged a rating of 4.15. Activities rated most successful were "meeting to discuss goals for child," "observation of the classroom," and "meeting with staff member prior to enrolling child." Those activities perceived to be generally successful but not as successful as those in the highest group included "making materials for use at home," "assisting with snack, field trips, parties, etc., for the classrooms," "meeting in your home," and "teaching in the classroom."

Five items on the Parent Questionnaires asked parents to indicate the degree to which their interaction with staff members had been helpful. The response choices for these five items and their weights ranged from Strongly Agree = 5, to Strongly Disagree = 1. In general the mean of 4.7 across all five items indicated that parents "Strongly Agree" that their contact with staff members had been helpful.

Parents' attitudes toward their own gains in knowledge and skills as a result of the family involvement program were generally favorable. Parents who responded at the end of the year to the questionnaire agreed with the statements that "I now know a lot more about my child's development," and that "I now know a lot more about how to help my child at home."

The Parent Questionnaire also asked parents to rate how much progress they felt their child had made in the five program skill areas: speech and language, social, self-help, fine motor, and gross motor. Parents rated their children's progress over all five areas as "Good Progress" with a mean of 4.12 at the end of the year.

Parent attitudes toward the program were also very positive. Parents were asked about the program's responsiveness to their child's needs, and about the degree to which they would recommend to their legislator that support for programs of this type be continued. For these three items the mean of 4.54 indicated a very positive overall parent evaluation. It should be noted that the most favorable mean rating on any item (4.77 out of a possible 5.0) among the questionnaire's 86 items was achieved in response to the statement, "I would recommend to my legislator that continued support be provided to preschool programs like this one."

Parent Involvement Models in Medical Centers

Two SEP-funded projects involving parents are located in neonatal intensive care units in medical colleges; one is in the College of Medicine at the University of Cincinnati, and the other is at the Loyola University Stritch School of Medicine in Maywood, Illinois. The Cincinnati project has been in existence for a longer period of time, but both are exemplary programs and can serve as models in settings where comprehensive services are needed to promote the growth and development of high-risk infants. Both models place a high value on educational intervention and parental competencies. In the interest of space, we will focus here on the Cincinnati program.

The Infant Stimulation/Mother Training Program at Cincinnati was funded in 1977 by SEP and is currently in its third year of development and demonstration. The origin of this program at the Medical Center of the University of Cincinnati, however, dates back to 1972, when the Cincinnati Maternal and Infant Care program brought together a multidisciplinary team of professionals interested in developing an intervention program for adolescent mothers and their high-risk infants. The agencies who participated in this planning were the Cincinnati Health Department, Fels Research Institute, Cincinnati General Hospital, Children's Hospital Research Foundation, and the Newborn Division at the University of Cincinnati Department of Pediatrics. A research project was established by this group. The major service goals of the project were: (1) infant stimulation and training of mothers; (2) medical and nutritional services, and (3) improved family adaptation through increased mother competence. The infant stimulation curriculum and the mother's training model (Badger, 1977) were originally developed and tested at the University of Illinois (Karnes, Teska, Hodgins, Badger, 1970) and at parent–child centers in Illinois and Georgia. Thus, the current program is built on previous experiences dating back to 1967–1969.

The research design of the initial project included 24 mother–infant pairs of low socioeconomic status (Badger, 1977). The experimental group attended weekly classes, while a comparison group received monthly home visits. Subjects were randomly assigned to either the experimental or control group, and groups were matched on race and sex.

The experimental group was subdivided into two groups—young mothers 16 years of age and under, and older mothers 18 years and older—which met separately. Classes met in the evenings at the medical center, and doctors, nurses, and social workers were available for consultation. The major goal of the training sessions was to stimulate infant development through training the mother to be a more competent teacher. The mother was considered to be the primary teacher. This pilot project continued until the infants were 12 months old.

The comparison group received home visits from a nurse or social worker. During these visits, the child's development was assessed, and problems related to health and nutrition were discussed with the mother. No attempt was made to teach the mother skills to stimulate infant development. Infants received the same toys provided to the experimental group in an instructional setting.

Data were collected on all infants when they were 12 months of age on the Uzgiris-Hunt Ordinal Scales of Psychological Development and the Bayley Infant Scales. Infants in the group of younger mothers receiving home-visiting began to fall behind in their development and were "at risk." On the other hand, infants of the same age mothers who were in the training program made significantly greater progress than their counterparts. The treatment effect was not evidenced in infants of mothers 18 years and older. Essentially, infants of these mothers did equally well in the experimental and comparison groups.

As a result of these data, the pilot training program was incorporated into an ongoing service model which included a broad health education program featuring instruction in health and nutrition as well as educational stimulation. The classes were structured:

1. to provide multiple opportunities for young women to experience satisfactions in their new role as mothers;
2. to train mothers to foster the sensorimotor, cognitive, and language development of their infants through an educational curriculum;
3. to develop the mothers' sense of dignity and self-esteem in their primary role as teachers of their infants;
4. to provide a setting where personal and family problems beyond the mother-infant focus could be openly discussed and resolved;
5. to increase the mothers' awareness of the health, nutritional, psychological, and educational needs of their infants;
6. to replace crisis-intervention medical treatment with comprehensive health care. (Badger, 1977, pp. 47–48)

The classes in this service model meet for 20 consecutive weeks and are initiated shortly after birth.

One innovative aspect of this service model was that teenage mothers received high school credit in child development for every 30 hours of class participation. In addition, individual attention from the clinic doctor or pediatric nurse was made available on request. Still another innovative feature of the program was the careful planning of training sessions, both from the standpoint of content as well as the physical arrangements of the room according to the ages of infants who accompanied mothers to the training sessions.

But perhaps the most innovative aspect of the Mothers' Training

Program was the delivery of training in a hospital setting and the focus on educational intervention as well as medical support. Badger, Burns, and Rhodes (1976), after one year's experience, suggested the following:

1. Intervention of high-risk adolescent mothers and their infants should begin as soon as possible after birth.
2. The early post-parturition period is an optimal time for recruitment.
3. The peer group holds a special appeal for adolescent mothers and serves as a motivating force in altering attitudes and behaviors.
4. Parenting classes for adolescents can be provided as adjunct services in health clinic and hospital facilities.
5. Health care professionals can be trained to assume a more definitive educational role while maintaining more traditional services; furthermore, they welcome training opportunities.
6. Wider community involvement is available when health care professionals assume a leadership role in meeting the multiple needs of the adolescent mother and her child. (p. 472)

In 1977, building on the previous experiences of this project, a BEH-funded project was initiated with premature, low-birthweight infants of teenage single parents. These infants, unlike those in the previous project, were premature and markedly at risk. About 150 mothers and infants were involved in the followup program. First, nurses involved parents in the physical and emotional care of their infants during their visits to the Special Care Nursery. A nursing protocol for infant stimulation techniques and modeled interactional behavior facilitated parent–infant interaction.

Second, weekly support group meetings for parents of infants in the Special Care Nursery were conducted by the neonatal physician's assistant and staff neonatologist. Medical information, anticipatory guidance in the care of their infants, and emotional support from other parents were provided in these meetings.

Third, supportive home visits by a child development specialist, paraprofessional teacher's aide, or social worker helped parents adjust to the many problems presented by premature infants after their discharge from the Special Care Nursery.

Fourth, weekly mother–infant classes were carried out in a pediatric outpatient clinic as part of the medical followup of these infants. Class goals of the Infant Stimulation/Mother Training Program were implemented.

Fifth, social events were scheduled regularly for parents and infants. These included swimming, trips to the zoo and parks, and parties.

Assessment at 6 months on the Uzgiris-Hunt Scales of infants who weighed less than 5 pounds at birth was completed for 51 infants; 12-month assessments were completed on 36 infants using the Uzgiris-Hunt and Bayley Scales (Badger, 1979). Comparison group data were provided by full-term infants delivered at the Cincinnati General Hospital whose mothers were socially at risk. The ages at which full-term infants passed items on the Uzgiris-Hunt Scales were used as the criteria for appropriate developmental performance. Premature infants did better than full-term infants on the object permanence scale ($X^2 = p < .02$) at 6 months corrected age. All other comparisons at 6 months and 23 months showed that the two groups of infants were not significantly different.

Forty-one of the premature infants were also tested on the Bayley Scales at 12 months corrected age. Their mean Mental Development Index (MDI) score was 105, with a range of 78–128. Their mean Psychomotor Development Index (PDI) score was 105, with a range of 80–134. The mean 12-month MDI score of eight premature infants who weighed less than 2½ pounds at birth was 101, with a range of 78–119; their mean PDI score was 90, with a range of 86–139. Thus, this program seems to have produced remarkable results in producing normal intellectual development among the premature infants of high-risk mothers.

These preliminary findings suggest that neonatal intensive care and followup medical, educational, and social services have a positive effect on infant progress at 12 months of age. Further analysis of data obtained during years 2 and 3 will provide evidence of the longer-term effects of the services provided in this project.

PUBLIC POLICY IMPLICATIONS OF PARENT INVOLVEMENT PROGRAMS FOR HANDICAPPED CHILDREN

All SEP-funded projects have parent involvement components, although some are stronger than others. When federal funding is withdrawn, however, information is no longer available regarding the extent to which projects continue to maintain parent involvement. Since parent involvement usually requires additional project funds, and with current levels of inflation and the consequent tightening of local and state funds, the federal government may well need to mandate and subsidize parent programs if they are to survive.

It is particularly difficult for the mother of a handicapped child, especially in single-parent and low-income families, to participate fully in her child's educational program. Many of these mothers must work outside the home. For such families, it seems apparent that the federal government must provide income support, if the mother is to stay at home and devote her time to childrearing. She then would be able to participate in parent education programs and become involved in activities which would enhance her competencies in working with her handicapped child. In turn, her contribution would enhance the child's chances to develop his/her potential to the fullest and minimize the handicap's impact on the child's future growth and development.

It is difficult to determine the appropriate division of funding between federal, state, and local governments in support of parent programs. Perhaps a formula could be devised to assure that monies would be forthcoming from the level best able to afford parent programs.

It is generally agreed and now confirmed by federal law (P.L. 94-142) that public schools should be responsible for the delivery of services to the handicapped child after age 3. But the responsibility for educating handicapped children under age 3 remains a problem. A few states have legislation that requires the public schools to educate infants under 3, and a number of states have permissive legislation that allows, but does not require, the public schools to educate infants. Even so, the large majority of public school programs are for handicapped children over age 3. Regardless of what institution has the major responsibility, educators should be involved in infant programs and in parent education.

Parent satisfaction with specific program activities and with program effectiveness as reflected in the growth of children are two paramount criteria. If parents do not approve of the program, do not see that their child is making progress, and do not believe they are a more competent parent because of the program, the parent involvement program will not prove successful. Further, if parents are involved in the handicapped child's educational program at an early age, the child will have a greater likelihood of overcoming the handicap or minimizing its effects. A parent that becomes involved early in the handicapped child's educational program will more likely continue that involvement as the child becomes older. Such a parent is more likely to serve as an advocate for the handicapped child in subsequent years, especially if the program offers advocacy training for parents.

Certain characteristics set apart successful and less successful parent involvement programs. Some of these characteristics are: (1) professionals working with parents must have the knowledge, skills, and personal attributes to work successfully with parents; (2) the needs of parents must be assessed, and parents must play a major role in assessing their own needs; (3) training must be an integral part of the parent involvement program, and this must reflect the expressed needs of parents—the more specific training is, the more helpful it will be to parents; (4) parent involvement programs must be flexible and individualized, recognizing that needs and interests vary from family to family and among individual members of a family; (5) parents must be kept informed about their child's progress as well as their own progress; and (6) parents need to feel that they have a right to help evaluate their child's program and their involvement in the program.

The major obstacle to increased support of parent education programs today is the continued reluctance of professionals to initiate such programs. Their resistance is often due to a lack of confidence among professionals in their ability to work with parents. It would appear that the preservice training of special educators should include course work in parent education and practicum experiences with parents. Stipends by the state or federal government to help special educators obtain formal training in working with parents of the handicapped appears to be a justifiable expenditure of public funds.

Another obstacle to increased support of parent education is the reluctance of parents of the handicapped to demand parent education. The federal government might well subsidize advocacy training program for parents of the handicapped at the local level. Those providing the training might be outside or inside the school program; regardless of affiliation, someone must provide the advocacy training needed by parents of the handicapped.

FOOTNOTE

[1] Outreach refers to projects that have completed 3 years of operation and receive funding to provide technical assistance to other projects.

REFERENCES

Badger, E. *The infant stimulation/mother training project progress report* (1979). University of Cincinnati, Mimeographed, 1979.

Badger, E. The infant stimulation/mother training program. In B. M. Caldwell & D. J. Slidman (Eds.), *A guide for helping handicapped children in the first three years*. New York: Walker, 1977.

Badger, E., Burns, D., & Rhodes, B. Education for adolescent mothers in a hospital setting. *American Journal of Public Health*, 1976, 66 (5), 469–472.

Bloom, B. S. *Taxonomy of education objectives, Handbook I: Cognitive domain*. New York: David McKay, 1956.

Gordon, I. J. Developing parent power. In E. H. Brotbert (Ed.), *Critical issues in research related to disadvantaged children*. Princeton, NJ: Educational Testing service, 1969.

Gray, S. *Home visiting programs for parents of young children*. Paper presented at the meeting of the National Association for the Education of Young Children, Boston, 1970.

Guilford, J. P. *The nature of human intelligence*. New York: McGraw-Hill, 1967.

Karnes, M. B., Teska, J. A., Hodgins, A. S., & Badger, E. D. Educational intervention at home by mothers of disadvantaged infants. *Child Development*, 1970, 41, 925–935.

Karnes, M. B., Studley, W. M., Wright, W. R., & Hodgins, A. S. An approach for working with mothers of preschool children. *Merrill-Palmer Quarterly*, 1968, 14, 174–184.

Karnes, M. B., & Zehrbach, R. R. Flexibility in getting parents involved in the school. *Teaching Exceptional Children*, Fall, 1972, 5(1), 6–19.

Leonard, J. *Chapel Hill services to the gifted/handicapped.* Chapel Hill, NC: The Chapel Hill Training-Outreach Project, 1978.

Levenstein, P. *Verbal interaction project: Aiding in cognitive growth in disadvantaged preschoolers through the mother-child home program, July 1, 1967-August 31, 1970, Final report of child welfare research and demonstration project R-300.* Washington, D.C.: Children's Bureau, Office of Child Development, U.S. Dept. of Health, Education, and Welfare, February, 1971.

Weikart, D. P., & Lambie, D. Z. *Ypsilanti-Carnegie infant education project progress report (Department of research and development).* Ypsilanti: Ypsilanti Public Schools, September, 1969.

Eight

Perspectives on Parent Involvement in Preschool Programs for Handicapped Children

Anne Hocutt and Ronald Wiegerink

INTRODUCTION

The purpose of this chapter is to examine the nature of parent involvement in preschool programs for handicapped children. A stated goal of many federal aid-to-education laws is to involve parents in activities which are: (1) related to their child's education, and (2) sponsored by the system or program providing the education service. In short, parent involvement has become a matter of national policy.

However, parent involvement is not a simple concept. There are many assumptions underlying parent participation, and there are a variety of contacts between the parent and school or between the parent and child which have been called involvement (Goodson & Hess, 1975). Two of the assumptions underlying parent involvement are: (1) that there are some "deficit" parents who must be taught ways to improve a child's chances for academic success; and (2) that it is the family (primarily the mother) which has the greatest impact on the child during the critical preschool years. Research regarding the efficacy of early intervention programs with at-risk and mildly handicapped children, particularly when such programs have a parent involvement component, has especially supported this last assumption (Bloom, 1964; Bronfenbrenner, 1975; Karnes & Teska, 1975; Lazar & Darlington, 1978; Schaefer, 1972; Weikart, Bond, & McNeil, 1978).

A primary reason for involving parents in education programs, then, is to promote beneficial changes early in life, particularly in children's cognitive functioning. This purpose is especially relevant when children are either at risk or handicapped; i.e., when they have special needs and when special intervention is required. Programs for parents of handicapped children may involve, first, instruction of the parent by the professional, and second, education of the child by the parent who uses the knowledge provided by the professional.

Other assumptions underlying parent involvement policies are that: (1) people have a right to share in decisions which affect them, and (2) consumers who are paying for a service have the right to receive the kinds and quality of services they want. This purpose is especially relevant when children traditionally have been refused services or given inappropriate services, as in the case of handicapped children. Programs for parents of handicapped children may give parents decision-making or policymaking responsibility. Such decisions usually have direct impact on the educational service provider, with indirect impact on the child.

An example of parent involvement policy which embodies many of the assumptions outlined above is P.L. 90-538. Enacted in 1968 (now section 623 of the Education of the Handicapped Act), this section authorizes an educational program called the Handicapped Children's Early Education Program (HCEEP). Since 1969, the Special Education Program [then the Bureau of Education for the Handicapped (BEH)] has funded several hundred projects (usually for a 3-year period) under this law to serve handicapped children and their parents. The purpose of these projects is to develop and demonstrate a variety of services for parents and preschool children, and then to promote the adoption of exemplary services by other, similar projects. This network of projects, called the "First Chance Network," is committed by law, regulations, and intent to foster and demonstrate parent involvement.

The law itself states that parents having children in these projects should be encouraged to "participate in the operation and evaluation of the projects" [Section 2(a) of P.L. 90-538]. The regulations designate

four general categories of involvement: planning, development, operation, and evaluation of the project; parent training; participation in the
educational and therapeutic components of the project; and dissemination of information about the project. The guidelines, while not having
the force of law, recommend the following services for parents:

1. assistance in understanding and coping with the child's behavior;
2. psychological or social work services;
3. information on child growth and development;
4. information on special education techniques;
5. observation of children in the project;
6. carry-over activities to the home; and
7. participation in planning and evaluation of the program.

   Since 1977, we have been studying parent involvement in the
HCEEP Network. In this chapter, we analyze parent involvement in
projects funded under this program from three different, but related,
perspectives. The first perspective is policy clarification: because of the
complexity of both concept and policy, we have used a Delphi procedure
to operationally define the meaning of the law, regulations, and guidelines from the point of view of five groups of experts. Second, we report
results from a survey of parent involvement as it was reported by HCEEP
projects in their third year of funding. These results permit us to draw
conclusions about how parent participation has actually been implemented in the network and to discuss factors related to the extent of
parent involvement. Finally, we examine parents' satisfaction with their
involvement in this program.

CLARIFICATION OF HCEEP PARENT INVOLVEMENT POLICY

Purpose

   The purpose of this study was to clarify HCEEP parent involvement
policy by soliciting expert opinion. A Delphi procedure (Delbecq, Van
de Ven, & Gustafson, 1975) was used to identify, collate, and prioritize
experts' interpretations of the practical meaning of the provisions of P.L.
90-538 and its regulations regarding parent involvement.

Rationale

   Federal policy requiring parent involvement in early childhood
education projects is a complex mandate which may allow a variety of
possible contacts between parents, professionals, and children. In addition, like many other mandates, this policy of parent participation is

not clearly defined: while the law appears to emphasize a decision-making role for parents vis-à-vis the individual project, the regulations and guidelines appear to emphasize more traditional parent activities, such as receiving information or educating their own children. While these roles are not necessarily incompatible, they are very different in purpose and rationale. Thus, a problem in implementing this mandate is that priorities regarding parent activities and roles have not been consistently established, and criteria regarding the appropriate amount of parent involvement have not been set. In order to study implementation practices and factors related to successful parent involvement, we thought it advisable to develop an operational definition of this policy.

Panel Selection and Characteristics

Members of the Advisory Board of the Carolina Institute for Research on Early Education of the Handicapped (Anderson, 1980) nominated individuals for the Delphi panel of experts. The nominees had to fall into one of the following five categories: Congressional staff, Bureau of Education for the Handicapped (BEH) staff, parents of handicapped children, directors of validated (i.e., funded beyond the usual three years) HCEEP projects, and experts in early childhood education and parent involvement. These groups were selected because they fall along a continuum from those who make to those who implement policy. Additional criteria were that the nominees should have experience in at least one of the following activities:

1. Active involvement in writing, interpreting, or implementing the law, regulations, or guidelines for the Education of the Handicapped Act;

2. Presentation of testimony to a legislative body or other concerned organization;

3. Publications concerning early childhood education and parent involvement; or

4. Consultation concerning either early childhood education or parent involvement.

The panel was composed of 12 men and 9 women. One subgroup (parents) was composed entirely of women; one subgroup (Congressional staff) was evenly divided between men and women; the rest had a ratio of 3 men to 1 woman. Of the 21 panelists, about half had doctoral degrees and all had at least a B.A. degree.

Delphi Method

The Delphi technique is a process through which group communication is structured so that individual judgments may be aggregated.

It consists of a series of structured questions: the first series (round #1) produces initial responses to an issue; the second (round #2) indicates initial positions; and the third (round #3) generates consensus and closure (Delbecq et al., 1975; Linstone & Turoff, 1975). Panelists receive feedback on all responses so that they may reconsider their responses in light of other expert opinion. This technique has been used successfully as a planning and policy clarification tool (Fendt, 1977; Jillson, 1975; Linstone & Turoff, 1975; Ludlow, 1975).

Our investigation followed the procedure outlined above. The first questionnaire was open-ended and asked the question: "What parent involvement activities do you think constitute effective and meaningful parent involvement in early education projects for handicapped children?" The second questionnaire asked the following question: "What rank of importance do you believe would be given to the implementation of *each* activity in order to fulfill the mandate/policy of parent involvement in First Chance Network projects?" A rank of 3 meant Very Important, 2 meant Important, 1 meant Slightly Important, and 0 meant Unimportant. In addition, respondents were asked to specify the percentages of parents they would expect to find in each activity they ranked 1, 2, or 3. The specific parent activities listed in the second questionnaire were taken from responses to the first questionnaire. The third questionnaire was based on only those activities for which agreement was not statistically significant; it asked essentially the same questions as the second questionnaire.

The statistic used to assess agreement among panelists was the Kendall Coefficient of Concordance, *W*, a descriptive measure of the extent of agreement or correlation among the five groups of panelists. In order to determine the extent of concordance, the specific parent activities generated by the panelists on the first round of the Delphi were grouped into four categories similar to those defined in the P.L. 90-538 regulations. These included: (1) parent training, i.e., parents receiving general information or instruction; (2) educational and therapeutic activities: passive, i.e., parents receiving reports, counseling, etc., specifically related to their child or the child's preschool project; (3) educational and therapeutic activities: active, i.e., parents acting as change agents for their children; and (4) planning, development, operation and evaluation, i.e., parents assisting education professionals in some regard with the project itself.

The extent of agreement was calculated between the five groups of panelists and the four categories of activities and between the panelists and all activities within each category. Further, agreement was calculated along the dimensions of relative importance (among categories, then on activities within each category) and the extent of involvement expected (as above).

Results

The panelists identified a total of 34 different activities they thought could constitute effective and meaningful parent involvement; panelists also rated the importance of each activity by assigning a score between 0 (unimportant) and 3 (very important) to each of the 34 parent activities. In addition, they identified the average percentage of parents they expected would participate in each activity. Table 1 shows the activities considered important, i.e., having an average rank value of 2.0 or greater; to a substantial degree, these activities emphasize the receipt of information or instruction by parents. Only three of the nineteen activities ranked in this range were considered decision-making activities (numbers 12, 13, and 14), and only five (numbers 1, 7, 11, 16, and 19) were considered active participation by parents in the projects' educational and/or therapeutic component.

The values of W, or Kendall's Coefficient of Concordance, will equal 1 when perfect agreement exists among judges and will equal 0 when maximum disagreement exists. The values of W were .94 for the relative importance of the four categories of activities as calculated among the five groups of panelists, and .90 for the extent of expected involvement. The parent training category was considered the most important by four of five groups (only the project directors dissented), and the planning, development, operation and evaluation category was considered least important by all groups.

Similarly, parent training as a category received the highest level of expected involvement from three of the five groups (project directors and BEH staff were the exceptions); and planning, development, operation and evaluation had the lowest levels of expected involvement across all judges. Overall, panelists expected 77% of parents to be involved in parent training, but only 36% to be involved in planning, development, operation and evaluation activities. When agreement across the groups of judges was calculated regarding the relative importance or extent of involvement expected for activities within a specific category, the values of W ranged from a low of .58 to a high of .86. Confidence levels for all analyses were .05 or higher.

Discussion

On the one hand, the results of this study confirmed the complexity of parent involvement in that a variety of parent–professional and parent–child contacts were considered appropriate by the panel members. Further, there was a wide range of values regarding the relative importance of the various activities (from .53 to 2.95 out of a possible 0 to 3.0)

**TABLE 1:   IMPORTANCE OF EACH ACTIVITY IN PROTOTYPIC PROJ-
ECT AND PERCENTAGE OF EXPECTED PARENT INVOLVE-
MENT**

Rank	Activity (parents should:)	Mean rank	Mean % involvement
1	Participate in development of child's Individual Education Plan	2.95	97.5
2	Receive information regarding support services or programs offered by other agencies	2.90	97.0
3	Receive systematic reports of child's progress	2.90	94.3
4	Receive information concerning the legal rights of child and parents	2.88	85.0
5	Receive instruction in educational techniques to use with child	2.84	85.0
6	Receive information concerning the behavioral and/or other effects of medicine	2.72	77.0
7	Work with child at home to carry out the child's educational or therapeutic program	2.70	84.1
8	Meet with child's teacher for informal exchange of information about the child	2.70	82.6
9	Observe child in activities at home at the request of project staff	2.68	84.5
10	Receive a formal orientation to the project (philosophy, methodologies, services, etc.)	2.60	74.8
11	Assist in the screening/assessment of their own child	2.53	83.4
12	Assist in setting project goals and objectives	2.45	69.4
13	Be members of project advisory board	2.45	34.3
14	Participate in project evaluation activities	2.33	74.6
15	Receive instruction in normal/exceptional child development	2.28	73.0
16	Participate in parent discussion groups to discuss problems associated with having a handicapped child	2.23	64.8
17	Receive regularly scheduled home visits	2.20	77.3
18[a]	Receive their own (the parents) individualized program	2.15	69.3
19[a]	Observe their child at the preschool on a regularly scheduled basis	2.15	69.0

[a] These activities are tied according to the mean value of importance. The activity which appears first has the highest percentage of expected parent involvement.

and the extent of participation expected (from 11.1% to 97.5% out of a possible 0% to 100%). On the other hand, the results also operationally defined the policy along two dimensions: (1) the nature and (2) the expected extent of involvement. Priorities were established through the ranking procedure used, and criteria regarding appropriate levels of involvement were set.

The extent to which this operational definition would be useful either for planning and evaluation or for research purposes depended upon the values of W in the statistical analysis. Because of the high levels of agreement, as indexed by the high values of W—especially in the among-categories analyses—the utility of this operational definition was strengthened. Just as impressive, perhaps, was the fact that agreement was achieved among panelists having very different backgrounds and experiences as administrators (government and project), consumers, policymakers, and researchers.

Finally, given the heavy emphasis on providing information to parents and involving parents in some way with the educational and/or therapeutic components of the projects, it was clear that this panel considered parents to be primarily learners and change agents for their children, not decision-makers. With regard to the underlying rationales for parent involvement policy presented in the introduction, the emphasis was on beneficial child outcomes, not on the consumer's ability to make some impact on the service delivery system. In summary, this operational definition was much closer to the language of the regulations and especially the guidelines than to the language of the law: while participation in project operation and evaluation was considered important, it certainly was not emphasized to the same extent as the more traditional pattern of participation embodied in the guidelines.

PROGRAM IMPLEMENTATION STUDY OF PARENT INVOLVEMENT

Rationale

The purposes of this study were to survey and document the parent involvement activities of third-year HCEEP projects and then to determine those factors which might be associated with the implementation of a parent involvement component congruent with the operational definition of the policy. Because First Chance Network projects are demonstration projects, they use a "variety of approaches in a wide range of settings and situations" (Martin, 1971, p. 662). The strategy is what Rivlin (1971) has called "random innovation," in which individual projects or facilities are encouraged to try new approaches to see how they work. Inherent in this strategy is a tension between policy and implementation: "The more general an idea and the more adaptable it is to a range of circumstances, the more likely it is to be realized in some form, but the less likely it is to emerge as intended in practice" (Majone

& Wildavsky, 1978, p. 114). With the operational definition of parent involvement policy established by the Delphi Panel as a standard for practice, the next step was to determine just how the policy had been realized and what project characteristics had promoted practices more congruent with the operational definition.

Project Characteristics

Third-year projects were selected for study because they had been in operation long enough to have their parent activities firmly in place. As would be expected because of the policy of random innovation, they were quite different from each other: they served between 13 and 250 children; they enrolled all ages of children between 0 and 8; they served the entire range of handicapping conditions and severity levels; they were home-based, center-based, or provided services in both settings; they were located in urban, rural, or suburban settings; and some served more than one catchment area.

Method

The 34 third-year projects were surveyed to determine both the type and amount of parent participation. The Parent Involvement Survey, based on a piloted survey of nine outreach projects, obtained information on the projects themselves (number of children enrolled, number of children on whom family data were reported, whether transportation was provided for parents, etc.) and required directors to report the percentages of parents (based on one parent per child) involved in specific activities. There was space for the directors to list activities and amounts of involvement for any activities not specifically listed in the survey. When the Delphi study generated additional activities, a followup instrument was designed.

While 28 projects (82%) responded to the original Parent Involvement Study, only 23 (67%) responded to the followup. Because of the problem of self-selection, the 23 projects responding to both survey instruments were compared with the 5 projects that responded only to the first survey and the 7 projects that did not respond at all. The comparison was made on the following project characteristics: sponsoring agency, size (number of children served) service delivery mode (home-based, center-based, or combination) and service area (rural, urban, suburban, or combination). There were no differences among the three sets of projects on these variables.

A t-test comparing the reported extent of parent involvement and involvement in each of the four categories used in the Delphi study was done for the 23 projects which responded to both instruments and the 5 responding only to the first. No differences were found.

Finally, several Chi Square analyses were carried out to determine whether a relationship existed between congruence with the operational definition of the policy and a number of project, staff, and parent characteristics. Among the variables selected on the basis of literature in this field and used in these analyses were: size (number of children served); type of sponsorship (public school or other organization); staffing patterns (extent of time spent with parents); existence of transportation for parents to project; director and staff training; the delivery system used (home-based, center-based, or combination); the type of catchment area served by the project (rural, urban, suburban, or a combination); and parent income and education level.

Results

The 28 projects offered all of the 34 activities identified as appropriate by the Delphi panel in the previous study, although no one project implemented all 34; the range was 13 to 31 activities offered. With regard to the categories of participation, involvement was greatest in educational and therapeutic:passive activities with 59% of the parents participating. These activities were ones in which parents received a service (as opposed to information) or in which they observed the child or met with the teacher. Nearly as high a percentage of parents—58.8%—were involved in parent training activities. At the other end of the continuum, only 15% of parents were involved in planning, development, operation, and evaluation activities (including information dissemination).

The only activities offered by all 28 projects were parent participation in the development of the child's Individualized Education Plan (IEP) and orientation to the project. There were nine individual activities in which an average of 80% or more of all parents were involved; of these nine activities, seven were also the most common ones offered by projects. One hundred percent of the parents received systematic reports of the child's progress. Ninety percent or more of the parents received a formal orientation to the project, met with the teacher for an informal exchange of information, received instruction in educational techniques to use with the child, or assisted in the screening or assessment of the child. Over 80% of parents participated in the development of the IEP, received information regarding other support services, observed their child at home, or received information concerning legal rights.

With regard to the analyses on the relationship between congruence with the operational definition (and also higher levels of involve-

TABLE 2:   SUMMARY OF SIGNIFICANT RESULTS OF FACTORS AS-
SOCIATED WITH PROJECTS LIKE AND UNLIKE PROTO-
TYPIC PROJECT

Variables	x^2 Values[a]	$p <$
Type of project sponsor (private, nonprofit; university-affiliated; public school)	5.77	.05
Percentage of time paid staff work directly with parents (less than 74%; 75% or more)	4.90	.05

[a] These values of x^2 were calculated using Yates's correction for continuity.

ment) and project, staff, and parent characteristics, the following statistically significant ($p < .05$) relationships were found (see Table 2).

Projects sponsored by private, nonprofit organizations were more congruent, and had higher levels of involvement than those sponsored by public schools.

Projects with a staff member designated to work with parents at least 75% time were more congruent and had higher parent involvement than did projects with a staff member spending less than 75% time on parent involvement and projects with no parent staff.

Discussion

While it was clear that there were a variety of practices with regard to the implementation of parent involvement policy, it was also clear that the actual practice of participation in these projects was roughly congruent with the operational definition of the policy arrived at in the previous study. The greatest levels were found (and had been expected) in the educational and therapeutic:passive and the parent training categories, and the least in the planning, development, operation, and evaluation category. In effect, overall practice appeared to emphasize the participation of parents in the roles of learners and/or change agents for their children, and not as decision-makers. Again, actual practice was closer to the guidelines than to the language of the law.

Further, involvement was found to be heaviest in the individual activities ranked highest by the Delphi panel (see Table 1). Of the 11 activities which had received average importance values of over 2.50, 9 were found to have high actual involvement levels. The two exceptions were parents' receiving information concerning the behavioral and/or other effects of medication and parents' working with children at home to carry out the educational or therapeutic program. The former exception obviously might apply to only a few parents and thus would logically be a very important, but not frequent, mode of participation. The latter involved actually working with—as opposed to observing—children in the home setting and might not be especially applicable for center-based projects. Thus, practice with regard to implementation of important activities was also quite consistent with the expectations of the Delphi panel in the previous study.

Determination of the factors related to greater or less involvement (and to greater or less congruence with the operational definition of the policy) yielded results which were interesting, but hardly surprising. The finding that involvement was greatest if a staff member were specifically designated to work with parents at least 75% time makes sense. On the face of it, the existence of a staff member whose job description emphasizes direct work with parents as the primary responsibility indicates a belief in the importance of parent involvement on the part of the project director. This finding clearly reinforces the opinion of Karnes and Zehrbach (1975) that a sympathetic staff is important in determining the quantity of parent participation. In any event, it clearly is not as effective in promoting parent involvement if several staff are designated to work with parents on a part-time basis. Given other responsibilities, work with parents might take a back seat and thus result in less parent involvement.

The result that public school sponsorship is associated with less parent involvement is somewhat troubling. There is a great deal of literature (Hocutt, 1979) showing that the educational system generally does not value parent involvement. There may be several reasons for this. First, public school teachers are usually taught to focus on the child, not on the family. Further, educational systems are designed to develop educational practices which relate more to professional expertise and convenience than to parent involvement. Thus, there is no history of the educational system being especially responsive to families.

In summary, it is clear that while the practice of involvement by third-year projects in the First Chance Network was a rough approximation of the policy of parent involvement as operationally defined by the Delphi panel, the extent of involvement of parents was somewhat less than the Panel desired. Based on the findings, those interested in increasing the participation of parents should ensure that staffing patterns promote involvement through assigning one person to work with parents as a major (i.e., at least 75% time) part of her job. Further, efforts should be made to keep the client load of the individual working directly with the parents relatively small. Finally, professionals who work with handicapped children—especially those working in public school settings—should be trained to consider the entire family, rather than attending solely to the child.

PARENT SATISFACTION STUDY

Purpose

The purpose of this study was to determine the level of satisfaction experienced by parents served in HCEEP projects. In addition, the study was designed to document the amount of parent involvement in projects and to determine if the level of parent satisfaction varies with amount and type of involvement or with family and child characteristics.

Rationale

Traditionally, parents and other consumers of human services for specialized populations have not been satisfied with the services they receive (Abramson, Gravink, Abramson, & Sommers, 1977; Anderson & Garner, 1973; Barclay, Goulet, Holtgrewe, & Sharp, 1962). Too often these services have been marked by repeated referrals, and consumers have had to search for services that do more than provide diagnosis and assessment. More recently, a few projects providing early childhood services have been able to achieve high levels of parent satisfaction. Studies of both Head Start (MIDCO, 1972) and the HCEEP network (Bureau of Education for the Handicapped, 1976) have documented parent satisfaction with the services they receive. Because these studies focused on overall levels of satisfaction as opposed to satisfaction with particular aspects of the service program, one is left with a picture of global approval of these projects. In order to more clearly understand the nature and extent of parent satisfaction with services, it is necessary to examine what particular program characteristics parents are and are not satisfied with and factors which relate to their satisfaction. It could be expected that satisfaction of parents of preschool handicapped children might vary with their child's degree and type of disability, the types of services provided, and family circumstances such as income and work patterns.

Method

Each of the 23 HCEEP projects which responded to the parent involvement survey was asked to participate in the parent satisfaction study. Projects were sent a packet of 10 Carolina Parent Questionnaires (Posante & Wiegerink, 1978) and instructions for randomly selecting 10 parents who had been served by the project for at least 1 full year. Parents were mailed the questionnaire and given a stamped envelope by which they could mail the questionnaire directly to the investigators.

Each questionnaire contained codes that identified both the project and the individual parents.

Results

Thirteen of the 23 projects participated in distributing the parent satisfaction surveys, and 77 of the 130 parent surveys were returned. Sixty-eight of the 77 respondents completed the entire questionnaire, and only these are presented here. The 13 projects represented a relatively diverse geographical distribution. The children averaged 3.75 years of age, were about equally distributed among the three disability categories (physically handicapped, developmentally delayed, multiply handicapped), and had been in the programs an average of 1.67 years. The parents' income represented a wide range (mean = $9,600), with 32% of the mothers working and 44% of the fathers with more than a high school education.

The parents' response to the satisfaction questionnaire indicated a relatively high level of satisfaction: 4.35 on a 5-point scale, with a range of 3.33 to 5.00. Six of the 68 parents provided all 5's on the 9–item scale indicating that they were very satisfied with all aspects of the program.

The responses did have sufficient variability, however, to provide a certain level of discrimination. On a series of 5-point scales of program satisfaction, parents had average ranges from 3.3 to 5.0. This range allowed for the more and less satisfied parents to be compared. Table 3 shows that the least satisfied parents ($N = 17$) had an average satisfaction level of 3.8 and a range of 3.3 to 4.0 compared with an average of 4.9 and a range of 4.8 to 5.0 for the most satisfied parents ($N = 15$). On most characteristics these two groups were alike; they came from six of the same projects, although an additional three projects were represented by less satisfied parents only, and two projects by more satisfied parents only. When projects with three or more highly satisfied parents are compared with projects with three or more less satisfied parents, interesting findings are evident. Although these projects are not different in most characteristics such as urbanity, income of parents, and model of service delivery, they are different in sponsoring agency and percent of parent involvement. Of great interest, all three projects with high proportions of least satisfied parents were affiliated with public schools.

Noticeable differences between the most and least satisfied parents were also evident in the number of hours spent with other parents and in the type of handicapping conditions characterizing their children. The least satisfied parents spent an average of 1.6 hours per month. Further, 73% of the more satisfied parents had developmentally delayed children

TABLE 3:   COMPARISON OF LEAST AND MOST SATISFIED PARENTS

	Least (N = 17)	Most (N = 15)
Mean satisfaction rating (highest score = 5.0)	3.8 (range = 3.3–4.0)	4.9 (range = 4.8–5.0)
Level of involvement		
At preschool	9.0 hrs.	11.4 hrs.
At home	52.0 hrs.	42.0 hrs.
With parents	1.6 hrs.	4.6 hrs.
Average time in program	21.7 mos.	17.8 mos.
Projects represented		
Total	9	8
In common	6	6
Type of handicap		
Physically handicapped	18%	20%
Developmentally delayed	35%	73%
Multiply handicapped	47%	7%
Child		
Sex male	65%	80%
Average age	51 mos.	45 mos.
Child progress	100%	100%
Ability to influence		
Child's education	82%	80%
School program	6%	73%

and 7% multiply-handicapped children, compared with 35% and 47%, respectively, for the less satisfied parents. In addition, the more satisfied parents were more often parents of boys than were the less satisfied parents. The most interesting finding is that, although both groups were equally satisfied with their child's progress (100%), and felt they had influence over their child's education (82% and 80%), a much higher percentage of the more satisfied parents felt they had acceptable levels of influence on the program or wished for more influence, whereas the less satisfied parents had little or no influence (73% compared with 6%).

Table 4 shows that the three projects with highly satisfied parents are in private, nonprofit organizations or universities whereas the three with less satisfied parents were found in public schools. Averaged across activities, projects with highly satisfied parents have 73% of their parents involved as opposed to only 45% for the projects with least satisfied parents.

Discussion

Unfortunately, the response rate of projects and parents was only slightly over 50%. This might indicate a response bias in favor of those

TABLE 4:   COMPARISON OF THREE PROJECTS WITH LEAST SAT-
ISFIED AND THREE PROJECTS WITH MOST SATISFIED
PARENTS

Parent characteristics	Least satisfied group	Most satisfied group
Average level of parental satisfaction	3.8	4.9
Average income	$9,200	$10,000
Location		
Urban	2	1
Rural	1	2
Sponsoring agency		
Public school	3	0
University	0	2
Private organization	0	1
% of involvement per project		
02	—	89
05	56	—
08	—	72
10	38	—
26	—	58
28	40	—
Average % of involvement across projects	45	73

projects and parents most positive about parent involvement. When this
is taken into account, the high level of parent satisfaction across projects
is not difficult to accept. These positive findings replicate the findings
of the Batelle Report (Bureau of Education for the Handicapped, 1976)
and Posante (1978) who found levels of over 90% very positive satisfaction with HCEEP services. They go beyond the results of these two
reports, however, in demonstrating that agency sponsorship, type of
child disability, and level of perceived influence by parents are related
to parent satisfaction.

CONCLUSIONS

This set of studies was both descriptive and exploratory in the
examination of parent involvement policy as implemented by projects
funded under the Handicapped Children's Early Education Program. In
general, the key policy questions asked involved the determination of
factors associated with better implementation practices (greater involvement, or involvement more congruent with the operationally defined
policy) and with parent satisfaction. While the results of each study have

been discussed previously in this chapter, two findings in particular draw together all three studies.

One interesting result was the low priority given to decision-making activities (in the planning, development, operation, and evaluation category) by the Delphi panel members, the very low level of involvement in these activities found in practice, and the low levels of satisfaction reported by parents not involved in these activities. From the perspective of beneficial parent outcomes (e.g., greater satisfaction with the project), as opposed to beneficial child outcomes, participation in decision-making activities appears more important than it does from either the operational definition of the policy or from actual practice. Thus, those professionals who wish to promote more parent satisfaction (and perhaps increase their involvement) should provide more opportunity for parents to have a voice in project decisions.

Another interesting finding was the crucial nature of agency sponsorship; both lower levels of involvement and satisfaction were found to be related to public school sponsorship. Given the assumptions behind the policy of parent participation—that it benefits the child and that consumers have the right to be involved in programs which affect them—it is desirable to somehow change this relationship between public school sponsorship and low levels of parent involvement and satisfaction.

There have been some findings in these studies that are not amenable to change or to intervention. However, those things which can be modified—staffing patterns, number of hours which parents spend working with children, opportunities for participation with regard to project operations—should be modified in order to increase involvement and satisfaction. Perhaps the unfortunate relationship between public school sponsorship and low levels of satisfaction or involvement may be changed by professional training which emphasizes the desirability of parent participation and the importance of the family. In the final analysis, we believe that it is worth struggling to realize the policy of parent involvement, and we hope that these studies have provided some data on which to base program changes designed to promote more participation and greater satisfaction.

REFERENCES

Abramson, P. R., Gravink, M. J., Abramson, L. M., & Sommers, D. Early diagnosis and intervention of retardation: A survey of parental reactions concerning the quality of service rendered. *Mental Retardation*, 1977, *15*, 28–31.

Anderson, K. (Ed.) *Status report: Carolina Institute for Research on Early Education for the Handicapped*, Chapel Hill: University of North Carolina, 1980.

Anderson, K., & Garner, A. Mothers of retarded children: Satisfaction with visits to professional people. *Mental Retardation*, 1973, *22*, 36–39.

Barclay, A., Goulet, L. R., Holtgrewe, M. M., & Sharp, A. R. Parental evaluations of clinical services for retarded children. *American Journal on Mental Deficiency*, 1962, *67*(2), 231–237.

Bloom, B. S. *Stability and change in human characteristics*. New York: Wiley, 1964.

Bronfenbrenner, U. Is early intervention effective? In M. Guttentag & E. Struening (Eds.), *Handbook of evaluation research* (Vol. 2). Beverly Hills, CA: Sage Publications, 1975.

Bureau of Education for the Handicapped. *Battelle Report: A summary of the evaluation of the Handicapped Children's Early Education Program* (HCEEP) (Prepared by the planning staff of the Office of Child Development). Washington, DC: Author, Department of Health, Education, and Welfare, 1976.

Delbecq, A. S., Van de Ven, A. H., & Gustafson, D. H. *Group techniques for program planning: A guide to nominal group and delphi processes*. Glenview, IL: Scott, Foresman, 1975.

Fendt, P. *North Carolina adult and continuing education future study.* Unpublished doctoral dissertation, University of North Carolina, 1977.

Goodson, D. O., & Hess, R. D. *Parents as teachers of young children: An evaluative review of some contemporary concepts and programs.* Stanford, CA: Stanford University, 1975.

Hocutt, A. M. Parent involvement policy and practice: A study of parental participation in early education projects for handicapped children (Doctoral dissertation, University of North Carolina, 1979). *Dissertation Abstracts International,* 1980, *41*(6), 2552-A.

Jillson, I. A. The national drug-abuse policy delphi: Progress report and findings to date. In H. Linstone & M. Turoff (Eds.), *The delphi method: Techniques and applications.* Reading, MA: Addison-Wesley, 1975.

Karnes, M. B., & Teska, J. A. Children's response to intervention programs. In J. J. Gallagher (Ed.), *The application of child development research to exceptional children.* Reston, VA: Council for Exceptional Children, 1975.

Karnes, M., & Zehrbach, R. Parental attitudes and education in the culture of poverty. *Journal of Research and Development in Education,* 1975, *8*(2), 45–53.

Lazar, I., & Darlington, R. D. *Lasting effects after preschool.* Washington, DC: Education Commission of the States, 1978.

Linstone, H., & Turoff, M. Introduction. In H. Linstone & M. Turoff (Eds.), *The Delphi method: Techniques and applications.* Reading, MA: Addison-Wesley, 1975.

Ludlow, J. Delphi inquiries and knowledge utilization. In H. Linstone & M. Turoff (Eds.), *The Delphi method: Techniques and applications.* Reading, MA: Addison-Wesley, 1975.

Majone, G., & Wildavsky, A. Implementation as evaluation. In H. E. Freeman (Ed.), *Policy Studies Review Annual* (Vol. 2). Beverly Hills: Sage Publications, 1978.

Martin, E. W. BEH commitment and program in early childhood education. *Exceptional Children,* 1971, *37*(9), 661–663.

MIDCO Educational Associates. *Investigation of the effects of parent participation in Head Start.* Washington, D.C.: Project Head Start, Office of Child Development, U.S. Department of Health, Education, and Welfare, 1972.

Posante, R. *Factors associated with parent satisfaction with a preschool program for the handicapped.* Unpublished doctoral dissertation, University of North Carolina, 1978.

Posante, R., & Wiegerink, R. *Carolina survey on parent involvement.* Chapel Hill: Carolina Institute for Research in Early Education of the Handicapped, Frank Porter Graham Child Development Center, Univ. of North Carolina, 1978.

Rivlin, A. M. *Systematic thinking for social action.* Washington, DC: Brookings Institution, 1971.

Schaefer, E. S. Parents as educators: Evidence from cross-sectional, longitudinal, and intervention research. *Young Children,* April, 1972, 227–239.

Weikart, D. P., Bond, J. T., & McNeil, J. T. *The Ypsilanti Perry Preschool Project: Preschool years and longitudinal results through fourth grade.* Ypsilanti, MI: High/Scope Educational Research Foundation, 1978.

NINE

PARENT PARTICIPATION IN FEDERAL EDUCATION PROGRAMS: FINDINGS FROM THE FEDERAL PROGRAMS SURVEY PHASE OF THE STUDY OF PARENTAL INVOLVEMENT*

J. WARD KEESLING AND RALPH J. MELARAGNO

INTRODUCTION

This chapter provides some initial findings from the Study of Parental Involvement in four Federal Education Programs (hereafter, the Study of Parental Involvement), which is being conducted by System Development Corporation (SDC) under a contract with the U.S. Education Department (ED). The present study is concerned with four federally funded educational programs:

1. Follow Through, created as part of the Economic Opportunity Act of 1964, which provides funds to support "comprehensive educa-

tional, health, nutritional, social, and other services as well as aid in the continued development of children (from low-income families) . . . to their full potential."

2. Title I of the Elementary and Secondary Education Act (ESEA) of 1965, which provides "financial assistance . . . to local educational agencies serving areas with concentrations of children from low-income families . . . (to meet) the special educational needs of educationally deprived children."

3. Title VI of the Elementary and Secondary Education Act (ESEA) of 1965, also called the Emergency School Aid Act (ESAA), which provides "financial assistance to meet the special needs incident to the elimination of minority group segregation and discrimination among students and faculty . . . and to encourage the voluntary elimination, reduction, or prevention of minority group isolation (in schools). . . ."

4. Title VII of the Elementary and Secondary Education Act (ESEA) of 1965, also called the Bilingual Education Act, which provides "financial assistance to local educational agencies . . . to enable (them) . . . to demonstrate effective ways of providing, for children of limited English proficiency, instruction designed to enable them, while using their native language, to achieve competence in the English language."

These four programs were selected by the Education Department for inclusion in the study because they address different educational concerns, serve different student populations, and have different legislative and regulatory requirements for parent participation. The cross-section of parent involvement incorporated in the study offers opportunities for more revealing policy analyses than would be possible in a study of any one of the programs by itself.

All four programs are subject to cycles of legislative reauthorization and rewriting of regulations. At the time of the survey, the Follow Through (FT) program was the only one of the four to have approved regulations. These regulations elaborate considerably on the legislation with respect to parent involvement.

Amending legislation for the other programs was enacted in October, 1978, (before we conducted the survey reported below), but regulations had not been approved by the time this study was written. Generally speaking, the proposed regulations for these three programs do not elaborate on the legislation with respect to parent involvement.

The findings reported in this chapter should not be construed as a comparative evaluation of parent involvement components across programs. Nor are they to be construed as a compliance audit. Very few specific statements in the legislation or regulations would permit one to construct a standard by which to assess the implementation of parent involvement components at the local level. There are even fewer instances in which the legislation or regulations are identical across programs and would permit a valid comparison of their parent involvement components. Finally, the information presented here is not intended to reveal the value of parent involvement to the districts, schools, teachers, parents, or children.

Rather, findings are a portrayal of the formal aspects of parent involvement at the local level in these four programs during the spring of 1979. They provide information on the extent of various types of parent involvement activities that will be useful in interpreting the richer data on the nature and value of these activities in subsequent reports from the study.

The chapter is divided into four sections. In the first section we present information on the four programs that are the focus of the study, provide historical information on the development of parent involvement in federal education programs, and trace the prior research findings in the area. The second section describes the Study of Parental Involvement, concentrating on the Federal Programs Survey phase. In the third section, we present certain key findings from the national survey. The final section contains conclusions drawn from our findings. We indicate some patterns that appear in the data, and then point out the types of research that are still needed to further our understanding of parent involvement and its effects in the public schools.

PARENT INVOLVEMENT IN FEDERAL PROGRAMS: ORIGINS AND PRESENT CONTEXT CONCEPTUALIZING PARENT INVOLVEMENT

Specifying the ways in which parents can participate in the educational process is fundamental to a conceptualization of parent involvement. Such a specification forms the basis for a description of parent involvement in the four programs that are the subject of this study.

Stearns and Peterson (1973), in a review of parent involvement in compensatory education programs, see three roles for parents: (1) tutors of their own children, (2) paid employees, and (3) advisors or decision-makers. While these three roles capture the principal ways in which parents take part in educational programs, they exclude others. More recently, a long-time student of parent participation in education, the late Ira Gordon, defined six roles for parents in the Parent Education model for Follow Through (Gordon, Olmsted, Rubin, & True, 1979): (1) classroom volunteer; (2) teacher of own child; (3) paraprofessional; (4) decision-maker; (5) learner; and (6) audience. Gordon's categories are somewhat imprecise, since it is particularly difficult to determine the operational difference between the last two roles. Nonetheless, we have found this schema quite consistent with the parental involvement functions that we have specified.

Our examination of contemporary thinking about parent involvement, derived from an extensive literature review and numerous discussions with educators and parents, led us to identify five parent involvement functions. These are: (1) governance (primarily defined as decision-making); (2) educational (as instructional paraprofessionals or volunteers, or as tutors of their own children); (3) school support (both tangible and intangible); (4) community–school relations (referring to communication and interpersonal relations); and (5) parent education (personal learning experiences). In this study of parent involvement in federal programs, we concentrate on the governance and educational functions to a greater degree than the other three functions since governance and education are the most closely related to the purposes of the four federal programs.

Descriptions of the Four Programs

Follow Through. Follow Through is an antipoverty program aimed at students who are at or below poverty level and who have participated in Head Start or a similar preschool program. Its goal is to sustain and expand, during grades kindergarten through three, gains students made in their preschool programs. A project is composed of one or more schools implementing a particular FT approach. Follow Through is the smallest of the four subject programs, there being but 161 local projects in the nation. However, as will be elaborated later, Follow Through has the richest prescribed parent involvement component.

Title I. In terms of both children served and funds allocated, Title I is the largest of the four programs we surveyed. In 1978, 93.7% of local education agencies (LEAs) received Title I funds (Wang et al., 1978) and one study (Hoepfner, Wellisch, & Zagorski, 1977) found that 67% of all elementary schools receive Title I funds. This program is truly national in scope, affecting every state, almost every LEA, and the majority of schools.

Title I is a categorical entitlement program, meaning that certain groups of students are entitled to receive its services. Its target population is composed of students who are educationally deprived and who reside in areas with high concentrations of low-income families. Its goal is to raise student achievement, especially in the areas of reading, language arts, and mathematics. Projects are carried out at either the school or LEA level.

ESAA. The second largest of the programs surveyed is the Emergency School Aid Act (ESAA). While ESAA projects are found throughout the United States, only about 5% of the LEAs currently receive ESAA funds. ESAA is a noncategorical education program. Its target population is composed of students in districts that are implementing or are planning to implement a desegregation plan. Its goals are to reduce racial isolation, treat problems arising from desegregation, and overcome the educational disadvantagement of racial isolation. Projects are carried out at the district level, at the school level, or through nonprofit organizations.

Title VII. Title VII of ESEA, often referred to as the Title VII Bilingual Program, is a categorical education program. Its target population is students of limited English proficiency. Its goal is to enable these students to achieve competence in the English language and to progress through the educational system through the use of a program of bilingual education. Projects are carried out at the district level, but students of limited English proficiency participate in their regular schools. Title VII is the third largest of the programs we studied. Given its specialized target population, the program is concentrated in locations in the nation where large proportions of students of limited English proficiency are found. While the largest number of participating students are Hispanic, more than a dozen languages are included. Approximately 5% of the LEAs in the nation receive bilingual program grants.

Historical Development of Parent Involvement in the Four Programs

The concept of parent involvement in federal education programs can be traced back to the Community Action Program of the Economic Opportunity Act (EOA) of 1964, administered by the Office of Economic Opportunity (OEO). Peterson and Greenstone (1977) indicate that EOA included community action to increase the political participation of citizens previously excluded from local politics, particularly members of ethnic minority groups. They note: "Taking its authority from EOA's celebrated requirement that poverty programs be developed with the 'maximum feasible participation of the residents of areas and the members of the groups served,' the OEO insisted that approximately one-third of local policymaking bodies consist of such residents or members, chosen 'whenever feasible' in accordance with democratic procedures" (pp. 241–242). Citizen participation in federal programs began in earnest with the EOA, based on the principle of participatory democracy: Affected citizens have the right to participate in the formation of policies that may affect their lives.

In terms of education, the Head Start program of EOA addressed the "maximum feasible participation" requirement by including parents on policymaking groups. In addition, parents of Head Start children were employed as staff members in Head Start centers, and center personnel had frequent contact with parents at the center and in the home. Head Start has provided a paradigm for parent involvement in subsequent federal education programs.

Close on the heels of EOA came ESEA of 1965. Seen by many as a continuation of the War on Poverty (Levin, 1977), ESEA broke the long tradition of opposition to federal support for public schools and gave the Commissioner of Education authority to establish basic criteria for implementation. Among the then-commissioner's criteria was the requirement that parents be involved in developing local project applications for Title I of the Act. Subsequently, regulations and guidelines were issued to clarify this criterion. In July, 1968, advisory committees were suggested; in November, 1968, "maximum practical involvement" of parents in all phases of Title I was required. In 1971 LEAs were required to provide parents with documents on planning, operating, and evaluating projects. In 1970 a Parent Advisory Council (PAC) was required at the district level; in 1974 the law was changed to include councils at both the district and school levels, with members selected by parents. Legislation in 1978 describes in detail the composition and training of PACs at both levels.

The Title VII Bilingual program was designed by Congress to provide LEAs with assistance for unique problems. Since Congress conceived of Title VII as a district-level program, the "participatory democracy" principle caused Congress to require district-level advisory groups. The recent reauthorization of ESEA continued to require parent advisory groups in participating districts, more specifically, parents are to be involved in developing the district's application and in the actual operation of the district project.

The legislation for Follow Through, as regards parental involvement, was modeled closely after that for Head Start. The Community Services Act funded Follow Through in OEO, although administrative control resided in the U.S. Office of Education. (This has since changed, and Follow Through is now funded and administered through the Department of Education.) Given its ancestry in OEO and its close relationship to Head Start, it is not surprising that the regulations for Follow Through specify more parent involvement than those of most federal programs.

Prior Research on Parent Involvement

The Study of Parental Involvement is the first effort on the part of the Department of Education to examine this component of federal education programs. While prior evaluations of each of the four programs have included some attention to parent involvement, none has addressed it in any substantial way. Therefore, little is presently known about the nature of parent involvement at the local level, as the following summary demonstrates.

The national evaluation of the Title VII Bilingual program (Danoff, Coles, McLaughlin, & Reynolds, 1978) did not touch on parent involvement, nor were effects of community advisory committees examined.

A little more is known about parental involvement in the ESAA program. In the longitudinal impact studies (Coulson et al., 1976), the degree of parent involvement was not influenced by various activities used to promote parent participation; however, more parents participated in schools where the principal assumed greater responsibility for school–community relations. In turn, degree of parent involvement was not found to be related to outcome measures. On the other hand, an in-depth study of a subset of ESAA schools (Wellisch, Marcus, MacQueen, & Duck, 1976) revealed greater gains in student achievement when parents were present in the classroom as instructional aides, volunteers, or visitors. By contrast, parent participation outside the classroom, such as through membership in advisory committees or as noninstructional aides, had no impact. Further, the use of parent aides in the classroom was found to influence student performance, but not so when the aides were outsiders.

The various volumes in the series on the "Follow Through Planned Variations Experiment" (Stebbins, St. Pierre, Proper, Anderson, & Cerva, 1977) have little to say about parent involvement, perhaps because the focus was on comparisons among the different FT models. Other studies have provided some information. For example, Nero and Associates (1976) report that a key element in facilitating the development of parent participation is the employment of a person at a FT school in the role of Parent Coordinator. This person was found to ease the contact between the school and the parent, and to facilitate communication at a personal rather than formal level. The Nero study also found that (1) the presence of classroom aides helps make parents feel more comfortable in interacting with the school, as do prior home visits by the Parent Coordinator; (2) parents become involved in decision-making when they perceive that their participation will be meaningful; (3) there is a tendency for more involvement when students are in the primary grades than later; and (4) middle-class, better educated parents tend to be more involved than lower-income parents. Since this study was based on brief visits to only 10 Follow Through sites, the findings outlined above must be considered tentative.

Given that Title I is the largest federal education program, it is not surprising that more studies that touch on parent involvement have been done with this program. This is not to imply that a great deal is known about parent involvement in Title I, for research to date would not support such a conclusion. Instead, the scattered findings are more provocative than definitive.

As part of the ongoing Sustaining Effects Study being carried out by System Development Corporation, 15,000 parents were interviewed in their homes. Certain questions dealt with parent involvement in the schools. Among the findings are that few parents of Title I children are aware of a school's Parent Advisory Council (PAC), few report voting in PAC elections, and few say that they are or have been PAC members. Even fewer parents are employed as paraprofessionals.

In a recent report to Congress, the National Institute of Education (1978) summarized findings from four NIE-sponsored studies that addressed, in part, district- and school-level Title I advisory groups. Highlights of the findings were that: principals often dominate school PACs, most PAC members are appointed rather than elected, few districts offer training to PAC members, PACs are seldom involved in planning or evaluating projects, and there is great variability in PAC operations and roles. Perhaps the most important conclusions drawn by NIE are that there is considerable confusion about PAC roles, and that there exists no clear federal policy about parent involvement.

Recently, a fifth study was completed for NIE that specifically addressed one aspect of parent involvement in Title I; namely, the PAC (CPI Associates, 1979). Conceived as an exploratory effort, the study was carried out in three states chosen to reflect variations in state support for PACs. Further, in each state LEAs were chosen to provide a spectrum of demonstrated LEA support for PACs. In all, eight LEA Parent Advisory Councils and 34 school PACs were included. Data were collected through interviews with LEA and school respondents. Four results concerning PAC impact on Title I projects were reported. First, district PACs had moderate impact. Second, school PACs had little impact. Third, the greatest PAC impact was found when the LEA staff sought change and obtained PAC support. Fourth, there was little impact when the PAC desired and attempted to obtain change on its own.

The five NIE-sponsored studies reviewed above provide some leads regarding parent involvement through advisory groups (which is a part of what we have defined as the "governance" function). An important difficulty with each study is that the methodologies employed do not allow for projection of findings to describe Title I PACs nationally.

Parent involvement has also been studied in work that is not directly tied to evaluation of federal programs. Three recent reviews are available that summarize findings from different studies (Center for Equal Education, 1977; Chong, 1976; Gordon, 1978). From these reviews it appears that parent participation in the classroom, parental assistance to their own children at home, and home visits by school–community liaison personnel result in an improved classroom atmosphere and in both cognitive and affective growth on the part of the students. These reviews also suggest that the involvement of parent advisory groups does not appear to have a great impact on schools and students, and that more extensive research is required in order to develop a theory of parent participation in decision-making that would aid in the evaluation and formulation of policy in this area. These reviews have helped shape our study, but the narrow focus for each of the above studies requires that findings be verified or rejected through detailed examinations of the four federal programs before policy decisions can be made.

THE STUDY OF PARENT INVOLVEMENT

Overview of the Study

Our study of parent involvement was divided into two major phases—a federal programs survey and a site study. Each of these phases is described below.

Federal programs survey. Given the paucity of information regarding parent involvement in the four programs, there is a need for basic descriptive data on formal parent involvement activities collected from a sample of districts and schools that is nationally representative. To this end a sample of districts and schools was selected for participation in a survey study. District-level program personnel were the primary respondents. Data of a factual nature were collected on funding arrangements; parent advisory groups; parents as paid aids, volunteers, and teachers of their own children at home; and the supervision and coordination of parent involvement. The data-collection effort for the national survey was carried out in spring, 1979. This report summarizes the findings of this national survey.

Site study. At the present time it is not possible to specify unequivocally the forces that help or hinder parent involvement nor the effects of parent involvement activities. Further, certain types of parent involvement activities are highly informal, and all activities are likely to have many subtle but important nuances. These dimensions of parent involvement are not amenable to study on the basis of information collected through survey methodology. Determining the factors that shape parent involvement activities and their effects requires intensive investigation by on-site researchers, with the investigation tailored in part to the unique aspects of each site. Participating sites were selected on the basis of certain background characteristics and the nature of parent involvement, as revealed by the Federal Programs Survey. The results of this study are now being analyzed and were therefore not available at the time this chapter was written.

Sample Design for the Federal Programs Survey

The sampling plan. The sampling plan for each of the four programs was designed to produce a self-weighting random sample of participating schools. Because nationwide lists of participating schools could not be generated in a timely fashion, it was decided to sample participating districts first, and then sample schools from within districts.

Many of the characteristics of interest in the study involve district-level activities (e.g., the district-level advisory group). In order to estimate values representing national averages it was necessary to have many districts participate in the survey. However, it was also desirable to have at least two participating schools in each sampled district so that school-to-school variation within districts could be examined, and so that there would be two schools to study in each district that was chosen for participation in the Site Study phase. Preliminary work indicated that a sample of about 100 districts per program would provide a sufficient basis for reasonably precise estimates of district-level population values. At the level of the school, it was determined that a sample of about 250 per program could be drawn within the budget constraints. This would provide for two or more schools to be drawn in each of the 100 sampled districts.

The size of the sample to be drawn for each program was determined by allocating districts such that the hypothetical sampling errors were equal across programs. Thus, the sample sizes reflect the different sizes of the programs: Title I has the largest sample and Follow Through the smallest. But both samples yielded the same estimated sampling error.

Samples of districts were drawn independently for each program using a technique known as probability proportional to size (PPS) sampling. The total district enrollment in grades K–8 was used as the size measure. This insured that larger districts with more-served schools would come into the sample with higher probability than smaller districts. This plan also tended to select districts with at least two schools to include in the sample. Lists of the served schools were obtained from the sampled districts and schools were drawn from this list. The probability of drawing a given school was proportional to the reciprocal of the size measure (enrollment) used to draw its district.

In order to minimize the burden on the respondent within a district (usually the district-level program director), it was decided to sample no more than four schools per district. Schools were randomly discarded within the sampled districts with more than four sampled schools to bring the number of sampled schools down to four. In order to reach the goal of 2.5 schools per district (on the average), the initial sample size was increased to more than 2.5 schools per district (for each program, as necessary) to allow for losses due to the process of discarding schools in districts where more than four schools were drawn into the sample.

Weighting. The sampling design described above requires that weights be used in estimating the population values for characteristics of districts and schools. These weights adjust the sampling probabilities so that each district in the sample of districts (or school in the sample of schools) represents its proper share of the population of districts (or schools). An example at the district level will illustrate this procedure. Suppose that in a hypothetical sample one district had 100,000 students and was drawn into the sample with a probability equal to 1.0 (i.e., it would always be selected into any sample drawn in a like fashion). Suppose that ten other districts in the population each have 10,000 students and one of them is drawn into the sample (its selection probability is 0.1). If the hours of parent coordination are averaged for these two districts in the sample, the resulting value represents what happens to the typical students (because each of the two sample values represents 100,000 students). Now, if one wishes to know what the typical district is like, then the two values should be multiplied by weights equal to the reciprocal of their sampling probabilities before the values are averaged. The weight for the larger district is $1.0/1.0 = 1.0$, because it represents only one district; while the weight for the smaller districts is $1.0/0.1 = 10$, because it represents 10 districts. The weights cause the smaller district to be treated as if there were nine more just like it in the data base.

Representativeness and precision. Many samples could have been drawn and each would have produced estimates that deviated from the average value of all such samples. One way of assessing the precision of a sample is to describe the sampling error. Analyses of the data indicate that for data involving proportions or percentages, the sampling error is about .05 or 5% at the maximum. Thus, if 50% of the participants respond that a given activity exists, then the standard error is about 5% and an interval of ± 1.6 standard errors, called a 90% confidence interval, would run from 42 to 58% (Gonzales, Qgus, Shapiro, & Tepping, 1975).

Nonsampling errors. The confidence intervals described above presume that the sampling design is valid and that there are no flaws in the data collection. However, even in complete censuses, where the population mean could be calculated directly, there are other sources of error that may invalidate the results. Examples include: inability to obtain information about all cases in the sample, definitional difficulties, differences in the interpretation of questions, inability or unwillingness to provide correct information on the part of respondents, and mistakes in recording or coding data.

Questionnaires used in the survey were field-tried on a limited number of cases to assure that they were not ambiguous. Data were rigorously screened during data collection and call-backs were made to correct inconsistencies and omissions that were noted by this process. In order to encourage frank reporting, provisions for maintaining confidentiality of the data were designed into the study and were explained to the respondents. These efforts must be balanced against the fact that the survey results are self-reported data in an area that does not have a well-established framework for inquiry. Thus, there is still the possibility that some of the data are the result of misunderstanding the intent of the questions or trying to report what it was thought the Education Department would like to hear.

Instrumentation for the Federal Programs Survey

Instruments for the Federal Programs Survey were developed to reflect three facets of the study: (1) the conceptual framework outlined above; (2) the hierarchical organization of school systems; and (3) differences and similarities across the four federal programs under study. For each of the four federal programs, a district-level and a school-level questionnaire were created. Each questionnaire addressed the parent involvement activities that are either mandated by the federal program or that may occur because the district or school chooses to implement such forms of parent involvement. Table 1 shows the correspondence between the areas of study in the conceptual framework and the content of the questionnaires. Questionnaires for all four programs addressed the same broad content areas.

Questionnaires used in the Federal Programs Survey (FPS) obtained information about the more formal aspects of the content areas listed in Table 1. They were designed to be completed by district-level personnel, with some assistance from local schools. Consequently, there are few questions asking for details of the processes engaged in under any of the functions. Much of the interest in the school support, school–community relations, and parent education functions, for example, would be centered on the processes and the content (rather than

TABLE 1: CORRESPONDENCE BETWEEN THE CONCEPTUAL FRAMEWORK AND THE CONTENT OF QUESTION-NAIRES USED IN THE FEDERAL PROGRAMS SURVEY

Conceptual framework for the study	Content areas in the Federal Program Survey	
	District-level questionnaire	School-level questionnaire
Context of implementation	District descriptive/demographic info.; district-level sources of funding[a]	School descriptive/demographic info.; school-level sources of funding[a]
Governance function	District advisory committee; composition/operation	School advisory committee; composition/operation
Educational function	Not addressed at the district level	School use of paid paraprofessionals; school use of volunteers; parents as teachers of their own children
School–community relations	Supervision and coordination of parental involvement	Coordination and promotion of parental involvement
School support function	Represented in certain response categories in other sections	Represented in certain response categories in other sections
Parent education function	Represented in certain response categories in other sections	Represented in certain response categories in other sections

[a] A substantial part of the district and school demographic information was to be obtained from data compiled by the Office of Civil Rights and the National Center for Educational Statistics. Such information was not available at the time this chapter was written.

simply the counts of participants), so these functions are less fully represented in the FPS questionnaires than the other functions. It was felt that the processes and content associated with these functions would not be easily determined by someone at the district level responding to the questionnaires.

In order to reduce respondent burden we agreed to use data on demographic characteristics that had been collected by federal agencies. The Common Core of Data (collected by the National Center for Educational Statistics in the fall of 1978) was to provide information on the grade-by-grade enrollment at the district-level, as well as information about which grades each district considered to be "elementary." The

Office of Civil Rights (OCR) survey was to supply racial and ethnic data for approximately 75% of the districts and schools in the FPS samples (the others were not in the OCR survey). Unfortunately, the OCR data base did not arrive in time to be included in this chapter.

Methodology for the Federal Programs Survey

The Federal Programs Survey was conducted in three phases: permission and enumeration, data collection, and followup. During the permission and enumeration phase, System Development Corporation (SDC) obtained permission from the chief state school officers to contact districts to obtain lists of schools served by the programs under study. Lists were obtained of those schools in each district that were participating in the program(s) for which that district had been chosen. These lists were then used to select schools for participation in the study. These contacts with each district (usually by phone) also established the name of a liaison person for SDC to deal with during the remainder of the survey data collection. Typically, this person was the local coordinator or director of federal program(s).

Copies of the appropriate district-level and school-level forms were sent to the liaison person in each district. This person was to fill out the district-level questionnaire and assign the school-level questionnaires to the staff members who were best acquainted with program operations at the schools. District personnel were allowed 2 weeks to review the questionnaire materials and begin filling them out. Two weeks after the questionnaires were mailed, a trained SDC representative called to establish a firm date for a second call to record questionnaire responses. This form of data collection was used to reduce the time needed for followup of incomplete, incorrect, and missing data that occurs in mail-out surveys.

FINDINGS FROM THE FEDERAL PROGRAMS SURVEY

District Characteristics

Data on the distribution of schools by type of locale are given in Table 2. Title I is by far the largest of the programs in terms of total grants and number of participating districts. Title I's nearly complete coverage of all districts in the country reflects the fact that the vast majority of districts are small and located in small towns and rural areas. By contrast, ESAA and Title VII grants are predominantly awarded to large-city districts. Follow Through seems more evenly split between the large-city and rural areas than the other programs.

TABLE 2: DISTRIBUTION OF SCHOOLS INCLUDED IN THE SAMPLE BY PROGRAM AND LOCALE[a]

Locale	Title I	ESAA	Title VII	Follow Through
Large cities (over 200,000 in population) and their suburbs	17	47	52	32
Middle-size cities (50,000–200,000) and their suburbs	13	17	13	19
Small cities or towns	31	20	17	17
Rural areas	39	16	19	33

[a] Entries are the percentages of served schools in each type of locale.

Financial Arrangements

Table 3 presents data on the average project size and funding levels. The ESAA programs gave the largest average awards, but served the greatest number of schools per participating district as well. Follow Through had the second largest average grant size and served the smallest number of schools per district. Consequently, Follow Through had a great deal more money to spend per school than the other programs.

The level of funding per served pupil also reveals differences from program to program. Title I and Follow Through provide nearly equal amounts per served pupil, while the Title VII program provides about 65% of this amount and the ESAA program provides 50%. The effects of these differences in funding levels on parent involvement are discussed below.

An attempt was made to gather information on the financial support that districts provided for parent involvement activities. Unfortunately, even within a program, there is no standard accounting practice

TABLE 3: AVERAGE INDICATORS OF PROJECT SIZE AND FUNDING LEVELS BY PROGRAM

Indication of project size	Title I	ESAA	Title VII	Follow Through[a]
Average number of participating schools	3.7	7.8	4.3	3.4
Average grant size	$175,000	$461,000	$216,000	$352,000
Average funding per served school	$40,000	$37,000	$34,600	$95,500
Average percentage of school enrollment served	24	49	21	74[b]
Average funding per served pupil	$500	$250	$360	$550

[a] Only enrollment in K-3 was considered for Follow Through.
[b] In the 1980—81 school year, the appropriation for Follow Through was cut by 31%.

across districts that permits reliable reporting of this information. For example, only 55% of all Title I projects reported using a line item form of accounting for parent involvement. Only 68% of these line items included advisory group meeting expenses. Since virtually all Title I districts have advisory groups, there seems to be little uniformity in reporting their expenses.

The problem becomes even more severe if one attempts to compare across programs. The FT directive to give preference to parents in hiring for paraprofessional positions, for example, can lead to reporting some of the costs of paraprofessionals as parent involvement costs. By contrast, a Title I district with a similar level of parent participation might be much less likely to report any of these costs as part of their parent involvement expenses, feeling that they are exclusively instructional costs. In short, the inconsistencies in reporting make it essentially impossible to report valid data on the absolute or relative costs to districts and programs of parent involvement activities.

Parent Participation in Project Governance

Membership characteristics of the district-level committees are influenced by the legislative and regulatory language as can be seen by the first two rows of Table 4. The Title I legislation specifically mentions only parents as members of this committee, without excluding others. The Title VII legislation mentions school staff, students, and community representatives as possible members, but stipulates that parents should not be less than half the membership. The FT regulations indicate that more than one half the membership must be low-income FT parents and that parents are to select other members from among community representatives. ESAA legislation specifies that after the grant is awarded, the project funded by the grant must be operated in consultation with parents of the served children and representatives of the served communities, including the committee that reviewed the application (which was to be composed of parents, teachers, and secondary-school students). These are, perhaps, subtle distinctions, but they produce noticeable differences in advisory committee composition. The major question raised by the data in Table 4 is why the FT projects have less involvement of community representatives than ESAA. The answer may lie in the fact that representation of low-income parents on the committee is emphasized in the criteria for evaluating project applications. In addition, the low-income parents may be regarded as appropriate representatives of the community interests and may not have been recorded as playing a dual role in answering the survey questions.

A second indicator of the influence of legislation and regulation

TABLE 4:   CHARACTERISTICS OF DISTRICT-LEVEL ADVISORY COMMIT-
             TEES BY PROGRAMS

Advisory committee characteristics	Title I	ESAA	Title VII	Follow Through
Committees that allow community representatives to vote	4	88	16	37
Committees in which all parents of service children are elected	30	20	42	86
Chaired by a committee member	57	79	58	85
Committees in which a school representative sets the agenda	34	27	9	17
Committees having a budget	42	30	49	98
Average budget[a]	$1,250	$880	$2,066	$2,655

[a] These budget figures are not directly comparable and should be interpreted with caution (see text).

has to do with the manner in which parents come to serve on the advisory committee. FT regulations specify that low-income FT parents are to be elected by their peers. Title VII legislation states that committee members are to be selected by parents of children participating in the project. ESAA legislation does not address this issue. Title I legislation presents an apparent anomaly: It clearly specifies that the committee members should be elected. However, this legislation was enacted after many of the committees had already been established for the 1978–79 school year. Presumably, Title I-served districts have moved into compliance with this legislation since the survey was conducted (in the spring of 1979).

TABLE 5:   PARTICIPATION OF DISTRICT-LEVEL ADVISORY GROUPS
             IN SELECTED MANAGEMENT ACTIVITIES BY PROGRAM[a]

Management activity	Title I	ESAA	Title VII	Follow Through
Develop project application	97	98	100	100
Plan project components	68	96	86	100
Evaluate meeting of goals	79	91	89	99
Sign-off parental involvement part of budget	55	79	74	100
Sign-off total project budget	55	65	60	94
Select project professionals	28	43	38	86
Select project paraprofessionals	21	47	32	97

[a] Entries in the table are the estimated percentages of district-level advisory groups that have at least an advisory role in the listed management activity.

The last four rows of Table 4 and all of Table 5, taken as a whole, provide further evidence that legislation and regulation influence parent involvement in project governance.

The FT regulations state that the project-level advisory committees are to "assist with the planning and operation of project activities and to actively participate in decision-making concerning these activities." The regulations go on to enumerate nine specific duties for the PACs to carry out, including: helping develop all components of the project proposal in its final form, helping develop criteria for selecting professional staff and recommending the selection of such staff, and exercising the primary responsibility in recommending the selection of paraprofessional staff. The regulations provide an incentive for achieving parent involvement in governance by noting that evidence that these specific duties are implemented will count toward continued funding of projects.

ESAA legislation indicates that projects should "be operated in consultation with, and with the involvement of" the advisory committee. The Title VII legislation states that projects should "provide for the continuing consultation with, and participation by," the advisory committee. Title I legislation states that advisory councils should have "responsibility for advising (the district) in planning for, and implementation and evaluation of, its . . . Title I projects." Thus, ESAA, Title VII, and Title I legislation fails to specify duties for the PAC. Furthermore, these programs evaluate proposals based upon the mere assurance that advisory groups will come into existence and function in the desired manner. Refunding decisions are not stated to be based on evidence of successful implementation.

Data in Table 5 show the percentages of district-level (project-level in the case of Follow Through) advisory groups that have at least an advisory role in the various management activities listed in the Table. This level of participation was chosen for presentation because it is the common denominator for all four programs.

Table 5 indicates that the specific nature of the FT regulations leads to their PACs more often having at least an advisement role. The clearest example of this is in the area of selection of professional and paraprofessional personnel. The large difference between Follow Through and the other three programs must surely be due to the specific mandate in the FT regulations. The next largest difference is in the area of budget where the FT mandate that PACs approve the proposal leads to the differences evident in the Table. Finally, the areas having to do with planning and evaluation show smaller differences because the differences in legislative mandate across the four programs are less sharply defined for these activities.

One measure of the support available for advisory committee activities is the budget that is allocated for their use. Follow Through is the only program of the four that mentions a budget for the advisory committee. The regulations state that it must be "sufficient to allow [the PAC] to effectively fulfill its responsibilities." Again, this specific requirement of Follow Through legislation results in a considerable difference in the proportion of advisory committees with budgets (Table 4).

The magnitude of the budgets is probably related to the available funding per pupil. The budgets for Title VII committees seem large given their funding level and their apparent activity level. Budget size may reflect activities of advisory committees that were not included in our study (such as training of the members or special events sponsored by the committees) in addition to the activities associated with governance. Thus, these budgets cannot be used to estimate the costs of parent participation in governance.

The last item to be discussed with respect to parent involvement in governance has to do with the conduct of the meetings of the district-level advisory committees (Table 4). Advisory committee meetings are not addressed by the legislation or regulation for any of these four programs. However, the differences across programs that are revealed in the middle two items in Table 4 are probably related to the emphasis on parent involvement in the legislation and regulation. The fact that FT regulations require evidence of parent participation as a condition of refunding provides an incentive that may account for some of its difference in tone and the resultant outcomes. Generally speaking, Follow Through PAC meetings are run by a PAC member using an agenda that was set by PAC members (often in collaboration with district personnel). By contrast, Title I PAC meetings are conducted by a PAC member only slightly more than half the time and the agenda is often set by a school representative. This is consistent with the Title I mandate to involve the PAC in advisement about project matters, as contrasted to the FT mandate to actively participate in decision-making about project activities. Title VII and ESAA advisory groups fall between these two extremes, as would be expected from the language of their enabling legislation.

Coordination of Parent Involvement Activities

Coordination of parent involvement activities is not addressed in the legislation or regulation for any of the four programs. However, it is reasonable to assume that the amount of coordination provided and the activities that coordinators engage in are related both to the amount of parent involvement mandated by the program and the financial resources available to provide the services.

Table 6 shows the differences across programs in the provision of coordination services. The following presentation discusses the program features liable to result in a need for these services.

Several sections of the FT regulations deal with aspects of parent involvement other than as PAC members, including: participation in the classroom as observers, volunteers, or paid employees, and participation in educational and community activities developed through other program components. FT projects are also required to have a social services component directed at the families of low-income FT children. A career development program is to be provided for paraprofessionals and non-professionals (FT parents are to have priority in access to both types of positions). The extent of these activities would seem to necessitate a high level of coordination, both to carry out the activities and to stimulate parent participation.

By contrast, both Title I and Title VII program legislation specifies roles for parents primarily as advisors. However, Title VII projects can involve a considerable amount of bicultural activity in which parents participate as exemplars of the culture. Coordinating these activities (e.g., classroom demonstrations, assemblies at which children perform skits, etc.) may account for some of the coordination time spent in Title VII projects.

The focus of ESAA—overcoming the problems of racial group isolation and the difficulties of implementing integration—suggests a stress on multicultural relations that would result in a need for a good deal of

TABLE 6:   DISTRICT- AND SCHOOL-LEVEL PROVISIONS FOR CO-ORDINATION OF PARENT INVOLVEMENT ACTIVITIES BY PROGRAM[a]

Types of provision for coordination	Title I	ESAA	Title VII	Follow Through
Average district-level hours of parent coordination per week	5.4	35	21	80
Two most frequent activities of district-level coordinators	G,M	M,R	G,R	G,R
Average school-level hours of parent coordination per week	3.2	7.4	7.0	36.8
Two most frequent activities of school-level coordinators	R,M	M,V	M,V	R,V

[a] Key:
G: informing parents about program guidelines and regulations.
M: attending meetings to inform parents about the district and school activities and policies.
V: coordinating visitations to parents to inform them about district and school activities and policies.
R: recruiting parents to participate in various activities.

parent coordination. The ESAA program legislation also requires that parents be shown preference in hiring for paraprofessional positions. Recruitment of parents for these positions would also require coordination. Finally, the larger average number of served schools per district might require parent coordination in order to establish and run the required advisory committee.

The data in Table 6 seem to be largely consistent with the types of activities that require coordination just discussed. In addition, the much larger number of coordination hours in the FT projects reflects not only the needs established above, but the availability of funds to support this activity. The emphasis of FT coordinators on recruitment reflects the strong regulatory mandate to involve parents in most aspects of the program. The emphasis on recruitment and home visitation in ESAA and Title VII probably reflects the multicultural concerns of those programs, and the fact that they have sufficient support to perform those services.

Title I projects, on the other hand, have only provided enough of these services to permit their coordinators to engage in making general presentations about the program's regulations and guidelines and about district and school activities and policies. Some recruitment does go on at the Title I schools, however. This is consistent with the Title I legislation which addresses parent involvement only in terms of participation on the advisory groups, and mandates such groups at the school level.

Parent Participation in Educational Programs

In this functional area, as in governance, there are differences in the specificity of the legislation and regulations defining parent participation in educational activities among the four programs that lead to differences in the degree of parent involvement. Table 7 shows the differences across programs in this area of participation.

Paraprofessionals. FT regulations state that: "Whenever an opening exists in project staff positions for nonprofessionals or paraprofessionals . . . the highest priority will be accorded to low-income persons who are parents of Follow Through children." The regulations also require projects to actively recruit parents for these positions. The ESAA legislation states that preference shall be given to parents of children affected by the project in recruiting and hiring teacher aides. The level of emphasis on parent involvement in the ESAA legislation is less than in the Follow Through regulations. Fewer ESAA schools employ paraprofessionals (66% vs. 100%) and they employ fewer people in these positions, on average (2.5 vs. 10.1). The survey did not inquire about

TABLE 7:   PARENT PARTICIPATION IN THE EDUCATIONAL FUNC-
             TION BY PROGRAM

Type of parent participation	Title I	ESAA	Title VII	Follow Through
Paid paraprofessionals	9	14	18	74
Volunteers	14	17	28	67
As teachers in their own homes, trained by:	27	35	50	76
Group training				
Workshops	39	26	50	71
Individual training	26	23	28	64

ᵃ Entries are percentage of schools in each program.

the recruitment processes, so it is not known whether the numbers of parents of served children employed in these positions by the projects represents preferential treatment.

Neither the legislation for Title I nor that for Title VII addresses the issue of hiring parents as paraprofessionals. The higher frequency of parent participation as paid paraprofessionals in Title VII, as contrasted to Title I, may reflect the fact that parents of served children are a likely source of bilingual adults needed in Title VII classrooms.

Volunteers.   The four programs are ordered in the same way with respect to frequency of parent participation in volunteer activities as they were with respect to employing parents as paraprofessionals. The specific language in the FT regulations (cited above) is one source of the large difference between this program and the other three. Another source, which was not investigated directly in this study, is the provision in the regulations for allowing certain in-kind contributions (such as volunteer time) to be counted in place of cash in payment of the non-federal share of the project costs (up to 20% of FT costs must be borne by the district). This incentive would surely contribute to the greater degree of volunteer activity in FT projects.

Parents as teachers of their own children at home.   This potential area of parent involvement is not addressed specifically in any of the legislation or regulations for the four programs. The frequency with which schools reported these activities (Table 7) is apparently linked to the program's emphasis on parent participation and on the availability of funds to support such activities. This is certainly the explanation for the greater emphasis on these activities, especially individual training, that occurs in Follow Through. The degree of emphasis in Title VII projects can be explained by the need to inform non-English speaking parents how they can help in the educational process.

SUMMARY AND CONCLUSIONS

The overall results of this study may be summarized in one succinct statement: Legislation and regulation can provide a powerful motivation to foster and support parent involvement. Furthermore, the data support the inference that differences between programs in the nature and extent of parent involvement are related to differences in the content of the legislation and regulations defining the programs. In particular, the specific content of the legislation and regulations influences the activities undertaken in the name of parent involvement at project sites in three ways:

1. By emphasizing parent involvement in the choice of language used to express the legislative or regulatory intent. This effect is seen in the generally higher levels of parent involvement in the Follow Through projects, even in areas where the nature of parent involvement is not specified in the regulations;

2. By specifying the activities in which parents are to engage. This effect is seen in the much higher levels of parent involvement in the Follow Through program in areas where the nature of parent involvement is specified in the regulations; and

3. By providing incentives for obtaining participation of parents. Follow Through is the only program to provide these incentives. The effect of tying refunding to evidence that parent involvement has taken place seems pervasive and is difficult to disentangle from other effects. The effect of allowing in-kind contributions to offset the nonfederal share of project costs probably has its greatest effect on the volunteer component.

This conclusion parallels that of Zerchykov, Davies, and Chrispeels (1980), who concluded from a study of state requirements for school-level advisory councils that strong action by central governments was necessary for the promotion and nurturing of local, grassroots democracy. Across the four programs in our study, it is clear that where the language of the mandate for parent involvement is less specific and emphatic, and where incentives are not provided, there is less activity.

The results of our survey also suggest two secondary conclusions: (1) the level of funding influences the extent of parent involvement activities; and (2) it is important to monitor the extent to which districts implement mandated activities.

Comparisons across programs reveal that the level of funding (on a per-pupil basis) influenced the availability of funds to provide certain services and activities related to parent involvement. However, the data were not sufficiently clear or specific to permit an accurate estimation of the costs of these services and activities.

Specifying in legislation and regulation that certain activities should take place within local projects probably does not guarantee that they will take place. While the survey did not inquire about monitoring practices, certain features of the data indicate that some monitoring of the implementation of required activities is desirable. In particular, the language in the FT regulations requiring evidence of parent involvement as a condition of refunding both provides an incentive and indicates a requirement for self-monitoring.

It bears repeating that the four programs under study have different purposes and goals. The legislation and regulations for such programs attempt to assure a role for parents in the context of that program's intent. Presumably, each program office believes that the roles it allocates to parents advance the goals of the program. The historical origins of the FT program have led it to emphasize parent involvement as one means to mobilize and coordinate community resources for the benefit of children (see Olmsted & Rubin, Chap. 5). The other programs, not sharing these historical antecedents, may have felt uncomfortable with specifying additional parent involvement components (and requiring assurances of compliance), unless there were compelling evidence that these components would advance the main purposes of the program.

Within the context of each program, the value of emphasizing parent involvement has to be weighed against the value assigned to other components demanding programmatic support, especially the provision of instructional services. The data from this study indicate that more parent involvement could be achieved if: (1) the legislation and regulations defining each program emphasized parent involvement, were specific about the desired forms of involvement, and provided incentives for involvement; (2) funding for the specified activities were provided, especially budgets for mandated advisory committees and for parent coordinators; and (3) some form of monitoring specific activities were provided.

Project managers at the local level generally do attempt to implement the mandated parent involvement components, going beyond the mandate to add other activities that seem suitable in the school context. These additional activities are chosen to promote the goals of the local project. Indeed, there are projects in all four programs that reported broad and intense involvement of parents in the management and operation of project activities. This suggests that there may be ways in which parent involvement can be an effective force in achieving the goals of each program.

Footnote

REFERENCES

CPI Associates. *An exploratory study of the impact of parent advisory councils on the management and administration of Title I programs at the local level*. Dallas: Author, 1979.

Center for Equal Education. Effects of parents on schooling. *Research Review of Equal Education*, 1977, *1*, 30–40.

Chong, M. *The role of parents as decision makers in compensatory education: A review of the literature*. Washington, DC: National Institute of Education, 1976.

Coulson, J., Ozenne, D., Bradford, C., Doherty, W., Duck, G., Hemenway, J., & Van Gelder, N. *The second year of the Emergency School Aid Act (ESAA) implementation*. Santa Monica, CA: System Development Corp., 1976.

Danoff, M., Coles, G., McLaughlin, D., & Reynolds, D. *Evaluation of the impact of ESEA Title VII Spanish/English bilingual education program* (Vol. III). Palo Alto, CA: American Institutes for Research, 1978.

Gonzalez, M., Qgus, J., Shapiro, G., & Tepping, B. Standards for discussion and presentation of errors in survey and census data. *Journal of the American Statistical Association*, 1975, *70*, 5–23.

Gordon, I. *What does research say about the effects of parent involvement on schooling?* Paper presented at the annual meeting of the Association for Supervision and Curriculum Development, 1978.

Gordon, I., Olmsted, P., Rubin, R., & True, J. *Aspects of parental involvement in the parent education Follow Through program*. Paper presented at the annual meeting of the American Educational Research Association, 1979.

Hoepfner, R., Wellisch, J., & Zagorski, H. *The sample for the sustaining effects study and projections of its characteristics to the national population*. Santa Monica, CA: System Development Corp., 1977.

Keesling, J. W. *Parents and federal education programs: Some preliminary findings from the study of parental involvement.* Santa Monica, CA: System Development Corp., 1980.

Levin, H. A decade of policy development in improving education and training for low-income populations. In R. Haveman (Ed.), *A decade of federal antipoverty programs.* New York: Academic Press, 1977.

National Institute of Education. *Compensatory education study.* Washington, DC: Author, 1978.

Nero and Associates. *Follow Through: A story of education change.* Portland, OR: Author, 1976.

Peterson, P., & Greenstone, J. Racial change and citizen participation: The mobilization of low-income communities through community action. In R. Haveman (Ed.), *A decade of federal antipoverty programs.* New York: Academic Press, 1977.

Stearns, M., & Peterson, S. Parental roles and underlying models in compensatory education programs. In *Parent involvement in compensatory education programs.* Menlo Park, CA: Stanford Research Institute, 1973.

Stebbins, L. G., St. Pierre, R. G., Proper, E. C., Anderson, R. B., & Cerva, T. R. *Education as experimentation: A planned variation model.* Cambridge, MA: Abt, 1977.

Wang, M., Hoepfner, R., Zagorski, H., Hemenway, J., Brown, C., & Bear, M. *The nature and recipients of compensatory education.* Santa Monica, CA: System Development Corp., 1978.

Wellisch, J., Marcus, A., MacQueen, A., & Duck, G. *An in-depth study of Emergency School Aid Act (ESAA) schools: 1974–1975.* Santa Monica, CA: System Development Corp., 1976.

Zerchykov, R., Davies, D., & Chrispeels, J. *Leading the way: State mandates for school advisory councils in California, Florida and South Carolina.* Boston: Institute for Responsive Education, 1980.

TEN

EXPLORING THE ASSUMPTIONS OF PARENT EDUCATION

K. ALISON CLARKE-STEWART

This volume amply illustrates the depth and variety of parent education efforts in the United States today. It details much of the program and evaluation work that has been done in this area and forewarns of the complexity of policy issues yet to be addressed. The general impression one gets from reading these chapters is that parent education is important and proven effective, and that we should proceed to solve the policy problems so we can set up more and more programs for more and more parents in more and more places. It looks as if the facts are in: we have seen parent education and it is good; we have tried parent education and it works.

But before we expand our parent education efforts in this era of scarce resources, I suggest we make sure we've got our facts straight. Support for parent education will inevitably come at the expense of other social programs; we need to make the most of our limited opportunities for social change. We will not get away for long with promising outcomes we can't deliver, and there is danger in basing parent education on the claim that it is "scientifically proven" if it is not. If the rationale for parent education were merely good will or good intentions, there would be no problem. But it is not—witness the many pages of program evaluations in this volume. Therefore, we need to examine very carefully this presumed empirical basis for parent education before we proceed. Personally, I support good intentions wholeheartedly, but I think our current parent education efforts are based on a bevy of unexplored and perhaps unfounded assumptions. My purpose in this chapter is to expose and explore some of these assumptions, so we can begin the examination our clients and Congressmen deserve.

There are (at least) five major assumptions underlying parent education, and each will be taken up in turn. These assumptions are:

1. There is an empirical foundation for parent education in the "basic" research literature in child development;

2. We have evaluated parent programs and know what the effects of parent education are;

3. We know what kinds of parent education programs work best;

4. We understand how parent education works;

5. Parent education is more effective than other kinds of social programs.

Let us examine each of these assumptions in some detail.

EMPIRICAL JUSTIFICATION IN "BASIC" CHILD DEVELOPMENT LITERATURE

It is impossible in the space of this brief chapter to describe in detail specific studies that have been cited to provide the basis and impetus for current parent education efforts. I can only suggest here the general lines of research that have been used.[1] First are studies demonstrating that differences in children's abilities by the time they enter school are related to the family's socioeconomic status. Second are observations of children raised in severely deprived environments, such as institutions, showing that these children are markedly retarded in intellectual and social development. Third are studies of children in "normal" home environments, documenting relations between children's development and the kind of parental care they receive, and indicating the kinds of care that are most beneficial. Fourth are studies pointing to a critical or sensitive period in infancy and early childhood during which children are particularly vulnerable to environmental impact. And fifth are studies demonstrating experimentally that adult behavior affects children's performance.

These kinds of basic research were used as the justification and basis for parent education programs in the 1970s. Unfortunately, each research paradigm has serious limitations. The social class literature has been reviewed and roundly criticized before (e.g., Clarke-Stewart & Apfel, 1979; Deutsch, 1973; Erlanger, 1974). To highlight only the most relevant criticisms: most studies of socioeconomic status (SES) have confounded SES with race, ethnicity, religion, and family structure. When variation due to these other factors is separated out, variability within socioeconomic levels turns out to be greater than that between levels, so SES is not such a good predictor of parental or child behavior after all. In fact, although the average frequency or level of behavior of parents and children in higher and lower social classes is different, their modal or most common behavior patterns are the same. But even if we accept a difference in average level as a sufficient basis for intervention, the average differences favoring middle-class mothers (such as being more affectionate, verbal, responsive, or egalitarian) are not present in infancy—the age most commonly recommended for starting parent education programs. And finally, there is no a priori assurance that education or training by itself will change parents' childrearing behavior, since SES is linked to income and occupation as well as to education—factors not affected by parent education programs. Clearly, the research on socioeconomic status does not provide a mandate for parent education.

The second kind of research—observation of severely retarded, apathetic children reared in orphanages or asylums or in extreme isolation-demonstrates dramatically the results of extreme caregiving failure (see Clarke & Clarke, 1976). However, the applicability of these studies to children being raised in families within the "normal" range is dubious. The correlational studies of child development and parental care in normal families are more directly applicable. These studies (see Clarke-Stewart, 1977; Clarke-Stewart & Apfel, 1979) show that as early as 6 months of age, an infant's abilities are related to the amount of stimulation provided by the mother's rocking, jiggling, talking, and playing, and that this relation continues and grows stronger as the child gets older. The more the mother gives the child play materials that are appropriate for his age, the more she shares, expands, and elaborates on his activities, entertains and talks to him, responds promptly and consistently to his signals, and offers consistent, clear, firm and rational control and approval, the better the child does in tests or behavioral assessments. Unfortunately, however, these observations in normal families have typically been made on small samples of white, middle-class subjects. Further, most were conducted in the laboratory or a constrained play situation. As a result, they cannot automatically be applied to the natural home situation of poor or black mothers who are the most common recipients of parent education. In fact, there is some suggestion that correlations between parental behavior and child competence are not the same in different racial groups (e.g., Baumrind, 1971; Clarke-Stewart, 1973).

Another serious problem with these findings as a basis for parent education is that the findings are merely correlational. They reflect statistical associations between parental behavior and child performance, but not necessarily causal direction from parent to child as is assumed in proposing parent education. There is now a growing body of research demonstrating how the child affects the parent and thus contributes to his own development (through individual differences in temperament, e.g., irritability or activity, and the demand characteristics of his behavior, e.g., a smile eliciting maternal smiling). What is necessary to prove that parental behavior influences or causes changes in the child's performance is causal analysis of relations between parental and child variables over time. To date, only a handful of studies have attempted this type of analysis (Belsky, Goode, & Most, 1980; Clarke-Stewart, 1973; Kessen, Fein, Clarke-Stewart, & Starr, 1973; Rogosa, Webb, & Radin, 1978), so the suggestion that direction of influence is from mother to child must still be regarded as tentative. What is also needed is an accounting of maternal styles as they interact with individual differences in children's characteristics. There is already a suggestion that things are not the same for boys and girls (Baumrind, 1977; Clarke-Stewart, 1973); for girls social competence is related to abrasive parental control, while for boys it is related to warm permissiveness; for boys, maternal responsiveness to crying is related to less frequent crying, while for girls it is related to either more or less crying. It is likely that maternal styles would also interact with differences in children's temperament. Even this research on parent–child interaction and relations, therefore, provides a tenuous basis for instituting parent education or designing parent education programs.

This observational research on child development in normal families may also be a basis for the assumption of parent educators that mother is the most important influence on the child's development and the appropriate target for intervention, because significant correlations between maternal behavior and child development have been found in all these studies. Unfortunately, however, these correlations of child development with maternal behavior have not been compared to correlations with the behavior of other persons in the child's environment. Very recently, research has begun to document the important role of the father in the family triad (e.g., Pedersen, 1980), suggesting that there is life beyond the mother–infant dyad. And as more and more mothers are taking jobs outside the home, we might expect that the behavior of other child-carers (grandmother, baby-sitters, day-care staff) will also become more important. The observational research on mother–child interaction is based almost exclusively on relations observed in "traditional" families, where mother does not work and is the exclusive or at least primary caregiver. Whether correlations between maternal and child behavior will continue to hold up for children in day care is not clear. There is already some suggestion they do not (Ramey, Farran, & Campbell, 1979). Certainly, observational studies to date cannot stand as proof that mother is the most important influence on child development.

Empirical evidence of a critical or sensitive period in infancy and early childhood comes from three sources: studies of young animals who were systematically deprived of various aspects of a normal environment; children raised from very young ages in institutions and thus naturally deprived of a normal upbringing; and studies documenting correlations between parent behavior and child performance at various ages. Again, support for early intervention on the basis of these studies is weak. With respect to the experimental studies of animals, although animals do appear to be particularly vulnerable to environmental assault in the early years or months, when effects are especially comprehensive and severe, even the dire effects of rearing in isolation can be overcome by later experience with "therapist" animals (e.g., baby monkeys or sheep dogs) (Cairns, 1977). Thus, even for animals subjected to complete social isolation, effects of early experience are not irreversible. So even if we could generalize from animals to humans (a risky proposition, since differences between species have been observed even among animals), these studies do not establish infancy as a definite critical period. Similarly, with children raised in institutions, although they too are especially vulnerable in the early years, when later adopted or given special training they also show substantial recovery (Clarke & Clarke, 1976). Thus, there is significant if not total reversibility of early effects for humans too.

The way in which correlational studies of children in normal families have been used to make a case that early childhood is a critical period is by showing that adult performance (e.g., intelligence) is increasingly predictable from tests given as the child gets older. The claim has been made that since predictability reaches an asymptote (maximum level of correlation) sometime toward the end of early childhood and does not increase after that, the environment no longer affects performance after this asymptote has been reached (e.g., Bloom, 1964; White, 1975). The problem with this conclusion is that it is based on studies of development in stable environments. The stability of individual differences in IQ based on children in stable environments does not mean that experience is less important at these later ages, but only that its importance does not change. If a child were suddenly placed in a poor environment (like a bad school or foster home) at age 8, it is quite likely his performance would show a significant decrement. It is clear that none of these lines of research establish infancy or early childhood as a critical period for development.

Finally, there are limitations to the experimental paradigm. Most experiments use an adult experimenter as a "parent substitute" who stimulates, reinforces, or punishes the child, or provides a model for the child to imitate. Such studies show effects on children's behavior related to characteristics of the adult experimenter, such as nurturance, power, or enthusiasm. But the question of generalizing to a home situation, real life, and a real mother is critical. Most studies have manipulated relatively trivial behavior, such as hitting a bobo doll or donating M & M's to a charity box, in highly constrained, laboratory situations. Only a few studies have examined the transfer of these behaviors to different situations or a different stimulus, and none have looked at long-term effects of the experimental manipulation. The laboratory and the experiment are artificially simplified, and although a particular manipulation works in the laboratory, what goes on at home where behavior is embedded in an immeasurably more complex context may be entirely different. As a matter of fact, apparently contrasting results regarding the effect of adult behavior on child behavior have been obtained in controlled laboratory experiments and uncontrolled home observations (e.g., results of adult responsiveness to infant crying reported by Ainsworth & Bell, 1977; Bell & Ainsworth, 1972; Etzel & Gewirtz, 1967; Gewirtz & Boyd, 1977).

In sum, then, the five lines of basic research that have been used to justify parent education—research on SES, children in institutions, mother-child interactions, critical periods, and laboratory manipulations—all may point in the same direction; namely, that parent behavior does seem to affect development throughout childhood and that important qualities of that behavior are stimulation, consistency, moderation, and responsiveness. But as I have suggested, each kind of research is seriously limited as a basis for parent education. In fact, the only true test of how parent behavior influences child development is what happens to children's development when parents change their behavior. This kind of evidence is potentially afforded by the very parent education programs at issue here. This brings us to the second assumption underlying parent education today: that we have evaluated parent education and know its effects.

PARENT EDUCATION EVALUATED AND PROVEN EFFECTIVE

This may be the most solidly supported of the five assumptions underlying parent education today. Parent education programs that have been evaluated do have generally positive outcomes, and the consistency of results showing such positive outcomes from such a wide variety of programs (as illustrated in chaps. 4, 6, and 7) is impressive. The conclusion of reviewers of these programs (e.g., Leler, this volume, for school-age programs; Goodson & Hess, 1976, for early childhood programs; and Beller, 1979, for infant programs) is inevitably favorable. Leler is typical: "In summary, the studies of parenting groups show generally favorable results. . . . 19 of 30 studies [using methods of parent education and involvement] revealed positive effects, and 11 showed no differences between experimental and control groups. None had significant negative results" (p. 163).

Thus, it is clear that parent training programs can have immediate effects on children's intellectual performance. Many programs demonstrate significant IQ gains for program children compared to control children. In addition, gains in children's language, when measured separately from IQ, have been observed. When studies have included other than cognitive variables, assessment of these variables suggests that children's sociability and cooperation may also be increased. For intellectual variables, furthermore, studies that have followed children after the program ended also show positive results. Global measures of program effectiveness in elementary school (such as placement in special education classes or grade failure) favor children from parent education programs, and IQ gains are maintained for several years after the program ends (see Clarke-Stewart & Apfel, 1979).

This is the most positive statement of parent education effectiveness possible. But before we bank on this simple conclusion that parent education "works," I must hasten to add some caveats. Most parent programs have simply not been evaluated. The positive results referred to above are based on evaluations of a relatively few, exemplary, model research-and-demonstration parent education programs. We don't know how widely they would generalize to less controlled, less expensive, run-of-the-mill programs. Moreover, even evaluation of these exemplary programs has been exceedingly simple. Of course, evaluation of such programs is challenging: it is difficult to find truly equivalent subjects for a comparison group or to justify or implement random assignments to a no-treatment control group; it is hard to keep different groups separated and parents in different groups incommunicado within the same geographical locale; it is not easy to keep samples comparable since subject attrition is related in complex ways to treatment and progress; and it is a problem to find or devise assessment instruments that are more informative than simple IQ or school achievement tests.

As a result of these difficulties, evaluations of parent education programs have typically been of the simplest possible sort: Tests of children's intellectual performance before the program started and after it ended with no control or comparison groups. Obviously this gives us very limited information about the effects of parent education. Nonprogram (e.g., Hawthorne) effects are not ruled out, nor are negative side effects. Effects on children's emotional development or effects on the mother have seldom been evaluated, and results of the scattered extant evaluations of these features are not consistent. Positive changes by the end of a few programs have been noted in maternal behavior and attitudes—mothers are more talkative, didactic, responsive, and active with their children; they use more complex speech, have less authoritarian attitudes toward childrearing, and feel more confident about being parents. But programs have been less successful in modifying other, more subtle and perhaps influential aspects of maternal behavior such as responding, caring, and playing (see Clarke-Stewart & Apfel, 1979).

Moreover, even for the outcome most typically assessed—the child's intelligence or academic performance—the degree of effect is not overwhelming. There are some studies that have not found any positive results; others have found positive effects on only some of the measures included. When Leler (Chap. 6) says 19 of 30 studies show positive effects on one or more outcomes, she does not report how many positive outcomes were possible. Clearly, it is stating things in the most optimistic way when credit is given for a positive outcome if only one of a dozen measures showed a significant effect. (It might be more accurate to say that, at least in terms of children's IQ gains, no parent education program has been reported to be harmful or worse than no treatment.) It should also be noted that differences reported, although statistically significant, are of moderate absolute size (not more than 15 IQ points). Finally, although immediate effects are achieved in general, most followup studies show effects are not permanent or even very long-lasting (see Clarke-Stewart & Apfel, 1979).

So when we say parent education works or is scientifically proven effective, we should be clear that what this means is that children whose parents have participated in a parent education program are likely to exhibit moderately increased levels of performance on an IQ or achievement test. We don't know very much about effects on noncognitive development, later development, the mother's behavior, or the family. We don't know whether any unevaluated parent education program has worked, is working, or will work. This brings us to the next major assumption in parent education: We know what kinds of parent education work best.

SOME PROGRAMS WORK BETTER THAN OTHERS

With all the variety in approaches that have been taken to parent education, one might expect that by this time—more than 10 years after the first programs began—we would be able to point to clear demonstrations that some programs work better than others. Parent education programs have varied in focus, format, and formulation. They have occurred in hospitals, homes, trailers, and backyards, lasted weeks or years, had sessions ranging from half an hour to half a day, and have occurred daily or monthly, in groups from one to a hundred. Instruction has included printed materials, modeling, reinforcement, videotapes, group discussion, formal classes, and dyadic tutorials. Unfortunately, when evaluations have been done, researchers have nearly always been concerned with demonstrating the overall effectiveness of a program; they have not examined effects according to variation in program dimensions (like length, intensity, or instructional method), or subject dimensions (like age, ability, or background), or delivery dimensions (like time, place, or target). Reviewers have tried, after the fact, to make generalizations across programs about what works best. But their efforts have been frustrated by the ubiquity of overlapping and confounded components among programs. To mention one example: In their comprehensive review of parent education programs, Goodson and Hess (1976) concluded that curriculum content was not related to program effectiveness. This conclusion was based on the finding that mean IQ score changes for different programs were unrelated to whether the program's content was cognitive, verbal, or sensorimotor. The problem with this conclusion, however, was that of the 28 programs they reviewed, 20 were cognitive in content, only 5 were verbal, and 3 sensorimotor. This hardly allowed a balanced or fair comparison of different curricular emphases. Beller (1979) gave up as hopeless the attempt to draw conclusions about more effective kinds of programs. Although Leler concludes: "The approaches which seem to have the most potential are those in which the parents have a definite role in the decision-making" (p. 173); and Karnes, Linnemeyer, and Myles (Chap. 7) similarly contend that parent involvement must be flexible and individualized, neither of these reviewers provides evidence of systematic quantification of outcome data or aggregation of program types. Even the most ambitious and valid of the efforts to generalize across programs—the work by the Consortium on Developmental Continuity (Lazar, Hubbell, Murray, Rosche, & Royce, 1977), which reanalyzed original raw data from 14 parent and early childhood education programs—could not establish the effect of particular dimensions unequivocally.

What is needed to answer questions about the relative effectiveness of different program approaches is probably not cross-program comparison—this may be impossible—but systematic investigation of dimensional variation within programs, while holding constant other potentially confounding factors. Unfortunately, most parent educators have put all their best bets about what will work into a single program.

They have not deliberately and systematically given one group treatment A and a second group treatment B. Consequently, if a program works, it is almost impossible to say what made it effective. A very few investigators have taken the within-program variation approach (Kessen et al., 1973; Slaughter, in press). The study by Kessen and his colleagues systematically varied curricular content while holding constant age, type of subjects (subjects were randomly assigned to curricular group), length and frequency of visits, instructional methods, and individual home visitors. In this study, as in Goodson and Hess's (1976) review, no differential effect on children's IQ of a cognitive, a language, and a social curriculum was found. But increases in children's language production and symbolic play and in their mothers' articulate, nondirectiveness were significantly more likely in the language and cognitive curriculum groups than in the social curriculum group. Clearly, the issue of differential effectiveness of curricula needs further within-program examination, before we will know what kind of parent education is best.

The issue of length of parent education programs is one which has received more attention than the issue of differential curriculum effectiveness, and studies of this dimension suggest that longer programs lead to longer-lasting gains (e.g., Gilmer, Miller, & Gray, 1970; Gordon, Guinagh, & Jester, 1977; Levenstein, 1977). Unfortunately, however, several of these studies confounded program length with children's age. Similarly, a more intense program schedule and longer visits may be more effective (e.g., Gilmer et al., 1970; Kessen et al., 1973), but studies examining these dimensions have confounded intensity with location, activities, focus on mother versus child, or age. Moreover, causal direction from visit length to greater effectiveness cannot be assumed. It may be that visits are shorter because the home visitor is unable to establish rapport with the mother or because mother or home visitor is discouraged by the child's lack of progress, rather than that longer visits cause larger gains in devleopment.

Instructional techniques are also likely to be related to program effectiveness, but evidence here, again, is inconclusive. Although there do seem to be benefits to more structured instruction (Goodson & Hess, 1976), this variable has been confounded with other aspects of the program. Although group discussion has been dismissed as not popular or effective by some reviewers (e.g., Brim, 1965; Chilman, 1973; Goodson & Hess, 1976), other studies using group discussion have found it more effective than individual home sessions (e.g., Badger, 1977; Slaughter, in press). Similarly, although merely giving the parent toys has not been very effective in some studies, programs that selected toys for their stimulating and age-appropriate properties proved to be effective (Badger, 1977; Levenstein, 1977; Slaughter, in press).

In sum, we are nowhere near a definite statement concerning the relative effectiveness of program curricula, instructional methods, or length and intensity of visits. The assumption that we know what kind of parent education works best is simply unfounded.

THE PROCESS OF PARENT EDUCATION IS FROM PARENT EDUCATOR TO MOTHER AND FROM MOTHER TO CHILD

The fourth assumption on which parent education is based is that we understand the process of change that occurs in parent education, and that the direction is from program planner and curriculum to mother and from mother to child. It is here, I think, we are on the weakest ground. For here there is a chain of untested assumptions that extends from the gleam in the program developer's eye to the last p-level in his final report. What is needed to test these assumptions is careful and detailed monitoring of what actually happens in parent education programs. A pre–post outcome evaluation design just does not shed light on the processes of change. And unfortunately, no program evaluation yet has done an adequate job of this kind of monitoring.

There are at least eight links in the chain of assumptions that guides current thinking about the process of change in parent programs. First is the assumption that what the program designer intends is what really happens. Home visitors, though given prior indoctrination and training in program techniques, have seldom been monitored *in situ* as they interpret and implement the program—and they should be.

The second assumption is that the message parent trainers intend is what gets through to the mother. The message that actually gets across may be distorted by the mother's uncertainty, anxiety, or ignorance into a more simple-minded form. We need to assess how the program is received.

Third is the assumption that all mothers are equally ready for parent training. Differences in mothers' circumstances and attitudes prior to the program have been observed to be related to their involvement in the program, their behavior, and their child's progress (Schaefer & Aaronson, 1977; Martin, 1977). Thus, our program evaluations need to consider effects of individual differences in parents' needs.

Fourth is the assumption that the mother's goals for herself and her child are the same as the program designer's—or would be if the mother knew better. Compatibility between parent and program goals has also been found to affect outcomes (Sonquist, 1975), but parents' goals have seldom been assessed in parent training studies. Goals should be assessed before the program even begins.

The fifth assumption is that giving the mother information or knowledge about child care will change her behavior. Although research does show that for families not in parent education programs knowledge about child development is associated with maternal behavior (mothers who were more knowledgeable were more affectionate, talkative, playful, and responsive), knowledge about child development is also related to the mother's general knowledge, education, and IQ (Clarke-Stewart, 1973)—factors that could account for both her specific knowledge about child development and her childrearing behavior.

Sixth is the assumption that the mother changes or will change in the desired direction. While there is some evidence that desired changes in maternal behavior occur (Lasater, Malone, Weisberg, & Ferguson, 1975), there is also evidence that some mothers in some programs change in the opposite direction from that intended—becoming more directive, more extreme, or less involved with their children (Badger, Hodgins, & Burns, 1977; Chilman, 1973; Kessen et al., 1973). It may be that the effect of parent training is to make the mother more anxious or unsure, which could make her adapt the program to strengthen rather than diminish her own natural inclinations. Moreover, the most essential and desirable aspects of mothers' natural behavior with their children—sociability, responsiveness, and effectiveness—may be particularly resistant to change (Kessen et al., 1973). Naturalistic assessment of the mother's behavior with her child before, during, and after the program is important for finding out what changes.

Seventh, there is the assumption that changing the mother's behavior causes the child's improved performance. What is needed to test this critical assumption is analysis of the relation between changes in maternal and child behavior over time. Only four studies offer evidence of this kind. In one (Kogan & Gordon, 1975), mothers' behavior changed during training sessions and children's behavior changed in the post-training period; but there was no correlation between maternal change and child change for individual mother–child pairs. In the second (Andrews, Blumenthal, Bache, & Wiener, 1975), mothers' behavior also changed prior to changes in children's IQ, but the time lags by which maternal change preceded changes in children's motor and cognitive performance were slight and could be at least partially attributed to asynchrony in scheduling mother and child assessments; these investigators did not analyze for correlations between maternal and child change. In the third study (Kessen et al., 1973), which examined both changes in group means and correlational patterns, the investigators found no evidence than changes in maternal behavior either preceded or caused increments in children's performance, and indeed, found that child changes preceded maternal changes on several factors. And finally, in the fourth study (Forrester, Boismier, & Gray, 1977) researchers found that the correlation between children's IQ at the beginning of the program and maternal stimulation at the end was stronger than that between maternal stimulation at the beginning and children's IQ at the end. Since the opposite direction of influence was observed in another comparable study of families not participating in a parent training program (Clarke-Stewart, 1973), this correlational pattern may reflect a treatment effect. What is needed, of course, is further breakdown by time periods during programs.

In addition to the results of these four investigations, consider the following three findings: the behavior of children in exclusively child-focused programs influences the mother's behavior (Falender & Heber, 1975); mother–child interaction and children's behavior are more susceptible to program-induced change than is maternal behavior or attitude alone (Kogan & Gordon, 1975; Lally & Honig, 1977; Leler, Johnson, Kahn, Hines, & Torres, 1975; Sonquist, 1975); and child-focused programs are at least as effective as mother or mother–child focused programs in producing child gains (Kessen et al., 1973; Love, Nauta, Coelen, Hewett, & Ruopp, 1976). Taken together, these findings make it only too clear that we have no basis for the assumption that parent training programs "work" strictly or simply through the mother's influence on the child.

Finally, the last assumption is that the benefits of parent training will continue after the program ends, because the mother learns principles she can adapt as the child gets older or can apply in her interaction with later-born children. Although younger siblings of children whose mothers are in a parent program have been observed to perform better than expected on intelligence tests (Gilmer, Miller, & Gray, 1970; Gray & Klaus, 1970; Levenstein, 1977), this apparent diffusion of the program is confounded by direct effects of the older siblings, the parent trainer, or her toys; it is not necessarily mediated by the mother's behavior. Moreover, evidence that mothers can adapt the principles learned in parent training programs as children get older has not yet been collected.

Clearly, we are a long way from understanding the process by which parent education works. This brings us to the last assumption on which current parent education is based; namely, that parent education is more effective than other forms of social reform.

PARENT EDUCATION IS THE MOST EFFECTIVE SOCIAL PROGRAM

Underlying the enthusiasm of social reformers for parent education seems to be the assumption that parent education will produce more social equality by improving children's development sooner, longer, more, and more cheaply than other forms of social programs such as child-centered early childhood education or day care programs. This assumption is based both on the logic that involving parents will create more permanent and pervasive environments of suitable stimulation for greater numbers of children, and on empirical evidence presented by Bronfenbrenner's (1974) comparative review of preschool and early intervention programs in which he concluded that parent education is more effective than center-based early childhood programs. Bronfenbrenner's review was based necessarily on a limited number of programs. Further, his favorable generalization about parent education was based primarily on gains reported by a single program (Levenstein's Mother–Child Home Program). Taking the child's intellectual performance as the criterion (as it was for Bronfenbrenner), further comparison of parent- and child-focused early childhood programs does not necessarily lead to the conclusion that involving parents is the most effective approach. In reviews or studies comparing mother–child-focused and child-focused (e.g., home visit vs. center) programs, in which mother–child has been touted as more effective (Beller, 1979; Bronfenbrenner, 1974; Goodson & Hess, 1976; Lazar et al., 1977) evidence has been weak: Lazar's comparison was between 13 high- or medium-parent involvement programs and only 1 low parent-involvement program; Goodson and Hess based their claim of superiority on gains of 6 versus 8 to 10 IQ points. Equally strong evidence exists for the claim that there is no difference between mother–child and child-focused programs (Gilmer, Miller, & Gray, 1970; Kessen et al., 1973; Miller & Dyer, 1975) or that child-focused are more effective than mother-child focused programs (Kessen et al., 1973; Love et al., 1976). In one study (Klaus & Gray, 1968), which combined home visiting and center programs, in fact, gains in children's intelligence occurred when children were attending the center (child-focused) and dropped when they had only home visits (mother–child-focused). Of studies comparing within-program effects of mother-focused versus child-focused programs, one (Lombard, 1973) found mother-focused superior; another found child-focused superior (Kessen et al., 1973); and a third (Stern, 1972) found no difference.

In sum, the suggestion that parent-focused (i.e., parent education) programs are more effective than those involving the child or focused exclusively on the child (i.e., early childhood education) is simply not supported. Nor is the evidence convincing that parent education has cost advantages by virtue of diffusion into later years or to siblings. Diffusion to sibs also occurred while the child was in child-focused programs (Garber & Heber, 1980), and the issue of maternal adaptation to older children has not yet been explored.

In conclusion, I have tried to expose some of the salient and critical assumptions underlying parent education and to suggest what evidence is available or needed to support or disconfirm them. Parent education in any form may provide a valuable service to children and the country, but as researchers concerned about science, or as policymakers concerned about economics, we need to be sure our arguments and their presumed scientific merit and effectiveness are well-founded. If time and resources allow us to put parent education on a firmer empirical foundation in the future, we may be able to strengthen our efforts to provide the best possible environment for all of America's children.

FOOTNOTE

[1] I have reviewed these studies and the parent education programs discussed below in a chapter entitled "Evaluating Parental Effects on Child Development" (Clarke-Stewart & Apfel, 1979).

REFERENCES

Ainsworth, M. D. S., & Bell, S. M. Infant crying and maternal responsiveness: A rejoinder to Gewirtz and Boyd. *Child Development*, 1977, *48*, 1208–1216.

Andrews, S. R., Blumenthal, J. B., Bache, W. L., & Wiener, G. *New Orleans Parent-Child Development Center* (Fourth Year Rep. OCD 90-C-381). New Orleans: University of New Orleans, March 1975.

Badger, E. The infant stimulation/mother training project. In B. M. Caldwell & D. J. Stedman (Eds.), *Infant education*. New York: Walker, 1977.

Badger, E., Hodgins, A., & Burns, D. *Altering the behavior of adolescent mothers: A follow-up evaluation of the Infant Stimulation/Mother Training Program*. Paper presented at the Nassau County Coalition for Family Planning Conference, Westbury, NY, November 1977.

Baumrind, D. Current patterns of parental authority. *Developmental Psychology Monograph*, 1971, *4* (1, Part 2).

Baumrind, D. *Socialization determinants of personal agency*. Paper presented at the biennial meeting of the Society for Research in Child Development, New Orleans, March 1977.

Bell, S. M., & Ainsworth, M. D. S. Infant crying and maternal responsiveness. *Child Development*, 1972, *43*, 1171–1190.

Beller, E. K. Early intervention programs. In J. Osofsky (Ed.), *Handbook of infant development*. New York: Wiley, 1979.

Belsky, J., Goode, M. K., & Most, R. K. Maternal stimulation and infant exploratory competence. *Child Development*, 1980, *51*, 1168–1178.

Bloom, B. S. *Stability and change in human characteristics*. New York: Wiley, 1964.

Brim, O. G. *Education for child rearing* (2nd ed.). New York: Free Press, 1965.

Bronfenbrenner, U. *Is early intervention effective? A report on longitudinal evaluations of preschool programs* (Vol. 2). Washington, DC: Department of Health, Education, and Welfare, 1974.

Cairns, R. B. Beyond social attachment: The dynamics of interactional development. In T. Alloway, P. Pliner, & L. Krames (Eds.), *Attachment behavior: Advances in the study of communication and affect* (Vol. 3). New York: Plenum Press, 1977.

Chilman, C. S. Programs for disadvantaged parents: Some major trends and related research. In B. M. Caldwell & H. N. Ricciuti (Eds.), *Review of child development research* (Vol. 3). Chicago: University of Chicago Press, 1973.

Clarke, A. M., & Clarke, A. D. B., (Eds.). *Early experience: Myth and evidence.* New York: Free Press, 1976.

Clarke-Stewart, K. A. Interactions between mothers and their young children: Characteristics and consequences. *Monographs of the Society for Research in Child Development*, 1973, *38*, (6–7, Serial No. 153).

Clarke-Stewart, K. A. *Child care in the family: A review of research and some propositions for policy.* New York: Academic Press, 1977.

Clarke-Stewart, K. A., & Apfel, N. Evaluating parental effects on child development. In L. S. Shulman (Ed.), *Review of research in education* (Vol. 6). Itasca, IL: Peacock, 1979.

Deutsch, C. P. Social class and child development. In B. M. Caldwell & H. N. Ricciuti (Eds.), *Review of child development research* (Vol. 3). Chicago: University of Chicago Press, 1973.

Erlanger, H. S. Social class and corporal punishment in childrearing: A reassessment. *American Sociological Review*, 1974, *39*, 68–85.

Etzel, B. C., & Gewirtz, J. L. Experimental modification of caretaker-maintained high rate operant crying in a 6- and a 20-week-old infant: Extinction of crying with reinforcement of eye contact and smiling. *Journal of Experimental Child Psychology*, 1967, *5*, 303–317.

Falender, C. A., & Heber, R. Mother–child interaction and participation in a longitudinal intervention program. *Developmental Psychology*, 1975, *11*, 830–836.

Forrester, B. J., Boismier, N. O., & Gray, S. W. *A home-based intervention program with mothers and infants.* Unpublished manuscript, George Peabody College for Teachers, Nashville, 1977.

Garber, H., & Heber, R. *Modification of predicted cognitive development in high-risk children through early intervention.* Paper presented at the American Educational Research Association, Boston, April 1980.

Gewirtz, J. L., & Boyd, E. F. Does maternal responding imply reduced infant crying? A critique of the 1972 Bell and Ainsworth report. *Child Development*, 1977, *48*, 1200–1207.

Gilmer, B., Miller, J. O., & Gray, S. W. *Intervention with mothers and young children: A study of intrafamily effects* (DARCEE Papers and Reports, 4, No. 1). Nashville, TN: George Peabody College for Teachers, 1970.

Goodson, D. B., & Hess, R. D. *The effects of parent training programs on child performance and parent behavior.* Unpublished manuscript, Stanford University, 1976.

Gordon, I. J., Guinagh, B., & Jester, R. E. The Florida Parent Education Infant and Toddler Programs. In M. C. Day & R. K. Parker (Eds.), *The preschool in action* (2nd ed.). Boston: Allyn & Bacon, 1977.

Gray, S. W., & Klaus, R. A. The early training project: A seventh-year report. *Child Development*, 1970, *41*, 908–924.

Kessen, W., Fein, G., Clarke-Stewart, A., & Starr, S. *Variations in home-based infant education: Language, play, and social development* (Final Rep., No. OCD-CB-98). New Haven, CT: Yale University, August 1975.

Klaus, R. A., & Gray, S. W. The early training project for disadvantaged children: A report after five years. *Monographs of the Society for Research in Child Development*, 1968, *33* (4, Serial No. 120).

Kogan, K. L., & Gordon, B. N. A mother-instruction program: Documenting change in mother–child interactions. *Child Psychiatry and Human Development*, 1975, *5*, 190–200.

Lally, J. R., & Honig, A. S. *The Family Development Research Program* (Final Rep., No. OCD-CB-100). Syracuse, NY, University of Syracuse, April 1977.

Lasater, T. M., Malone, P., Weisberg, P., & Ferguson, C. *Birmingham Parent-Child Development Center*. (Progress Rep., Office of Child Development) Birmingham, AL: University of Alabama, March 1975.

Lazar, I., Hubbell, R., Murray, H., Rosche, M., & Royce, J. *The persistence of preschool effects: A long-term follow-up of fourteen infant and preschool experiments* (Final Rep., Grant No. 18-76-07843). Office of Human Development Services. Ithaca, NY: Community Services Laboratory, Cornell University, September 1977.

Leler, H., Johnson, D. L., Kahn, A. J., Hines, R. P., & Torres, M. *Houston Parent-Child Development Center*. (Progress Rep., Grant No. CG60925, Office of Child Development). Houston, Tex: University of Houston, May 1975.

Levenstein, P. *Verbal Interaction Project—Mother–Child Home Project*. (Progress Rep., Grant No. R01-MH-18471-08.) (National Institute of Mental Health) Freeport, NY: Family Service Association of Nassau County and State University of New York, June 1977.

Lombard, A. D. *Home instruction program for preschool youngsters* (HIPPY). Jerusalem: The National Council of Jewish Women and Center for Research in Education of the Disadvantaged, Hebrew University of Jerusalem, September 1973.

Love, J. M., Nauta, M. J., Coelen, C. G., Hewett, K., & Ruopp, R. R. *National Home Start evaluation*(Final Rep., HEW-105-72-1100). Cambridge, MA: Abt Associates, March 1976.

Martin, B. *Modification of family interaction* (Final Rep., Grant No. R01-MH-22750). Chapel Hill, NC: University of North Carolina, Psychology Dept., January 1977.

Miller, L. B., & Dyer, J. L. Four preschool programs: Their dimensions and effects. *Monographs of the Society for Research in Child Development*, 1975, *40* (5-6, Serial No. 162).

Pedersen, F. A. *The father–infant relationship*. NY: Praeger Special Studies, 1980.

Ramey, C. T., Farran, D. C., & Campbell, F. A. Predicting IQ from mother–infant interactions. *Child Development*, 1979, *50*, 804–814.

Rogosa, D. R., Webb, N., & Radin, N. *An application of causal models to data on cognitive development in lower-class children*. Unpublished manuscript, University of Chicago, 1978.

Schaefer, E. S., & Aaronson, M. Infant education project: Implementation and implications of the home-tutoring program. In M. C. Day & R. K. Parker (Eds.), *The preschool in action* (2nd ed.). Boston: Allyn & Bacon, 1977.

Slaughter, D. T. Early intervention: Maternal and child development. *Monographs of the Society for Research in Child Development*, in press.

Sonquist, H. *A model for low-income and Chicano parent education.* Santa Barbara, CA: Santa Barbara Family Care Center, 1975. (ERIC Document Reproduction Service No. ED 113 063).

Stern, C. Developing the role of parent-as-teacher with Head Start populations. In J. B. Lazar & J. E. Chapman, *The present status and future research needs of programs to develop parenting skills.* Washington, DC: Social Research Group, George Washington University, 1972.

White, B. L. *The first three years of life.* Englewood Cliffs, NJ: Prentice-Hall, 1975.

SECTION III

ASSOCIATED ISSUES

There are several issues concerning parent education that usually receive only indirect attention from researchers, and yet are of substantial concern for those interested in public policy. Four of the more important issues of this type are dealt with in this section on associated issues.

Earl Schaefer, a long-time student of parent education, raises several concerns about whether and how the professions and institutions that deal with families can accommodate parents' needs for information and involvement. Schaefer's argument has four essential parts. First, he holds that parents are the central influence on children's development. Second, sounding very much like Dokecki and Moroney (Chap. 2), he presents several arguments favoring the view that parents need support from professionals and institutions in order to effectively fulfill their family responsibilities under modern conditions.

Third, in the central and most controversial part of the argument, Schaefer maintains that in their current condition, the professions and institutions are not prepared to provide the type of support families need. For one thing, professionals have developed an "individualistic and pathological" perspective on the world. As a result, they focus on problems and ignore health, favor interventions that involve one sick individual while ignoring the individual's social and cultural milieu (or, as Schaefer says, "ecology"), and overlook the importance of preventive measures while preferring to await the onset of acute conditions and then recommend treatment. For a second thing, professionals simply lack the training to see beyond their individualistic and pathological paradigm. Without training that shows professionals how to look for and capitalize on family strengths, involve parents as partners in the maintenance of health or the treatment of problems, and eschew the use of institutions in favor of community-based treatment, professionals simply cannot effectively serve families.

Fourth, in place of the individualistic and pathological model, Schaefer argues for what he calls an "ecological-developmental" model to guide service delivery to families. Thus, he argues for policies that place parent education and support in both traditional institutions with which most parents have contact, such as hospitals and schools, and in less traditional "institutions" such as neighborhood and community peer and friendship networks. Schaefer even goes so far as to suggest that current institutions and professionals may be too rigid to handle these changes, in which case "new programs and professions should be developed" (p. 298).

Whether one agrees with the basic outline of Schaefer's argument, he does make a consistent case for rather substantial government support of new professions, institutions, and programs to support parents in their childrearing function. He differs from many analysts in his forthright suggestion that currently existing professions and institutions may be too myopic and self-serving to effectively implement expanded parent support programs. This is an argument that deserves very careful scrutiny.

An approach to parent education that avoids many of the problems summarized by Schaefer is the simple provision of information through accessible channels of communication. If one could ascertain parents' needs for information about family life and childrearing and deliver this information to them in effective and inexpensive ways, several ends could be achieved simultaneously. First, the mere provision of information avoids the frequently heard criticism of parent programs that they reject or denigrate their clients' childrearing practices—otherwise why would programs be trying to get parents to change? Providing information to parents avoids this problem because it allows them to use their own judgment in deciding what to use and what to reject. Moreover, most methods of giving parents information would keep social workers, educators, and other professionals out of their clients' homes and away from other types of direct contact with the family.

Second, issues of compulsion and stigma can be largely avoided by information programs. Third, information programs have the potential of being quite efficient, particularly if they can be used in a preventive fashion, since they can be developed and disseminated for relatively little money. The major questions in this regard are whether inexpensive yet effective methods of delivery can be found, and whether mere exposure to information can alter behavior.

In any case, it seems wise to devote some consideration to the information needs of parents. Unfortunately, few empirical studies of parent information needs have been conducted. For this reason, the chapter by Sparling and Lowman is particularly interesting. These investigators surveyed a stratified probability sample of 2,088 parents with children 0–36 months; of these parents, 1,458 (70%) returned usable questionnaires. In addition, a sample of 100 low-income families were interviewed with the same questionnaire.

Using parents' ratings both of their interests and problems as indexes of their needs, Sparling and Lowman report several noteworthy results. Among these is the reassuring finding that, although the perceived information needs of parents were substantially influenced by demographic factors, promoting general learning and development in the child is seen as a top priority need of all parents by both the interest and problems analysis. The research also revealed that books were a valued information source, but that interpersonal contacts with family and friends, doctors and nurses, and teachers were also highly preferred sources of information. Television, by contrast, was a favored source of information for very few parents. The questionnaire information also produced the interesting result that information needs of parents depend heavily on the age of their children as well as their parents' income level. Clearly, primarily because of the high efficiency and low stigma of information approaches to parent education, this approach deserves more attention than it has received thus far.

Another important issue concerning parent education programs is the relation between these programs and other social programs. Many advocates of parent programs seem to envision entirely new and separate programs devoted to educating and supporting parents. Programs such as the Parent Child Development Centers (Chap. 4) typify this approach. A second approach to expanding parent participation would be to include parent involvement, education, or support components in currently existing social programs (and in social programs enacted by Congress in the future). Thus, for example, Congress has required parent involvement on advisory boards, in proposal writing, and in other types of decision-making in several federal programs, such as Title I of the Elementary and Secondary Education Act, Bilingual Education, and the Education of All Handicapped Children Act (P.L. 94-142). It would seem to be a relatively straightforward matter to amend other social legislation, including Aid to Families with Dependent Children, Title XX, and health programs such as WIN, Title V, and Community Mental Health Centers, to either require parent participation or to strengthen existing parent involvement requirements.

Issues associated with requiring parent participation in social programs are discussed in the chapter by Edith Grotberg. After presenting a useful set of definitions to clarify various types of parent participation, and after discussing several examples of public and private programs intended to enhance parent participation, Grotberg examines a number of obstacles to increased parent participation in social programs, in particular, the public schools. To address these obstacles, Grotberg then suggests 11 areas in which research could produce information needed to establish a firm basis for parent participation.

Finally, Grotberg presents several specific policy recommendations. Interestingly, she asserts that, as a matter of principle and not empirical data, "child care, education, health, nutrition, [and] social service [programs affecting parents and children] must empower parents to participate in decision-making and in developing and carrying out the program" (p. 329). Her recommendations constitute a very strong case for parent participation and would require substantial changes in many current federal programs.

The final chapter in this section, by Luis Laosa, is a careful examination of perhaps the most controversial issue associated with parent education in contemporary social policy; namely, the possibility of ethnic and cultural bias in both the programs and in the concepts on which the programs are based. Only Laosa, Mundel, and Clarke-Stewart among the authors represented in this volume are skeptical about parent education. Like Clarke-Stewart, Laosa is concerned with the validity of research on which parent programs are based. But his greatest concerns are directed to the assumptions underlying parent programs.

As Ogbu (1978, 1981), Valentine (1976), Stack (1974), and several other authors have argued, social scientists have tended to view differences between the white, middle-class and other groups as deficits in the behavior or values of the other groups. Parent programs can easily slip into this trap if they are directed primarily to changing the child-rearing practices of low-income and minority parents. The underlying problem here is that many social scientists (e.g., Bernstein, 1960; Deutsch, 1967; Hunt, 1961) have identified deficits in the home as a primary cause of subnormal development. Thus, no matter what justification is actually used for intervening in homes and for trying to change parents' childrearing practices, the justification often *seems* to be that the parents' normal behavior is deficient. In practice, this problem is usually further exacerbated because the people who design and deliver the programs are from different socioeconomic, and often ethnic, backgrounds than program participants. This situation is ripe for abuse, and has led some investigators to outright rejection of parent programs that involve manipulations of parents' behavior (Ogbu, 1978; Valentine, 1968).

It seems prudent, then, to pay careful attention to Laosa's argument. He begins with the assertion that, the claims of parent educators notwithstanding, current parent education programs are based on assumptions that are not essentially different than those that supported the old compensatory education programs. In particular, Laosa states, they are based on a "deficit or social pathology paradigm" for which empirical support is questionable.

Laosa also discusses two associated issues concerning parent programs and minority families. First, these programs raise serious privacy issues. As Dokecki and Moroney (Chap. 2) point out, a long-established assumption of American social policy is that public programs can intrude on family privacy only in the most extraordinary circumstances, such as child abuse or financial destitution. The poor, however, are not always covered by this assumption—as made clear by the AFDC requirement that mothers must sign over to the state their children's claim rights against the father. Similarly, Laosa wonders whether some publicly supported parent programs might seem to "dictate standards of behavior within the family"—an outcome that is clearly inconsistent with most conceptions of the limits of social policy.

Laosa also wonders whether it is reasonable to expect parent programs to solve major social ills. Rather, the solution to these problems may be found in income redistribution programs, job programs, or housing programs. One is reminded of Mundel's (Chap. 3) claim that a major reason policymakers do not support expansion of parent programs is that they fail to see that these programs can contribute to the solution of major social ills. In any case, Laosa raises this issue to express concern that when parent education programs, like compensatory education programs, are found to "fail," social scientists and practitioners will have created a new occasion for blaming the victim.

References

Bernstein, B. Language and social class. *British Journal of Sociology*, 1960, *11*, 271–276.

Deutsch, M. *The disadvantaged child*. London: Basic Books, 1967.

Hunt, J. McV. *Intelligence and experience*. New York: Ronald Press, 1961.

Ogbu, J. U. *Minority education and caste: The American system in cross-cultural perspective*. New York: Academic Press, 1978.

Ogbu, J. Origins of human competence: A cultural ecological perspective. *Child Development*, 1981, *52*, 413–429.

Stack, C. B. *All our kin: Strategies for survival in a Black community*. New York: Harper, 1974.

Valentine, C. A. *Culture and poverty*. Chicago: University of Chicago Press, 1968.

ELEVEN

PARENT–PROFESSIONAL INTERACTION: RESEARCH, PARENTAL, PROFESSIONAL, AND POLICY PERSPECTIVES

EARL S. SCHAEFER

INTRODUCTION

Progress in research on the influence of parents on child development and on parent-centered and family-centered early intervention should be applied in the professions and institutions that provide services for children and families. Unless special research, development, evaluation, and demonstration programs influence the major professions and institutions, they will have little influence on child development. Current health and education practices and policies have focused on providing care and education for the child, rather than on supporting parental care and education. Increased consciousness of the parent role in child development and of methods for supporting parental care and education might contribute to professional–institutional change.

Evidence of the major influence of parents on child development will be reviewed below. A discussion of the current focus of parent–professional interaction will provide a basis for analysis of current and potential roles of parents and professionals in child care and education. An analysis of the individualistic, pathological paradigm that guides delivery of services to children suggests the need for services guided by an ecological, developmental paradigm that emphasizes professional support for family care. However, professional–institutional change will require the support of researchers, parents, and policymakers as well as professionals. Although support for parent education and involvement has been provided by parents and policymakers in the past, additional public policy support for professional change is needed. A feasible objective would be further development of a knowledge base and of professional education and training for more effective parent–professional interaction.

THE INFLUENCE OF PARENTAL CARE AND EDUCATION OF THE CHILD

The need for a professional focus on strengthening and supporting rather than supplementing family care is suggested by the characteristics of family as contrasted to professional care of children (Schaefer, 1972). Priority of parental influence upon the child during the prenatal, infancy, and preschool period, the duration of parental care from conception to maturity, and the continuity of parental child care that is related to the parent's full-time responsibility for the child suggest the significance of parent care for child development. The scope of parental care and sharing of experiences and situations with the child, the pervasiveness of parental influence on the child's life style and experiences, the intensity of parent–child relationships, the consistency of patterns of parental care and education of the child, and the great variability among families in child care have an early, continuing, and cumulative impact on child health, welfare, and education. The cost of further substitution of professional care for family care is shown by the high staff-to-child ratios required by institutional care and by day care. Yet the need for support for family care of children is shown by statistical data on trends in family functioning, child care, and child development (National Research Council, 1976).

The significance of parental care for the child's intellectual development and academic achievement is shown by the fact that the mean mental test scores of different socioeconomic status groups tend to stabilize as early as 3 years of age, after the period of rapid language development (Hindley, 1965; Terman & Merrill, 1937). Both Bradway (1945) and Bayley (1970) report that early verbal scores give better predictions of later intelligence than nonverbal scores. Evidence that school entrance does not typically change the level of functioning developed during the preschool years and maintained by the family environment suggests the need to support the child's early and continuing language development in the family as the basis for intellectual functioning and academic achievement.

Research on parent behavior during infancy and at school entrance implies that stable patterns of parent behaviors may have an early and continuing influence on the child's intellectual development. Maternal interaction with and stimulation of the infant as shown by talking, praising, and playing games during bathing, dressing, and play for a sample of low-income mothers was stable from 4 to 12 months in one recent study. In addition, maternal interaction with the child was correlated with the mother's receptive vocabulary, internal locus of control, self-directing versus conforming values for the child, and approval of a high level of interaction with the infant as well as with the mother's education, age, and marital status (Schaefer, Siegel, Bauman, & Hosking, 1979). Maternal characteristics and behaviors during infancy were interpreted as a pattern of modernity in childrearing that might predict the child's future intellectual development and academic achievement. Support for this hypothesis was provided by a cross-sectional study of maternal characteristics and of child competence in kindergarten and of reading achievement at the end of first grade (Schaefer & Edgerton, 1979). Talking with the child about the mother's friends, interests, and childhood experiences, sharing activities such as reading books and magazines, working with plants and gardens, and cooking with the child were correlated with the child's academic competence. The child's mental test scores during kindergarten and reading scores at the end of first grade were also correlated with parental self-directing values as contrasted with conforming values for children and with progressive educational attitudes of encouraging imagination and verbalization of ideas. Parental attitudes, beliefs, values, and behaviors were as highly correlated as sociodemographic characteristics of the mother with the child's reading scores, suggesting that these parent characteristics may be mediating variables between socioeconomic status and the child's intellectual development (Schaefer & Edgerton, 1979).

A hypothesis that correlations between parent characteristics and child intellectual development and academic competence might be largely due to hereditary influences is contradicted by findings that levels of intellectual competence and of academic achievement of adopted children are more similar to those of their adopted than their natural parents (Skeels & Harms, 1948; Schiff et al., 1978). Similarly, findings that mentally retarded adolescents and young adults reared in severely deprived family environments show substantial IQ gains after leaving those environments suggest that the family environment has a continuing influence on the development of intellectual potential (Clarke & Clarke, 1959). Gains made by children in both parent-centered and child-centered early intervention programs show that with higher levels of intellectual stimulation children achieve higher levels of intellectual functioning (Bronfenbrenner, 1974). The importance of support for family functioning is also shown by the correlations between family relationships and the socialization of children. Rutter (1971) reported that mother–child, father–child, and father–mother relationships are correlated with delinquent behavior of boys. Research on family systems (Lewis, Beavers, Gossett, & Phillips, 1976) and on marital adjustment, parent–child relationships, and child maladjustment (Johnson & Lobitz, 1974) support the significance of family functioning for social and emotional development of children.

THE NEED FOR PROFESSIONAL SUPPORT FOR PARENTAL CARE AND EDUCATION

The major role of the parent in care, education, and socialization of the child demonstrates the need for parent education and for the availability of guidance, consultation, and counseling for parents. Parenting requires more skills than the many human service occupations, yet it is often an avocation rather than a full-time occupation. The parenting role requires skills in the care and education of children at all ages and knowledge of the many disciplines that promote the health, education, and welfare of the child. Although the skills of a nutritionist, nurse, physician, teacher, and recreation leader would contribute to parental competence, the array of skills required to be an effective parent has hardly been defined and seldom taught. In stable, cohesive communities with large nuclear and extended families that include adults and children at various age levels, the child learns basic parental skills through everyday experience in the family and community. In the past, variability in parenting competence as well as variability in child health and education were accepted; yet current national goals for improved health, welfare, and education of all children may be impossible to achieve without developing a system for strengthening and supporting family care and education of children.

Increased knowledge of early intellectual development and the role of experience in intellectual development, as well as interest in fostering the academic competence of all children, contributed to the development of infant and preschool education and parent-centered intervention (Bloom, 1964; Hunt, 1961). Despite the success of early child-centered intervention, comparisons of child-centered and parent-centered programs suggest that parent-centered programs are most cost-effective (Bronfenbrenner, 1974; Schaefer, 1972). Although this conclusion is disputed, findings that more successful programs began at young ages, had goals for parents, included home visits, and had more favorable staff-to-child ratios provide support for early parent-centered programs (Vopava & Royce, 1978). Many of the early parent-centered programs had a limited focus on intellectual and academic competence, but more recently the Parent and Child Development Centers and the Child and Family Resource Programs have developed broader objectives of child and family development. However, funding for expansion of these programs is limited despite the conclusion of the report by the Comptroller General (1979) that such programs "can result in reduced health, social, and educational problems in young children" (p. i).

Documentation in the report *Lasting Effects After Preschool* (Consortium for Longitudinal Studies, 1978) would also support a conclusion that early parent-centered intervention has long-term effects on academic achievement. The need for and the effectiveness of support for family care and education of children have been demonstrated; yet progress in developing funding for such programs has been limited.

A review of the history of child care and education and the development of a model for parent–professional interaction may provide a basis for further planning for professional support of family care. Initially, the child's care and education were almost solely the responsibility of the family, extended family, and community. Recognition of the need for professional health care and education led to rapid development of the professions, initially through private funding but increasingly through government funding with acceptance of public responsibility for children's education and health. If the initial period might be called the "Age of Family and Community," the immediate past might be called the "Age of Professions and Institutions" that led to rapid development, with increasing public funding, of schools, colleges, preschools, day care centers, hospitals, and clinics. Although the professions and institutions were developed to supplement family care and education, some critics suggest that they have begun to supplant the family. Illich (1975), for example, has noted a trend during the past half century toward both birth and death in the hospital. Other critics have noted that institutional policies at the time of birth have separated the mother from father and from the newborn infant (Klaus & Kennell, 1976). Schooling has also moved to earlier ages, with a rapid progression from elementary schooling, to kindergarten, to preschool education, and with increasing emphasis on developmental day care during infancy.

During the rapid development of institutional health care and education, the role of the family in child health and education has been

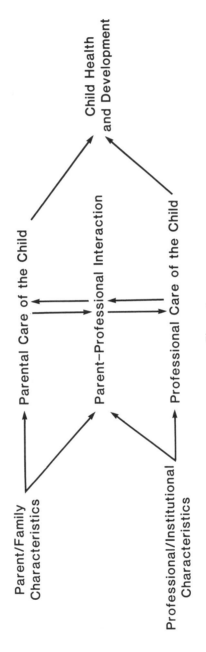

Figure 1.
A model for parent and professional care and interaction.

to a great extent ignored and neglected. Perhaps parental and professional concerns about privacy, territoriality, and dominance have contributed to the professionals' emphasis on the child's care and education in institutions (Lightfoot, 1978). Parents have continued to provide care and education for their children, but with little communication and collaboration between parents and professionals.

In the emphasis on the role of professions and institutions in child care, parent–teacher interaction has focused on the contributions of the professional and on parental support for the professional role. However, increasing evidence of the importance of the family for the health, education, and welfare of children and evidence of the cost-effectiveness of parent-centered intervention suggest the need for professions to contribute to the effectiveness of family care. Bronfenbrenner's (1979) concept of ecological intervention implies that one goal of the professions might be to strengthen the child's interactions in the family and community.

A conceptual model of antecedents and correlates of professional care, parental care, and parent–professional interaction is reproduced in Fig. 1 (Schaefer, 1982). In the Age of the Family, the emphasis was on parental care; in the Age of Professions and Institutions, the emphasis has been on professional care. By contrast, in the current Age of Ecology, the emphasis might be on parent–professional interaction in a total system of child care. The model suggests that parent–professional interaction might influence the quality of both parental and professional care of children. Yet different emphases in parent–professional interaction and in parent involvement can lead to very different programs.

A matrix of child care settings—family and institution—and of parent and professional roles is proposed in Fig. 2. Parental roles in the family and professional roles of teacher, caregiver, and model for the child stress the independent contributions of parents and professionals. Interpretations of parent involvement in the institution have often stressed parental roles of volunteer, service giver, or paraprofessional; of the parent as observer or student; and of parents as decision-makers on policy boards. These parental roles in the institution often do not have direct effects on parental care of the child in the home. Professional roles of parent educator and consultant or counselor are designed to strengthen parental care, whereas emphasis on the professional as rescuer and law enforcer emphasizes supplementing or supplanting parent care. Growing recognition of shared and reciprocal roles of parents and professionals as advocates, planners, organizers, case managers, coordinators, and collaborators in child care and education may contribute to more active, responsible roles for parents in an ecological approach to child care and education. Yet few professionals have been educated

	Family	Institution
Parent Roles	Caregiver Teacher Model	Volunteer fund–raiser Paraprofessional Observer/Student Decision maker
Reciprocal and Shared Roles	Advocate Planner/Organizer Case Manager/Coordinator Collaborator	
Professional Roles	Rescuer/Law Enforcer Parent Educator Parent Consultant	Caregiver Teacher Model

Figure 2.
A matrix of child care settings and of parent and professional roles.

to understand the parental contribution to child care and education and to collaborate with parents in organizing an integrated system of child care and education in the family, community, and institution.

TOWARD A PARADIGMATIC BASIS FOR PARENT–PROFESSIONAL INTERACTION

Fleck's (1979) analysis, *Genesis and Development of a Scientific Fact*, shows the need for translating scientific findings concerning the major role of the family in child development and the effectiveness of parent-centered intervention into social facts that influence policies, programs, and professions. Fleck observed that as scientific findings are communicated to a wider audience, they become accepted as hard facts. Such findings may then contribute to a new "thought style" that leads to the development of a new perception of reality. An analysis of the current "thought style" in the professions that provide services to children and their families and of the emerging "thought style" that would be supported by recent research on parent and professional contributions to child development might contribute to the development of new perspectives and programs within the existing professions and institutions.

Kuhn (1970) acknowledged Fleck's contribution to his own analysis of how scientific paradigms influence perceptions of problems and of their possible solutions. Kuhn also discussed how new findings might lead to a paradigm shift that would contribute to a change in a discipline. Piaget's (1954) identification of a tendency to assimilate new findings to an existing conceptual scheme as contrasted to accommodating the conceptual scheme to new findings describes the behavior of adults as well as children. Etzioni's (1968) discussion of bit criticism as contrasted to radical criticism of the professional–institutional context also notes the difficulty of developing new perspectives of problems and their potential solutions. Development of new "thought styles," paradigms, and perspectives are now needed in order to change the professional–institutional context.

Early intervention research has contributed to the development of new perspectives for the professions that provide services to children and their families. Accumulating research on families and children has contributed to the development of an ecological perspective as contrasted to the individualistic perspective on delivery of services to children (Bronfenbrenner, 1974, 1979; Schaefer, 1970, 1976b). The individualistic perspective focuses on delivery of services to the isolated individual, whereas the ecological perspective focuses on the effects of the organism's interactions with the environment as the primary determinant of development. Examples of the individualistic perspective would be individual psychotherapy, child-centered tutoring, and provision of health and education services to the isolated child in the clinic or classroom. Examples of ecological interventions would be parent-centered early intervention such as Home Start, the Child and Family Resource Program that analyzes family needs and assists in establishing and achieving family goals, and family therapy that focuses on the interactions of family members. Reports by young adults that family and community members contributed more to their development than professionals (Werner & Smith, 1977) would support the development of programs and professions that have a primary goal of strengthening interaction among family and community members.

A pathological perspective that focuses on screening, diagnosis, and treatment of pathology has also limited investment in fostering development in the family and community. To a great extent psychology and psychiatry have contributed to the pathological perspective the conceptual schemes that emphasize symptoms, deficiencies, and deviations in behavior and development. Government policies of supporting programs that address specific pathologies have also limited the funds available for health promotion and for research that would contribute to a developmental perspective in programs and professions. Positive conceptualizations of self-actualization (Maslow, 1954) and competence (White, 1959) have been followed by a conceptualization of social competence that was motivated by goals of the Head Start program (Zigler & Trickett, 1978). A shift to a developmental perspective would contribute to enhancing the strengths and skills of the individual and to the development of social supports in the family and community. Evidence that focusing parental attention on positive behavior has positive effects on child development (Baer et al., 1976) and evidence that parents who perceive and spontaneously comment on the positive qualities of their children contribute to positive development (Schaefer & Bayley, 1963) suggest that a shift to a positive developmental, as contrasted to a pathological, perspective would contribute to child development.

A developmental perspective would also have major implications for professional training, including an emphasis on recognition of strengths and skills of children, parents, and community members; and for public policy, including increasing support for health promotion and primary prevention through fostering development. A developmental perspective would stress parent education that emphasized the nurture and reinforcement of strengths, skills, and positive behavior as contrasted to screening, diagnosis, and treatment of pathology.

The complementary developmental, ecological perspectives on child development would emphasize the role of the family and community, as contrasted to the role of professions and institutions, in promoting child health, education, and welfare. To continue the current emphasis on supplementing family care would require the further growth of preschools and developmental day care to provide for the early social, emotional, and intellectual development of children, as well as further extension of the school day, school week, and school year to provide education during the time currently spent in family and community. Such extension of professional and institutional care of children would approach a "brave new world" of total institutional care envisioned by Huxley (1946). The alternative solution to the provision of equality of education opportunity (Coleman, 1966) and of improved child care would be to increase support for family and community care of children. The failure of bureaucratic solutions has shown the need for community organization to provide for community needs (Doughton, 1980). The success of parent-centered and family-centered intervention programs suggests that strengthening and coordinating family and community resources would improve child care, education, and child development (Comptroller General, 1979).

Fleck's (1979) and Kuhn's (1970) analyses of the function of research

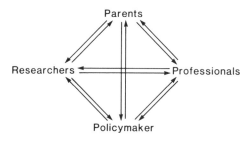

Figure 3.
Interactions that influence professional–institutional change.

in changing paradigms and thought styles and Etzioni's (1968) discussion of the role of the knowledge industry in *The Active Society* imply both the importance of research and the interpretation and dissemination of research for professional–institutional change. Figure 3 suggests that further research on families and family-centered interventions might influence parents, policymakers, and professionals. Despite the stability of the professional–institutional context derived from shared perspectives of parents, professionals, and policymakers, research findings do influence professional policies. Examples are the impact of Klaus and Kennell's (1976) research on the effects of extended contact on maternal attachment to the infant and Bowlby's (1951) integration of research on maternal separation upon hospital policies for children and parents. Although the relative influence of researchers, parents, policymakers, and professionals is difficult to determine, the examples given above demonstrate that interpretation and dissemination of research findings can contribute to professional–institutional change.

PARENT, POLICYMAKER, AND PROFESSIONAL VIEWS OF PARENT–PROFESSIONAL INTERACTION

Analysis of the interactions among persons who share responsibility for the care and education of children—parents, policymakers, and professionals—suggests that each group must be involved in the process of professional–institutional change. The degree of acceptance of the parent's major role in child care and education and the degree of support for programs that would strengthen the family's contribution to child care vary both within and among these three groups. National surveys find broad support among parents for parent education (Elam, 1973). Available data on professional attitudes toward implementation of parent education, however, seem to indicate that professionals have not seen parent education as a major professional responsibility. When political support and an adequate rationale for parent involvement have been provided, policymakers have mandated parent involvement in programs for children. A major obstacle to progress in parent education and parent involvement may be the individualistic, pathological, professional–institutional paradigm that is acquired in professional training and that guides the provision of services to children and their families.

That parents recognize their major responsibility for child development is shown by parent responses in the *Gallup Polls of Attitudes toward Education* (Elam, 1973). When asked where they would place the chief blame when some children do poorly in school, the majority of parents blamed the children's home life, and few blamed teachers or schools. When asked to select among reasons that have been given to explain the decline in national test scores, a majority of parents chose the response, "Less parental attention, concern, and supervision of the child." In response to the question, "As a regular part of the public school educational system, it has been suggested that courses be offered at convenient times to parents in order to help them help their children in school. Do you think this is a good idea or poor idea?" 78% of public school parents replied that it was a good idea. In reply to the followup question, "Would you be able to pay additional taxes to support such a program?" 52% replied "Yes" and only 21% "No." Younger, nonwhite, and college-educated respondents showed the highest levels of approval. Evidently, parents accept more responsibility and express more interest in parent education than is provided by parent–teacher interaction patterns. Parents who had participated in several parent-centered intervention programs also overwhelmingly agreed that the program was a good thing for their child (Consortium on Developmental Continuity, 1977), a finding that has been supported in other parent programs.

Despite the increasing interest in "home/school/community interaction" (Wallat & Goldman, 1979), most teachers have little training and little orientation toward collaborating with parents in the child's education. In an unpublished survey (Schaefer, 1976a) of 320 kindergarten and first-grade teachers in rural and suburban communities in North Carolina, teachers rank-ordered their objectives in parent–teacher interaction. Table 1 shows that the major focus was on the child's school work and that the lowest ranked objective was "to provide support for the parent's educational role in the home." In a second unpublished survey of 24 teachers in a university town (Schaefer, 1976a), the highest ranked goals were "for the teachers to tell the parent how the child is doing in school" and "for the teacher to familiarize the parent with the classroom and class activities." A middle ranked goal was "for the teacher to suggest home activities that would enrich the child's learn-

TABLE 1:   RANK ORDER GIVEN BY TEACHERS TO OBJECTIVES OF PARENT–TEACHER INTERACTIONS

	Ranking[a]						
Objective	1	2	3	4	5	6	Mean rank
To inform parents about their child's school work	53	21	11	8	6	2	1.99
To discuss child's school-related problems	13	40	22	14	7	3	2.71
To inform parents about teacher's expectations for the child	7	14	19	27	17	16	3.82
To discuss child's home-related problems	5	9	31	21	19	14	3.84
To gain parental support of the school	17	10	8	13	28	25	4.01
To provide support for parent's educational role in the home	8	8	12	16	20	36	4.42

[a] Data in the first six columns are the percentage of 320 teachers who assigned each of six ranks to the objectives: 1 = high, 6 = low.

ing," and very low ranked goals were "for the parent to give the teacher suggestions about how the teacher can help the child" and "for the parent to express ideas about effective education." The highest priority was to communicate the teacher's role in the classroom and the lowest priority was to listen to the parents' views on education and on the education of their own child.

Apparently, teachers do not accept the role of supporting the parent's education of the child in the home or the role of egalitarian collaboration with the parent—although individual teachers do rank these goals of parent–teacher interaction highly. An individualistic, rather than an ecological, and a professional–institutional, rather than a family and community, perspective continue to be a major focus in parent–teacher interaction. The finding that the objective, "for the parent to discuss with the teacher any social or emotional problems the child might have" was ranked higher than the objective, "for the parent to give the teacher suggestions about how the teacher can help the child" suggests a pathological rather than a developmental perspective.

Parent education and anticipatory guidance have been goals of well–child care (American Academy of Pediatrics, 1977). Although contacts with pediatricians might provide support for the parental role during infancy, available research suggests that these activities are rarely included in well-child visits. Few urban mothers reported anticipatory guidance during visits to Child Health Stations or to pediatricians and general practitioners during the infant's first year of life (Mindlin & Denson, 1971). Stine's (1962) observations of pediatric visits also found little discussion of child behavior or development, and Starfield and Barkowf's (1969) observations revealed that parents' questions were often unacknowledged and unanswered. Chamberlin's (1974) interviews with middle-class mothers receiving pediatric care showed that a majority of mothers who identified conflicts with, or concerns about, the child or who identified definite behavioral or emotional problems of their children had not talked with a professional about the problem. Apparently, parent education, anticipatory guidance, and support in coping with developmental problems are not widely available from pediatricians nor from other professionals during infancy and early childhood. Yet positive results have been reported from parent education during pediatric visits in the early months of life (Casey & Whitt, 1980) and from home visits by a public health nurse during the early years of life (Gutelius, Kirsch, McDonald, Brooks, & McErlean, 1977). If health professionals were motivated and trained in parent education, the child-health system could contribute significantly to parent effectiveness. However, the finding that mothers with higher levels of parent education reported more symptoms of their children to pediatricians suggests that parent education, guided by the pathological perspective of identifying, diagnosing, and treating symptoms and deviations, might contribute to negative perceptions of children (Chamberlin, Szumowski, & Zastowny, 1979).

An analysis of legislative provisions for parent involvement by Gotts (1979) suggests that policymakers often support parent involvement in programs for children. Head Start and related parent-centered and family-centered early intervention programs, including the Parent–Child Centers, Home Start, and Child and Family Resource Program, have specific provisions for parent involvement (U.S. Dept. of Health, Education and Welfare, 1975). Head Start included provisions for parent participation in the classroom as employees, volunteers, and observers; for direct involvement in decision-making; and for working with their own children. The requirement of a plan for voluntary participation of parents in Head Start has resulted in varying but often low amounts of parent participation. However, Home Start, the Parent–Child Centers, and the Child and Family Resource Program have a major focus on parent involvement as contrasted to Head Start which has a major focus on the classroom. A focus on working only with parents, rather than a dual focus of providing a center-based program for children as well as a parent-involvement program, apparently is a more effective way to support parental care and education of the child in the home.

Perhaps the emphasis on compensatory education in Title I of the

Elementary and Secondary Education Act (U.S. Dept. of Health, Education, and Welfare, 1969) has resulted in the emphasis on parent involvement through Parent Advisory Councils. The parent-involvement provision of the Education of All Handicapped Children Act (P.L. 94-142) emphasizes parental rights to be involved in planning an Individual Education Program (IEP) for their child. Thus, the focus in these programs is on parent involvement in the child's education in the school rather than in the home.

Gotts (1979) contrasted the conception of parent involvement as parental control of the school with the conception of parent involvement as partnership and the development of parental skills and suggests that this latter goal conception may be more attainable within the framework of public school governance. The research literature can be interpreted as suggesting that the goal of developing parental skills may also have greater effectiveness in influencing the educational attainment of children (Bronfenbrenner, 1974). Greater consciousness by policymakers of an ecological, developmental, family and community paradigm for human services would contribute to explicit legislative provisions for parent education and involvement that is oriented toward improving parent effectiveness in care and education of the child in the home.

THE ROLE OF GOVERNMENT POLICY IN PARENT–PROFESSIONAL INTERACTIONS

The major investment of government funds in child health and education and the history of legislative support for parent involvement in comprehensive child development programs demonstrate that policymakers have an interest in, and have established precedents for, government involvement in parent–professional interaction. Government's interest in the development of cost-effective services for children might be best advanced by strengthening families. Yet concerns that government policy might supplant or interfere with family care of the child have contributed to the defeat of the Child and Family Services Act of 1975 (S. 626 and H.R. 2996), despite the Act's explicit recognition that "the family is the primary and the most fundamental influence on children" and that "child and family service programs must build upon and strengthen the role of the family. . . ." However, high levels of public support for parent education and high levels of satisfaction in parent-centered early intervention programs suggest that an informed public would support a government role in promoting constructive parent–professional interaction.

If government policies are adopted that would strengthen and support parental care and education of the child through parent–professional interaction, questions concerning when, where, and by whom these programs will be implemented must be addressed. The major health and education professions that provide services to all parents and children at different stages in the life cycle would appear to offer greater opportunities for parent education than the child-care and welfare professions that offer services to selected populations. Yet the major commitment of the health professions to physical health, to a biomedical rather than a biopsychosocial perspective (Engel, 1977), and to a pathological rather than developmental perspective (Schaefer, 1979) has limited the amount of parent education offered by pediatricians. Similarly, the major commitment of educators to education of the individual child in the classroom has limited their involvement in the education of current and future parents. The need for accessible, continuing support for parental care before the birth of the child, during infancy and the preschool years, and during the years of school enrollment suggests either that the existing professions and institutions should include parent education and support as a major component of existing programs or that new programs and professions should be developed. Perhaps radical criticism of the current institutional context might contribute to professional change, but researchers, parents, and policymakers must provide incentives and support for change.

What are some of the options of government support for professional–institutional change and for development of new parent education and support systems? The research on early intervention reviewed elsewhere in this volume (see Clarke-Stewart, Chap. 10) implies that research, development, and evaluation of parent education and parent support programs can contribute to change. The process of disseminating that research to the public, professionals, and policymakers is also an essential component of translating scientific findings into social facts that influence programs for children and families (Fleck, 1979). Experience with legislatively mandated parent involvement suggests that development of professional education and of preservice and inservice education for professionals is essential for effective implementation of parent education and involvement. Although such education and training programs have begun, they have not influenced many current health and education professionals. When an adequate research, development, evaluation, professional education, and training basis has been established for parent education programs, demonstrations of parent programs within existing institutions, such as the Parent Education Follow-Through Program, can contribute to professional–institutional change. Legislative mandates for parent education and parent involvement would contribute more to effective programs after research, education, and demonstration programs have been successfully implemented.

The approach to program development for children during the War on Poverty was first to initiate a major program and then to do the research, development, evaluation, and training required to improve the program. Current financial limitations suggest the need for a different approach. Perhaps available funds could be used to develop a knowledge and manpower basis for professional–institutional change. After effective parent education and parent support programs have been developed and demonstrated, and after professional education and training programs have been developed, government policy and government funding might support the development of a comprehensive system that would provide continuing support for parental care and education of children.

REFERENCES

American Academy of Pediatrics. *Standards of child health care* (3rd ed.), Evanston, IL: Author, 1977.

Baer, D. M., Robury, T., Baer, A. M., Herbert, E., Clark, H. B., & Nelson, A. A programmatic test of behavior technology: Can it recover deviant children for normal public schooling? In T. D. Tjossem (Ed.), *Intervention strategies for high risk infants and young children*. Baltimore: University Park Press, 1976.

Bayley, N. Development of mental abilities. In P. H. Mussen (Ed.), *Manual of child psychology* (3rd ed., Vol. 2). New York: Wiley, 1970.

Bloom, B. J. *Stability and change in human characteristics*. New York: Wiley, 1964.

Bowlby, J. *Maternal care and mental health* (Monograph Series, No. 2). Geneva: World Health Organization, 1951.

Bradway, K. P. Predictive value of Stanford-Binet preschool items. *Journal of Educational Psychology*, 1945, *36*, 1–16.

Bronfenbrenner, U. *A report on longitudinal evaluation of preschool programs* (Vol. 2). Is early intervention effective? Washington, DC: DHEW Publication No. (OHD) 74-25, 1974.

Bronfenbrenner, U. *The ecology of human development*. Cambridge, MA: Harvard University Press, 1979.

Casey, P. H., & Whitt, J. K. Effect of the pediatrician on the mother–infant relationship. *Pediatrics*, 1980, *65*, 815–820.

Chamberlin, R. W. Management of preschool behavior problems. *Pediatric Clinics of North America*, 1974, *21*, 33–47.

Chamberlin, R. W., Szumowski, E. K., & Zastowny, R. R. An evaluation of efforts to educate mothers about child development in pediatric office practices. *American Journal of Public Health,* 1979, *69,* 875–886.

Clarke, A. D. B., & Clarke, A. M. Recovery from the effects of deprivation. *Acta Psychologica,* 1959, *16,* 137–144.

Coleman, J. S. *Equality of educational opportunity.* Washington, DC: U.S. Government Printing Office, 1966.

Comptroller General of the United States. *Early childhood and family development programs influence the quality of life for low-income families* (HRD-79-40). Washington, DC: U.S. General Accounting Office, 1979.

Consortium for Longitudinal Studies. *Lasting effects after preschool* (OHDS 79-30178). Washington, DC: U.S. Department of Health, Education, and Welfare, 1978.

Consortium on Developmental Continuity. *The persistence of preschool effects* (OHDS 78-30130). Washington, DC: U.S. Department of Health, Education, and Welfare, 1977.

Doughton, M. J. People power: An alternative to runaway bureaucracy. *The Futurist,* 1980, *14,* 13–22.

Elam, S. (Ed.). *The Gallup Polls of attitudes toward education, 1969–1973.* Bloomington, IN: Phi Delta Kappa, 1973.

Engel, G. L. The need for a new medical model: A challenge for biomedicine. *Science,* 1977, *196,* 129–136.

Etzioni, A. *The active society: A theory of societal and political processes.* New York: Free Press, 1968.

Fleck, L. *Genesis and development of a scientific fact.* Chicago: University of Chicago Press, 1979.

Gotts E. E. *Legislated roles of parent involvement and current school practices.* Paper presented at the National Institute of Education conference on What Opportunities Are There for Parents to be Educators?, Washington, DC, December, 1979.

Gutelius, M., Kirsch, A., McDonald, S., Brooks, M. R., & McErlean, T. Controlled study of child health supervision: Behavioral results. *Pediatrics,* 1977, *60,* 294–304.

Hindley, C. B. Stability and change in abilities up to five years: Group trends. *Journal of Child Psychology and Psychiatry,* 1965, *6,* 85–99.

Hunt, J. McV. *Intelligence and experience.* New York: Ronald Press, 1961.

Huxley, A. *Brave new world.* New York: Harper, 1946.

Illich, I. *Medical nemesis.* London: Galder & Boyars, 1975.

Johnson, S. M., & Lobitz, G. K. The personal and marital adjustment of parents as related to observed child deviance and parenting behavior. *Journal of Abnormal Child Psychology,* 1974, *2,* 193–204.

Klaus, M. H., & Kennell, J. H. *Maternal–infant bonding.* St. Louis: C. V. Mosby, 1976.

Kuhn, T. S. *The structure of scientific revolutions* (2nd ed.). Chicago: University of Chicago Press, 1970.

Lewis, J., Beavers, W., Gossett, J., & Phillips, V. *No single thread: Psychological health in family systems.* New York: Brunner/Mazel, 1976.

Lightfoot, S. L. *Worlds apart: Relationships between families and schools.* New York: Basic Books, 1978.

Maslow, A. H. *Motivation and personality.* New York: Harper, 1954.

Mindlin, R., & Denson, P. Medical care of urban infants: Health supervision. *American Journal of Public Health,* 1971, *61,* 617–697.

National Research Council. *Toward a national policy for children and families*. Washington, DC: National Academy of Sciences, 1976.

Piaget, J. *The construction of reality in the child*. New York: Basic Books, 1954.

Rutter, M. Parent–child separation: Psychological effects on the children. *Journal of Child Psychology and Psychiatry*, 1971, *12*, 233–260.

Schaefer, E. S. Need for early and continuing education. In V. Dennenberg, (Ed.), *Education of the infant and young child*. New York: Academic Press, 1970.

Schaefer, E. S. Parents as educators: Evidence from cross-sectional longitudinal and intervention research. *Young Children*, 1972, *27*, 227–239.

Schaefer, E. S. *Parent–professional–child interaction and involvement* (Second annual report to U.S. Office of Child Development). Chapel Hill, NC: University of North Carolina, Frank Porter Graham Child Development Center, March 1976. (a)

Schaefer, E. S. Scope and focus of research relevant to intervention: A socio-ecological perspective. In T. Tjossem (Ed.), *Early intervention with high risk infants and young children*. Baltimore: University Park Press, 1976. (b)

Schaefer, E. S. Professional paradigms in child and family health programs. *American Journal of Public Health*, 1979, *69*, 849–850.

Schaefer, E. S. Professional support for family care of children. In H. M. Wallace, E. M. Gold, & A. C. Oglesby (Eds.) *Maternal and child health practices: Problems, resources, and methods of delivery* (2nd ed.). New York: John Wiley, 1982.

Schaefer, E. S., & Bayley, N. Maternal behavior, child behavior and their intercorrelations from infancy through adolescence. *Monographs of the Society for Research in Child Development*, 1963, *28*, (3, Serial No. 87).

Schaefer, E. S., & Edgerton, M. *Parent interview and sociodemographic predictors of adaptation and achievement*. Paper presented at the meeting of the American Psychological Association, New York, September 1979.

Schaefer, E. S., Siegel, E., Bauman, K. E., & Hosking, J. *Sociodemographic and early maternal behavior correlates of infant behavior at one year*. Paper presented at the meeting of the American Public Health Association, New York, November 1979.

Schiff, M., Huyme, M., Dumaret, A., Stewart, J., Tomkiewicz, S., & Feingold, J. Intellectual status of working-class children adopted early into upper-middle class families. *Science*, 1978, *200*, 1503–1504.

Skeels, H. M., & Harms, I. Children with inferior social histories: Their mental development in adoptive homes. *Journal of Genetic Psychology*, 1948, *72*, 283–294.

Starfield, B., & Barkowf, S. Physician's recognition of complaints made by parents of their children's health. *Pediatrics*, 1969, *43*, 168–172.

Stine, O. Content and method of health supervision by physicians in child health conferences in Baltimore. *American Journal of Public Health*, 1962, *52*, 168–172.

Terman, L. M., & Merrill, M. A. *Measuring intelligence: A guide to the administration of the new revised Stanford-Binet Tests of Intelligence*. New York: Houghton Mifflin, 1937.

U.S. Department of Health, Education, and Welfare. *E.S.E.A., Title I program guide* (No. 45A). Washington, DC: U.S. Office of Education, 1969.

U.S. Department of Health, Education, and Welfare. *Head Start policy manual:*

Head Start program performance standards. Washington, DC: U.S. Government Printing Office, 1975.

Vopava, J., & Royce, J. *Comparison of the long-term effects of infant and preschool programs on academic performance.* Paper presented at the meeting of the American Educational Research Association, Toronto, March 1978.

Wallat, C., & Goldman, R. *Home/school/community interaction.* Columbus: Charles E. Merrill, 1979.

Werner, E. E., & Smith, R. S. *Kauai's children come of age.* Honolulu: University Press of Hawaii, 1977.

White, R. W. Motivation reconsidered: The concept of competence. *Psychological Review*, 1959, *66*, 297–333.

Zigler, E., & Trickett, P. K. I.Q., social competence, and evaluation of early childhood intervention programs. *American Psychologist*, 1978, *33*, 789–798.

TWELVE

PARENT INFORMATION NEEDS AS REVEALED THROUGH INTERESTS, PROBLEMS, ATTITUDES, AND PREFERENCES*

JOSEPH SPARLING AND
BETSY LOWMAN

Family social services can be delivered through a variety of modes. However, the modality of clinical or individual casework service in response to an already-existing problem has been by far the most common (Kamerman & Kahn, 1978) and most criticized (Fischer, 1976) family social service. But other service alternatives such as information and education might be equally or more effective in some areas of family need—and these services might be brought into play before problems are manifested, acting in some degree as a preventive (Ramey & Haskins, 1979). The research in this chapter attempts to profile parenting information as a potentially effective element of preventive services.

PROBLEM

The growing tendency toward small two-generation families (Tietze, 1971) has cut off or at least impeded some of the more traditional and informal channels for transmitting child development information. The importance of communicating with parents regarding what is known about children and their development hardly needs emphasis. Early attempts to facilitate such communication with parents through programs like Head Start (Lazar & Chapman, 1972) have clearly indicated that the transmission of information or skills to parents is an extraordinarily complex process with success always dependent on more than a simple, one-way technique. The awareness is growing that a program of services or education should begin with a thorough needs assessment of the prospective clients (Popham, 1972) and should proceed as an interactive process.

The present study of information for parents was designed to contribute to (1) the future development of information strategies or products for parents, (2) the sensitive implementation of parent education programs or program components, and (3) the needs assessment process through which future programs will be planned and designed.

BACKGROUND LITERATURE THAT INFLUENCED THE DESIGN OF THE PRESENT STUDY

Warner, Murray, and Palmour (1973), in a survey of the general information needs of Baltimore residents, found that less than 10% of those surveyed indicated a need for more information about education or child care. Yet Dervin (1976) found that problems about child care ranked high among those cited by a cross section of Seattle residents. One explanation for these differences, which was anticipated by Warner et al. is that many people (particularly the urban poor) may not typically relate information to the solution of their problems; they express their problems as complaints, rather than as a need for information. Therefore, survey respondents may answer questions about the kinds of information they want quite differently from the way they answer questions about what needs or problems they have. We interpreted this distinction as having implications for the way in which survey questions were worded. In the present survey, questionnaires used a dual approach to elicit the maximum response from both middle- and lower-class respondents. Some of the questions were asked in terms of information: e.g., ''Please indicate your interest in reading each article by giving it a score." Others were asked in problem terms: e.g., "Listed below are some problems parents face. Have any of them troubled you recently?"

In a recent study (Granoff, 1977) mothers identified, selected, and rank-ordered the most important needs of mothers and newborns. The rank-ordered lists (including the most frequently mentioned problems of sleeping, crying, and physical discomforts) provided a useful resource in the development of the problems section of the present survey instrument. Equally useful was a report by Mesibov, Schroeder, and Wessen (1977) in which they categorized the problems parents "called in" to a large pediatric practice.

Finally, Walters (1977) investigated parent information needs which might be met by television. Of the 1,300 persons contacted by telephone, fewer than half thought that TV was a helpful information source. A group of 40 expert analysts believed that to attract a parent audience to a public television educational program would require a massive promotional campaign. The finding of equivocal interest in TV as an information source spurred the present study to explore a more complete range of sources and their interactions with information content.

SURVEY METHOD

Sample

To obtain 1,400 responses, 2,088 questionnaires were mailed to a stratified random sample of mothers who were previously identified and maintained as a marketing research panel.[1] The sample was stratified by birth month of the youngest child in the household. Approximately 58 questionnaires per month of age from 0 to 36 months were mailed; 1,516 (72.6%) were returned and 1,458 (69.8%) were usable for the study.

Because the mail-out data collection technique is unsuccessful with many low-income households, the general sample was augmented with 100 personal interviews of high-risk parents in which the same items were administered verbally. The interviews were conducted in eight cities: Atlanta, Birmingham, Chicago, Dallas, Denver, Kansas City, Los Angeles, and New York. Typically, they were conducted in pediatric clinic waiting rooms as parents arrived for well-baby appointments. Minority parents at or below the poverty level made up the high-risk sample.

Basic Instrumentation Considerations

The purpose of the survey was to learn about parent information needs. However, experience in needs assessment (Lillie & Black, 1976) suggests that an awareness and clear statement of needs is best explored and developed through a direct and extended interaction between client and researcher. Therefore, the necessity of collecting data rapidly (and typically without personal contact) forced us to abandon the "needs" concept and to use instead several related concepts from which needs might be inferred. The related concepts used in the instrument were: (1) preferences (for information sources); (2) interests (in information topics); (3) attitudes (about childrearing); and (4) problems (in childrearing).

While an adequate theory or knowledge base is not available regarding the relationships of these concepts, it seems likely that needs incorporate all problems and some interests, as illustrated in Fig. 1. If these relationships in fact exist, it means that needs are a "mixed bag." The individual's awareness of some needs (as problems) has a negative tone. His awareness of some needs (as interests) has a positive tone. And for some needs, represented by shaded areas in the diagram, the individual may have no awareness at all. This last group is illustrated by the parent's need for information about the Heimlich Maneuver (a technique for reviving a choking child), whether or not he has ever heard of the maneuver. These various types of needs, and there may be others, make it difficult or impossible for the naive respondent to

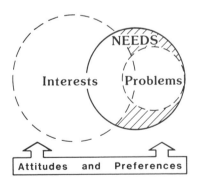

Figure 1.
Needs as an hypothesized relationship among interests, problems, attitudes, and preferences.

answer the straightforward question, "What are your information needs?"

By measuring interests and problems, the present instrument has tapped the two major aspects of need to which parents can readily respond. The instrument is flawed by its inability to tap the parent's unperceived needs or to separate those interests which are need-based from those which are simply curiosity-based. However, these flaws are accepted, since a much more expensive and complex approach would have been required to remedy them.

The concepts of preference and attitude are not a direct aspect of need, but may be thought of as mediating variables which impinge on need in various ways. For example, attitudes can shape (or be shaped by) interests and can define the borders of problems. Preferences can determine which information channels will be "open" and how much information may be received in response to need.

The instrumentation of the survey attempts to get a snapshot of two major areas of the needs domain (interests and problems) and to include two externally shaping factors (attitudes and preferences) in the picture.

Questionnaire

The general design of the questionnaire included four parts made up of closed-ended questions. The first part identified the sources of information parents prefer; the second assessed parents' information-seeking interests; the third measured parent attitudes; and the fourth assessed parenting problems. The survey instrument and a discussion of item development and pilot testing are provided in a report to the Administration for Children, Youth, and Families (Sparling, Lowman, Lewis, & Bartel, 1979, pp. 52–56).

SURVEY ANALYSES AND RESULTS

Basic descriptive statistics were computed and are supplied as percentages of responses throughout this report. Factor analysis of the interest scores was completed to identify and differentiate the conceptual areas of parent information interests. With each of the specific information interest topics, "readership" was calculated for the total sample and for each of the demographically defined subgroups. Information interest factor scores were computed for each parent and used to examine broad interest trends. The sample was divided into eight segments, each associated with an information factor, and the demographic characteristics of these segments were studied. And finally, correlations were examined to determine the ability of the attitude scores to predict the information interest factor scores. In the following sections, results are organized sequentially on interests, problems, attitudes, and preferences.

Information Interests and Parenting Problems

Interests and problems were the two concepts used to elicit responses that might be interpreted as parent information needs. The interest scores were analyzed first in terms of readership.

Readership of specific information articles. In the survey questionnaire, potential interests of parents were expressed as hypothetical article titles, and each title was rated in terms of the respondent's interest in reading it. For example, parents were asked how much they would like to read an article entitled "Build Your Child's Self-Confidence" rather than being asked if they wanted more information on self-confidence. When a 100-point interest scale is used, as in this survey, the estimated readership of an article is the proportion of respondents who score it 90 or higher. Validation studies have shown that, using this criterion, the mean error of prediction is about 6–7% (Haskins, 1975; McLaughlin, Haskins, & Feinberg, 1970; Stevenson, 1973), which is only slightly higher than the sampling variation in the most elaborate and time-consuming readership research.

Survey results show that the estimated readership of the 50 information topics (represented as article titles) ranges from 62% to 6%. These rates are comparable to those found in a recent study of readership in a daily newspaper (Stevenson, 1977). Total readership figures for the 50 articles, arranged in five arbitrary groups indicating readership levels, are shown in Table 1. The articles which fall in the highest readership category reflect broad and eclectic interests. Four of these titles concern the child's learning and/or cognitive development; three, the parents' management of emotional growth; one, health; and one, family dynamics. Seven of the nine top articles concern positive activity on the part of the parent. Phrases like "build your child's. . . ," "what to do. . . ," "prepare your child. . . ," "games to enhance. . . ," and "help . . ." suggest that parents clearly see themselves in a facilitative and skillful role vis-à-vis their young children.

Both the general population and the high-risk group gave high ratings to these titles, suggesting that information on certain topics may have an almost universal appeal. The demographic variations that did occur were in expected directions. For the article "The sick child: What to do," 71% of the teenage mothers were included in the readership

TABLE 1:   **ESTIMATED READERSHIP FOR 50 INFORMATION ARTI-CLES**[a]

Article title	% of mothers who are likely readers
Highest Readership	
Build your child's self-confidence	62%
The sick child: what to do	53
Prepare your child for learning	52
How mental abilities develop in children	49
Active learning: games to enhance academic skills	48
Help brothers and sisters get along with each other	47
The difference between loving and spoiling	45
A child's imagination: activities for growth	45
Parent–infant games that can help a baby learn	45
High Readership	
Learning in the first year of life: how can parents raise smarter kids?	43%
Teach your child to talk	43
Independence: how much, how soon?	42
Identify mental handicaps in preschoolers	41
Prevent common childhood illnesses	41
Protect your child's teeth	39
How do babies learn trust?	39
Moderate Readership	
When does punishment become child abuse?	36%
Immunize your child	36
How well does your child see?	36
Baby exercises to develop motor skills	36
Family changes that come with adding children	35
For kids' sake, think toy safety	35
When a child is angry	35
What to do with angry feelings toward your baby	33
Impact of TV on today's children	32
Is my baby all right? A guide to birth defects	31
How your child's diet changes as he grows	31
When does an infant begin to understand speech?	29
Boy or girl: how different are they—how alike?	29
Pregnancy disorders: 8 symptoms to report to your doctor	28
How to respond to stuttering and other speech problems in children	27

Low Readership

Put together your own playground	25%
A reading list for story time	24
Myths and facts about the working mother	24
What infant movements mean—arm waving has a purpose	23
How can I tell what my baby wants when she's crying?	22
Choose a balanced diet from the grocer's baby shelves	21
Establish a partnership with your child's preschool	20
The challenge of being a teenage parent	20
What does it cost to raise a child these days?	19
Using community services for your baby: do you know how?	18
Knowing your community's special resources	18

Lowest Readership

When it comes to your baby, does your mother really know best?	16%
When is your infant ready for a babysitter?	14
Caring for the premature baby	14
Explaining divorce to children	12
Raising a family as a single parent	11
What do other parents do about naps?	9
Techniques for the baby's bath	7
Be a successful stepparent	6

[a] The five levels of readership are arbitrary and are provided to make the table more readable. The cutoffs were identified as natural breaks in the distribution.

compared to only 43% of mothers from the 30–39 age group. For the article on sibling harmony, 29% of the mothers with one child were likely readers compared to 63% of the mothers with three or more children.

In addition to identifying the titles with wide audience appeal, the readership analysis demonstrates that some titles represent particularly strong concerns of the high-risk population. For example, 61% of the high-risk sample were included in the readership of "Raising a family as a single parent," while only 6% of the general population sample were included.[2] As might be expected due to overlap in the groups, topics of strong interest at high-risk parents are also of high interest to parents under 20 years of age. For example, readership of "The challenge of being a teenage parent" includes 17% of the general sample, 53% of the high-risk sample, and 80% of the parents under age 20.

General reading interests. In addition to looking at readership of specific titles, it is important to gain a more general view of readership or interest. In general, what kinds of parents are interested in what kinds of information?

Information titles in the questionnaire were carefully selected to cover a variety of conceptual areas of possible information interests or needs. Child development, child health and physical well-being, child problems, and special needs were some of the broad areas suggested by previous research (Sparling, 1976), and a cluster analysis of a pilot form of the titles (Sparling et al., 1979) tentatively supported these four categories of parent interests. Factor analysis of the survey data was used to try to validate these broad interest areas.

In the factor analysis, principal components factoring technique with iteration, varimax rotation, and orthogonal solutions was used. An Eigen value criterion of 1.0 resulted in 8 factors incorporating 42 of the 50 titles. Factor scores were generated from this solution for all respondents for use in further analyses.

Factor 1 was given the title, "Promoting General Learning and Development." While the analysis does not reveal anything about the importance of the factors, the fact that learning and development was the first factor indicates that parents respond to the component items in a highly consistent manner.

The second factor emerging from the analysis, entitled "Family Coping," contains several items reflecting stress on the family: financial concerns, anger toward children, advice from grandma.

Factors 3, 4, and 5 were entitled "Promoting Infant Learning and Development," "Promoting Health," and "Nontraditional Parenthood," respectively. Factor 3 represents a concept similar to Factor 1, but it demonstrates that parents have an awareness of the learning potential of very young infants which is distinct and additional to their awareness of learning in general. The health factor is clear and consistent with other surveys of parent information needs. Nontraditional parenthood, emerging here as a factor, again underscores the specialized needs of particular groups of new mothers.

The three remaining factors were labeled "Community Resources," "Social–emotional Development," and "Continuing Child Development" (having to do with older children). Factor 6, the Community Resources factor, was not revealed in most previous studies and therefore is of particular interest. Social–emotional development of the child as managed by the parent is the interest expressed in Factor 7. Here the emphasis is on the child rather than the parent, as it is in Factor 2. Finally, the general development of older children, particularly siblings, is Factor 8. These eight general categories provide a summary of the interests on the parent survey.

In order to gain a broad view of how various groups in the sample were responding to general information categories, the total sample was divided into eight segments. This analysis attempted to isolate the kinds of parents who are particularly interested in one kind of content. Based on factor scores, each mother was assigned to the one group in which she had expressed greatest interest. Most parents, of course, are interested in more than one general content category. Thus, the segmentation analysis distorts the readership patterns in the sense that an individual can be assigned to only one segment, even when she has other information interests as well. However, this analysis is useful in that it suggests something about the parent's top priority.

The first segment of the sample, that is, the group whose highest choice was Factor 1 (Promoting General Learning and Development), contained an over-representation of individuals with college education. Forty-three percent of the segment had college education, compared to only 31% of the total sample.

The Promoting Infant Learning and Development segment contained proportionately more respondents with only one child. While 36% of the total sample had only one child, 63% of the Promoting Infant Learning segment were one-child families. Parents with their youngest child less than 12 months of age were also over-represented in the Promoting Infant Learning segment. These variations between the total sample and the segment of the sample with infant learning as their first interest underscore the importance of getting information to parents at the right time—when they and their children are ready for it.

High-risk parents comprised only 6% of the total sample, yet they accounted for 14% of the sample segment having Promoting Health as their top interest. It seems likely that the health needs of these high-risk parents are inadequately served and this accounts for a relative increase in interest in health information.

The Nontraditional Parenthood segment contained a surprise. It included more parents (54%) with family income over $15,000 than the total sample (which contained 42%). Perhaps the fact that divorce is common among some high-income groups explains their interest in this factor which has a number of items dealing with divorce, single parents, and step-parents. Distribution within the Social–emotional Development segment of the sample paralleled the total sample, except that this segment contained 10% more families with two children (48% for this segment, 38% for the total sample). Other segments including Family

Coping, Community Resources, and Continuing Child Development had demographic profiles paralleling the general sample. This suggests that these broad topics are of average interest to all groups.

Parenting Problems

But what about information needs that are based not on likes or interests, but on worries, concerns, or problems? Part of the survey questionnaire was designed to cover content similar to the interests section but from a problem perspective. It was hoped that the responses to problems would reveal a different aspect of these parents' information needs than was revealed by their interests.

It was something of a surprise, then, when the top problem, parents' concern about supporting the child's developmental potential (see Table 2), did not reveal a new need but reconfirmed one that was well-established by the interest data. The largest group of highly rated problems seemed to relate to Factor 2, Family Coping. These problems included time alone for the mother, babysitters, crying, accidents, the demanding child, parent fatigue, spoiling, difficulty with toilet training, and unwanted advice. The remaining two problems from the top 12 (data were gathered on 26) had to do with when to call the doctor and the child's tantrums, items which related clearly to the Promoting Health factor and the Social–emotional Development factor, respectively.

TABLE 2: PERCENTAGE OF PARENTS WHO ARE OFTEN CONCERNED ABOUT TWELVE PROBLEMS

Problems	% of high-risk mothers	% of general population mothers
I wonder how I can help my baby develop her full potential	34	40
I wish I had more time for myself	30	27
It's hard to find a good babysitter	26	23
I'm having trouble getting my child to respond to toilet training	11	18
I wonder what my baby wants when he is crying	39	14
I worry that my child will get hurt around the house	27	14
My child is impatient and demanding	21	13
My child's activity wears me out	20	13
I wonder if I am spoiling my baby	22	13
I get advice I don't want from family and friends	16	13
I wonder when I should call the doctor	24	10
My child throws tantrums	25	8

Several interesting demographic trends were observed. For example, "I wonder when I should call the doctor" was often a concern of 38% of the teenage mothers, but of only 9% of the mothers over age 20. Time for one's self, negativism, and toilet training were problem areas which were proportionately of more frequent concern to older mothers and mothers with older children, especially 2-year-olds.

While the general content of the most frequent problems seemed to relate to the broad interest categories or factors (perhaps because of the redundancy built into the questionnaire), the correlations between specific problems and specific titles were small, adding some credence to the belief that the problems might tap some separate area of information need. Where significant correlations existed, the general sample and the high-risk sample often were seen to respond in different ways. For example, between the problems "I wonder if I am spoiling my baby" and the interest title "The difference between loving and spoiling," the high-risk sample had a nonsignificant Pearson correlation coefficient ($r = .06$, $n = 97$, N.S.) while the general sample had a significant correlation ($r = .19$, $n = 1457$, $p < .001$). This pattern of significant, though small, correlations occurring in the general sample and near-zero correlations occurring in the high-risk sample was repeated for several apparently related problem/interest pairs.

However, the problem, "I worry that my child will get hurt around the house" had a small significant correlation with a health interest, "The sick child: what to do" for both groups (high-risk, $r = .24$, $n = 94$, $p < .021$; general, $r = .14$, $n = 1460$, $p < .001$). Furthermore, the safety problem for the high-risk group was correlated at the .001 level of significance with five additional interests including such varied topics as independence, understanding speech, trust, angry feelings, and self-confidence. A number of other correlations significant at least at the .05 level of confidence also existed with this safety item, suggesting that for the high-risk group some concern about household safety as a problem may be a bellwether response that signals the presence of a variety of positive interests regarding the child.

It is interesting to note that two apparently parallel items, the problem "My child seems to lack confidence—I wish I could help" and the interest title "Build your child's self-confidence" had very small correlations for both groups (high-risk, $r = .03$; general $r = .08$). This was in contrast to other parallel topics which did produce a small significant relationship, at least in the general sample. In addition, the self-confidence title received the highest mean interest score, and its parallel problem received the lowest mean problem score, an apparent contradiction. This pattern may demonstrate the separate perceptions that the interests and problems were meant to elicit, or it may be due to the fact that since children in the study were below age 36 months, most were too young for a problem with self-confidence to have yet occurred. It is a hopeful sign that parents recognize the importance of this area regardless of the existence of a current problem.

The data on problems added some new knowledge to the needs picture. There were weak but frequent parallels between the problems and interest sections for the general sample. Perhaps when problems are of a more moderate degree, as with the general sample parents, rather than being acute, as with the high-risk sample parents, they may have a modest but persistent relationship to interests. The generally smaller correlations for the high-risk sample may indicate that it is mainly for this population that the problems area stands separately from interests and adds substantially to the understanding of information needs.

Parent Attitudes

Attitudes toward childrearing were measured by a forced-choice rank ordering of characteristics which parents value in their children. This measure, adopted from Schaefer and Edgerton (1979), taps bipolar attitudes which they term "progressive" and "traditional."

The top-valued child quality for the general population sample, the progressive value "to feel they are good persons" (see Table 3), was valued fourth by the high-risk population sample. Such sharp group differences suggest that these attitude scales might act as good predictors of parent-information interests. Indeed, of all variables, including the demographics, the child qualities attitude scale was the most consistently related to interests. For example, parents' interest in promoting general learning and development (Factor 1) was correlated with traditional child qualities attitude at a higher level ($r = .20$, $n = 1,549$, $p < .001$) than

TABLE 3:   MEAN ATTITUDE SCORES FOR VALUED CHILD QUALI-
             TIES BY PARENT RISK STATUS[a]

Attitudes	High-risk	General
Progressive		
To feel they are good persons	2.9	5.1
To think for themselves	3.5	4.2
To be curious about many things	2.8	3.1
Traditional		
To obey parents	5.5	4.3
To be polite to adults	4.1	2.8
To keep themselves and their clothes clean	2.2	1.5

[a] Range for any item = 1–6.

it was correlated with any of the socio-demographic variables. (Higher scores on Factor 1 were seen to be related to lower traditional attitudes on which qualities.) In the present sample, the attitude measures showed wide variation, paralleling differences in the demographic characteristics of the respondents. Progressive values increased with mother's age, education, and family income, whereas traditional values decreased. A typical regional effect was also noted, with Southern respondents reporting the most traditional values, Eastern and North Central respondents reporting the most progressive values, and Western respondents falling in an intermediate position. Since attitude scales relate in a consistent way to many demographic variables, the scales may at times act as a kind of convenient summary of these variables.

Sources of Information

Parents are accustomed to using a variety of sources of information to help them with the tasks they face in raising young children. In an earlier study (Sparling, 1976), parents reported that they frequently obtained information about children from their friends and family, books, doctors, and television. The present study attempted to clarify our understanding of parents' use of information sources by exploring two additional questions:

1. Which sources would parents prefer to use if the information were equally available from all sources? This question was raised because it seemed from the previous study that sources parents reported using were the ones which were most accessible to them, but not necessarily those which they would prefer. Data on preferences rather than actual use seemed more useful for developers and disseminators to consider, since they typically have the task of choosing future rather than current channels for disseminating new information.

2. Which sources of information would parents prefer for various types or content areas of information about children? The previous survey considered only information about children in general, and did not attempt to determine if there might be different preference patterns for different types of information.

Preferred sources. Parents were asked to choose the three information sources they would prefer to use among a set of nine options. They did this for each of five content areas, and in each case they indicated their choices in rank order from first to third. Table 4 shows the frequency of choices given to each information source averaged across all content areas. The sources are arranged in the table from most-frequently to least-frequently chosen, based on the total of all three levels of choice.

TABLE 4:   PREFERENCES FOR INFORMATION SOURCES[a]

Sources	% of first choices	% of second choices	% of third choices
Books	17	20	19
Family and Friends	28	14	13
Doctors and Nurses	18	15	9
Courses and Teachers	14	14	10
Magazines	5	12	15
Social Agencies	9	9	8
Pamphlets	3	8	14
Television	5	5	8
Films	1	3	4

[a] Each of over 1,500 mothers gave three choices for each of five information content areas; this produced a total of almost 24,000 choices.

Books and Family and Friends were the most frequent choices for preferred information sources. The next most frequent choice, Doctors and Nurses, was followed closely by Courses and Teachers and might be thought of as a second level of priority. Magazines, Social Agencies, and Pamphlets clustered closely together as somewhat less frequent choices. Of last priority were Television and Films in that order. In general, the majority of choices were for interpersonal sources followed by print media and lastly by the audiovisual media. (Books and Social Agencies deviated from this pattern.)

The strong preference for interpersonal sources is shown even more clearly when the first or primary choice selections are examined separately. Among the primary choices, both Family and Friends and Doctors and Nurses were named more often than Books, and Social Agencies were named more than Magazines.

Second and third choice sources in the present survey appear to be ones which may best be used in conjunction with other sources. Print media were more frequently selected as strong second and third choice sources. Books, Magazines, and Pamphlets in that order head the list among other choices. Audiovisual media remain at the bottom of the list among all choice levels, although they increase slightly in popularity as second and third choices.

Sources vs. content areas.   Since it seemed logical that parents might vary their preferred sources of information depending on the content of their information need, five broad content areas were built into the sources question. We hoped these five areas would parallel the factors derived from the article title section (see Table 1). The match was adequate, but not perfect. In effect, the sources question asked parents to cross-tabulate on a priority basis the preferred sources within the information content areas.

For information on the content area "How children grow and develop," two of the nine sources accounted for over half of all first choices: parents gave most of their primary choices to Doctors and Nurses (39%) and Books (20%). In contrast, parents chose most frequently Courses and Teachers (35%), and about evenly Family and Friends (23%) and Books (22%), for information on "How to teach children." For this information content area, Doctors and Nurses were first choice for a mere 4% of the parents.

Family and Friends and Doctors and Nurses were the favorite first choices (32% and 25%, respectively) of parents when they wanted information on "How to cope with children's problems." For "How to cope with family problems," Family and Friends was again the most frequent (36%) primary choice, but was followed by Social Agencies (25%) as the other source receiving substantial first choice nominations. The area of family problems is the only information area for which Social Agencies was a high priority source for the total sample.

For the final content area, "How to manage your child's environment," the source Family and Friends (32%) was the most frequent first choice with none of the other response options gaining even as much as 20% of the nominations.

In broad summary, close acquaintances were the most frequently desired primary source of information on problem areas or management of environment; the medical profession was the most frequently desired first source of information on child development; and the education profession was the most frequently desired first source of information on teaching children. The first choices show where the clearly preferred information channels are. The remaining choices suggest that the top channels may be supplemented, augmented, or even replaced by other information sources if the need arises.

DISCUSSION OF RESULTS

That parents want comprehensive and not narrowly defined information is supported by the broad spectrum of topics chosen in the interest section of this survey. The highest-rated topics from the survey suggested that most parents have an eclectic, whole-child approach to information interests with selected aspects of intellectual and creative development coming near the top. The factor structure of the interest topics seemed to confirm this view and placed some social–emotional topics with the cognitive topics in the first factor, Promoting General Learning and Development. The segmentation analysis supported health as the most frequent broad area identified by forced choice.

The survey revealed relationships among attitudes, information interests, and a variety of demographic variables. For example, interest in information on Promoting General Learning and Development was more likely, if the mother had lower traditional attitudes, higher income, and more education. We expected younger mothers to have some topics of particular interest to them. In fact, teen mothers expressed high interest in the information topic, "The sick child, what to do," and reported the problem, "I wonder when I should call the doctor," as being a frequent concern. It is instructive to note that while younger mothers in an earlier study (Sparling, 1976) identified toilet training as an important information topic, in the present survey only mothers over 20 years old reported problems with toilet training. Perhaps the first study reflected anticipation, while the second reflected coping. Both points in time may mark a period of receptivity to information on this topic.

Some other types of information may need to be available at even more specific points in the family history to be useful in childrearing—too early, and it will not be assimilated; too late, and it will be useless. Also the information must be available through a trusted source.

According to this survey, Friends and Family and Doctors and Nurses are preferred primary information sources, although each has its own area of information content primacy. Books were identified as the most frequent first-choice print material, and other forms of print were seen to be second or third choices—presumably used in conjunction with some other source. Courses and Teachers were shown to be a primary source when the information topic was "How to teach children." Television was notable in its absence as a primary source or a source that appealed more to younger or poorer parents.

The survey description of preferred information sources has particular relevance for professionals who plan parent education or parent involvement programs. Parents want to receive information through relatives or friends. Program developers might do well to encourage parent-to-parent information flow and to help professional home visitors to become "a friend of the family." Certain authorities such as doctors or teachers might contribute in their recognized areas, but should not be the exclusive source of information in a parent education program. The most important aspect of any programming effort in parent education may be to coordinate and time a variety of useful messages from an array of sources.

Footnotes

* The authors wish to thank Joan M. Bartel for questionnaire development, Isabelle S. Lewis for field testing, and ParaTest Marketing, Inc., for national data collection. Support for this research was provided by the Administration for Children, Youth and Families (Grant 90-C-1263). Opinions expressed are those of the authors.

[1] Sample selection and data collection were subcontracted to ParaTest Marketing, Inc. This firm maintains the National Baby Panel, a sample of 7,000 households described by ParaTest as "quota controlled demographically to conform with census estimates among geographic division, population density, age of homemaker and family income. The panel is pre-screened for respondent participation and for the collection of demographic data, and is updated monthly. Weights were applied to the sample to compensate for under-representation of mothers younger than 21 years and older than 36 years. Figures throughout the study represent weighted N's.

[2] Base rates are important to the interpretation of these and all percentage figures. While the single parent topic is of interest to a much higher proportion of the high-risk sample, this represents about the same absolute number of high-risk and general sample individuals, vis., $61\% \times 144 = 88$; $6\% \times 1480 = 89$.

REFERENCES

Dervin, B. *The development of strategies for dealing with the information needs of urban residents: Phase I; citizen study. Final report.* Washington: U.S. Department of Health, Education and Welfare, 1976. (ERIC No. ED 125 640)

Fischer, J. *The effectiveness of social casework.* Springfield, IL: Charles C. Thomas, 1976.

Granoff, M. K. *Assessing needs in early childhood education: Development of a questionnaire.* (A dissertation completed under the direction of Ira J. Gordon.) Unpublished manuscript, University of Florida, 1977.

Haskins, J. B. Pretesting interest in messages. *Journal of Advertising Research,* 1975, 15, 31–35.

Kamerman, S. B., & Kahn, A. J. *Family policy: Government and families in fourteen countries.* New York: Columbia University Press, 1978.

Lazar, J. B., & Chapman, J. E. *A review of the present status and future research needs of programs to develop parenting skills.* Washington, DC: George Washington University, 1972.

Lillie, D. L., & Black, T. Principles and procedures in technical assistance: An approach to educational change. *Educational Technology,* October, 1976, 33–36.

McLaughlin, H., Haskins, J. B., & Feinberg, B. M. An economical technique for pretesting communications campaigns. *Journal of Applied Psychology,* 1970, 50, 690–696.

Mesibov, G. B., Schroeder, C. S., & Wesson, L. Parental concerns about their children. *Journal of Pediatric Psychology,* 1977, 2, 13–17.

Popham, J. *An evaluation guidebook: A set of practical guidelines for the educational educator.* Los Angeles: Instructional Objectives Exchange, 1972.

Ramey, C. T., & Haskins, R. H. The causes and treatment of school failure: Insights from the Carolina Abecedarian Project. In M. Begab, H. Garber, & H. C. Haywood (Eds.), *Causes and prevention of retarded development in psychosocially disadvantaged children.* Baltimore: University Park Press, 1979.

Schaefer, E. S., & Edgerton, M.D. *Parent interview and socio-demographic 67edictors of adaptation and achievement.* Paper presented at the American Psychological Association Annual Convention, New York, 1979.

Sparling, J. J. *Infant Development and Education Needs-Assessment Survey.* Unpublished report. Chapel Hill: University of North Carolina, Frank Porter Graham Child Development Center, 1976.

Sparling, J. J., Lowman, B. C., Lewis, I. S., & Bartel, J. M. *What mothers say about their information needs, Volume I.* Final Report to the Administration for Children, Youth & Families. Chapel Hill: University of North Carolina, Frank Porter Graham Child Development Center, 1979.

Stevenson, R. L. Cross-cultural validation of a readership prediction technique. *Journalism Quarterly,* 1973, *50,* 690–696.

Stevenson, R. L. *Readership of the High Point Enterprise* (Report). Chapel Hill: University of North Carolina, 1977.

Tietze, C. Prevalence and effectiveness of family planning. *Millbank Memorial Fund Quarterly,* 1971, *49*(4), 132–142.

Walters, P. B. *An assessment of parent education and general needs that can be served by educational programming for television.* (OE-300-76-0398), Silver Spring, MD: Applied Management Sciences, 1977.

Warner, E. S., Murray, A. D., & Palmour, V. E. *Information needs of urban residents: Final Report.* Washington: U.S. Department of Health, Education, and Welfare, 1973. (ERIC No. ED 088 464)

THIRTEEN

INTEGRATION OF PARENT EDUCATION INTO HUMAN SERVICE PROGRAMS

EDITH GROTBERG

Many current human service programs support, educate, or involve parents. Some of these programs, such as Aid to Families with Dependent Children, are largely financial support, but may include referral to needed services, housing, or resources. Other programs, such as Title I of the Elementary and Secondary Education Act (ESEA), are largely educational in nature, with the education focused on children, but may include a Parent Advisory Council to stimulate parent involvement. Still other programs, such as the Comprehensive Education and Training Act (CETA), are largely job training for adults, but may include parent education or support services to trainees with young children. Head Start requires parent involvement at an advisory level, encourages parent participation in the Head Start program, and provides opportunities for parenting education.

Granted the existence of a broad array of service programs that affect families, one might be concerned with the extent to which parent education could or should be integrated into these programs. This chapter, based on discussions held during the Parent Education and Public Policy Conference, addresses five issues concerning integration of parent education into human service programs: (1) clarification of types of parent participation; (2) recognition of the need to have government, non-government, and informal groups work together; (3) identification of obstacles to parent participation; (4) summary of research needs; and (5) description of needed policy or policy changes.

TYPES OF PARENT PARTICIPATION

There is no generic term to incorporate the various types of parent participation or the different concepts of parent education, parent supports, and parent involvement. This lack of a generic term complicates any discussion of concerns for parents in human service programs. Thus, it is helpful to use the term "parent participation" as a generic term incorporating three more specific types of parent participation:

1. *Parent Involvement*. Parent involvement refers to parent participation in the formulation, management, and substance of particular programs that affect their lives. This definition accepts the principle of participation as a democratic right and acknowledges the literature on the benefits to children when their parents become involved in the programs. The literature draws primarily on studies of families with low income, but the principle of involvement is probably valid for other families as well. Parent involvement as defined here includes empowerment, sharing of knowledge and skills with professionals, and expecting accountability.

2. *Parent Education*. Parent education includes the dissemination or acquisition of the information and skills that help parents fulfill their functions as parents. Also included here is information, learning, training, acquisition of knowledge and skills about institutions that affect parents in their parenting roles. The intent of parent education is to have parents develop their ability to use information and services effectively without the need for extensive institutional support.

3. *Parent Support*. Support for parents may be informal, with friends and relatives providing the support. It may also be a mutual support system or self-help group where common needs are met. Support may be of a more formal nature including churches, community organizations, the PTA, or child care facilities. Finally, formal institutional support may be needed, including hospitals, social services agencies, or educational institutions.

Human service programs should attempt to consider all three kinds of parent participation. Thus, if parents need institutional support, they should be provided with parent education relating to the need that required institutional support and should have a role to play in parent involvement. Parent participation in many programs for handicapped children (see Chaps. 7 & 8) is an example where all three kinds of participation occur.

COOPERATION BY GOVERNMENT AND NONGOVERNMENT AGENCIES

Parent participation, as defined above, cannot be limited to government programs, but must include nongovernment programs and informal, self-help, mutual support programs as well. The importance of this broader perspective is: (1) to be consistent with the democratic philosophy of participation in social programs; and (2) to prevent disparate systems and programs from development in ways that reduce the potential for cooperation.

The government can require parent participation in programs and may, as in the case of Head Start or Title I, be quite specific about the types of parent participation required. The Congress of Parents and Teachers, contrary to the required parent participation in government programs, can address parent participation throughout its organizations, potentially involving parents and future parents of the entire educational system of the country. Parent education, for example, is a part of most public school programs, encouraged and supported by the PTA, and also appears in many parent groups outside the school. The PTA has lobbied for a comprehensive health act which would include parent education and has also held 16 conferences in recent years to develop parent awareness of the need for parent education. After these PTA conferences, meetings were held with public school officials to describe models of parent education recommended by the PTA. The entire process took four years. These health programs have now been demonstrated in eight states. Young people in the schools attend conferences conducted by the PTA to learn about the health programs and to indicate their preferences. The intent is to generate consumer support for these programs in which parents, through the PTA, have been part of the process of development and dissemination of parent education through health education. The PTA urges parent participation in program development and a parent component in all programs affecting families.

Government programs and PTA programs are both enhanced and extended through the different target populations addressed and the different structures of policy performance and services.

The Center for Parent Involvement is another example of a nongovernment organization concerned with family needs and supports which frequently cooperates with government groups. The Center provides a base for self-help and mutual support groups, which organize around their own specific needs rather than meeting eligibility requirements more common in public programs. Because many parents and professionals are concerned about ways community workers can bring parents and programs together without fostering a dependency relationship, the Center has its community workers trained so they provide information to parents about the health, education, nutrition, and service needs to their families, and then advise them on programs, formal and informal, public and private, where these needs may be met. The newly developed concept of mediating groups is consistent with the Center's use of community workers, who may include friends, neighbors, and those from churches and local organizations such as the PTA. The critical fact is that public and private services and institutions are frequently difficult for families to negotiate and mediators are sought. Cooperation between government and nongovernment programs is often made possible through such mediators.

OBSTACLES TO PARENT PARTICIPATION

In programs like Head Start, parent participation, although mandated, does not involve more than one third of the parent population. Many parents do not have the time to participate, or they are given tasks in the centers that do not challenge them. They often lack sufficient information or training to contribute to the program, and many staff members are not clear on how to help parents. In the public schools, parent participation is prevented in a number of ways. Unions tend to oppose the teacher time required to work with parents, and peer pressure is exerted to prevent teachers from becoming involved with parents. The Parent Advisory Councils (PACs) under Title I, ESEA, have not fared much better. In a recent study of over forty PAC's across the country, each had been bypassed or undermined by the school system. In most cases the PACs did virtually nothing, and the members were usually mere recipients of information rather than participants in advising or in teaching their children.

Obstacles to increased parent participation in these and similar programs occur at two levels. One is the legal level. Many school systems point out that the laws hold schools, not parents, accountable for education. When schools share their power with parents, they cannot share accountability. The second level is interpersonal. Relationships between parents and teachers are fraught with tensions and misunderstandings. The PTA experience has been that teachers and parents do not have much contact. This is especially true of low-income parents who resist going to school because it seems foreign to their values and ways.

There already exists a good deal of information about effective parenting, about effective institutions, and about effective parent participation. And there are models of effective advisory boards. But there seems to be a block between parents and institutions, and this block disrupts the communication of information and, more important, the involvement of parents in meaningful roles.

RESEARCH NEEDS

At least 11 research areas concerning parent participation are in need of empirical information. These research areas are built on the premise that parent participation in programs is important and, in fact, is a right:

1. Research is needed to determine what parents want in parent participation; i.e., what types of involvement, education, and supports parents themselves see as important. Provisions for group and cultural differences must be included in these studies.

2. What types of parent participation produce what effects for parents, children, and society?

3. What factors reduce or increase parent effectiveness, e.g., what skills do parents need? What can parents do to help their children succeed in school?

4. How are informal, mutual support, self-help groups formed? What incentives can be used to encourage the emergence of such groups?

5. How can family networks and friendship networks be used to increase parent participation?

6. What roles can teachers play in parent involvement, parent education, and parent support? What roles can the school play?

7. How can parent advisory boards be more effective and have more influence on programs?

8. What do children learn when parents interact with institutions and programs?

9. How can institutions be changed to increase parent participation?

10. What kinds of parent participation are most effective with what types of families?

11. What are critical characteristics and roles of effective mediators?

POLICY AND POLICY CHANGES

Experience with parent participation resulting from programs in the Department of Housing and Urban Development, the Department of Agriculture, and the Department of Health and Human Services provides a basis for examining current policies and determining policy changes or innovations. Increased national concern for families has already caused these and other agencies to study the impact of policies on families and suggests the need to be more sensitive to family needs. Added to that increased concern for families is an increased awareness that parents should be involved in programs affecting them and their children. This awareness leads to a suggested policy guide:

> Each program affecting parents and children, whether child care, education, health, nutrition, or social services, must empower parents to participate in decision-making and in developing and carrying out the program.

Increased awareness of the role of parents in the development and education of their children and evidence that parents make a critical difference in the lives of their children suggest further examination of ways to help parents become more effective in their roles. The fact that professionals can share knowledge, information, and skills with parents enhances the abilities of parents and promotes more professional–parent cooperation and equity. Parent education in programs or as part of programs suggests the following policy guide:

> Each program which is intended to affect the lives of children must have a parent education component so that parents might develop skills, acquire information, and become knowledgeable about parenting. The parent education component should be linked to informal networks (such as mutual support or self-help groups) and to the formal program structure.

The shift to concern for support of the entire family makes new requirements on programs. Not only do programs need to examine the impact of their efforts on family stability and functioning, but they need to examine new ways to assure family integrity. Closely aligned to family supports is the concern for prevention of family breakup. These concerns suggest the following policy guide:

> Each program which is intended to serve the needs of family members must demonstrate the ways in which the program will provide support to the entire family, preserve its integrity, and respect its uniqueness. Programs emphasizing prevention of family break-up must clarify the elements of the program that are preventive.

SUMMARY AND CONCLUSION

Current and proposed programs supported by public and private funds have a unprecedented challenge in this country: to find ways to integrate parent involvement in the decisions and policies of major social programs, increase parent education and thereby promote parent effectiveness, and stimulate parent supports to assure continued family functioning. The task is so large and the stakes so high that nongovernment and government organizations and formal and informal groups must work together to assure parent participation. There are many obstacles to parent participation; these need to be studied and eliminated. Finally, current and proposed policies must reflect the need to assure parent participation and to integrate this participation into recognizable components of the programs. The shift is moderate, but basic, and has far-reaching implications for stronger families in the nation.

FOURTEEN

PARENT EDUCATION, CULTURAL PLURALISM, AND PUBLIC POLICY: THE UNCERTAIN CONNECTION

LUIS M. LAOSA

Longstanding concerns about the academic underachievement of poor and ethnic minority children are being translated today into a movement that seeks solutions to this serious and refractory problem by means of direct interventions into families. The purpose of these interventions is to modify childrearing practices and thus indirectly influence the level of academic achievement of children who traditionally have performed poorly in schools. The ultimate goal is to enable the children of low-income and ethnic-minority families to move, upon reaching adulthood, into middle-class social and economic status. Parent education has thus emerged as a major social policy issue for the 1980s.[1]

My intent in this chapter is to raise some questions and review some research findings that bear on what I think is a critical, although too frequently neglected, issue in parent education today: the connection between the policymaking process and the families or individuals who ultimately are affected by the policy. The goals of current parent education programs are similar in invoking *implicit standards of parenting* that are considered most likely to produce well-adjusted, intelligent, and academically successful children. My concerns center on the research, the values, and the assumptions on which we base our choice of these standards and on the processes by which we arrive at them.

Because the term "parent involvement in education" has diffuse meanings, I shall be more explicit about my focus. Indeed, the term can refer to a broad range of contacts between parents and educators, and between parents and children. It is useful to differentiate, as Goodson and Hess (1975, 1978) do, four distinct types of parent involvement in education. Each type represents an approach used by current intervention programs. Each type also represents, to some degree, the implicit or explicit goals of the program or activity for the parents: (1) parents as more effective teachers of their own children; (2) parents as better parents; (3) parents as supporting resources for the school; and (4) parents as policymakers. The extent to which the priority and focus of the intervention is on modifying the parent–child interaction in the home varies greatly from one type of program to another. Although all four types of intervention programs have the potential to affect interactions in the family, the first two types explicitly state it as a goal. Therefore, because my concern here is on policy decisions that aim to affect the educational and caregiving interactions between parents and children, I will focus on the first two types of intervention. These are interventions designed to give parents new competencies and new knowledge to guide their relationships with their children. These types of interventions typically specify desirable parental behaviors to be acquired; such new behaviors are intended to support increased cognitive and social development of the children.

Parent education has come to replace compensatory education as a popular strategy for social and economic reform. Compensatory education, like parent education, was an attempt to remedy the poor academic achievement of low-income and ethnic minority children and thus enable them to move up from their parents' social class. Conceived and launched in the 1960s, compensatory education was based on the premise that there was some deficiency in these children, their families, and their cultures that had to be corrected (Laosa, 1977d, 1981a). Schools were designated as the agents of change responsible for exposing these children to a set of experiences that their "culturally deprived" families were unable to provide. Compensatory education would ensure that the minority child participated in school activities designed to foster the development of intellectual skills and attitudes that enabled the typical child from a middle-class family to attain academic success. According to this reasoning, once the poor and ethnic minorities were skilled and educated, they could achieve middle-class economic and social status and thus break out of the "cycle of poverty."

Wherein, then, lies the difference between the approaches embodied by compensatory education on the one hand and by parent education on the other? Compensatory education was child-centered: The schools were to be the agents of change to compensate for the continuing "cultural deprivation" of the home. In parent education, by contrast, parents become the agents of change: poor and ethnic minority parents are taught childrearing techniques that are considered to produce children with the intellectual skills and attitudes necessary for successful academic competition with their middle-class peers.

Although statements to the contrary are now fashionable among parent educators, a careful examination of the two approaches reveals profound similarities. Historically, both approaches are deeply rooted in the same conceptual foundation, and both emanate from the same research base.

Much of the research and development that served to shape the conceptual basis for policy and programs in both compensatory education and parent education drew strongly from Basil Bernstein's (1961) theoretical formulations. Bernstein, in contrast to those who sought a biological explanation of social-class and ethnic-group differences in school performance, aimed toward an understanding on the basis of environmental explanations (see Ginsburg, 1972). He proposed that middle- and lower-class parents employ different childrearing techniques, which result in different patterns of language and thought. In Bernstein's (1961) view, middle-class life is oriented around the values of order, rationality, stability, planning for long-range goals, and the control of emotion. Children in middle-class homes are encouraged to verbalize emotions, to control them, and to try to understand feelings rationally. In their use of discipline, middle-class parents tend to use verbal rather than physical punishment, to elaborate on a rationale for an interdiction, and to explore the child's motivation. This style of interaction is seen to foster the development of a language that is complex and that can carry subtle shades of meaning. Exposure to this kind of language—which Bernstein called the "elaborated code"—and to these childrearing practices is seen to cause the middle-class child to develop a superior abstract-reasoning ability that permits complex and subtle intellectual activity.

In contrast, Bernstein viewed lower-class socialization and its results as almost the opposite. He theorized that lower-class parents do not present to the child an ordered, planned, and rational system of living. Moreover, the discipline administered by lower-class parents was seen as arbitrary and their expression as emotional, direct, and often volatile. Their language was considered to be ill-suited for the expression of subtle shades of meaning or the elaboration of thought. Consequently, in Bernstein's view, the lower-class child was not faced with the problem of comprehending complex chains of reasoning involving relations and abstract categories. He was seen as acquiring a language that was considered to be, in many respects, deficient—a poor vehicle for thought. This "restricted code" was seen to have the effect of limiting the generality and abstraction of thought and to result in a

> low level of conceptualization, an orientation to a low order of causality, a disinterest in processes, a preference to be aroused by, and respond to, that which is immediately given. . . . This partly conditions the intensity and extent of curiosity. . . . There will be a tendency to accept and respond to an authority that inheres in the form of social relationships, rather than in reasoned or logical principles. (Bernstein, 1961, pp. 302–303)

These alleged characteristics have been presumed to inhibit the lower-class child's ability to learn from the environment.

Many social scientists whose research and development work involved low-income and minority populations found Bernstein's views highly appealing and were influenced by them. Thus, operating within Bernstein's (1961) theoretical formulation, Hess and Shipman (1968) concluded from their observations of maternal teaching behavior in Black families of varied socioeconomic levels that:

> The cognitive environment of the culturally disadvantaged child is one in which behavior is controlled by imperatives rather than by attention to the individual characteristics of a specific situation, and one in which behavior is neither mediated by verbal cues which offer opportunities for using language as a tool for labeling, ordering, and manipulating stimuli in the environment, nor mediated by teaching that relates events to one another and the present to the future. The meaning of deprivation would thus seem to be a deprivation of meaning in the early cognitive relationships between mother and child. (p. 103)

In a similar vein, Bee, Van Egeren, Streissguth, Nyman, and Leckie (1969) made the following interpretations of their data on maternal teaching behavior:

> Our findings, as those of Hess and Shipman, provide evidence of an impoverished language environment and ineffectual teaching strategies experienced by the lower-class child. Such a child may learn a good deal about what *not* to do, or at least about global rules of conduct, but he may not be well equipped with the language tools or learning sets required for a systematic approach to the analysis of problems. He has not, judging from our results, been encouraged to learn general techniques of problem-solving, and he has not been exposed to the highly differentiated language structure that is most suitable for verbally mediated analysis of the environment. (pp. 733–734)

The inference that Kamii and Radin (1967) made from their data is also typical of a "deficit" or "pathology" interpretation:

> The influence techniques used by disadvantaged mothers may in part account for the lack of inner controls observed in school among lower-class children. . . . The lower-class Negro child, whose socioemotional needs are not met and who does not develop an emotional dependence on his mother, is known, in general, to fail to behave in accordance with society's norms. (pp. 308–309)

I should make explicit here my belief that the writings of these researchers, as well as the research of others who adhere to similar views, reflect a conscious and definite intention that humane and progressive results in public understanding, policymaking, and community programs should flow from their work. Thus, for example, after concluding from their data that the learning styles and information-processing strategies that the child obtains in the process of interacting with the mother may set limits upon the potential mental growth of the child, Hess and Shipman (1968) called for new programs to remedy the situation as they saw it. These were to be programs that *"resocialize* or *reeducate* the child toward more effective cognitive strategies" (p. 103). Other investigators recommend that programs be designed to effect permanent change in the behavior of poor and ethnic-minority mothers. For example, Kamii and Radin (1967) concluded from their data that "compensatory education must include an attempt to alter the socialization practices of disadvantaged mothers" (p. 309). Such interventions would act directly on the perceived cause of the lower-class and ethnic-minority child's lack of success in school: the mother's behavior (fathers were assumed to be absent).

Although certainly well-intentioned, the work of these and other social science professionals reinforced popular misconceptions and stereotypes on the basis of rather limited research. Not only their interpretations of the data, but also the designs of their studies—including their selection of variables—were cast within the deficit or social pathology paradigm, which at the time was a popular conceptual framework for the conduct of research and development in education (see Laosa, 1981a).

Like the research on other ethnic minorities, much of the literature concerning Chicano families is limited to historical and stereotypic treatises; discussions of socialization in Chicano families generally have occurred within a comparative model of Euro-American, middle-class milieux, and often from the perspective of a social pathology model. Much of this literature has relied on only a very few dimensions that become the undergirding variables for explaining Chicano socialization and child development. These dimensions have included, for example, the stereotypic constructs of "machismo" and "passivity." Hence, a rash of generalizations ensued that viewed *"the* Mexican-American family" from the perspective of social pathology. This approach, to say the least, has not contributed positively to knowledge useful for developing relevant policy and programs for Chicano parents and children.

Today, a growing minority of scholars question the adequacy of the assumptions underlying the deficit and social pathology paradigm, as well as the concepts, theories, and methods that emanate from it. Critics of the deficit and social pathology views have argued that much of the research and development work centered on ethnic-minority and low-income populations is biased by a Euro-American, middle-class point of view. They further contend that conceptual and methodological approaches based on such viewpoints prejudice our understanding of the reality of those populations. Because those who operate within a "deficit" viewpoint—or any other aggressively ethnocentric framework—are predisposed to identify order and organization with conformity to the norms of their own sociocultural group, any possibility of finding another kind of social organization or cultural patterning in their observations is confounded from the outset (Laosa, 1981a).

Even when a deficit or social pathology framework is not apparent, research findings must be viewed and used with some caution, questioning whether the full range of existing variation has been examined, and realizing that the research questions and even the results are likely to be influenced by the value orientations of the investigators. Although the findings may be replicable, recurrent, and apparently robust, they should not be exempt from this caveat (Clarke-Stewart, 1977). Indeed, one's ability to understand the reality of a given social or cultural group is limited if the interpretive framework for the analysis of that reality is based on assumptions associated with a different kind of reality (Nobles, 1978). The orientations characteristic of those who study ethnic minority families has been based largely on an understanding and perception of reality different from that of the families studied. One needs only turn to fashions and the mass media to find examples of the critical relationship that exists between the interpretive framework in research and the validity of the information it yields. For example, in the 1940s and 1950s it was the style for Black women to straighten their hair. Some White sociologists interpreted this as evidence of self-hatred among Black people—that it meant they were trying to be White. In the past five years, White women have had their hair frizzed, Afro-ed, and now cornrowed; we have yet to hear any sociologist suggest that this reflects deep self-loathing on the part of White women.

A major concern in the study of parental behavior has been how to define socially competent parenting. This is indeed a difficult endeavor in a pluralistic, complex, and rapidly evolving nation such as ours, where families of varied social and cultural backgrounds live side by side and contribute their share to the society's development. One finds in such a society a strikingly rich diversity in preferred styles of behavior. There is diversity among and within groups, and the variation is perhaps widest in the beliefs, attitudes, and behaviors surrounding family life and especially the rearing of the young. Different groups value different patterns of family interaction; they hold varied beliefs concerning what is exemplary behavior; they also differ in their views of what constitutes desirable behavior on the part of children; they differ, moreover, in their conceptions of the attributes that define "optimal development" (Laosa, 1974a, 1978, 1979b, 1980a, 1981a, 1982a, 1982b). There is, of course, sufficient evidence and general agreement that extreme environmental deprivation and certain forms of physical abuse are severely detrimental to the child (see, for example, Dennis, 1960; Spitz, 1946). The lack of agreement over the definition of competent parenting focuses not on this but on the patterns of parental behavior that fall within the normal range in each sociocultural group. Although the goal of many parent education programs—producing academically successful children—is widely shared, the preferred means of attaining the goal varies both among and within the different cultural and socioeconomic groups.

To some, the current parent education movement seems yet another attempt to melt away sociocultural diversity by imposing one group's standard of parenting over the others. The "melting pot" view of American society called for the amalgamation of all subcultures into a new and superior culture. It is becoming increasingly apparent, however, that such a model may not provide a healthy outcome for certain groups (Laosa, 1974b; Laosa, Burstein, & Martin, 1975). It now seems clear that an amalgamation model, when directed by a dominant class, leads to the melting away of the other subcultures and to the preponderance of one group over the others.

Increasingly aware of the challenges to the deficit, social pathology, and melting pot views, parent educators have begun to state—in forceful and sometimes vehement language—that their programs are not based on such viewpoints. Although these claims are easily stated, the evidence to support them is not so easily adduced, and indeed in most cases it is rather meager and almost always unconvincing. As we have seen, most of the research in which these programs are rooted was carried out within a deficit and social pathology framework, and at a time when that framework had not been sufficiently challenged and thus was still very much in vogue among the vast majority of research producers. A more subtle and perhaps more important limitation of the available research is that almost all of the data have been collected in studies designed and executed by Euro-American, middle-class researchers. Thus, even when a deficit or social pathology framework is not apparent, we must view and use the data with caution, knowing, as we have already seen, that not only the interpretation of results, but also the research questions posed, are likely to be influenced by the value orientation of the investigators. It is also important to note that almost all evaluations of the impact of parent education programs on children employ as a principal assessment instrument a standardized intelligence test; yet many of those instruments are considered by some to measure conformity to certain norms of behavior characteristic of the Euro-American middle-class (see Laosa, 1977c, 1982b).

As a cornerstone of our free nation, sociocultural diversity presents us with an awesome dilemma: In an open society where the movement toward cultural pluralism is ascending in recognition and acceptance, can there be a single and broadly applicable set of standards for "good" parenting behavior? How should policy decisions of this sort be made? Who shall determine what standards of behavior are to be encouraged or even imposed? Indeed, beyond a minimum set of universally accepted codes designed to ensure the physical health and safety of its members, should public policy dictate standards of behavior within the family?

Although it is now generally agreed that sociocultural diversity in the behavior of parents toward their own children does exist, heated controversies continue concerning alternative interpretations of the observed differences. The debate centers on several major questions (Laosa, 1981a; 1982b): Should we measure and interpret behavior in social and cultural settings different from ours, employing our own methods and conceptual categories which may be inappropriate or irrelevant in those settings? Do the observed differences between groups indicate that the behavior of minority and poor mothers toward their own children is in some way deficient or inferior to the maternal behavior typically found in middle-class homes? Are the norms for behavior adhered to by certain cultural groups inherently superior to the norms exhibited by other groups? And who, indeed, is qualified to make decisions about the relative value of the norms reflected in the behavior of the various sociocultural groups?

Much work is yet needed before an adequate research base is available. The needed research should be based on models that accurately reflect the reality of life among socioculturally diverse families. Families in America must be understood within the shaping sociocultural, historical, and economic context that determines their place within a complex and rapidly changing society. Without such a research base, the connection between, on one hand, the information available to policymakers and program developers, and, on the other hand, the world of those who are affected by the policies and programs, will continue to be weak and uncertain.

Although this type of research is only just beginning, there is growing evidence of differences in parenting styles not only among but also *within* ethnic groups. For example, in a recent series of observational studies, I uncovered great individual variability in the teaching strategies of Chicano mothers (Laosa, 1977b, 1978, 1982a), a finding that dispels the common misconception that certain ethnic minority groups are homogeneous with regard to parenting styles. Indeed, frequently one hears people talk about families from a particular geographical area and describe the members as, say, "Spanish Americans," "Spanish-speaking," or "Hispanic Americans." Not only are there several distinct Hispanic groups in the United States with quite different cultural, linguistic, and socioeconomic characteristics, but even within each of the subgroups there is considerable variability. This fact was clearly demonstrated in another study of three Hispanic communities, which I conducted several years ago (Laosa, 1975). That study examined the contextual use of language by parents and their children in Chicano, Cuban-American, and Puerto Rican families in different geographic regions of the United States. The results showed that the implicit sociolinguistic "rules" associated with the use of Spanish and English were important sources of variance both *among* and *within* the communities. These and other sources of variability, when ignored, can result in policies and programs that are inappropriate or inadequate for certain groups.

As part of the series of studies I have been conducting to examine sociocultural diversity in patterns of family interaction, I recently set out to determine whether differences exist between Chicano and non-Hispanic White families in young children's first experiences with activities involving teaching and learning in relation to their mothers (Laosa, 1979a, 1980a, 1981a). Mothers were observed in their homes while they taught their own children how to solve problems involving perceptual, cognitive, and motor abilities. What have the results shown? Comparisons of Chicano and non-Hispanic White mothers revealed that there were no ethnic-group differences in the *total number* of teaching behaviors directed to the children. Both the Chicano and non-Hispanic White mothers directed approximately the same number of teaching behaviors to their children. When these interactions were analyzed by the types of teaching strategies involved, however, the results showed that, as a group, Chicano mothers used different teaching strategies from those used by the non-Hispanic White mothers.

As yet, there is little evidence that any of the teaching strategies that distinguish, say, Chicano and non-Hispanic White mothers make for "better mothering" in any general sense of the term (LeVine, 1980). Not surprisingly, however, school teachers appear to use the teaching strategies that are characteristic of non-Hispanic White mothers, rather than the teaching strategies observed most frequently in Chicano homes. Might such a discontinuity between the teaching strategies of home and school account at least in part for the low academic achievement of Chicano children (cf. Laosa, 1977a, 1982a)? If this proves to be the case, one must then decide (1) whether to attempt to modify the patterns of behavior in Chicano families to conform to the non-Hispanic White patterns of interaction, or (2) whether school teachers should diversify their teaching repertoires to provide greater home–school continuity for Chicano children.

Not only do we find sociocultural-group differences in family interaction patterns, but, to complicate matters further, it appears that the same parental behavior may have different meanings—therefore different consequences for children's development—across different sociocultural groups. Support for this "differential meaning" hypothesis comes from two recent studies. In one study (Laosa, 1976), I examined the relationship between various maternal teaching behaviors and measures of children's development in Chicano and non-Hispanic White families. An important finding was that the pattern of correlations between specific maternal behaviors and the children's cognitive development varied by ethnic group. In another study (Laosa, 1980b, 1981b), I examined the structural organization of various maternal teaching behaviors, again in Chicano and non-Hispanic White families. The results suggest that maternal behaviors are organized into distinct structures that differ when one compares the two sociocultural groups. Together, these findings suggest that a given class of parental behavior that has one kind of influence on children's development for one sociocultural group does not necessarily have the same effect or "meaning" for another sociocultural group.

Research such as this is necessary in order to identify how parent educators can be more responsive to the needs and characteristics of diverse families; we are only just beginning to catch a glimpse of the rich complexity involved in the study of family diversity. Certainly there are deficiencies in each group. However, the better we understand behavior relative to the sociocultural context in which it occurs, the better able we will be to design policies and programs that capitalize on the instructional styles and other characteristics that are distinctive of each group. Thus, the heretofore weak and uncertain connection between parent education, cultural pluralism, and public policy will be strengthened.

In closing, I would like to address briefly at a different level of policy analysis the issues I have thus far discussed. It behooves us to examine our expectations for parent education as a tool of social reform. Is it realistic to expect parent education to solve effectively the problems of social and economic inequality that face so many of the nation's ethnic minority families? As we have seen, parent education may be replacing compensatory education as the preferred national policy for equalizing opportunity among the children of poor and ethnic minority families. As Schlossman (1978) recently has argued, this change may also shift the burden of accountability for failure from the school and the government-sponsored education professional to the family. Indeed, parent education isolates the parents (most often mothers) as the principal agents for change. Ironically, this occurs in an era when the state of our economy requires that women (and men, for that matter) work more than ever before outside the home, an era when the time available to parents is so rapidly shrinking. We should, in any event, guard against placing on families an inordinate share of the blame for our social problems; the real sources of the problems may lie elsewhere.

FOOTNOTE

[1] Interest in parent education is indeed not new in America. For each period of history, however, this interest has reflected different concerns and has found expression in ways unique to the times (see Brim, 1959; Chilman, 1970; Harman & Brim, 1980; Schlossman, 1976).

References

Bee, L., Van Egeren, L. R., Streissguth, P., Nyman, B. A., & Leckie, S. Social class differences in maternal teaching strategies and speech patterns. *Developmental Psychology*, 1969, *1*, 726–734.

Bernstein, B. Social class and linguistic development: A theory of social learning. In A. H. Halsey, J. Floud, & C. A. Anderson (Eds.), *Education, economy, and society*. New York: Free Press, 1961.

Brim, O. G. *Education for child rearing*. New York: Russell Sage Foundation, 1959.

Chilman, C. S. Programs for disadvantaged parents: Some major trends and related research. In B. M. Caldwell and H. N. Ricciuti (Eds.), *Review of child development research* (Vol. 3). Chicago: University of Chicago Press, 1970.

Clarke-Stewart, A. *Child care in the family: A review of research and some propositions for policy*. New York: Academic Press, 1977.

Dennis, W. Causes of retardation among institutional children: Iran. *Journal of Genetic Psychology*, 1960, *96*, 47–59.

Ginsburg, H. *The myth of the deprived child: Poor children's intellect and education*. Englewood Cliffs, NJ: Prentice Hall, 1972.

Goodson, B. D., & Hess, R. D. *Parents as teachers of young children: An evaluative review of some contemporary concepts and programs*. Stanford, CA: Stanford University, May 1975. (ERIC Document Reproduction Service No. ED 136 967)

Goodson, B. D., & Hess, R. D. The effects of parent training programs on child performance and parent behavior. In B. Brown (Ed.), *Found: Long-term gains from early intervention*. Boulder, CO: Westview Press, 1978.

Harman, D., & Brim, O. G., Jr. *Learning to be parents: Principles, programs, and methods*. Beverly Hills, CA: Sage, 1980.

Hess, R. D., & Shipman, V. C. Maternal influences upon early learning: The cognitive environments of urban pre-school children. In R. D. Hess and R. M. Bear (Eds.), *Early education: Current theory, research, and action*. Chicago: Aldine, 1968.

Kamii, C. K., & Radin, N. L. Class differences in the socialization practices of Negro mothers. *Journal of Marriage and the Family*, 1967, *29*, 302–310.

Laosa, L. M. Child care and the culturally different child. *Child Care Quarterly*, 1974, *3*, 214–224. (a)

Laosa, L. M. Toward a research model of multicultural competency-based teacher education. In W. A. Hunter (Ed.), *Multicultural education through competency-based teacher education*. Washington, DC: American Association of Colleges for Teacher Education, 1974. (b)

Laosa, L. M. Bilingualism in three United States Hispanic groups: Contextual use of language by children and adults in their families. *Journal of Educational Psychology*, 1975, *67*, 617–627.

Laosa, L. M. *Teaching problem-solving to their young children: Strategies used by Mexican-American and Anglo-American mothers—preliminary analyses*. Paper presented at the XVI Interamerican Congress of Psychology, Miami Beach, FL, December, 1976.

Laosa, L. M. Inequality in the classroom: Observational research on teacher–student interactions. *Aztlán International Journal of Chicano Studies Research*, 1977, *8*, 51–67. (a)

Laosa, L. M. *Maternal teaching strategies in Mexican American families: Factors affecting intra-group variability in how mothers teach their children*. Paper presented at the annual meeting of the American Educational Research Association, New York, April 1977. (b)

Laosa, L. M. Nonbiased assessment of children's abilities: Historical antecedents and current issues. In T. Oakland (Ed.), *Psychological and educational assessment of minority children*. New York: Brunner/Mazel, 1977. (c)

Laosa, L. M. Socialization, education, and continuity: The importance of the sociocultural context. *Young Children*, 1977, *32*, 21–27. (d)

Laosa, L. M. Maternal teaching strategies in Chicano families of varied educational and socioeconomic levels. *Child Development*, 1978, *49*, 1129–1135.

Laosa, L. M. *Estrategias de enseñanza maternas en familias Chicanas y Angloamericanas: La influencia de la cultura y la escolaridad en la conducta materna*. Paper presented at the XVII Interamerican Congress of Psychology, Lima, Peru, July 1979. (a)

Laosa, L. M. Social competence in childhood: Toward a developmental, socioculturally relativistic paradigm. In M. W. Kent & J. E. Rolf (Eds.), *Primary prevention of psychopathology (Vol. 3): Social competence in children*. Hanover, NH: University Press of New England, 1979. (b)

Laosa, L. M. Maternal teaching strategies in Chicano and Anglo-American families: The influence of culture and education on maternal behavior. *Child Development*, 1980, *51*, 759–765. (a)

Laosa, L. M. Measures for the study of maternal teaching strategies. *Applied Psychological Measurement*, 1980, *4*, 355–366. (b)

Laosa, L. M. Maternal behavior: Sociocultural diversity in modes of family interaction. In R. W. Henderson (Ed.), *Parent–child interaction: Theory, research, and prospects*. New York: Academic Press, 1981. (a)

Laosa, L. M. *Statistical explorations of the structural organization of maternal teaching behaviors in Chicano and non-Hispanic White families.* Paper presented at the Conference on the Influences of Home Environments on School Achievement, Wisconsin Research and Development Center for Individualized Schooling, School of Education, University of Wisconsin, Madison, October 1981. (b)

Laosa, L. M. School, occupation, culture, and family: The impact of parental schooling on the parent–child relationship. *Journal of Educational Psychology*, 1982, *74*, 791–827. (a)

Laosa, L. M. The sociocultural context of evaluation. In B. Spodek (Ed.), *Handbook of research in early childhood education*. New York: Free Press, 1982. (b)

Laosa, L. M., Burstein, A. G., & Martin, H. W. Mental health consultation in a rural Chicano community: Crystal City, *Áztlán International Journal of Chicano Studies Research*, 1975, *6*, 433–453.

LeVine, R. A. Influence of women's schooling on maternal behavior in the third world. *Comparative Education Review*, 1980, *24*, (No. 2, Part 2), S78–S105.

Nobles, W. W. Toward an empirical and theoretical framework for defining black families. *Journal of Marriage and the Family*, 1978, *40*, 679–688.

Schlossman, S. Before Home Start: Notes toward a history of parent education in America, 1897–1929. *Harvard Educational Review*, 1976, *46*, 436–467.

Schlossman, S. The parent education game: The politics of child psychology in the 1970s. *Teachers College Record*, 1978, *79*, 788–808.

Spitz, R. A. Hospitalism: An inquiry into the genesis of psychiatric conditions in early childhood. *Psychoanalytic Study of the Child*, 1946, *1*, 53–74.

FIFTEEN

PARENT EDUCATION AND PUBLIC POLICY: SYNTHESIS AND RECOMMENDATIONS[1]

RON HASKINS AND DIANE ADAMS

The intent of this chapter is to address Mundel's (Chap. 3) admonition to determine whether social scientists have anything important to say to policymakers about parent education. We will pursue this intent by providing a brief overview of federal involvement in parent education programs and summarizing the current status of parent involvement in several federal programs aimed at educating preschool and school age children. Following a discussion of social science data and policy making, we turn to an analysis of parent education and public policy. The analysis employs several criteria applicable to a broad range of social programs, and uses these criteria to synthesize much of the material covered in the

*We thank Jim Gallagher for comments on an earlier version of this chapter, and Florine Purdie, Brenda Brady, Ann Rhyne, and Stacy Reynolds for help in preparing the manuscript. The views expressed in this chapter do not represent the consensus of people at the conference on Parent Education and Public Policy.

preceding chapters. We conclude with three recommendations concerning public policy.

FEDERAL INVOLVEMENT IN PARENT EDUCATION: AN HISTORICAL OVERVIEW

The Great Society

Parent involvement in the education of young children began with the Smith Lever and Smith Hughes Acts, passed in 1914 and 1917 respectively, which established parent education as a function of Agricultural Extension agencies. At this early date, parent education was characterized by a belief in the importance of motherhood. At least three national groups—the American Association of University Women, the Child Study Association of America, and the National Congress of Parents and Teachers (later the PTA)—attempted to educate mothers in child development so they could be more effective in childrearing. Although parent education appears to have shifted its focus from moral and religious development in the nineteenth century to emotional, physical, and mental health in the early twentieth century, until the last 2 decades it was primarily a middle-class movement (see Schlossman, Chap 1). Indeed, during much of the twentieth century, the parent education movement permeated middle-class American family life. Magazines, discussion groups, and other vehicles for parent education expanded as communication systems were refined.

However, when poverty was "rediscovered" during the administration of John Kennedy (1961–63), parent education was seen as a way to help eliminate the disadvantages of poverty and prejudice. Renewed concern with poverty stimulated academic debates on whether poverty was caused by personal characteristics and behaviors of the poor (Lewis, 1966) or by structural deficits in American society (Piven & Cloward, 1971; see also Valentine, 1968). Indeed, as with the Moynihan (1965) report on black families, these debates sometimes extended into the national media. Only a few writers, such as Riessman (1962), who emphasized the "overlooked positives" of disadvantaged groups, and Chilman (1966), who wrote extensively about the strengths of poor families, favored the latter interpretation. The overwhelming evidence seemed to be on the side of a more pathological view of the poor. They could not cope with life, their children, their economic status, the schools, nor society in general. Thus, the poor became the focus of large-scale social programs intended primarily to improve their children and themselves. Throughout the 1960s and 1970s, such parent programs gained momentum with support from the social and behavioral sciences. In addition, there was local pressure from disadvantaged groups themselves for greater opportunities, power, and influence.

Head Start

The earliest embodiment of the new role for poor and minority parents was the Economic Opportunity Act of 1964, which set in motion the most diverse, expensive, and studied attack on poverty in American history. Head Start was created as a result of that legislation. Started in the summer of 1965, Head Start was originally intended to serve about 100,000 children with a preschool program of compensatory education. As it turned out, over 500,000 children were actually enrolled that first summer, and Head Start has consistently served more than 350,000 children per year since 1966 (Zigler & Anderson, 1979). A panel of experts chaired by Dr. Robert Cooke, whose work outlined the Head Start program in some detail, viewed Head Start as a way to enrich the environments of a significant portion of poor children otherwise doomed to educational failure. Although Head Start programs varied widely across the country, in accord with the political and practical vicissitudes of different communities (Zigler, 1979), Head Start was built on the concept that families rather than schools were the primary source of values and behaviors of children. This approach led logically to the concept of parent and family involvement in programs for children, which has remained an integral part of Head Start programs ever since (O'Keefe, 1978).

The Cooke Panel, in attempting to create a program for disadvantaged children that would not only prepare them for school but ameliorate some of the institutional factors causing poverty, developed seven objectives for Head Start. Two of these objectives were to assist parents in advocating for their children and to teach parents methods of stimulating the child's intellectual growth at home. Moreover, when the first Policy Manual for Head Start (Office of Child Development, 1967) was written, it contained a strong mandate for parent involvement:

> Project Head Start is a program for the economically disadvantaged preschool child. It is based on the philosophy that (1) a child can benefit most from a comprehensive interdisciplinary attack on his problems at the local level, and (2) the child's entire family, as well as the community, must be involved in solving his problems. Every Head Start program must have effective parent participation. (p. 1)

During the summer of 1965, when those thousands of children were enrolled in Head Start programs for the first time, the actual parent participation level was probably quite low; the rush of getting the program off the ground precluded much attention to parents. But by the fall, when Head Start was to be a full-year program, the mandate for a "parent specialist" in every program indicated a serious commitment to involving parents. Several parent roles (volunteering in the classrooms, receiving home visits, participating in parent groups, policy making, employment) were outlined in the revised Policy Manual (Office of Child Development, 1969), and by 1970 the Manual removed the word "advisory" from the policy committee's function, thereby giving parents even more potential control of Head Start programs. As suggested by the title, the policy committee was intended to make policy, and even to wrest some authority from whoever created the proposal for the local Head Start program, whether a school board, a local community action agency, or a nonprofit agency.

As Head Start programs proliferated, and as guidelines and performance standards were refined, objectives relating to parents and families permeated the program. And because of its rather heady beginnings and its continued Congressional support, Head Start has been seen as the "parent" of parent involvement.

Elementary and Secondary Education Act

Soon after the creation of Head Start, Congress enacted the Elementary and Secondary Education Act (ESEA) of 1965, called by Robert McKay (1966) "the most significant achievement of any Congress in this century, indeed if not in the entire history of the nation" (p. 212). This exhuberant view of ESEA was based primarily on what many social critics and policymakers deemed an appropriate and long-overdue federal role; namely, to assure adequate educational opportunity for all children. President Johnson said the decision to attack the long-standing failure of the public schools to educate poor and minority children was "the greatest breakthrough in the advance of education since the Constitution was written" (McKay, 1966, p. 213).

One of the requirements of ESEA programs was a Parent Advisory Council (PAC). The PACs were originally conceived to be the information vehicle for local school administrators to help design Title I and other programs, and to approve the proposals sent to Washington. This form of parent involvement took a more simplistic approach than parent involvement in Head Start. Head Start was intended to be a comprehensive family development program; ESEA programs were intended to infuse public education with more dollars and more materials to better serve low-income children. But the schools did not view parents or the family as critical to the successful education of children. As a result, Title I gave parents the right to approve the proposal for federal funds and have some voice in planning for their own children, but these parent involvement requirements were not as strong as those in the Head Start program. Thus, we can find in the early history of these compensatory programs a clear differentiation of the role parents should play.

Follow Through

Established by Congress in 1967, Follow Through was designed to assist Head Start children after they entered the public schools (see Olmsted and Rubin, Chap. 5). Follow Through provided special instructional programs, as well as health, nutrition, and other related services to families, under the direction of a sponsor. Each sponsor's program or model emphasized different educational philosophies and therefore different activities. However, all the models were committed to a substantial degree of parent involvement—more on the order of Head Start, rather than Title I, parent involvement.

In fact, there is a vast difference between Follow Through policy concerning parents and traditional public school policy. The schools, for example, have no mandate for parents to be given preference in hiring, to be in the majority on advisory councils, or to have fiscal oversight—all of which are required by Follow Through. Further, low-income parents must be involved, and their involvement must be documented, for Follow Through projects to be refunded. By contrast, even middle- and upper-income parents have none of these rights and responsibilities in regular public school programs. These strong Follow Through parent involvement requirements seem to be based on the assumption that Head Start had laid the groundwork for parents to have success in decision making and working on policy committees. Whether this link is, in fact, made by low-income parents is unknown.

Education for All Handicapped Children

The Education for All Handicapped Children Act (P.L. 94-142), passed in 1975, has been widely hailed as landmark legislation. Before 1975, the public schools could—and often did—refuse services to handicapped children. Even when they were served by the schools, handicapped children were often not educated together with nonhandicapped children. P.L. 94-142, however, required the schools to educate all handicapped children, and to do so by placing them in "the least restrictive environment." Thus, "mainstreaming"—integration of the handicapped with their nonhandicapped peers—became a legally required approach for assuring that handicapped children are guaranteed a free, appropriate public education.

P.L. 94-142 became the law of the land because there was consensus

among parents, special education teachers, advocates for the handicapped, and policymakers that it was not appropriate to remove handicapped children from the mainstream of school life. Parent advocacy
was in no small measure responsible for the passage of the federal law.
Thus, it is not surprising that strong parent participation requirements
and procedural safeguards became embedded in the law.

This legislation does not require comprehensive services to families, nor does it include a mandate for giving preference in hiring to
parents. It does, however, guarantee parental oversight in creating each
child's educational plan and consultation with teachers concerning the
child's progress. Parent support groups and handicapped children's
Parent Advisory Councils are also guaranteed. In a somewhat perverse
way, the law mandates integration of the children in public school settings while at the same time mandating separate parent councils, not
integrated with ESEA Title I or other parent advisory groups.

Thus, we find in the law outlining educational services for all
handicapped children substantial requirements for parent involvement
because the parents' advice must be sought and considered in planning
their children's educational program. Moreover, parents have the right
to challenge the planning and conduct of the programs offered their
child.

Other Federal Programs

Other federal education programs do not mandate the high level
of parent involvement required by Head Start, Follow Through, and
P.L. 94-142. The legislation assisting bilingual children (under Title VII
of ESEA, passed in 1974) and minorities (under Title VI of ESEA, passed
in 1972) requires what might be termed "moderate" parent involvement.
Parent participation on advisory committees is required and parents are
to be "consulted" about the agency application. The Indian Education
Act (P.L. 93-638) and the Migrant Education Act (ESEA, Title I-B) are
examples of minimal parent involvement: parents are to be "represented" in decisions concerning the educational opportunities planned
for their children, though such representation may be provided by someone other than the parents themselves.

Summary: The Status Quo in Federal Programs

Figure 1 summarizes the status of parent involvement requirements in the federal programs outlined above. The primary conclusion
to be drawn from Figure 1 is that current federal programs demonstrate
a great diversity in parent involvement requirements. Some programs,

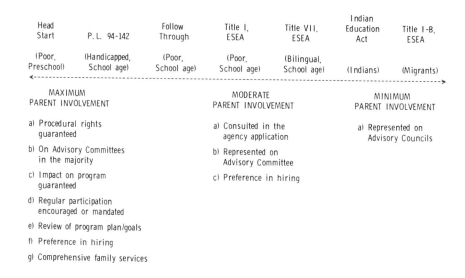

Head Start	P. L. 94-142	Follow Through	Title I, ESEA	Title VII, ESEA	Indian Education Act	Title I-B, ESEA
(Poor, Preschool)	(Handicapped, School age)	(Poor, School age)	(Poor, School age)	(Bilingual, School age)	(Indians)	(Migrants)

MAXIMUM PARENT INVOLVEMENT	MODERATE PARENT INVOLVEMENT	MINIMUM PARENT INVOLVEMENT
a) Procedural rights guaranteed	a) Consulted in the agency application	a) Represented on Advisory Councils
b) On Advisory Committees in the majority	b) Represented on Advisory Committee	
c) Impact on program guaranteed	c) Preference in hiring	
d) Regular participation encouraged or mandated		
e) Review of program plan/goals		
f) Preference in hiring		
g) Comprehensive family services		

Figure 1. A continuum of parent involvement requirements in federal programs.

like Head Start, Follow Through, and P.L. 94-142, have very strong parent involvement requirements. To use Schaefer's (Chap. 11) language, these programs are based on the belief that parents and professionals can create a full partnership in planning, administering, and conducting educational programs for children. By contrast, programs like the Migrant Children's title of ESEA and the Indian Education Act provide only weak mandates for parent involvement. The major role given to parents in these programs is merely advisory.

It may be worthwhile to note that when programs are arranged on a continuum like that shown in Figure 1, those involving middle-class or black parents seem to require substantial parent involvement, while programs addressed to less powerful minorities, such as Chicanos, migrants, and Indians, require little parent involvement. It may be that parents in these latter groups are, in fact, less competent, which would constitute a reasonable basis for minimizing their involvement, but we are not aware of evidence supporting this generalization, and none was presented to the Congress during Congressional testimony for these programs. In fact, the remarkable differences between these programs in mandated parent involvement does not seem to be based on any rational approach to decision making. Rather, they seem to be based on the vicissitudes of the policymaking process. We will return to this point below.

POLICY AND DATA

Before turning to the analysis of parent education programs, we would like first to comment on the role that social science data should play in policy making. The major benefit that social science brings to policy making is the generation of data to assist in reaching policy decisions. To be sure, there are other and even more important factors that influence decision-making (Lindblom & Cohen, 1979), but data can play a valuable role. On the other hand, the use of social science data can cause mischief in the decision-making process because there is no set of principles that specifies the relation between data quantity or quality and policy choice. One might argue that a tacit principle held by most social scientists is that relatively strong data should constitute relatively strong support for policy.

This principle, however, leaves a great deal unstated. Rarely do data on a particular phenomenon help a policymaker decide that a given type of policy (e.g., policy to establish parent programs) is preferable to policy in another domain (e.g., policy to provide families with money). Nor do data tell a policymaker how much money should be invested in a given program. Data also have the serious limitation of ignoring the political and economic forces that inevitably shape policy choice.

The beginning of wisdom in using data to inform policy choice, then, is to recognize the limited role they can play under any circumstances. In short, we must flatly acknowledge that data are only one among several factors that can, should, and do influence policy choice. Nonetheless, having recognized their circumscribed role, we would propose four rules for determining the suitability of data for policy making.

Replication

First and foremost, a finding must be replicated. Never, absolutely never, should social scientists or those who popularize social science findings begin to agitate for public action on the basis of a single study. Rather, confidence should reflect the number of times various studies have produced the same finding, and confidence should be relatively stronger as replication is achieved with samples from different parts of the country, with samples of differing demographic backgrounds, and with different outcome measures obtained in different laboratory and naturalistic settings. Further, particular attention should be paid to replication failures. Social scientists should read no-difference findings as a caution light, and proceed to discover explanations for their failures to replicate. Differences in study design, sample characteristics, measurement devices, or statistical procedures should occasion limitations in the generality of a finding.

Significance

A second rule for determining the policy relevance of social science results involves assessing the significance of particular findings. Unfortunately, social scientists typically have a precise but narrow understanding of "significance." By convention, a social science finding is significant if it meets the criterion of not being produced by chance alone; more specifically, we usually call a finding significant if our statistical methods tell us that a difference of that particular size or a correlation of that particular magnitude could have occurred by chance no more than 5 times in 100.

But such a statistically significant difference may be meaningless in a policy context. If, for example, we had ten studies showing that a statistically significant 4-point difference in child IQ could be produced by a given parent program, it would not follow that this finding is "significant" in the way most people—including policymakers—use the term. What is needed here is some better and more direct criterion of significance.

Two closely related approaches to this problem seem feasible. First, social scientists should attempt to select variables that are direct measures of policy outcomes. Criticisms of IQ and achievement test scores in the social science literature are legion, but few have attempted to convert criticism to action. It is true that IQ and achievement test scores have intrinsic meaning to social scientists, but when pressed for translating IQ or achievement test results to some policy relevant variables, social scientists necessarily attempt to convert these measures to variables such as earnings (e.g., Weber, Foster, & Weikart, 1978). These approaches, however, are frought with peril, primarily because there are few studies that have directly measured the relation between IQ increments and job market earnings (see Featherman, 1980; Jencks, 1972, 1979).

In general, good policy variables are ones that can be easily translated to dollars saved or earned. Thus, policymakers will have direct and understandable information for making policy choices if they know that a particular program will result in a particular level of savings or will add to the subsequent productivity of people who participate in the program.

One recent study demonstrates the value of collecting data that can be converted to policy-relevant variables. A consortium of investigators organized by Irving Lazar and Richard Darlington attempted to discover the long-term effects of preschool programs (Lazar et al., 1977; Lazar & Darlington, 1978; Darlington et al., 1980). Former participants and their controls from 14 preschool programs were located when they were between 9 and 19 years old. In addition to the typical measures such as family demographics, IQ, and school achievement, investigators in the consortium had the foresight to obtain two valuable pieces of information from school records. In particular, they collected information on grade retention and placement in special education classes. Like IQ and school achievement, these variables have intrinsic meaning to social scientists and educators, and perhaps to most policymakers. Their real advantage, however, is that they can be directly translated into something everyone can understand; namely, dollars invested or saved by local school systems.

As it turned out, most of the 14 projects discovered that children who had been in preschool programs had lower rates of grade retention and special education placement than control children who had not attended preschool programs. As Weber, Foster, and Weikart (1978) have demonstrated by obtaining data from a Michigan school system on the cost of grade retention and special education placement, it is possible to directly convert reduced rates of grade retention and special class placement to dollars saved. Needless to say, if the latter sum is greater than the former, policymakers have an excellent set of information that could help them decide to fund preschool programs.

This brings us to the second procedure social scientists can employ to improve the usefulness of their measures for decision makers. We are referring, of course, to benefit–cost analysis. The essence of the political process is allocation of scarce resources. Other things being equal, policymakers want to spend money in ways that will either generate new money or will prevent greater expenditures later. Thus, social scientists are well advised to collect data that can be translated to costs and benefits as measured by dollars. In this regard, measures such as grade retention, special education placement, employment rates, college attendance, crime or delinquency reduction, teenage pregnancy reduction, and so on are preferable to measures such as IQ and school achievement.

Longitudinal Data

Another way to increase the policy relevance of social science findings is to emphasize longitudinal data. In addition to a host of technical reasons that demonstrate the superiority of longitudinal data (see Gallagher, Ramey, Haskins, & Finkelstein, 1976), there is reason to doubt the policy relevance of most cross-sectional data. The types of studies normally thought to be important for policymaking are those that show the effect of some treatment or intervention (e.g., training parents to work with infants produces elevated levels of infant IQ). But effects at the time of or shortly following intervention are not nearly as important for policy decisions as long-term effects. Social scientists should not be in the position of basing their claims on contemporaneous effects, or at least should always make it clear in their writing, speeches, and testimony that short-term effects are less important for policymaking than long-term effects. An implication of this point, of course, is that social scientists should do everything possible to obtain funds to follow their subjects for years following intervention. The Lazar (1977) consortium has shown that such efforts are feasible and may produce results that have very clear implications for public policy.

Large-scale Implementation

A fourth consideration for applying social science findings to policy decisions is that the results of small-scale studies—even those replicated by other small-scale studies—may not generalize to large populations (see Dokecki, 1982). Many small-scale studies are high quality efforts with substantial budgets. Staff members are likely to be well trained and highly motivated, investigators are often implementing a program in which they have a personal stake, and facilities are likely to be adequate or better. Further, investigators are likely to carefully train staff members in the goals and methods of their particular program, and may conduct periodic checks—some of which may even be based on outcome data—to ensure that the program is being appropriately implemented and is producing acceptable results. By contrast, when a program is being implemented on a large scale, local staff may have no special commitment to the particular form of intervention, they may not have complete understanding of the intervention goals, methods, and underlying theory, and they may be less highly trained than staff in the original project. In addition, several other factors—such as poor facilities, different participant characteristics, and local mores incompatible with the program—may conspire to produce inferior results when programs are implemented on a large scale.

All of which suggests that social scientists should make only modest claims for their interventions until they have been implemented in several locations over a period of time. A serious problem with this generalization is that it runs counter to what many observers would say is political wisdom. Head Start is a case in point. As Sargent Shriver (1979) has pointed out, political wisdom dictated an immediate build up of Head Start to a large-scale program in the summer of 1965. The President and Congress had been sold on Head Start; thus, Shriver concluded that the best thing to do was create as large a program as possible as quickly as possible. The result was that Head Start enrolled well over half a million children during its first summer—more than five times the number originally planned.

As this example shows, political reality is that there is no ideal moment for a program, "only a time when action is possible" (Sugarman, 1979, p. 115). By contrast, the view of social science is that program build-up should be gradual, should include several types of quality control, and should permit delays in implementation when problems turn up.

In a word, social science and political considerations may dictate opposite courses of action for program implementation. Although there may be no solution to this dilemma, let it be clear that rapid program expansion was not done with the blessing of social scientists. There seems to be something almost self-defeating in this attitude; after all, if data from small-scale studies are persuasive, if we believe in the objectives of the program, and above all, if the program might help children and families, how can we fail to support program implementation?

The answer is that it all depends on one's view of social science. Our view is that science, if it is to be worthy of its name, tradition, and place in society, must judge by overt and strict criteria. It is not that we must avoid judgments—probabilities are at the heart of the social sciences—but that we must make these judgments on the basis of criteria which specify the strength of policy conclusions from the status of social science data. The argument presented above is that our judgment should be predicated on four types of data; namely, replications, benefit–cost information, longitudinal data, and data from large-scale implementation under field conditions.

To keep matters interesting, of course, it is necessary to admit that all four criteria are almost never met. Thus, social scientists who would inform policymakers, or policy analysts who would base their policy choice—in part, at least—on social science data, are forced to couch their predictions in probabilistic terms. Humility, based on the status of knowledge, will usually force us to say that approach A is a good bet, a moderate bet, or a bad bet.

Finally, it can hardly be overemphasized that these judgments allow no room for advocacy. Indeed, one is nearly tempted to say that to the extent a given social scientist or policy analyst is an advocate for children, their judgments will be clouded and hence unreliable. In this case, we would do well to observe the dictum of diplomacy; to wit, *Surtout pas de zèle* (above all, no zeal).

PARENT PROGRAMS AND POLICY ANALYSIS

The Policy Problem

Even when data meet or approach the criteria described above, they do not have immediate application to public policy. Rather, data must be interpreted within a framework dictated by an understanding of the policy problem at hand and by the analysts' values. In the sections that follow, therefore, we define the policy problem of parent education in greater detail and define the values we are trying to promote by using parent programs.

Parent programs are not a policy problem in the sense that policy problems are usually defined (Haskins, 1980; Haskins & Gallagher, 1981; MacRae & Wilde, 1979; Wildavsky, 1979). Rather, parent programs are a strategy or technique for addressing particular problems of child and family development. This is an important distinction from the analyst's perspective because policy analysis usually begins with the identification and definition of a societal problem that effects the public interest. Readers of this volume will undoubtedly be impressed by the range of problems included under the rubric "parent education"—programs for parents of handicapped children, for parents of poor children, for parents of low achievers in the schools, for parents of children with special problems of a medical or psychological nature, and for middle- and upper-class parents seeking to learn more about childrearing. Indeed, Dokecki and Moroney (Chap. 2) seem to suggest that all parents can use help rearing their children and therefore could profit from government-sponsored parent programs.

In fact, the current interest in parent education and other parent programs is due, at least in part, to the belief by many social scientists, practitioners, and advocates that such programs are effective in solving a variety of societal problems. As Schlossman (Chap. 1) shows, this belief is not a recent development, but has a long history within the academic disciplines concerned with child development, the foundations and government agencies that fund parent programs, and the popular media.

Nonetheless, in this review chapter we are going to define the societal problem as one of inadequate child development. Our primary focus will be on programs to promote the development of low-income children of preschool age (0–5), though our conclusions may apply as well to programs for low-income children of school-age (5–11) and handicapped children of any age (0–18).

Analysis Criteria

If the policy problem is one of inadequate child development, what values do we want to maximize in selecting public policy to address the problem? In other words, by what yardstick will we identify good policy? Following our previous work in this area (Haskins, 1980), we stipulate four "universal criteria" by which social programs—including parent programs—are frequently analyzed; namely, preference satisfaction, efficiency, equity, and stigma. Preference satisfaction defines good policy as policy that maximizes the preferences of program participants. The underlying justification for this approach to preference satisfaction is that individuals know their own preferences best and are therefore most satisfied when they have a range of program alternatives from which to select. At minimum, parents should be free to decide whether they want to participate in a given program.

The efficiency criterion is perhaps best defined by the economic dictum that policymakers should spend the last dollar of public money where it will do the most good. A related definition of efficiency, as discussed previously, is that public investments should be cost efficient in the sense that they either avoid a greater expenditure in the future or produce a surplus in the short run. What is wanted for purposes of decision making, then, is evidence that parent programs will justify their costs by (1) increasing the productivity of parents, their children, or both or (2) reducing the necessity for larger investments in treatment programs at some later date.

The equity criterion of greatest interest for our purposes, sometimes called "vertical equity," is that citizens with fewer resources receive the greatest benefits from government expenditures. As applied to parent programs, this criterion stipulates that the most desirable programs are those addressed to low-income and minority families and to families with handicapped children.

The final universal criterion—stigma—defines good public programs as those that cause the least unjustified discredit to their participants. Sigma has two aspects which, presumably, are causally related. In the first, because of negative attributions by fellow citizens, program participants are viewed as inferior—as, for example, in need of education or other services because of personal failings. In the second, exposure to intense or prolonged stigma produces actual feelings of inferiority, perhaps leading to undesirable changes in behavior (such as increased apathy) among program participants. Thus, stigma is bad for two reasons which correspond to its two primary aspects. Like the targets of gossip or slander, stigmatized citizens are treated unfairly. Even more important, stigma is bad because it can be dysfunctional by reducing the probability that program participants will exhibit the behaviors the program is designed to help them achieve.

Having defined the policy problem and identified the criteria by which we will judge policies aimed at solving the problem, we are now in position to analyze parent programs.

ANALYSIS OF PARENT PROGRAMS

Preference satisfaction

Theoretically, parent programs should have little trouble in meeting the criterion of preference satisfaction. In one way or another, nearly every type of parent program aims to help mothers, and sometimes fathers, do a better job of rearing their children. Since almost no one questions that parents of all income and ethnic backgrounds love their children and want the best for them, parent programs should have a visceral appeal to mothers and fathers. And indeed, most available evidence indicates that parents are pleased with the types of programs described in this volume. The survey evidence from parents in the Handicapped Children's Early Education Program presented by Karnes and her associates (Chap. 7) and by Hocutt and Wiegerink (Chap. 8), as well as evidence from the Follow Through program summarized by Olmsted and Rubin (Chap. 5), demonstrates that parents show remarkably high levels of satisfaction with parent programs. These results indicate that parent preferences are being met by at least some federally sponsored programs.

By contrast, the thrust of both the Schaefer (Chap. 11) and Laosa (Chap. 14) chapters is that many current parent programs are meeting neither the needs nor desires of parents. Schaefer cites national surveys (e.g., Elam, 1973) and other evidence to argue that parents accept responsibility for child development and would even be willing to pay higher taxes to support public school programs aimed at helping parents assist their children in school. Yet direct parent participation in the educational activities of the public schools is strikingly infrequent, and the Hocutt and Wiegerink (Chap. 8) data suggest that parents of handicapped children are least satisfied with programs sponsored by the public schools. Schaefer also holds that professionals, including social workers, pediatricians, and teachers, jealously protect their turf against parents, and as a result deny parents the level of participation in their children's development that survey research indicates they want. In this respect, professionals, and institutions such as schools, hospitals, and clinics, deny parents an adequate level of involvement, and thus should be considered deficient by the criterion of preference satisfaction.

Like Schaefer, Laosa (Chap. 14) is concerned that professionals and program planners have adopted a deficit, pathological model of low-income and minority families. Further, Laosa is especially concerned that program designers have accepted "a single and broadly applicable set of standards for 'good' parenting" (p. 338) which is inconsistent with the standards held by several minority groups in American society. Even more to the point, Laosa questions whether public policy is ethical when it supports any particular set of standards over against another set of standards. Laosa's concern, then, is precisely that many parent programs violate the preferences of minority group parents by encouraging, or even forcing, them to behave in ways that are inconsistent with their cultural values.

Considerations such as those reviewed above lead us to three conclusions about parent programs and the preference satisfaction criteria. First, there is no inherent reason why parent programs cannot receive high scores for maximizing preference satisfaction. It is axiomatic that parents are concerned with their children's development, and national surveys indicate both that parents recognize and accept their responsibility for child development and that they are anxious to participate in programs designed to help them fulfill this responsibility. Moreover, several chapters in this volume (Chaps. 5, 7, and 8) indicate that various types of parent programs, but especially those involving parents of handicapped children, are highly favored by parents. We conclude that, under some circumstances, parent programs should be rated highly on the criterion of preference satisfaction.

Second, some parent programs may be quite deficient in meeting preference satisfaction. Schaefer's (Chap. 11) concern that professionals view families with problems as pathological and Laosa's (Chap. 14) concern with the rights of ethnic minorities seem to be the two primary factors that impede preference satisfaction. The common problem underlying both cases is that professionals believe that what parents are currently doing is wrong, or at least not optimum, and that professionals know how parents should change.

No doubt, professionals do often impose their views on parents, and no doubt these views are sometimes based on ignorance, prejudice, or both. On the other hand, professionals are sometimes right and occasionally do know more about what is good for children than parents. Further, some professionals can help parents become more skilled in executing their responsibilities. There is a tension between parents and professionals, the outcome of which may be to reduce preference satisfaction by parents. But this problem is not an inherent characteristic of parent programs. Rather, it must be counted a failing of particular programs and particular professionals.

Third, at least in our view, it follows from the two previous conclusions that parent programs do have a problem with preference satisfaction. Since the major cause of these problems (where they occur) is the beliefs and attitudes of professionals, we are not optimistic that tinkering with legislation or regulatory provisions can solve the problem. Nor are we optimistic that better training of professionals will solve the problem.

On the whole, then, we rate parent programs (as currently practiced) as only moderately successful on the preference satisfaction criterion.

Efficiency

The strongest efficiency criterion requires that money spent on parent programs could not be better spent on any other program. A more moderate efficiency criterion is that investments in parent programs pay for themselves. Nothing definitive can be said about either of these criteria as they apply to parent programs. Confining ourselves to only the latter criterion, we face a situation in which there are few social science studies directly relevant to the point; i.e., few studies testing whether parent programs produce effects in parents and children that resulted in more "good" (as measured in dollars) than was invested in the program. Information of this type is what Mundel (Chap. 3) asks for; if it were available, and if it showed parent programs to be efficient, we would have something quite important to say to policymakers.

As argued above, the benefit–cost study that comes closest to being applicable to parent programs is a 1978 publication by Weber, Foster, and Weikart. Using grade retention and special education placement as outcome variables, the authors were able to translate into dollars the experimental–control differences in grade retention and special education placements produced by a preschool program. The authors also performed other analyses—such as estimating the value of released parental time because their child was in day care—which further strengthened the conclusion that the preschool program produced long-term savings.

Unfortunately, this valuable study is only indirectly related to the issue of parent programs. This is the case because children in Weikart's preschool program enjoyed both center-based intervention and parent training. Thus, it is not possible to separate the effects of these two program characteristics. The strongest conclusion that could be drawn, based in turn on the conclusion that Weikart's program produced long-term results superior to those of preschool programs that did not include a parent component (see Bronfenbrenner, 1975), is that parent training *may* be an essential component of successful preschool intervention.

Despite the absence of benefit–cost studies of parent programs, we might speculate on what such studies would show if they were available. What is needed to support such speculation are data from parent programs demonstrating positive outcomes—elevated IQ levels or school achievement, for example. Even more pertinent would be studies showing that the effects of parent programs were superior to those of programs delivered by professionals or paraprofessionals.

With regard to the former possibility, Clarke-Stewart (Chap. 10) concludes that the most solidly supported finding about parent programs is that they produce positive outcomes. The thorough reviews by Goodson and Hess (1976) and Bronfenbrenner (1975) reached the same conclusion. The primary variable on which this conclusion is based, of course, is IQ. Thus, if we had a good way to translate IQ points into dollars (by, for example, estimating the effect of IQ elevation on lifetime earnings, as Weber, Foster, and Wiekart, 1978, have attempted to do) it might be possible to demonstrate the efficiency of parent programs. As matters now stand, however, we cannot draw the unequivocal conclusion that parent programs are cost efficient.

Moreover, as suggested above, what is really wanted are data showing that parent programs are more effective than other intervention programs. If they are not, then why should they be recommended to policymakers for additional funding? Perhaps the most comprehensive evaluation of this type (Lazar & Darlington, 1978), however, failed to find strong evidence that "Parental Involvement" (p. 150) was significantly associated with program effects as measured by special education placement. Interestingly, this conclusion seems to be more conservative than that reached in an earlier analysis of the same data (Vopava & Royce, 1978). Further, as Clarke-Stewart (Chap. 10) argues, other studies or reviews of parent-focused vs. center-based programs are equivocal; reviews which have concluded that parent programs were superior to center-based programs were based on differences of only about 4 IQ points (Goodson & Hess, 1976) or were based primarily on a few studies (Bronfenbrenner, 1975). Finally, one of the programs most frequently cited as demonstrating the superiority of parent training has published data showing that attempts to replicate the earlier findings ended in failure (Madden, Levenstein, & Levenstein, 1976).

Three additional considerations about efficiency and parent programs will round out our case. First, it is clear that the four criteria specifying the relation between social science research and policy conclusions (see above) are only partially met by empirical research on parent programs. As Clarke-Stewart (Chap. 10) shows, the criteria of replication is satisfied; in fact, it would appear that there have been more replications of the result that parent intervention programs can lead to increased, and relatively long-lasting, IQ levels in children than for most other phenomenon of policy interest studied by social scientists.

Regarding the significance criterion, we face the usual case of statistically significant findings in search of a social interpretation. Thus, children in parent programs enjoy gains of at most 10–15 IQ points compared with untreated control children, though only 5 or so points as compared with children in a center-based program (Bronfenbrenner, 1975; Clarke-Stewart, Chap. 10). As argued above, however, we can make no solid claims about parent programs in benefit–cost terms.

Turning to the criterion of longitudinal data, we must again label the evidence as equivocal. Several of the primary studies, such as those of Gordon (1973) and Levenstein (1975), collected IQ data over a several year period, including data after termination of the intervention program. The children seemed to maintain their gains after 2 or 3 years, but longer-term followup (Lazar & Darlington, 1978, Table 5, p. 47) revealed that at about age 10 only the Levenstein children maintained a statistically significant IQ advantage over controls. As mentioned above, however, more recent studies by Levenstein have placed this finding in doubt (Madden et al., 1976). Nonetheless, one must be impressed by such longitudinal results. Even a conservative interpretation would indicate that parent intervention programs can, under some circumstances, produce long-term IQ gains in children.

On the whole, then, data on parent programs seem relatively strong if measured by the first three criteria of social science data proposed above. Which brings us to the final criterion of large-scale implementation. Although there have been only moderate amounts of outcome data on the effects of parent programs from large-scale programs such as Follow Through, the Parent Child Development Center (PCDC) experiment discussed in detail by Dokecki, Hargrove, and Sandler (Chap. 4) is a remarkable attempt to produce this type of data (see also Andrews et al., 1982). Leaving aside questions of political feasibility, such as those that governed the implementation of Head Start in 1965, we would argue that the PCDC experiment represents precisely what social scientists should attempt to do when they can control the course of implementation. In particular, the PCDC approach was carefully planned in advance; several initial sites were identified to design, describe, and disseminate the curriculum; common outcome measures were collected longitudinally; several waves of increasingly broad implementation were envisioned; several geographical regions were involved; clients varied in demographic profile; and true experimental designs were employed.

Our interpretation of the PCDC outcome data varies in degree, albeit not in kind, from the conclusions drawn by Dokecki and his associates (Chap. 4). First, with regard to maternal behavior, the fact that all three original PCDC programs showed some differences favoring experimental mothers in their home environment, teaching ability, and behavior in various test situations is quite remarkable. In fact, when the children were 24 and 36 months old respectively, 10 of 15 and 7 of 11 tests of some aspects of maternal behavior toward children were significant and favored experimental mothers in the Birmingham sample, 2 of 12 and 7 of 12 favored experimental mothers in the Houston sample, and 4 of 10 and 5 of 10 favored experimental mothers in the New Orleans sample (see Andrews et al., 1982). These data provide convincing evidence that the behavior of mothers can be successfully changed by intervention programs. Further, these effects were accompanied by similar behavioral differences in the experimental and control children at all three sites, and experimental children in two of the three programs had significantly higher IQs than control children at 36 months. Averaged over the three programs, the mean IQ difference between experimentals and controls was about 6 points. Moreover, both projects that produced significant IQ effects at 36 months were also found to have similar and even increasing effects about 1 year after the projects ended.

As remarkable as the PCDC data appear to be, they do have two shortcomings that cause us to be moderate in drawing conclusions. First, the fact that one of these sites failed to produce an IQ difference in children at age 3 is reason for caution. Second, data from the three replication sites in Detroit, San Antonio, and Indianapolis are not yet available. Thus, we cannot be confident that the original PCDC programs can generalize their impressive effects to other centers.

In sum, the PCDC experiment provides strong evidence that parent programs can change the behavior of low-income mothers, and moderately strong evidence that such programs are associated with increased IQ scores of children that seem to persist for 1 year after the end of the program. The PCDC experiment has not, however, provided evidence on the replication process.

Summarizing information on the efficiency criterion, then, no direct evidence can be cited to support the superiority of parent education programs as compared with other programs. On the other hand, based on the Weber, Foster, and Weikert (1978) study, we should conclude that parent involvement may be a necessary component of efficient preschool programs. Further, based on studies of outcome variables that may be related to cost effectiveness—and especially IQ results from the PCDC study—there is direct evidence that parent programs are effective, and at least some evidence that they may produce longer-lasting gains than intervention programs without parent participation. All in all, we rate parent programs as moderately strong on the efficiency criterion.

Equity

The equity criterion of greatest interest to us is vertical equity. This criterion stipulates that good programs should redistribute resources. As with the case of preference satisfaction, there is no inherent reason why parent programs cannot satisfy the equity criterion. Indeed, there is at least some reason to believe that parent programs can be rated very high on the equity criterion. Like many social programs, parent programs can be focused on exactly the group of parents most in need of assistance. In fact, virtually all of the parent programs discussed in this volume involved low-income parents or parents of handicapped children. As long as legislation specifies that eligible parents must have incomes below some amount—such as the Department of Agriculture's poverty level income—parent programs can receive high ratings on the equity criterion.

On the other hand, two additional considerations are pertinent to evaluating parent programs on the equity criterion. First, Bronfenbrenner (1975, p. 593), based primarily on research by Klaus and Gray (1968) and Radin and Weikart (1967), concluded that parent programs for preschool children were not effective for families at the lower end of the disadvantaged range. These families, he argued, were "so overburdened with the task of survival" that they did not have the "energy or psychological resources" necessary to participate effectively in parent programs. If Bronfenbrenner is correct, it does not follow that parent programs should be rated any lower on the equity criterion, only that there may be a tradeoff between equity and efficiency such that serving the lowest, low-income families and thereby maximizing on the equity criterion is likely to reduce the program's efficiency because of attenuated effects on parent and child development.

Second, as with any social program, if parent programs maximize the equity criterion, they will thereby produce two further tradeoffs. The first is between equity and segregation by income and ethnic group. Although integration is not an explicit criterion in this analysis, many observers (e.g., St. John, 1975) consider it to be a value of major importance. The second tradeoff is between equity and stigma—isolation of low-income parents may increase stigma by singling them out as the only ones in need of services, or at least the ones most in need of services. This consideration prompts us to turn to a broader discussion of stigma.

Stigma

It is almost axiomatic that nonuniversal programs produce stigma. If nearly all citizens are eligible for and participate in a given program, the program will produce little stigma; by contrast, programs focused on specific and identifiable subgroups create the conditions for stigmatizing participants. The difference between stigma produced by Supplemental Security Income and Aid to Families with Dependent Children is instructive in this regard.

Again, of course, we are faced with a tradeoff—in this case between equity and stigma. On the one hand, we might argue, as we have in considering the preference satisfaction and equity criteria, that parent programs have no special problems not shared with other social programs on the stigma criterion. After all, any program designed to help people that focuses on subgroups within the population runs the risk of stigmatizing its participants.

On the other hand, there may be some reason to believe that parent programs have special problems with the stigma criterion. In particular, four characteristics of these programs may produce stigma. First, as argued above, there would be little need for parent programs if parents were doing an excellent job of rearing their children. Thus, many parent programs—particularly those teaching parents how to stimulate their child's intellectual growth—are based on the assumption that the parents' natural behaviors are deficient in some way.

This leads rather directly to the second problem associated with stigma; namely, that professionals sometimes believe they know more about what is good for children's development than parents. In this regard, the cautions raised by Schaefer (Chap. 11) and Laosa (Chap. 14) are again applicable. To a major degree, the problem here is one of attitude, particularly as attitudes are conveyed in the behaviors of professionals. Sensitive and experienced professionals or paraprofessionals can often get parents to change behavior without making parents feel ignorant or incompetent. Other professionals, however, communicate a kind of superiority to parents and thereby stigmatize them. Schaefer's solution is to emphasize the positive, to call out and build upon the existing strengths of parents, and to train professionals to view themselves as partners with parents in promoting child development. Whether this approach will work is questionable, and Schaefer himself seems to have doubts.

A third aspect of stigma raised by parent programs is outlined by Laosa (Chap. 14). The problem of cultural differences between low-income and minority-group parents on the one hand, and middle-class professionals on the other, is essentially a more intense version of the concerns raised by Schaefer (Chap. 11). In this case, it is not simply that professionals stigmatize parents by viewing—and treating them—as deficient. Rather, the problem is intensified because cultural differences, stemming perhaps from concrete difficulties inherent in the parents' life circumstances (Ogbu, 1981), produce substantial differences between parents and professionals in their beliefs about desirable childrearing practices. These may include such practices as punishment, expectations for school achievement, verbal stimulation, and so forth. Laosa's view is that some, perhaps many, professionals are incapable of even understanding why minority parents behave the way they do because their cultural background, and the research based precisely on assumptions implicit in middle-class values, render the professionals blind—or at least myopic. Stigma is an inevitable consequence of such differences in cultural backgrounds (see also Ogbu, 1978, 1981).

Finally, Schlossman (1978) has argued that parent programs raise the possibility of a particularly virulent form of stigma. Schlossman's argument is that a major reason the federal government and child development experts have come to favor parent programs is that, in the event such programs fail, parents can be blamed for the failure. This form of blaming the victim (Ryan, 1971) is perhaps the starkest form of stigma, holding in effect that problems of the poor and the minorities are hopeless because of the overwhelming deficiencies of these people. This perspective, needless to say, has not gone unchallenged (Fein, 1978).

Where does this leave us in analyzing parent programs on the stigma criterion? As is so often the case in policy analysis, we cannot resolve the issues by appealing to definitive social science research. Some programs stigmatize parents, others do not. Surely there must be ways to minimize stigma—by, for example, training professionals more effectively, making programs voluntary, involving parents in decision making, and employing minorities as staff members. It is easy enough to conclude—and we hereby do so—that all these approaches should be built into federal legislation and local program requirements. Nonetheless, we are not sanguine about the effectiveness of public policy in reducing the stigmatizing aspects of parent programs. Thus, our conclusion is that parent programs share with other social programs, and perhaps in a somewhat intensified manner, the problem of stigmatizing participants. In this regard, parent programs as typically practiced cannot be considered benign; we conclude that they should receive a moderately unfavorable rating on the stigma criterion.

RECOMMENDATIONS

Our analysis of parent programs brings us to three recommendations. First, the available information does not permit us to conclude that parent programs should be rated highly on the criteria of preference satisfaction, efficiency, or stigma. With certain qualifications, parent programs could be rated highly on the criterion of equity. Defining the societal problem as one of inadequate child development, and conceptualizing parent programs as a method of attacking this problem, we have not found empirical evidence to strongly support the efficacy of the approach. The strongest conclusion that seems permitted by the evidence is that parent programs are moderately effective in solving the problem. It follows that there is no basis for a major expansion of government support for parent programs. We can think of no better statement of the justification for this moderate conclusion than that given by Clarke-Stewart (Chap. 10):

> Before we expand our parent education efforts in this era of scarce resources, I suggest we make sure we've got our facts straight. Support for parent education will inevitably come at the expense of other social programs; we need to be sure we make the most of our limited opportunities for social change. We will not get away for long with promising outcomes we can't deliver. . . . (p. 257)

Second, our major conclusion should not be construed to mean that we favor a cutback in current parent education efforts. Indeed, we can see no reason for the inconsistencies in current parent involvement requirements characteristic of the federal programs highlighted in Fig. 1. Thus, we recommend that the parent involvement requirements of programs such as the Indian Education Act and Migrant Education be strengthened to bring them in line with Head Start or at least Follow Through provisions.

The justification for this recommendation is twofold. First, such changes do not constitute a major initiative and will not be expensive. Second, the War on Poverty concept of "maximum feasible participation" captures a justification for direct citizen involvement in programs that does not depend on outcome data of the type emphasized in our analysis. Rather, this justification is simply an application of the democratic concept that citizens should have a voice in public programs that affect their lives—and even more to the point, the lives of their children. In our view, parents have this right, regardless of whether such involvement produces performance gains in their children.

Our third conclusion is that the federal government should fund—at the level of perhaps 2 or 3 million dollars, growing to 10 to 12 million dollars, per year over 7 to 10 years—an implementation effort along the lines of the PCDC experiment. The focus population should be preschool children from low-income and minority families, it should begin with 4 or 5 sites and expand to 20 or 30, and an ongoing external evaluation should be part of the effort. Extant data on parent programs justifies this rather modest investment.

Parent programs began in an era of middle-class mothers' desire to improve their childrearing skills and to maximize their children's potential. Parent programs reached their zenith during the years of the Great Society. Today these programs have filtered throughout public education to such an extent that scarcely a school district in the nation has not been affected by the presence of a parent advisory committee. Parent education has been an intentional experiment on a grand scale.

The experiment has been long-lasting and effective in altering the educational lives of several million children, especially children from low-income families. Whether this is enough to generate broad support for the above recommendations remains to be seen in a period of federal retrenchment. We can only conclude that parent involvement is a policy matter of some importance; the "transforming of society" urged by Lawrence Frank in the 1920s may not be brought about entirely by having "educated" parents, but the complexity and persistence of social problems leads us to believe that parent programs can continue to play a limited but important role in solving some of them.

REFERENCES

Andrews, S. R., Blumenthal, J. B., Johnson, D. L., Kahn, A. J., Ferguson, C. J., Lasater, T. M., Malone, P. E., & Wallace, D. B. The skills of mothering: A study of Parent Child Development Centers. *Monographs of the Society for Research in Child Development*, 1982, 47 (6, Serial No. 198).

Bronfenbrenner, U. Is early intervention effective? In M. Guttentag & E. L. Struening (Eds.), *Handbook of evaluation research* (Vol. 2). Beverly Hills, CA: Sage, 1975.

Chilman, C. S. *Growing up poor*. Washington, DC: U.S. Department of Health, Education, and Welfare, 1966.

Darlington, R. B., Royce, J. M., Snipper, A. S., Murray, H. W., & Lazar, I. Preschool programs and later school competence of children from low-income families. *Science*, 1980, *208*, 202–204.

Dokecki, P. R. The vicissitudes of program development: Commentary on Tharp and Gallimore. *Journal of Community Psychology*, 1982, *10*, 119–124.

Elam, S. (Ed.). *The Gallup Poll of attitudes toward education, 1969–1973*. Bloomington, IN: Phi Delta Kappa, 1973.

Featherman, D. L. Schooling and Occupational Careers: Constancy and change in worldly success. In O. G. Brim & J. Kagan (Eds.), *Constancy and change in human development*. Cambridge, MA: Harvard University Press, 1980.

Fein, G. G. *The game of social criticism: A commentary*. Unpublished manuscript, Merrill-Palmer Institute, 1978.

Gallagher, J. J., Ramey, C. T., Haskins, R. T., & Finkelstein, N. W. Use of longitudinal research in the study of child development. In T. D. Tjossem (Ed.), *Intervention strategies for high risk infants and young children*. Baltimore, MD: University Park Press, 1976.

Goodson, D. B., & Hess, R. D. *The effects of parent training programs on child performance and parent behavior.* Unpublished manuscript, Stanford University, 1976.

Gordon, I. J. *An early intervention project: A longitudinal look.* Gainesville, FL: University of Florida, Institute for Development of Human Resources, 1973.

Haskins, R. A model for analyzing social policies. In R. Haskins & J. J. Gallagher (Eds.), *Care and education of young children in America: Policy, politics, and social science.* Norwood, NJ: Ablex, 1980.

Haskins, R., & Gallagher, J. J. (Eds.). *Models for analysis of social policy: An introduction.* Norwood, NJ: Ablex, 1981.

Jencks, C. *Inequality.* New York: Basic Books, 1972.

Jencks, C. *Who gets ahead?* New York: Basic Books, 1979.

Klaus, R. A., & Gray, S. W. The early training project for disadvantaged children: A report after five years. *Monographs of the Society for Research in Child Development,* 1968, *33* (4, Serial No. 120).

Lazar, I., & Darlington, R. B. *Lasting effects after preschool.* Ithaca, NY: Consortium for Longitudinal Studies, Cornell University, 1978.

Lazar, I., Hubbell, V. R., Murray, H., Rosche, M., & Royce, J. *The persistence of preschool effects: A long-term follow-up of fourteen infant and preschool experiments* (Final Report for Grant #18-76-07843). Ithaca, NY: Cornell University, Community Service Laboratory, September 1977.

Levenstein, P. A message from home: Findings from a program for non-retarded low-income preschoolers. In M. J. Begat & S. A. Richardson (Eds.), *The mentally retarded and society.* Baltimore, MD: University Park Press, 1975.

Lewis, O. *La vida: A Puerto Rican family in the culture of poverty.* New York: Random House, 1966.

Lindblom, C. E., & Cohen, D. K. *Usable knowledge: Social science and social problem solving.* New Haven, CN: Yale University Press, 1979.

Madden, J., Levenstein, P., & Levenstein, S. Longitudinal IQ outcomes of the mother–child home program. *Child Development,* 1976, *47,* 1015–1025.

MacRae, D., & Wilde, J. *Policy analysis for public decisions.* North Scituate, MA: Duxbury Press, 1979.

McKay, R. E. The President's program: A new commitment to quality and equality in education. In J. Frost & G. R. Hawkes (Eds.), *The disadvantaged child.* Boston, MA: Houghton-Mifflin, 1966.

Moynihan, D. P. *The Negro family: The case for national action.* Washington, DC: Office of Policy Planning and Research, U.S. Department of Labor, 1965.

Office of Child Development. *Head Start policy manual.* Washington, DC: Children's Bureau, U.S. Department of Health, Education, and Welfare, 1967, 1969, and 1970.

Ogbu, J. U. *Minority education and caste: The American system in cross-cultural perspective.* New York: Academic Press, 1978.

Ogbu, J. Origins of human competence: A cultural ecological perspective. *Child Development,* 1981, *52,* 413–429.

O'Keefe, A. *What Head Start means to families* (Head Start Bureau). Washington, DC: U.S. Government Printing Office, 1978.

Piven, F. F., & Cloward, R. A. *Regulating the poor: The functions of public welfare.* New York: Vintage, 1971.

Radin, N., & Weikart, D. A home teaching program for disadvantaged preschool children. *Journal of Special Education,* 1967, *1,* 183–190.

Riessman, F. *The culturally deprived child*. New York: Harper & Row, 1962.

Ryan, W. *Blaming the victim*. New York: Vintage Books, 1971.

St. John, N. H. *School desegregation: Outcomes for children*. New York: Wiley, 1975.

Schlossman, S. L. The parent education game: The politics of child psychology in the 1970s. *Teachers College Record*, 1978, *79*, 788–808.

Shriver, S. Personal statement on "Head Start, A retrospective view: The founders." In E. Zigler & J. Valentine (Eds.), *Project Head Start: A legacy of the War on Poverty*. New York: Free Press, 1979.

Sugarman, J. M. Personal statement on "Head Start, A retrospective view: The founders." In E. Zigler & J. Valentine (Eds.), *Project Head Start: A legacy of the War on Poverty*. New York: Free Press, 1979.

Valentine, C. A. *Culture and poverty: Critique and counter-proposals*. Chicago, IL: University of Chicago Press, 1968.

Vopava, J., & Royce, J. *Comparison of the long-term effects of infant and preschool programs on academic performance*. Paper presented at the meeting of the American Educational Research Association, Toronto, March, 1978.

Weber, C. U., Foster, P. W., & Weikart, D. P. *An economic analysis of the Ypsilanti Perry preschool project*. Ypsilanti, MI: High Scope, 1978.

Wildavsky, A. *Speaking truth to power: The art and craft of policy analysis*. Boston, MA: Little, Brown, 1979.

Zigler, E., & Anderson, K. An idea whose time had come: The intellectual and political climate. In E. Zigler & J. Valentine, *Project Head Start: A legacy of the War on Poverty*. New York: Free Press, 1979.

Name Index

Italicized numbers show pages where complete references can be found.

A

Aaron, H. J., 83, 92, 98, *110*
Aaronson, M., 267, *275*
Abramson, L. M., 223, *228*
Abramson, P. R., 223, *228*
Acland, A., 113, *139*
Adler, A., 157-160, *175*
Ainsworth, M. D. S., 262, *273*
Allen, J. E., 147, *176*
Altman, N., 119, *140*
American Academy of Pediatrics, 295, *300*
Anchel, G., 145, *177*
Anderson, K., 214, 223, *228*, 348, *373*
Anderson, R. B., 72, *79*, 84, 103, *110*, 129, *140*, 236, *256*
Andrews, S. R., 80, 95-97, *110*, 268, *273*, 364-365, *371*
Antler, J., 35n, *37*
Apfel, N., 1, *6*, 78, *79*, 259, 263-264, 272n, *274*

B

Bache, W. L., 268, *273*
Badger, E., 202-204, *209*, 266, 268, *273*
Baer, A. M., 292, *300*
Baer, D. M., 292, *300*
Bane, M. J., 43, 51, *62*, 113, *139*
Bank Street Follow Through Model, 127, *138*
Barclay, A., 223, *228*
Barkowf, S., 296, *302*
Bar-Lev, Y., 157, *175*
Barnard, D. P., 152, *180*
Barnes, L., 52, *64*
Bartel, J. M., 308, 312, *323*
Bauer, M. T., 159, *175*
Bauman, K. E., 285, 302
Baumrind, D., 260, *273*
Bayley, N., 284, 292, *300, 302*
Beady, C. H., 113, *138*
Bear, M., 233, *256*
Beaton, Jr., A. E., 113, *139*, 142, *178*

SUBJECT INDEX

A

Administration for Children, Youth, and Families (ACYF), 87, 105
Adult education, 90-91
Advocates, 5
American Association of University Women, 18

B

Bank Street College of Education, 88, 104, 125-127
Behavior Analysis Model (University of Kansas), 127-128
Beveridge Report, 46
Budget cuts, 66, 69

C

Child care, 45
Child Development Institutes, 2, 14-16
Child Study, 17
Child Study Association of America (CSA), 2, 13-19, 30
Child Welfare Research Stations, 15-16
Committee on Child Development (National Research Council), 15
Community Impact Model, 144-145
Consortium for Longitudinal Studies, 265, 287, 354-355, 363

D

Delphi Method, 75, 214-215

E

The Early Childhood Education for the Severely/Multiply Handicapped Program, 198-199
Economic Opportunity Act, 114-115
Education for All Handicapped Children Act, 350-351
Education for Severely Handicapped Outreach, 197